Industrial Labour in India

Rajendra Kumar Sharma

ATLANTIC
PUBLISHERS & DISTRIBUTORS (P) LTD

Published by
ATLANTIC
PUBLISHERS & DISTRIBUTORS (P) LTD
7/22, Ansari Road, Darya Ganj, New Delhi-110002
Phones : +91-11-40775252, 40775214, 23273880, 23275880
Fax: +91-11-23285873
Web: www.atlanticbooks.com
E-mail: orders@atlanticbooks.com

Printed & bound in India by Atlantic Print Services

PREFACE

This book has been written according to syllabi prescribed in M.A. (Sociology) and M.A. (Economics) in Indian Universities in the papers entitled: Labour Problems; Labour Problems in India; Labour Problems and Welfare; Labour Problems and Social Security etc. With analytic presentation of the material drawn from authentic sources; holistic approach in controversial matters; narration in simple language; examples drawn from Indian life and questions for exercise at the end of each chapter, this book seeks to serve as an ideal textbook for the students and a reference book for the teachers.

Starting from History of Industrial Development and Industrial Planning in India this book covers the topics: Labour and Labour Force; Labour and Personnel Policy; Industrial Organisation and Human Relations; Personnel Selection, Recruitment and Placement; Personnel Management; Manpower Planning; Industrial Leadership and Supervision; Theories of Motivation in Industry; Industrial Morale, Wage Administration and Policies; Systems of Wage Payment; Non-Wage Incentives and Fringe Benefits; Specialization; Rationalization; Automation; Workers' Adjustment; Unemployment and Employment; Problems of Housing; Training and Development of Personnel; Industrial Disputes; Trade Unionism in India; Labour Legislation; Labour Welfare; Workers' Participation in Management and Profit Sharing; Collective Bargaining; Grievance Procedure and Discipline; Social Welfare in India, Social Security in Other Countries; Social Security in India; Employees' State Insurance; India and I.L.O.

Suggestions for improvement are invited from the indulgent readers.

RAJENDRA K. SHARMA

Contents

1

History of Industrial Development

Today as we hear the words "industry" or "industrial system" or just think of them, we automatically recall to our minds a picture of huge mill or factory fitted with giant machines electrically and power operated covering vast tracts of land, having wide and huge expanse of buildings and employing hundreds of men. We also associate with the roar and rattling of machines, sky-high chimneys emitting thick clouds of smoke. However, even prior to the development of modern sophisticated industry, man was industrious. He was engaged in some industry, however crude and underdeveloped that may have been in comparison to modern industry. We define man as a rational animal; but we may equally define him with full justification as 'an industrious animal'. Thus, we find that the history of industry is as long as the history of man; they are co-eval. With the advancement of civilisation, man has advanced industrially. For the sake of convenience, we can divide the history of industrial development into three periods: Ancient Industry, Medieval Industry and Modern Industry. This division is done with a view to chronology and development.

ANCIENT PERIOD

In the ancient or primitive period of industry are included those works which were performed by man when he was neither literate nor civilised. In this period no systematic industry had developed. The main concern of man during these days was merely to provide for food and physical protection. The means which were adopted by him to meet these ends were symbolic of his industrial effort. For food the primitive man used to hunt animals and gather wild vegetables and fruits. For hunting he employed bow and arrow and certain instruments made by sharpening stone. All primitive weapons were made either of wood or stone. These weapons were symbols of industrial development of that period. Besides, making fire by friction of stone or bamboos was industrial miracle of that time. For a pretty long time this state of affairs persisted.

MEDIEVAL PERIOD

In medieval period there was sufficient development in industry. In this period the signs of industry became quite visible in the efforts of man. A number of manually operated machines were fabricated. Man also began using animal power to meet his ends. The signs of industrialisation, production of goods in excess of consumption and stocking of these came in evidence at this time. The exchange of goods and division of labour also came into vogue. As a consequence of this, different industries started operating separately. For example, blacksmith, carpenter and weaver set up independent units. Thus, began the specialization of jobs. The artistic spirit of the artisans was awakened.

The medieval industrial age in the West can be divided into three distinct industrial systems. This division is based on the nature of the industrial system. These industrial systems are:

(1) Feudal system

(2) Guild system

(3) Domestic system.

1. Feudal system: Under this system, the primary industry was agriculture. Few persons controlled vast tracts of lands each and they engaged and employed hundreds of workers to do the farming. This system was in vogue in Europe between 9th and 12th centuries. Under this system the owner of the land was called feudal lord and persons engaged by him were called serfs. The serfs were virtual slaves of the feudal lord. Besides agriculture, other important professions were those of carpentry, blacksmithy, pottery and weaving. Even these artisans were dependent upon feudal lords.

Under the feudal system, the serfs were required to give all kinds of services to their respective lords. In case required, they had to wage war against the enemies of their lord.

From 11th century onward, urban towns started coming up in Europe. With urbanization feudal system got a setback. The labour or the working class now had an alternative to working as serfs. They could migrate to towns and find work there. As a result of urbanization, Guild system came into vogue.

2. Guild system: The urbanization in Europe emancipated the serfs from their traditional slavery. Having emancipated themselves from serfdom under feudal lords, the worker started learning new trades and skills. As a result of specialization and proficiency in trades acquired by workers, centres of trade came up. Gradually this process gave rise to Guild system.

In Guild system, trade associations representing various trades came into being. These trade associations worked for the promotion and development of their respective trades. These associations supervised the quality and quantity of goods being produced by the members of their association. They also fixed and regulated the prices of goods. Various kinds of relations obtained among the members of a guild. They were related, besided economic relations, by social, political and religious relations.

Under Guild system there used to be two kinds of guilds: the Merchant Guilds and Craft Guilds. The main task of the Merchant Guilds was to look after the interests of businessmen. They used to demand justice from government in a manner in which Chambers of Commerce of today function. The Craft Guilds were associations formed by craftsmen carrying on a particular craft. The Craft guilds worked for the promotion of the crafts and protection of the interests of craftsmen. The craft guilds used to arrange weekly markets where craftsmen could sell their products. In Craft guilds, master craftsmen played crucial role, though less skilful Craftsmen were also given due share. They were helped to acquire proficiency in their skill. The master craftsmen used to belong to families of master craftsmen. The craftsmanship was supposed to be hereditary. In these days, the Craft guilds of blacksmiths, carpenters and weavers were particularly prominent.

The guild system occupies a place of pride in the history of Industrial Development. This system was important in maintaining social harmony and unity. Remarking about the merits of this system Raj Kohli says, "The builders of the great cathedrals of Europe (at the period) had achieved a unity of feeling and thought which the modern world has apparently lost."[1]

Decline of Guilds

The guild system lasted for a pretty long time, but gradually it declined. From 16th Century there was a gradual decline and deterioration in this

1. Kohli, R. K., *The Education of Henery Adams, An American Odyssey*, The American Review, New Delhi, July 1968, p. 73.

system. There were two chief causes for the decline of this system. The first cause was internal and the second was external.

The first internal cause of the decline of the guild system was that its functions and the rights of its officials were not well-defined. This gave rise to myriad conflicts. For example, the guild of goldsmiths was always warring with the guild of silversmiths. Moreover, there was gradual fragmentation of the guilds. Originally, there was only one guild of cloth merchant. But soon many sub-guilds like association of weavers, tailors, embroiderers etc., were formed.

The second cause of the decline of the guild system was external. Under this system there was one group of traders who were manufacturers and the other was that of middle men. This group of middle men later began exploitation of the manufacturers. It acted in the manner and style of modern capitalist. The middle men took over the control of all levers of production and arbitrarily used them for their own selfish ends. Generally they took over the control of raw material. The arbitrary acts of these middle men gave severe set back to the guild system.

Besides these two reasons, there were certain local and immediate causes of this decline. At this time America was discovered. The way to commerce and trade with East also opened. Due to this the trade and commerce was deeply affected. In the production and demand of goods there was sudden upward surge. During these days a religious factor also contributed its share in the decline of guilds. The protestant sect of Christianity had greater dominance at this juncture. The rise of protestant religion spelt the rise of individualism and this, too, proved inimical to guild system which was based on a sense of co-operation. In these days another factor which gave death blow to guild system was the invention and use of big machine and introduction of sophisticated techniques of production.

3. Domestic system: After the decline of guild system, domestic system came into vogue. This system was a kind of capitalism. As far as the method of production was concerned, it was not much different from that of guild system. However, under domestic system there was no place and no role for various guilds and trade associations. Under domestic system a head of family who normally was a master craftsman controlled the entire production and everything was under his personal ownership. The head of the family used to provide for the raw material and also the manufactured goods. All processes or stages of production were under his individual control and survision. Under this system the craftsmen had not much freedom. The system is to be seen today in the form of cottage industries.

It was again the role of middle-man and the money-lender which ruined the domestic system. The head of a trade in domestic system required from time to time extra funds for the purchase of the raw material. This extra amount came from the money-lender and he usually exploited the opportunity to the fullest. Besides, mechanization of industry rendered this system obsolete and economically non-viable. The capitalist by investing huge amount into industry and mechanizing it to the hilt completely ruined the domestic system. Thus, the domestic system came to an end and modern industry came into being.

MUGHAL PERIOD

In Mughal period India was industrially advanced. In the reign of Akbar and Jahangir the state of industry was fairly well developed and advanced. During the reign of these rulers, India was famous world over for its industrial products. At this time spices, cloth and indigo used to be exported to Europe from India. The muslin of Dacca was world-renowned. A number of industrial centres had sprung up at this time from which goods used to be exported abroad.

Under the Mughals, industry in India was quite widespread. There were industrial centres in rural as well as urban areas. The aim of the industry in rural areas was mostly to cater to needs of local people. The goods of daily need were available in villages. The industry in urban areas was highly developed and was carried on vast scale. The primary aim of industry in towns was to produce fine quality goods for the purposes of export. The industry at this period was not privately owned but was under the control of guilds. At certain places middle-men used to play a role. These middle-men used to pay in advance for the goods needed by them.

During the reign of Mughals Indian industry was at its peak. After the Mughals there began a gradual decline and deterioration of the Indian industry. The chief reason for this decline was the industrial revolution in the West. As a result of the industrial revolution the pattern and nature of industrial production in England underwent such a change that the demand there for the Indian goods completely dried up. There were a number of reasons for this radical change. Firstly, industry in England was becoming highly mechanized. The mechanisation led to an increase in the production and also improvement in the quality of goods. Thus, there was competition between machine-made foreign goods and hand-made Indian goods. The machine-made goods were cheap, standard and available in bulk. For pretty obvious reasons Indian goods failed to compete with their Western counterparts. This led to drying up demand of Indian goods in Europe. This had deleterious effect on the Indian industry. Besides drying up of export, the foreign goods became popular in India. The result was that there was steep decline in the demand for Indian products which, in turn, led to closure of many manufacturing units. The skilled Indian craftsmen perished or took to job under foreign controlled companies.

BRITISH PERIOD

The progress of Indian industry has not been steady. In old days the Indian industry was highly developed. In fact it had no match in the world. But with the industrial revolution in the West it has been losing ground gradually. The old pattern of industry is all but ruined. The modern industry in India began after the British took over the reigns of India. Between 1850-60, jute mills were established in India. About this time railway system was started. In the beginning rail track between mining centres in Bihar and Calcutta were laid. Along with the development of means of communication there was rapid industrial growth in India. About this time foreign merchants established textile mills in Bombay and Ahmedabad. In Kanpur woollen and leather factories were established. These factories were under British ownership though the raw material was supplied by Indians and the labour working in these factories was also Indian. The profit was made by the British at the expense of Indians.

The British Government used to export the raw materials from India and import into India the finished goods at exhorbitant prices. The British had little sympathy for the development of local industry. In 1911, Jamshedji Tata ushered in an era of Indian Industrial revolution by setting up a steel mill in Jamshedpur. However, its production was not adequate to meet the local demand. About this time there was sufficient progress in means of communication and the production of coal and iron ore. On the whole, however, Indian industry was backward.

INDIAN INDUSTRY DURING WARS

In the First World War the British had to suffer and face grave difficulties on account of the undeveloped state of Indian industry. The situation arose where the sea-routes were blocked and it became impossible to export raw materials from India and to import finished goods into India. On account of this the army based in India was put to great hardships. Therefore, after the war the British encouraged setting up industries in India. However, the real progress in industry came after the Second World War.

POST-INDEPENDENCE PERIOD

India got independence on August 15, 1947. The Indian government began a herculean effort to develop the Indian industry. The government wanted to achieve self-sufficiency.

During the last three decades of planned development industrial production has made rapid strides both in terms of variety and quality. The production increased at an average growth rate of about 5 per cent per annum during 1970-1983. While almost all groups of industries contributed to this increase, the growth has been particularly marked in areas, such as, petroleum products, chemicals and chemical products, metal products, electronics and other electrical machinery, transport equipment and power generation. The share of manufacturing sector in the net domestic product at constant prices increased from 13.4 per cent in 1970-71 to 15 per cent in 1982-83.

The different five year plan periods saw the expansion and diversification of the industrial structure with the establishment of new units in the existing fields as well as the setting up of new enterprises. As a result, the number of industrial units has increased significantly. In 1951, there were only two major units producing iron and steel. There are now six major steel plants with a capacity of about 87 lakh tonnes. They produced about 73 lakh tonnes of saleable steel during 1982-83. The steel produced by these plants has provided the basis for achieving the self-sufficiency in making a number of engineering goods from pin to giant machinery. In the field of new industries, agricultural tractors, electronics and fertilizer industries, which practically did not exist in 1951, have progressed to such an extent that the import of these products has been brought down to the minimum. The drug and chemical industries have also made rapid progress. The textile industry is no longer confined to the cotton and jute textiles. Today, there are quite a few units producing different types of synthetic fibres. The machine building industry, too, has made rapid strides. The engineering industry can supply virtually the entire requirement of power generating equipment, equipment for railways, road transport and communications. Self-sufficiency has been reached with regard to sugar and cement machinery, power boilers, material handling equipment and a large number of consumer durables.

An important feature of industrial growth in the country after Independence has been the rapid expansion of the public sector. In 1951, there were only five non-departmental public undertakings, with an investment of ₹ 29 crore. On 1 April 1983, they numbered 209 with an investment of ₹ 30,033 crore. These enterprises produce diverse products such as steel, coal, aluminium, copper, heavy and light engineering products, fertilizers, basic chemicals, drugs, minerals, petroleum products, locomotives, aircraft and ships.

INDUSTRIAL POLICY

Independent India's industrial policy was first announced in 1948. This envisaged a mixed economy with an overall responsibility of the Government for planned development of industries and their regulation in the national interest. While it reiterated the right of the State to acquire an industrial undertaking in public interest, it reserved an appropriate sphere for private enterprise. The policy was revised in 1956 following Parliament's acceptance in 1954 of a socialistic pattern of society as the national objective. Under the revised policy, industries specified in Schedule A (enumerated below) are the exclusive responsibility of the State while industries in Schedule B (also enumerated below) are to be progressively State-owned, but private enterprise is expected to supplement the efforts of the State in these fields. Future development of industries falling outside the two Schedules would, in general, be left to private enterprise. Notwithstanding this demarcation it is always open to the State to undertake any type of industrial production.

A. *Schedule A Industries*: Arms and ammunition and allied items of defence equipment; atomic energy; iron and steel, heavy castings and forgings of iron and steel, heavy plant and machinery required for iron and steel production, for mining, for machine tool manufacture and for such other basic industries as may be specified by the Government; heavy electrical plant including large hydraulic and steam turbines; coal and lignite; mineral oils; mining of iron ore, manganese ore, chrome ore, gypsum, sulphur, gold and diamonds; mining and processing of copper, lead, zinc, molybdenum and wolfram; minerals specified in the Schedule to the Atomic Energy (Control of Production and Use) Order 1953; aircraft, air transport; railway transport; shipbuilding; telephones and telephone cables, telegraph and wireless apparatus (excluding radio receiving sets), generation and distribution of electricity.

B. *Schedule B Industries*: All other minerals except minor minerals as defined in Section 3 of the Minerals Concession Rules, 1949; aluminium and other non-ferrous metals not included in Schedule A; machine tools;

ferro-alloy and tool steel; basic and intermediate products required by chemical industries, such as the manufacture of drugs, dyestuffs and plastics, antibiotics and other essential drugs, fertilizer; synthetic rubber; carbonisation of coal; chemical pulp; road transport and sea transport.

Regulation of Industry

In line with the policy first announced in 1948, the Constitution was amended and the Industries (Development and Regulation) Act, 1951, was enacted. Under this, industries listed in the Schedule A to the Act are required to be licensed by the Government. The Act authorises the Government to examine the working of any such industrial undertaking and to issue directions which it considers necessary. If the undertaking continues to be mismanaged the Government is empowered to take over its management of control. The Act empowers the Government to secure equitable distribution and fair prices of any article produced by the scheduled industries.

PRESENT INDUSTRIAL DEVELOPMENT

Attainment of industrialisation over the last 46 years has been a striking feature of Indian economic development process which was launched as a conscious and deliberate policy in the early fifties. In pursuance of this policy, large investment has been made in building up capacity over a wide spectrum of industries. Industrial production has made rapid strides in terms of variety, quality and quantity. There has been a substantial diversification of industrial base during this period with the consequent ability to produce a very broad range of industrial good. Self-reliance has been achieved in basic and capital goods. Indigenous capabilities have now been established to the point of virtual self-sufficiency so that further expansion in various sectors such as mining, irrigation, power, chemicals, transport and communication can be based primarily on indigenous equipment. Process of industrialisation has also fostered entrepreneurship and development of a wide variety of technical, managerial and operative skills. Today, the country is in a position to provide consultancy services as well as managers, technicians and skilled workers for setting up industrial projects abroad.

A significant aspect of industrial development during the above period has been the predominant role assigned to public sector in establishment of basic industries. Public sector has taken initiative for development of various industries such as steel, non-ferrous metals, petroleum, coal, fertilizers and heavy engineering. It has also made investment in consumer industries like textiles, drugs and pharmaceuticals, cement and sugar. Number of public sector enterprises which was only five in March 1951 rose to 244 in March 1991. In 1985-86, Government initiated a number of measures aimed at removing constraints on industrial growth and providing a more congenial environment for development. These include delicensing of industries, re-endorsement of capacity, broad banding etc. As a result of these measures, industrial production achieved an average growth of 8.5 per cent in the Seventh Plan period. New policy initiatives announced in the Statement on Industrial Policy of 1991 provide the basic framework for the overall industrial policy of the government.

INDUSTRIAL LICENSING POLICY

Industrial licensing is governed by the Industries (Development and Regulation) Act, 1951. Over the years, keeping in view the changing industrial scene in the country, the industrial licensing policy has undergone modifications. Accordingly a new industrial policy was announced on 24 July 1991. Government has decided to do away with industrial licensing for all industries except those industries specified in Annexure-II of the policy (please see list at the end of this sub-head) irrespective of levels of investment. Compulsory licensing has been considered necessary for security and strategic consideration, safety reasons and over-riding environmental concerns and the need to regulate production of articles of elitist consumption. Besides, entrepreneurs will be allowed to freely develop their industries, become more competitive nationally and internationally, more efficient and modern.

The theme of the policy is continuity with change. While freedom has been given to the major industries to grow, reservation of items for small-scale will continue so as to promote the industrial and agro-industrial employment base. While proposing major changes in licensing policy, the pre-eminent place of the public sector in eight core areas will be continued. These include arms and ammunition, atomic energy, mineral oils, rail transport and mining of coal and minerals. The exemption from licensing will be particularly helpful to the many dynamic, small and medium entrepreneurs who have been unnecessarily hampered by the licensing system. As a whole, the Indian economy will benefit by becoming more competitive, more efficient and modern.

List of Industrial in respect of which Industrial Licensing will be Compulsory

(*i*) Coal and lignite; (*ii*) petroleum (other than crude) and its distillation products; (*iii*) distillation and brewing of alcoholic drinks; (*iv*) sugar; (*v*) animal fats and oils; (*vi*) cigars and cigarettes of tobacco and manufactured tobacco substitutes; (*vii*) asbestos and asbestos-based products; (*viii*) plywood, veneers of all types and other wood-based products such as particle board, medium density fibre board and black board; (*ix*) chamois leather; (*x*) tanned or dressed furskins; (*xi*) paper and newsprint except bagasse-based units; (*xii*) electronic aerospace and defence equipment of all types; (*xiii*) industrial explosives, including detonating fuse, safety fuse, gun powder, nitrocellulose and matches; (*xiv*) hazardous chemicals; (*xv*) drugs and pharmaceuticals; (according to Drug Policy) (*xvi*) entertainment electronics (VCRs, Colour TVs, CD players, Tape Recorders).

Broad-Banding Facility

Existing and new industrial units will be provided with a broad-banding facility to enable them to produce any article so long as no additional investment in plant and machinery is involved. Further, exemption from licensing will apply to all substantial expansions of existing units.

Change in Convertibility Clause

The mandatory convertibility clause which enables financial institutions to convert loans into equity will no longer be applicable for term loans extended by financial institutions for new projects.

Direct Foreign Investment

Government welcomes foreign investment which is in the interest of the country's industrial development. The new policy welcomes foreign investment with its attendant advantages of technology transfer, marketing expertise, introduction of modern managerial techniques in the country and export promotion.

Approval will be given by the Reserve Bank of India for direct investment upto 51 per cent equity in high priority industries which include areas like metallurgy, electrical equipment, transportation, food processing, software, hotel and tourism industry. There shall be no bottlenecks of any kind in this clearance of proposals for foreign equity participation. Such clearance will be available if foreign equity covers the foreign exchange requirement for imported capital goods. Direct foreign investment beyond 51 per cent or in sectors other than those 34 specified industrial sectors is also permissible but would require the approval by the government.

Dividends to be expatriated by companies in consumer goods sector with foreign equity will have to be met through export earnings over a period of time. All payments flowing from approval of foreign technology agreements will have to be made through foreign exchange purchased at market rates.

Similarly companies with foreign equity upto 51 per cent will be given automatic approval by the Reserve Bank of India to act as trading houses primarily engaged in export activities. This will generate greater passage of Indian goods to export markets.

FOREIGN TECHNOLOGY AGREEMENTS IN HIGH-PRIORITY AREAS

There is a great need for promoting an industrial environment where acquisition of technological capability receives priority. With a view to injecting the desired level of technological dynamism in Indian industry, Government will provide automatic approval for technology agreements related to high-priority industries within specified parameters upto a (*a*) lumpsum payment of ₹ one crore, (*b*) five per cent royalty for domestic sale, and (*c*) eight per cent for exports, subject to payment of eight per cent of sales over a ten-year period from the date of agreement or seven years from the commencement of production. Similar facilities will be available for other industries as well if such agreements do not require the expenditure of free foreign exchange. Predictability and independence of action that this measure is providing to the Indian industry will induce them to develop indigenous competence for the efficient absorption of foreign technology.

Special Empowered Board

In pursuance of the decision contained in the Statement on Industrial Policy, a special empowered Foreign Investment Promotion Board has been constituted. The objective of this Board is to invite and facilitate investment in concentration areas to extend inputs such as raw materials, common facilities, design development and other related services to craftpersons.

Small Industries Developments Organisations

A new department called Small Scale Industries and Agro and Rural Industries has been created in the Ministry of Industry headed by a Secretary to the Government. The office of the Development

Commissioner functions as the nodal agency for formulating, co-ordinating and monitoring the policies and programmes for promotion and development of small scale industries in the country. It maintains close liaison with other ministries, Planning Commission, state government financial institutions, voluntary organisations and other agencies concerned with development of small scale industries. It provides a comprehensive range of facilities and services including consultancy in techno-economic, managerial aspects, training, common facility services, common processing and testing facilities, tooling facilities and marketing assistance etc., to small scale units. The office of the DC (SSI) commonly called SIDO (Small Industries Development Organisation) provides these services through a network of 28 small industries service institutes (SISIs), 30 branch institutes, 4 regional testing centres, 2 central footwear training centres, 2 production centres and 15 field testing stations in areas of concentration of specific types of industries.

In addition, there are also specialised institutions like Central Institute of Tool Design, Hyderabad; Central Institute of Hand Tools, Jalandhar; Hand Tool Design Development and Training Centre, Nagpur; Central Tool Room and Training Centres, Ludhiana and Calcutta; Institute for Design of Electrical Measuring Instruments (IDEMI), Bombay; Integrated Training Centre Nilokheri; National Institute of Small Industry Extension Training (NISIET), Hyderabad, National Institute for Entrepreneurship and Business Development (NIESBUD); New Delhi, Product-*cum*-Process Development Centres for Foundary and Forging at Agra and for Sports Goods and Leisure Time Equipment at Meerut and Electronic Service and Training Centre, Ramnagar (UP) which provide training and technical services in specialised fields.

Besides three Indo-German Tool Room at Indore, Ahmedabad and Aurangabad and two Indo-Danish Tool Rooms at Bhubaneshwar and Jamshedpur are being set up. Efforts continue to augment the facilities provided in the various institutes/centres under the SIDO especially those located in the backward areas.

VILLAGE AND SMALL SCALE INDUSTRIES

Modern small scale industries and unorganised traditional industries are known as village and small industries (VSI). This sector is divided into eight sub-sectors. Small scale industries and powerlooms represent modern small industries and *Khadi*, village industries, handlooms, sericulture, handicrafts and coir represent the traditional industries.

DIRECTORATE GENERAL OF TECHNICAL DEVELOPMENT

The Directorate General of Technical Development (DGTD) is the principal advisory organisation of the Government of India on all matters relating to industrial development in the country. Being a nodal technical advisory body it has changed its orientation to a promotional and developmental agency.

The new industrial policy aims to dismantle the regime of controls in order to provide the much needed freedom to entrepreneurs to set up projects on the basis of their best commercial judgement. DGTD is a multi-disciplinary technical organisation geared to provide the facility for interaction between various technological inputs and thus make available unified advice at one point in accelerating the development process.

To facilitate implementation of the new industrial and foreign investment policies, DGTD organises regional seminars in various states. The objective of the seminars is to focus attention on the opportunities available in the concerned state based upon local raw materials and resources in order to promote industrial development and to convey the message of liberalisation to all concerned with the implementation and use of new industrial policies including the state government industrial promotion agencies as well as entrepreneurs. It also gives advice to entrepreneurs in the selection of product, choice of technology, availability of capital equipment as well as other inputs for setting up of industries.

An Industrial Technology Data Bank has been set up in DGTD with the object of collecting, analysing, storing and disseminating information on industrial technologies available abroad and within the country. The data is being stored on a computer having user-friendly programming. It contains detailed description and techno-economic parameters on alternative routes of technologies as well as different sources in order to help the user in choosing a technology which is best suited to him for achieving international competitiveness.

Various publications are being brought out by DGTD. The Handbook of *Indigenous Manufacturers Both Engineering and Non-Engineering Items* serves as a major buyers' guide for procurement of items manufactured within the country. Industrial profiles, monographs, industrial reviews, etc., are also published and these are of immense help to the entrepreneurs to take investment decisions. Reports of Technology Advisory Groups in different sectors are also being brought out to help industries in planning their long-term technology strategy. In order to share current developments and exchange of views with the industry on technology trends, production and analysis and policy changes, a quarterly newsletter has also been started of which seven issues have already been brought out. The access to latest production data on 252 industries which play an important role in working out the industrial index is available in order to provide the required transparency.

QUESTIONS FOR EXERCISE

1. Describe pre-independence scene of industrial development in India.
2. Describe post-independence development of industries in India.

2

Industrial Planning in India

DEVELOPMENT OF INDUSTRIES

The history of the organised industry in India may be traced to 1854 when the real beginning of the cotton-mill industry was made in Bombay with predominantly Indian capital and enterprise. The foundations of the jute industry were laid near Calcutta in 1855, mostly with foreign capital and enterprise. Coal-mining also progressed about this time. During and after the First and Second World Wars, a somewhat more liberal policy was adopted by the authorities, such as a discriminating protection policy which gave impetus to industrial development. Several industries rapidly expanded, and a number of new industries came up such as steel, sugar, cement, glass, industrial chemicals, soap, vanaspati and some branches of engineering. But their production was neither adequate in quantity for meeting even the low-level of internal demand nor was diversified in character.

Progress during First and Second Plans

During the First and Second Plans, the growth and diversification of industry were remarkable particularly in the Second Plan. Three new steel plants, each of 10 lakh ingot tonnes capacity, were set-up in the public sector and the capacity of the two existing steel works in the private sector was doubled. Foundations were laid of heavy electrical and heavy machine tool industries and heavy machine building and other branches of heavy engineering industries. The production of machinery for cement and paper industries was started for the first time. In chemical industries, the advance was on a wide front, leading not only to large units and greatly increased output of basic chemicals such as nitrogenous fertilizers, caustic soda, soda ash and sulphuric acid but also in the manufacture of a number of new products like urea, ammonium phosphate, penicillin, synthetic fibres, industrial explosives, polyethylene and dyestuffs. The output of many other industries like bicycles, sewing machines, telephone and electrical goods increased substantially. New skills were learnt by the workers and a large and growing class of industrial managers came into being. Organised industrial production practically doubled in these ten years; the index of industrial production rose from 100 in 1950-51 to 194 in 1960-61. New industrial townships and factories sprang up in the environs of the main cities of the country.

Progress during the Third Plan and Annual Plans

Industrial progress was markedly uneven during the eight years which comprised the Third Plan and the subsequent Annual Plans. In the first four years, conditions were relatively favourable for industrial investment and growth and the progress achieved was significant. Thereafter for nearly three years, the economy was subjected to considerable stress and strain and growth rate in industrial production declined firstly slowly and then steeply till it reached virtual stagnation. But in the last year of this period *i.e.* 1968-69, there were distinct signs of recovery. The decline after 1964-65 was attributable to several factors of which the most important were series of dislocations caused by hostilities in 1965 and two successive droughts in 1965-66 and 1966-67. Many industries were severely affected by shortage of raw materials and components arising from pause in external aid in 1965.

Among industries in which Third Plan production targets were fully or early realised by 1965-66 were aluminium, automobiles, electric transformers, cotton textile machinery, machine tools, sugar, jute, textiles, power-driven pumps, diesel engines and petroleum products. On the other hand, in some important industries like steel and fertilizers, there was a considerable shortfall in production. In subsequent years, there was step-up in production in certain industries such as fertilizers, heavy chemicals, cement and petroleum products. In spite of this uneven performance, significant achievements contributing towards realisation of diversified industrial structure were made during this period. Several large projects launched at the commencement of Third Plan were completed and brought into production in particular, in heavy engineering and different units in Heavy Engineering Corporation. Mining and Allied Machinery Corporation and of heavy electrical projects made it possible largely through indigenous efforts, expansion of further capacity in vital sectors like iron and steel, mining and power generation. In rail and road transport and communications, virtual self-sufficiency for supply of equipment and rolling stock was achieved.

Machinery manufacturing capacity for a variety of traditional industries like textiles, sugar and cement was developed and designed and engineering capabilities were expanded. Process technology was either acquired or developed to enable planning, designing and construction of industrial projects with maximum indigenous efforts in fields like fertilizers, rayons and dissolving pulp. There was an appreciable increase in production capacity of steel and non-ferrous metals. Progress was made in expansion of capacity in petroleum, fertilizer and petrochemical industries.

Progress during Fourth Plan

In Fourth Plan, performance of industrial sector fell short of expectations both in terms of production and investment. Investment of industrial development in public sector was estimated to be about ₹ 2,700 crore as against provision of ₹ 3,050 crore. While pace of investment in some sectors like iron ore and petrochemicals was generally satisfactory, this was not so in respect of other sectors like iron and steel, non-ferrous metals, fertilizers and coal. In fact, shortfall in overall investment was much larger if account was taken of the escalation in project costs.

A number of factors were responsible for the unsatisfactory growth in industrial production. While in some of the critical industries like steel and fertilizer, production remained substantially below the installed capacity on account of operational problems in different units, other agro-based industries like sugar and textile showed an erratic trend. The inadequate pace of investment resulted in a reduced demand for industrial machinery adversely affecting the level of output of the capital goods industries. Production in other engineering industries was also hit by the shortage of steel and non-ferrous metals.

On the positive side, there was a substantial production increase in several industries like alloy and special steels, aluminium, automobile tyres, petroleum refinery products, electronics, machine tools, tractors and heavy electrical equipment. The production in the public sector undertakings also showed an encouraging rise towards the closing years of the Fourth Plan. Apart from this, the industrial base was further expanded and greater degree of sophistication and self-reliance achieved.

Progress during Fifth Plan

The Fifth Plan laid emphasis on rapid growth of core sector industries and increase in the production of export-oriented goods and articles of mass consumption. The average rate of growth of industrial sector was estimated at seven per cent per annum in the revised plan. The sharp increase in the prices of foodgrains, fertilizers and oil seriously upset the assumptions on which the Fifth Plan had been framed. These new developments also lent urgency to a time-bound programme of action in order to achieve a measure of self-reliance in food and energy. The successive Annual Plans had to be formulated on the basis of these considerations.

The Fifth Plan envisaged a total outlay of ₹ 53,411 crore comprising ₹ 37,250 crore for public sector and ₹ 16,161 crore for private sector respectively. However, due to the emergence of an unprecedented inflationary situation as a result of a steep increase in oil prices in November 1973, the Plan had to be drastically modified in 1976. The revised plan envisaged a total outlay of ₹ 69,351 crore comprising ₹ 42,303 for public sector and ₹ 27,408 crore for the private sector respectively. The public sector outlay included ₹ 3,000 crore as investment on inventories; the remaining public sector outlay of ₹ 39,303 crore was as current outlay. Of the revised public sector outlay of ₹ 39,303 crore during the Fifth Plan, the share of industries and minerals sector amounted to ₹ 10,201 crore of the total outlay. The outlay for large and medium industries was ₹ 9,691 crore and that of village and small industries ₹ 510 crore.

Progress During Sixth Plan

The Sixth Plan envisaged a total public sector plan outlay of ₹ 97,500 crore. The overall outlay earmarked for large industries and minerals sector is ₹ 20,407 crore including coal and petroleum. A major part of the outlay amounting to ₹ 19,018 crore is in the central sector and the balance of ₹ 1,389 crore is for the state sector. Besides this, private sector investment during 1980-1985 is estimated at ₹ 30,323 crore. The outlay for village and small industries is ₹ 1,780 crore.

Industrial policy during the Sixth Plan aimed at optimum utilisation of existing capacities, quantitative increase in output of consumer intermediate, capital goods and improvement of productivity. It aims at an annual growth rate of eight per cent of industrial production during the five-year period. As per the index of industrial production, the average growth rate achieved during the Sixth Plan was 5.5 per cent per annum compound. The growth during the years was rather uneven: four per cent in 1980-81, 8.6 per cent in 1981-82, 3.9 per cent in 1982-83, 5.3 per in 1983-84 and 5.8 per cent in 1984-85. It may however be mentioned that the above growth rates as indicated by the index of industrial production are generally of a lower order as compared to the actual growth in the overall manufacturing sector. The index (base 1970=100) has serious limitations in terms of inadequate coverage of newly emerging growth areas like electronics, petrochemicals, etc., which were virtually non-existent in 1970. The index also does not reflect the high levels of growth in the small-scale sector. A review of performance of industries in the Sixth Plan reveals that targets of capacity creation have been achieved for industries like aluminium, zinc, lead, thermoplastics, petrochemicals intermediates, electrical equipment, automobiles and consumer durables. Production targets were achieved in industries like petroleum, machine tools, passenger cars, motor cycle and scooters, TV receivers, etc. However, shortfall in production was reported for coal, steel, non-ferrous metals, cement, drugs and pharmaceuticals, textiles, jute manufacture, commercial vehicles, railway wagons, sugar, etc. Some of the major technology achievements of the Sixth Plan are: commissioning of 500 mw power generation unit, commencement of manufacture of 500 mw turbo generator and boiler and manufacture of fuel-efficient 800 cc passenger cars of contemporary technology of international level. In the fertilizer sector, manufacture of 1,350 tonnes per day fertilizer plant has commenced. In the steel sector, fully indigenous 3,200 cubic meter blast furnace and seven meter tall coke oven battery and equipment are now manufactured in the country. Similarly, large-sized heavy machinery for mining are now being manufactured, *e.g.*, long-wall mining equipment, eight cubic meter hydraulic excavators, etc.

In electronic industry, which has been identified as a sunrise industry in the Seventh Plan, higher production level than targeted has been achieved in the Sixth Plan, Higher levels of technology have been achieved in fields like LSI/VLSI circuits, manufacture of eight and 16 bit micro-computer chips, computers and micro-processors, communication equipments, broadcasting and TV transmission equipments, micro-electronics, electronic materials and components, etc.

During the Seventh Five Year Plan, the overall performance of industrial sector has been quite satisfactoiy. The average growth rate of the industrial sector comprising mining, manufacturing and electricity generation during the Seventh Plan period was 8.5 per cent. Though marginally short of the target of 8.7 per cent, this was much higher than the 3.5 per cent growth achieved during the Sixth Five Year Plan. Year-wise achievements during the Seventh Plan were 8.7 per cent in 1985-86, 9.1 per cent in 1986-87, 7.3 per cent in 1987-88, 8.8 per cent in 1988-89 and 8.4 per cent in 1989-90.

The manufacturing sector, which achieved an average growth rate of 8.9 per cent during the Seventh Plan period, contributed significantly to the achievement of the higher growth rate in the economy. Within the manufacturing sector, two industry groups, manufacture of electrical machinery and chemicals and chemical products achieved growth rates of 25.8 per cent and 11.7 per cent respectively. These two groups contributed about 61 per cent of the industrial growth in the manufacturing sector.

The significant growth in industrial production during the Seventh Plan is attributable to a number of factors, the most important being improvement in the performance of infrastructure namely power, coal, etc. The other contributory factors were: (*a*) changes in the area of licensing and procedures; (*b*) import of technology; (*c*) higher import of capital goods; (*d*) better utilisation of installed capacities; and (*e*) allowing broad-bending of products in a number of industries. The Seventh Plan also witnessed a higher dose of liberalisation measures such as (*i*) raising the assets limit for exemption to companies from the purview of MRTP Act; (*ii*) exempting 83 industries under the MRTP Act for entry of dominant industries; (*iii*) grant of exemption from licensing for industrial units with an investment of upto ₹ 50 crore in backward areas and ₹ 15 crore in other areas on the basis of a negative list; and (*iv*) delicensing non-MRTP, non-FERA companies for 31 industry groups and MRTP/FERA Companies in backward areas for 72 industry groups.

During the Seventh Plan, manufacturing and electricity sectors achieved a higher annual growth rates as compared to that of the Sixth Plan. The mining sector, however, witnessed a substantial slowdown in growth rate from 12.7 per cent in the Sixth Plan to 5.6 per cent in the Seventh Plan.

The growth of industrial production was lower at 8.4 per cent in 1990-91 as compared to 8.6 per cent in 1989-90. The manufacturing sector which accounts for more than three-fourth of the total weight in Index of Industrial Production, however, performed better by achieving a higher growth of 9.2 per cent as against 8.6 per cent in 1989-90. The two infrastructural industries namely mining and electricity registered a sharp decline in growth rates from 6.3 per cent to 3.5 per cent in the case of former and from 10.8 per cent to 8.6 per cent in the case of latter.

The statement of Industrial Policy announced by the Government of India on 24 July, 1991 has brought about far-reaching changes both in the policy and procedures. The major highlights of the New Industrial Policy are: abolition of industrial licensing except for short list of 18 industries, liberalisation in respect of foreign investment, technological dynamism, amendment of MRTP Act and stress on profitability of the public sector.

The New Policy emphasises privatisation. The only areas where security and strategic concerns predominate are to be reserved for the public sector.

The growth of industrial production was 'NIL' in 1991-92 as compared to 8.4 per cent in 1990-91. The manufacturing sector showed a negative growth rate of –1.5 per cent in 1991-92. The growth rate achieved in mining and quarrying sector was 0.8 per cent. However, electricity registered a marginal increase from 7.8 per cent in 1990-91 to 8.4 per cent in 1991-92.

PROGRAMME IMPLEMENTATION

The Ministry of Programme Implementation (now Department of Programme Implementation in the Ministry of Planning and Programme Implementation) was set up in September 1985, to usher in a new system of goal-oriented management to closely monitor implementation of anti-poverty programmes, performance of all industrial infrastructure sectors of economy and implementation of Central sector industrial projects costing over ₹ 20 crore each. The Department, through its efficient system, prompt facilitative action and computerised network provided by the National Informatics Centre, is ensuring effective implementation of projects and programmes.

Infrastructure Monitoring by the Department of Programme Implementation aims at reviewing the physical performance with reference to the targets for the financial year of nine industrial infrastructure sectors namely powder, coal, steel railways, telecommunications, shipping and ports, fertilizers, cement and petroleum and natural gas, which have a pivotal role in the economic development of the nation. This involves identifying problem areas requiring action on a priority basis and coordinating the efforts of administrative ministries with a view to overcoming critical bottlenecks, determining intersectoral linkages for achieving optimal results with emphasis on better capacity utilisation.

Physical targets (for each area in respect of each infrastructure sector) are examined at the beginning of the year.

All Central sector projects costing ₹ 20 crore and above are continuously monitored, aggregating 311 projects with a total anticipated investment of ₹ 1,01,828 crore as on 30 September, 1992 on scientific basis using computer based project management systems. For the purpose of close monitoring 30 mega projects costing ₹ 1,000 crore and above and 112 major projects costing ₹ 100 crore to less than ₹ 1,000 crore, are monitored through the online computerised Flash Reporting System.

All the 311 projects along with 169 medium projects are covered in a detailed quarterly report called Quarter Project Implementation Status Report. Besides continuous monitoring, review and problem solving role, the Department continuously reviews the system of project formulation, appraisal and implementation and gives suggestions to improve the system and then it brings innovative changes after the Governments' concurrence. The DPI has also made efforts to improve the art of project management by increasing awareness through training programmes on the latest techniques of project management. This innovative system would help adoption of the strategic and tactical decisions without delay and would help speedy implementation of projects in the long run.

20-POINT PROGRAMME

The concern for human poverty and its eradication to improve human environment have been the central focus of our development planning in the country since the inception of the planning era. The explicit manifestation of the government's concern for poverty alleviation got its expression when the first 20-Point Programme was launched on 1 July, 1975 under the connotation of *'Garibi Hatao'* which was conceived by the late Prime Minister Smt. Indira Gandhi. This programme was implemented with a fair success during 1975-76 and 1976-77 Annual Plans. Needless to mention that the Sixth Five Year Plan (1980-85) incorporated these programmes as guiding factors in the planning process. Taking the past experience, the original 20-Point Programme was further redefined, revitalized and announced to the Nation on 14 January, 1982.

Objectives

(*i*) Increase irrigation potential, develop and disseminate technologies and inputs for dry land agriculture; (*ii*) Make special efforts to increase production of pulses and vegetable oil seeds; (*iii*) Strengthen and expand coverage of integrated rural development and national rural employment programmes; (*iv*) Implement agricultural land ceilings, distribute surplus land and complete compilation of land records by removing all administrative and legal obstacles; (*v*) Review and effectively enforce minimum wages for agricultural labour; (*vi*) Rehabilitate bonded labour; (*vii*) Accelerate programmes for the development of scheduled castes and scheduled tribes; (*viii*) Supply drinking water to all problem villages; (*ix*) Allot house sites to rural families who are without them and expand programmes for construction assistance to them;

(*x*) Improve the environment of slums, implement programmes of house building for economically weaker sections and take measures to arrest unwarranted increase in land prices; (*xi*) Maximise power generation, improve the functioning of electricity authorities and electrify all villages; (*xii*) Pursue vigorously programmes of afforestation, social and farm forestry and the development of bio-gas and other alternative energy sources; (*xiii*) Promote family planning on a voluntary basis as a people's movement; (*xiv*) Substantially augment universal primary health care facilities and control of leprosy, TB and blindness; (*xv*) Accelerate programmes of welfare for women and children and nutrition programmes for pregnant women, nursing mothers and children, specially in tribal hill and backward areas; (*xvi*) Spread universal elementary education for the age-group 6-14 years with special emphasis on girls and simultaneously involve students and voluntary' agencies in programmes for the removal of adult illiteracy; (*xvii*) Expand the public distribution system through more fair price shops, including mobile shops in far flung areas and shops to cater to industrial workers, students' hostels, and make available to students text-books and exercise books on a priority basis and to promote a strong consumer protection movement; (*xviii*) Liberalise investment procedures and streamline industrial policies to ensure timely completion of projects. Give handicrafts, handlooms, small and village industries all facilities to grow and to update their technology; (*xix*) Continue strict action against smugglers, hoarders and tax evaders and check black money; and (*xx*) Improve the working of the public enterprises by increasing efficiency, capacity utilisation and the generation of internal resources.

Various programmes were formulated to achieve the above objectives focusing mostly on the critical socio-economic constraints to development. The existence of human poverty was considered the single most adverse constraint to human development. The Sixth Five Year Plan was designed taking note of the micro-objectives of 20-Point Programme in the critical sectors which were accorded high priority in the planning process. The emphasis on agricultural productivity, rural employment, provision of safe drinking water, allotment of house sites to the rural families, improvement of slums, voluntary family planning, provision of basic health care, concern for environmental degradation, spread of elementary education, accelerating welfare programmes for the women and the children were the most positive features of the revised 20-Point Programme which were spelt out keeping in view the basic objective of the development planning that the fruits of planning must ensure the 'basic needs' of human beings if development process is at all to be sustainable.

While the various evaluation reports indicate different positive impacts, the major impact of the 20-Point Programme in the country was the re-distribution of productive assets in favour of the less privileged who are the backbone of the economy. From the point of view of a sustainable growth, these programmes not only improve the productivity in the rural sector but also increased the overall quality of life in the villages to a perceptible degree.

20-POINT PROGRAMME 1986

In the light of the experience and achievements of the revised 20-Point Programme-1980 and the emerging new socio-economic problems during the Seventh Plan (1985-90), the programmes were restructured in 1986 with the directions given by the then Prime Minister Shri Rajiv Gandhi, which was popularly known as 20-Point Programme-1986. The restructured programmes came into effect from 1 April, 1987 along with Annual Plan of 1987-88.

Objectives

1. Attack on rural poverty: (*i*) Ensure that poverty alleviation programmes reach all the poor in every village; (*ii*) dovetail wage employment programmes with programmes for area development and human resource development and create national and community assets like school buildings, road, tanks, fuel and fodder reserves; (*iii*) correlate the various rural development programmes to improve productivity and production-expand rural employment; (*iv*) promote handlooms, handicrafts, village and small industries and improve skills for self-employment, and (*v*) revitalize *Panchayats,* co-operatives and local bodies.

2. Strategy for rain-fed agriculture: (*i*) improve the technology for conserving moisture and ensure better management of land and water resources; (*ii*) develop and distribute appropriate and improved seeds; (*iii*) reduce vulnerability to drought through suitable changes in drought-prone areas and drought-relief programmes.

3. Better use of irrigation water: (*i*) develop the catchment areas and improve drainage in basins and deltas; (*ii*) improve irrigation management in command areas; (*iii*) prevent water logging, salinity and wasteful use; (*iv*) co-ordinate the use of surface and ground water.

4. Bigger harvests: (*i*) revolutionise rice production in the Eastern Region and other areas of low productivity; (*ii*) achieve self-reliance in edible oils; (*iii*) secure greater production of pulses; (*iv*) intensify the cultivation of fruit and vegetables; (*v*) augment facilities for modern storage, processing and marketing of agricultural produce; (*vi*) help livestock and dairy farmers to increase productivity; (*vii*) develop fish farming and sea fishing.

5. Enforcement of land reforms: (*i*) complete compilation of land records; (*ii*) implement agricultural land ceilings; (*iii*) distribute surplus land to the landless.

6. Special programmes for rural labour: (*i*) enforce minimum wages for unorganised labour in agriculture and industry; (*ii*) fully implement law abolishing bonded labour; (*iii*) involve voluntary agencies in programmes for the rehabilitation of bonded labour.

7. Clean drinking water: (*i*) provide safe water for all villages; (*ii*) assist local communities to maintain the sources of such water supply in good condition; (*iii*) pay special attention to water supply for SCs and STs.

8. Health for all: (*i*) improve the quality of primary health care; (*ii*) fight leprosy, TB, malaria, goitre, blindness and other major diseases; (*iii*) provide immunisation for all infants and children; (*iv*) improve sanitation facilities in rural areas, particularly for women; (*v*) pay special attention to programmes for the rehabilitation of the handicapped.

9. Two-child norm: (*i*) bring about voluntary acceptance of the two-child norm; (*ii*) promote responsible parenthood; (*iii*) reduce infant mortality; (*iv*) expand maternity and child care facilities.

10. Expansion of education: (*i*) universalise elementary education with special emphasis on girls' education; (*ii*) improve the content of education at all levels; (*iii*) promote non-formal education and functional literacy programmes, including promotion of skills; (*iv*) stimulate adult literacy programmes, with the participation of students and voluntary agencies; (*v*) emphasis on national integration and social and moral values and instill pride in our heritage.

11. Justice to Scheduled Castes and Scheduled Tribes: (*i*) ensure compliance with the constitutional provisions and laws for the SCs and STs; (*ii*) ensure possession of land allotted to SCs and STs; (*iii*) revitalise the land allotment programme; (*iv*) organise and assist special coaching programmes to improve educational standards; (*v*) eradicate scavenging and undertake special pro-grammes for the rehabilitation of *Safai Karamcharis;* (*vi*) provide better direction and adequate funds for the Special Component Programmes; (*vii*) pursue programmes for the fuller integration of SCs and STs with the rest of the society; (*viii*) ensure the rehabilitation of tribals displaced from their habitat.

12. Equality for women: (*i*) raise the status of women; (*ii*) enhance awareness of the problems of women; (*iii*) create mass consciousness about women's rights; (*iv*) implement a national programme of training and employment for women; (*v*) enable women to participate with equality in socio-economic development and nation-building; (*vi*) rouse public opinion against dowry and ensure effective implementation of anti-dowry legislation.

13. New opportunities for youth: (*i*) enlarge opportunities for youth in sports, adventure and cultural activities; (*ii*) promote physical fitness; (*iii*) involve youth on a massive scale in projects of national development such as: (*a*) the cleaning of the Ganga (*b*) the conservation and enrichment of the environment (*c*) mass education; (*iv*) identify outstanding young persons in all fields to encourage and develop their talents; (*v*) involve youth in promoting national integration, cultural values, secularism and scientific temper; (*vi*) expand the network of *Nehru Yuvak Kendras;* (*vii*) strengthen the National Service Scheme and the National Cadet Corps; (*viii*) encourage voluntary agencies working for the welfare of rural youth.

14. Housing for the people: (*i*) make available house sites to the rural poor; (*ii*) expand programmes of house construction; (*iii*) lay special emphasis on construction of houses for SCs and STs; (*iv*) develop low cost building materials.

15. Improvement of slums: (*i*) restrict the growth of slums; (*ii*) provide basic facilities in existing slum areas; (*iii*) encourage planned house building in urban areas.

16. New strategy for forestry: (*i*) grow more trees and raise more forest, with the full involvement of the people; (*ii*) protect the traditional rights of tribal populations and local communities of access to fuel wood and forest produce; (*iii*) reclaim wastelands for productive use; (*iv*) plant appropriate vegetation in hilly desert and coastal areas.

17. Protection of the environment: (*i*) enhance public awareness of the dangers of environmental degradation; (*ii*) mobilise popular support for environmental protection; (*iii*) promote recognition that enduring development demands preservation of the ecology; (*iv*) ensure judicious site selection for project and proper choice of technology.

18. Concern for the consumers: (*i*) bring essential consumption goods within easy reach of the poor; (*ii*) build a consumer protection movement; (*iii*) restructure the distribution system so that subsidies reach the most needy; (*iv*) strengthen the Public Distribution System.

19. Energy for the villages: (*i*) expand the supply of electricity for productive use in the villages; (*ii*) develop alternative sources of energy, particularly biogas; (*iii*) promote integrated area specific programmes for rural energy.

20. A responsive administration: (*i*) simplify procedures, (*ii*) delegate authority; (*iii*) enforce accountability; (*iv*) evolve monitoring systems from block to national level; (*v*) attend promptly and sympathetically to public grievances.

While the restructured 20-Point Programme renewed the Nation's commitment to eradicate povery, it laid balanced emphasis on how to raise overall productivity, reduce income inequalities and remove social and economic disparities so that the ultimate fruits of development resulted in improvement of quality of human life. The coverage of the programme was broadened to bring within its ambit a number of major areas of social concern for fulfilling not only the "basic needs" like adequate provision of food, clean drinking water, housing and health facilities, it laid more emphasis on human dignity and individual rights by encouraging 'responsible' parenthood, equality for women, opportunities for the youth, rights of consumers, justice to scheduled castes and scheduled tribes, etc.

Monitoring and Evaluation

Three tier systems for monitoring and evaluation of the implementation of the programmes are carried out *i.e.:* (*a*) at the agency level which are entrusted with the execution of the programmes in the field; (*b*) at the state level which provide infrastructure and direction for programme execution; and (*c*) at the Central level not only by the sectoral Ministries and Departments but also by the Department of Programme Implementation, under the Ministry of Planning and Programme Implementation, which oversees the monitoring and evaluation system on a continuous basis and reports to the Cabinet Secretariat and the Prime Minister's Office.

Assessment of Impact of 20-Point Programmes

A statement showing the targets and achievements of the major-20-Point Programmes on all India basis for 1989-90, 1990-91, 1991-92 and 1992-93 (April-December) is given in table 2.1 which shows the relative success and failure of the programme.

QUESTIONS FOR EXERCISE

1. Trace the development of Industries in India through five year plans.
2. Write Short note on 20-Point Programme.

TABLE 2.1

Targets and Achievements

Sl.	Item	Unit	Achievements			Target	Achievements
			1989-90	1990-91	1991-92	1992-93	April-Dec.'92
1	2	3	4	5	6	7	8
1.	IRDP (Families)	000 Nos.	3,301.2	2,877.3	2,437.2	1,875.1	1,185.2
2.	Jawahar Rozgar Yojana	Lakh Mandays	8,285.8	8,425.9	7,765.3	7,762:5	3,901.2
3.	SSI Units (Regd.)	000 Nos.	162.0	174.6	183.3	140.3	119.3
4.	Distribution of Surplus Land	000 Acres	118.1	89.9	143.6	150.7	63.2
5.	Banded Labour Rehabilitation	Nos.	9,759	2,679.0	1,824.0	2,279	1,331
6.	Drinking Water Problems (VLG)	Nos.	5,4180	40,969.0	34,122.0	35,493	19,152
7.	Community Health Centres	Nos.	177	76.0	116.0	259	52
8.	Primary Health Centres	Nos.	1,489	1,648.0	195.0	759	86
9.	Sub Centres	Nos.	8,934.0	496.0	—	—	—
10.	Immunisation of Children	Lakh Nos.	181.8	214.9	199.1	242.9	137.0
11.	F.P. Sterilisation	000 Nos.	4,061.1	4,053.0	3,930.6	5,224.6	2,376.2
12.	Eqv. of Sterilisation	000 Nos.	2,275.4	2,503.1	2,105.0	2,961.7	1,460.8
13.	ICDS Blocks Oprl. (Cum)	000 Nos.	1803	2,017.0	2,428.0	2,595	2,598
14.	Anganwadies (Cum)	000 Nos.	196.5	215.9	249.3	282.8	270.9
15.	SC Families Assisted	000 Nos.	2,227.0	2,084.4	2,083.3	2,595.6	1,018.8
16.	ST Families Assisted	000 Nos.	978.5	822.4	830.2	895.9	468.9

Contd...

Sl.	Item	Unit	Achievements			Target	Achievements April-
			1989-90	1990-91	1991-92	1992-93	Dec.'92
1	2	3	4	5	6	7	8
17.	House Sites Allotted (Families)	000 Nos.	884.2	771.5	1,215.7	601.4	628.0
18.	Construction Assistance (Families)	000 Nos.	410.9	421.1	478.2	360.3	350.8
19.	Indira Awas Yojana for SC/ST (Houses)	000 Nos.	167.3	147.4	208.6	117.6	124.3
20.	EWS Houses Provided	000 Nos.	34.5	76.8	97.1	115.2	42.9
21.	LIG Houses	000 Nos.	64.8	59.0	59.1	53.7	20.3
22.	Slum Improvement (Pop)	000 Nos.	2,013.2	1,922.7	1,608.0	1,177.7	721.5
23.	(*i*) Tree Plantation	Lakh Nos.	34,186	26,341.1	17,657.9	14,500.0	13,196.3
	(*ii*) Area to be Covered[1]	000 Hectares	—	701.1	947.0	1,064.0	895.6
24.	Fair Price Shops Opened	Nos.	4,262.0	2,427.0	5,643.0	1,512	2,899
25.	Villages Electrified	Nos.	15,892	10,203.0	5,819.0	4,240	1,358
26.	Pumpsets Energised	000 Nos.	528.8	551.8	543.9	256.8	226.7
27.	Improved Chullahs	000 Nos.	1,913.8	1,756.6	1,713.8	1,625.0	627.2
28.	Bio-gas Plants (States)	000 Nos.	134.50	136.4	135.6	114.4	67.4

1. Prior to 1990-91, the targets were fixed in terms of Tree Plantation only.

3

Labour and Labour Force

What is Labour?

According to *The Concise Oxford Dictionary*, labour means bodily or mental work, exertion, toil leading to supply wants of the community, body of those who contribute by toil to production, labourers, the labouring class as a political force, the labour group etc. Labour party means the political party representing interests specially of workers. Labour exchange means employment exchange. Labour force means the body or the number of workers employed. Labour union means trade union of labourers. Labour market means the market of supply of labour with reference to its demand. A labourer has been defined as one who labours, the man doing bodily exertion for wages, work that requires strength or patience rather than skill or training. Again, to labour means to exert oneself and to work hard, to strive for purpose to make living. All these explanations are a necessary prelude for the understanding of labour problems, labour welfare and other things concerning the labourers.

Characteristics of Labour

The following are the chief characteristics of labour as it is understood in economics, sociology and other social sciences concerned with labour:

1. Source of wealth: According to most of the thinkers labour is the factor in production process which is the main source of all wealth. In the words of Frederic Engels, "Labour is the source of all wealth, the political economists assert. It is this—next to nature, which supplies it with the material that it converts into wealth. But it is even infinitely more than this. It is the prime basic condition for all human existence; and this to such an extent that, in a sense we have to say that labour created man himself." The Marxist theory of surplus value is based upon this idea.

Therefore, Karl Marx recommends that the surplus value should be distributed among the workers.

2. Living thing: Labour is a living thing. It is inseparable from the personality of the labourer. It is not a commodity. It cannot be bargained or sold and used like things. Therefore, it has been recommended that a humane behaviour and environment for labourers must be ensured by the employers.

3. Saleable: However, labour is saleable, though the worker retains his own property. His training and efficiency are very important in this connection. A skilled worker gets better price for his labour. Therefore, it has been advised that the labourers must be given opportunity for training to develop their skill and efficiency.

4. Perishable commodity: Labour is a perishable commodity. If it is not used now or today it is lost for ever. It cannot be stored up. It has no reserve price. The worker cannot afford to wait. Hence, he is in a weak bargaining position in comparison to the employers. A significant corollary from this characteristic of labour is that the employers and the government and the trade unions must take special care not to waste mandays since labour lost is lost for ever.

5. No rapid adjustment with demand: As labour is not a commodity it cannot always rapidly adjust with the law of demand and supply. Neither can its supply be curtailed in the condition of low demand nor its supply can be increased in the case of increase in demand. This characteristic is important both for the workers and employers.

6. Less productive than capital: Capital may buy machine which is more productive than the labourer. A man stands poor in comparison with the productive capacity of the modern machine. Today, complex and improved automatic machines require no human effort. They are solely run by power. The labourer cannot compete with them. Therefore, in the capitalist competitive economy, the owners of the capital claim the major share of the profits. They take away the largest share of the national income. On the other hand, Marxist ideology does not accept this capital theory, since according to it capital is amassed by exploitation of labourers. Therefore, ultimately the major share of profits should go to the labourers.

7. Human factor: The most important characteristic of labour, from the point of view of social welfare and security, is the human factor. The labourer is a human being. Therefore, moral and social considerations must be taken into account in any discussion of labour problems and social welfare.

8. Less mobile than capital: Labour being human is less mobile than capital. Capital may be stored and converted into currency which can be transacted through paper money and bank cheques and drafts etc. Thus, capital is very mobile. In comparison labour is less mobile. Therefore, the capital always dominates the labour. Indian labourers are particularly less mobile since in this country there is a wide variety of natural and social environments everywhere.

The above characteristics of labour lay down the fundamentals for planning the policies for amelioration of the problems of labour welfare.

An important characteristic of the population of a country is the size and quality of labour force. Labour force is influenced by morality, fertility and migration. All these factors determine labour force in a country.

Definition of Labour Force

According to the United Nations, labour force has been defined as, "An economically active population." According to S.N. Agarwala, "Labour force is defined to include persons who actually work for wages and salaries, own-account workers, employers and unpaid family workers and also those who are unemployed but seeking work. It does not include persons employed in activities which are economically unproductive like rentiers, pensioners, beggars and dependents."[1] In the words used by *Multilingual Demographic Dictionary*, "For a statistical measurement of the working population, the gainful worker concept or the labour force concept may be used. According to this concept, the working population is defined as being composed of those persons who have a gainful occupation which they normally engage in. According to the labour force concept, the working population is defined as a group of persons who are working at a gainful occupation or wanting or seeking such work during a specific period preceding the inquiry."[2]

Labour force has been equated to economically active population or working population which has been defined by the Multilingual Demographic Dictionary as follows: "Generally speaking the working population consists of those individuals who take part in the production of economic goods and services, including unpaid family workers in an economic enterprise as well as persons who work for pay or profit."[3]

1. Agarwala S.N., *India's Population Problem*, p. 186.
2. United Nations Multilingual Demographic Dictionary, *op. cit.* p. 23.
3. *Ibid.*, p. 23.

Economically active population has been defined by the United Nations as follows: "An economically active population comprises all persons of either sex, who furnish the supply of labour available for the production of economic goods and services during the time reference period chosen for the investigation. It includes both persons in the civilian labour force and those serving in the armed forces."[1] Economically active population again has been classified as (*a*) Employed, (*b*) Unemployed. The population other than economically active comprises the following four groups : (*a*) Home makers, (*b*) Students, (*c*) Income recipients, (*d*) Others. The size of employed and unemployed population is calculated in a certain reference period which, according to the United Nations, has been recommended as one week. Statistical measurement of the working population is measured in terms of the gainful workers concept of the labour force.

SOURCES OF DATA

The most important source of data concerning labour force is the population Census. In India information on employment has been collected in all the Censuses beginning from 1881. However, each Census has defined the term 'worker' differently. In the 1951 Census the classification of worker and non-worker was based on the dependency approach in which persons were classified as earners, earning dependents and non-earning dependents on the basis of their gainful occupation. In the Censuses 1961 and 1971 however, a dual approach was adopted. In this approach those employed in traditional activities like agriculture, their activity during the last season was recorded, on the other hand in the case of those in regular employment, a reference period was adopted and the activity during the period recorded. The data concerning developed and developing countries is compiled by Demographic Year Book published by the United Nations, particularly in the year 1972-73. Besides, data concerning labour force is also collected by special Manpower Surveys or Labour Force Surveys. For example, in India the various rounds of the National Sample Survey (NSS) estimates of the labour force are collected in terms of sex, age, material status, rural or urban region and educational attainment, etc.

Analysis of Labour Force Data

Analysis of labour force data is generally conducted by labour force participation rates or economic activity rates. Crude as well as refined measures are used for the study of the labour force. The Crude Labour Force Participation Rate or Crude Activity Rate indicates the size of the labour force in proportion to the size of the total population. Besides,

1. United Nations, *Principles and Recommendations for 1970.*

there are other measures such as the General Labour Force Participation Rate and the Standardised Labour Force Participation Rate. These are as follows:

1. Crude Labour Force Participation Rate or Crude Activity Rate: This is calculated by computing the total number of persons in the labour force in the numerator and the total population in the denominator and then multiplying the quotient by 100. For example, the male labour force participation rate in 1971 in India was 52.50. This was computed as follows:

The total number of male workers = 14,90,75,136

The total male population = 28,39,36,614

$$\text{The male labour force participation rate} = \frac{14,90,75,136}{28,39,36,614} \times 100 = 52.50$$

The measurement suffers from the following limitations:

(*i*) The data are affected by the age distribution of the population.

(*ii*) The data suffer from all the weaknesses from all the crude rate used in demographic analysis in any country.

(*iii*) Very young persons and very old persons are not exposed to the risk of labour force participation.

2. The General Labour Force Participation Rate: The measurement is useful to calculate the refined labour force participation rate. It is calculated by relating the total labour force only to the population above the specified minimum age. Thus, it is computed only in the working age groups. It often specifies minimum as well as maximum age. For example, in 1971 the general labour force participation rate in India was 86.89 which was computed as follows:

Number of male workers in the age group 15-59 = 12,87,23,291

Number of males in the age group 15-59 = 14,81,40,059

$$\text{General labour force participation rate males} = \frac{12,87,23,291}{14,81,40,059} \times 100 = 86.89$$

3. The Age-sex Specific Labour Participation Rates: This measurement is useful for comparisons between the various regions of a country or between various countries. The data are not affected by the age composition of the population. All the three above mentioned measures may be computed separately. In 1971 in India the labour force participation rate in 20-24 age group was 81.30 for males and 17.85 for females. In the case of males it was computed as follows:

Total population = 2,15,52,684
Males engaged in labour force = 1,75.29,831
Labour force participation rate = 81.30.

This was calculated by dividing the number of males engaged in labour force from the total number of population and multiplying it by 100. For example, the labour force participation rate in the case of females for the same age group was calculated as follows:

$$= \frac{2,15,19,694}{34,40,492} \times 100 = 17.85$$

Similar rates may be calculated for other age groups such as 15-19, 25-29, 30-39, 40-49 and so on upto 60 years of age after which generally people do not work. It has been found by comparisons of specific labour force participation rate in different ages that before age 25 it increases with each successive age group but after 45 years of age it declines with each successive age group and very sharply after 65 years of age. No significant variations are observed in the average activity rates between the ages 20 and 55, at different levels of development in different countries. However, differences are observed in the higher ages. For example, in the least developed countries the average male participation rates in the age group 55-65 are highest. In agricultural countries economic necessity compels men to continue to work as long as they are physically fit. Therefore, one finds a more pronounced participation rate in higher ages in these countries. Similarly, in agricultural and developing countries children start working at a very young age. On the other hand, in economically advanced countries the participation of children in the activity group is very limited due to enforcement of compulsory education and the labour laws. It may be understood why in India the labour force participation rate is higher among children and old persons due to the above mentioned reasons concerning agricultural and developing countries.

4. Standardized Labour Force Participation Rate: This fulfils the need for a summary measure which will not suffer from the weakness of the crude participation rate. It is useful for comparing the degree of participation of persons in the labour force in various countries It is calculated for all age groups whose total is divided by the total number of persons working in all ages and multiplied by 100. In India it was 61.32 in 1971. This indicates that 61.32 would have been participation rate for males in India if the Indian age distribution of males had been like that of United States.

LEVELS OF LABOUR FORCE PARTICIPATION

According to the United Nations Publication *The Determinants and Consequences of Population Trends, Vol. I* the following are the important points of variations in the Census operations of various countries, making it difficult to compare labour force participation :[1]

(*a*) The time reference period of the Census question on economic activities. This may vary from a single day to one year, or may vaguely refer to an individual's "usual" status;

(*b*) The treatment of persons engaged both in economic and non-economic activities;

(*c*) The criteria for identifying unemployed persons; and

(*d*) The distinction in farm households between members to be classified as being in the labour force and those not economically active. The measurement of the labour force is extremely difficult under conditions prevailing in the rural areas of many less developed countries, where a marked labour scarcely exists.

Besides the above mentioned variations, different types of errors and biases make comparisons difficult. However, such comparisons have been made. It has been found that the age-specific participation rate for those below 15 years of age is the highest in Thailand where it is 43.7%. This rate for this age group is zero in developed countries like United Kingdom and Japan. Similarly, for the age groups 65-70 the participation rate in Thailand was 44.6 whereas it was only 2.5 in Sweden. This shows that very few people work in developed countries while almost half of the population in developing countries goes on working in this age. The labour force participation rate for male in India 1971 was 55.54 in the age group 15-19 and 73.79 in the age group above 60 which shows the poverty of the country. Similar results may be observed about crude labour force participation rates for females. However, in developed countries more females join the working force. And yet the situation is almost similar, to that of the male labour force. For example, in Thailand in 1970 the crude labour force participation rate among females was 46.0 while it was only 33.2 in U.K. and 29.5 in USA. However, it was 45.5 in USSR since the communist countries insist upon equality of sexes in labour force. Again, in Muslim countries the females do not participate in labour force, therefore, the percentage of female population in labour force has been very low in these countries. For example in 1971 it was 8.0 in Morocco. In 1970 it was 5.2 in Kuwait. In India also the situation

1. *Op. cit., Population Studies No.* 50. New York, 1973, pp. 294-95.

is very much similar since the percentage was 11.9 in 1971. This shows that female labour force participation rates tremendously vary from one country to another due to different reasons. It should be remembered here that in most countries housewives are not counted in active working force despite the fact that their working hours are sufficiently long within the home. Cultural influences have been very important in this respect. For example, one finds a very high female labour force participation rate in African countries while among Muslims it is very low. Similarly, it is very high in Socialist countries while it is low in Capitalist societies.

LABOUR FORCE IN INDIA

In India information on labour has been collected since the beginning of the Census in 1881. The data for the 1911, 1921 and 1961 Censuses were found quite comparable. The data for the Censuses 1931 and 1951 were not strictly comparable, due to undercounting. In 1971 Census the data for females had become entirely incomparable due to very large undercounting. According to S.N. Agarwala, "The 1971 Census departed from the previous Censuses to such an extent that the data for females have become entirely incomparable with those of the earlier Censuses. It has been estimated that if the 1971 Census had not so departed from the 1961 Census, the working force in 1971 would have been 156 million males and 71 million females instead of 149 million males and 31 million females. The very large undercount of females is spread over agricultural as well as unorganized non-agricultural activities. The view that definitional changes have resulted in a difference of 47 million in the working force is not borne out by the sample survery carried out after the 1971 Census to test such a thesis."[1]

Level of Labour Force

In 1971 the total labour force in the country was 180.4 million. Thus, 52.5% males and 11.9% females were engaged in work, making the total of 32.9%. The activity rate was higher in rural areas as compared to the urban areas. There was a striking difference in the activity rates of females in the urban and rural areas. The following table shows the labour force by sex and residence in 1971:

1. Agarwala, S.N. *India's Population Problem*, p. 187.

TABLE 3.1

Labour Force by Sex and Rural-Urban Residence, 1971[1]

Sex	Number of Workers (in millions)			Percentage of Workers		
	Rural	Urban	Total	Rural	Urban	Total
Male	120.4	28.7	149.1	53.5	48.8	52.5
Female	28.0	3.3	31.3	13.1	6.6	11.9
Total	148.4	32.0	180.4	33.8	29.3	31.9

Age Specific Activity Rate

In 1971 out of the 180.4 million workers, 10.7 million were children below the age of 15. Again, 14.1 million were old persons above the age of 60 years and more. The majority of the labour was from rural areas, since 80% of Indian population lives in villages. A high activity rate was found in the age group 20-60. The males aged 60 and above were working 52% in urban and 77% in rural areas. A short difference was noticeable in the activity rates of males and females. This is partly due to distinctions among rural and urban social mores and economic status. This may be visualised by the following table:

TABLE 3.2

Activity Rate by Age, Sex and Rural-Urban Residence, 1971[2]

Age	Rural		Urban		Total	
	Male	Female	Male	Female	Male	Female
0-15	7.5	3.0	2.8	0.8	6.6	2.6
15-20	62.1	18.4	33.1	5.5	55.2	15.5
20-25	86.3	2.2	67.4	9.5	81.3	17.9
25-30	95.3	21.8	90.5	11.6	94.2	19.7
30-40	97.6	23.4	95.5	13.1	97.1	21.4
40-50	97.6	24.1	95.2	14.5	97.1	22.4
50-60	95.5	20.8	87.9	12.7	94.0	19.4
60+	17.4	11.3	55.4	6.4	73.8	10.5

Activity Rate by Educational Level

There is hardly any question of activity rate according to educational attainments in rural areas due to widespread illiteracy in rural India. Therefore, such rates have been computed only about the urban areas. The table 3.3 given on page 34, shows activity rate by educational level in urban areas, in India in 1971.

1. *Census of India*, 1971, Economic Characteristics of Population Series I, Paper No. 3, pp. 1-73.
2. *Ibid.*

Activity Pattern of Workers

Indian Censuses divide activity pattern of workers by sector of employment. These sectors are three—Primary, Secondary and Tertiary. In 1961 the percentages of workers in these sectors of employment were 69.18, 11.48 and 19.34. In 1971, the corresponding percentages were 70.38, 11.33 and 18.29. This shows that there has been no appreciable change in the activity pattern of workers during the period 1961-1971. The distribution of female workers also shows the same pattern. In 1971 their percentage in the above mentioned sectors was 82.97, 7.67 and 9.36 respectively. This percentage will gradually change with the rise of industrialisation and economic development. Today the primary sector continues to be the most important field of worker's activity. This is clear by the above 70% total average secured by it since 1901 to 1971. The lowest position has been occupied by secondary sector which has occupied only slightly more than 10% of the total percentage of workers during the period 1901-1971. The total average for tertiary sector of employment has varied from 14 to 17% during the above mentioned period. This is equally applicable to the activity pattern of the female workers.

TABLE 3.3

Labour Force Participation Rate for Males and Females by Educational Attainment, India 1971[1]

	Educational Attainment	Labour Force Participation Rate (per 100 persons)	
		Males	Females
1.	Matriculation or Higher Secondary	63.49	13.34
2.	Non-technical diploma or certificate not equal to degree	64.12	22.22
3.	Technical diploma of certificate not equal to degree	79.31	60.85
4.	Graduate degree other than technical degree	73.48	21.58
5.	Post-graduate degree other than technical degree	84.67	42.89
6.	Technical degree or diploma equal to degree or P.G. degree	81.13	63.17
7.	(*a*) Engineering and technology	81.95	32.55
	(*b*) Medicine	76.12	71.23
	(*c*) Agriculture veterinary and dairying	89.47	16.67
	(*d*) Teaching	84.82	63.71
	(*e*) Others	77.50	56.62

1. *Pocket Book of Population Statistics*, New Delhi: Office of Registrar General of India, 1922, pp. 88-89.

Workers by Industrial Categories

It is well-known that most of the Indian males are employed in agriculture either as cultivators or agricultural labourers. While among the males the number of cultivators has been larger among females the number of agricultural labourers has been larger. It is particularly so since most of the land is owned by males in rural areas. One finds a significant difference between rural and urban people in this respect since the majority of the urban people are engaged in various industries. This also makes significant difference in the pattern of female employment in rural and urban areas. This will be clear by the table 3.4.

Workers by Employment Status

The data gathered by the 1971 Census were classified into four categories: Employer, Employee, Single worker and Family worker. As is clear by the table 3.5 the proportion of single workers and family workers was found to be higher in the rural areas. In the urban areas, on the other hand, there was a predominance of employer and the employee categories. As is clear by the table 3.5, the proportion of the female workers was high both in urban and rural areas.

TABLE 3.4

Workers by Industrial Categories Sex and Rural-Urban Residence, 1971[1]

	Rural		Urban		Total	
	Male	Female	Male	Female	Male	Female
1. Cultivators	67.4	9.1	1.5	0.2	68.9	9.3
2. Agricultural laboures	30.4	15.2	1.3	0.6	31.7	15.8
3. Livestock, forestry, fishing hunting etc.	3.0	0.7	0.5	0.1	3.5	0.8
4. Mining and quarrying	0.5	0.1	0.3	—	0.8	0.1
5. Manufacturing, processing, servicing etc.						
(*a*) Household industry	3.8	1.0	1.2	0.4	5.0	1.4
(*b*) Other than house-hold industry	2.9	0.5	6.9	0.4	9.8	0.9
6. Construction	1.0	0.1	1.0	0.1	2.0	0.2
7. Trade and commerce	3.3	0.3	6.2	0.2	9.5	0.5
8. Transport, storage and communication	1.2	–	3.1	0.1	4.3	0.1
9. Other services	6.9	1.0	6.7	1.2	13.6	2.2
Total Workers	120.4	28.0	28.7	3.3	149.1	31.3

1. *Census of India*, 1971, Economic Characteristics of Population Series, Paper No. 3, pp. 1-73.

TABLE 3.5

Percentage of Workers by Employment Status, Rural-Urban Residence and Sex, 1971

Employment	Rural		Urban		Total	
	Male	Female	Male	Female	Male	Female
Employer	3.4	1.1	6.1	1.4	5.2	1.2
Employee	55.1	57.1	66.6	73.5	61.7	64.7
Single worker	34.5	29.6	24.5	21.6	28.8	25.9
Family worker	7.0	12.2	2.8	3.5	4.5	8.2

According to Instructions to Enumerators for filing up the individual slip, issued by Census of India 1971, "A Single worker is a person who works by himself but not as head of household in a household industry. He is not employed by anyone else and in his turn does not employ anybody else, not even members of his household, except casually."[1]

Workers by Occupational Divisions

Total workers including the female workers in Census 1971 data were classified in ten major divisions of national classification of occupations, excluding the categories of cultivators and agricultural workers. The term farmer was used for planters, livestock farmers, dairy farmers, poultry farmers, etc., and not cultivators. The table given below shows percentage of occupational distribution of workers by rural-urban residence in 1971:

TABLE 3.6

Percentage of Occupational Distributed of Workers by Rural-Urban Residence, 1971[2]

	Divisional Description	Male Workers			Female Workers		
		Total	Rural	Urban	Total	Rural	Urban
0-1	Profession, technical and related workers	8.88	9.61	8.23	13.73	8.60	20.83
2.	Administrative, executive and managerial workers	2.26	1.22	3.19	0.34	0.16	0.59
3.	Clerical and related workers	9.87	6.36	13.03	3.46	0.91	6.97
4.	Sales workers	14.01	11.75	16.04	7.53	7.16	8.05

Contd...

1. *Census of India*, 1971, pp. 32-33.
2. *Ibid.*

	Divisional Description	Male Workers			Female Workers		
		Total	Rural	Urban	Total	Rural	Urban
5.	Service workers	10.54	10.19	10.86	15.35	12.53	19.23
6.	Farmers, fishermen, hunters, loggers and other workers	7.72	14.07	2.01	12.31	19.17	2.85
7, 8 & 9	Production and related workers, transport equipment operators and labourers	44.99	44.17	44.21	44.99	48.81	39.70
10.	Workers not classified by occupations	2.53	2.63	2.43	2.28	2.64	1.78
	All Workers	100.00	100.00	100.00	100.00	100.00	100.00

Workers by Occupation and Industry

Further, workers data in 1971 Census were further classified by occupation and industry. The occupational divisions included: 1. Professional, technical and related workers, 2. Administrative, executive and managerial workers, 3. Clerical and related workers, 4. Sales workers, 5. Service workers, 6. Farmers, fishermen, hunters and loggers, etc. 7, 8 and 9. Production and related workers, transport equipment operators and labourers. These were further divided into industrial categories, III to IX. It was found that 88% of the professional, technical and related workers were concentrated in other services. 95% of the sales workers were employed in trade and commerce. The rural and urban areas did not show much difference except in the case of 7, 8 and 9 categories.

Secondary Work Workers

In the Census 1971, every worker and non-worker was asked to tell his secondary activity. This secondary activity was undertaken in addition to the main activity. If any person participated in some economic activity other than his main work that type of activity was identified as secondary work. However, most of the females who reported secondary work were non-workers. On the other hand, most of the males who reported a secondary activity were workers. While the former were mainly engaged in agricultural labour as secondary activity, the secondary activity of the males was in non-household industry, trade, business or service etc. Of the total number of persons reporting secondary activity (51.37 million), about 92.5% or 4.94 million were from rural areas. The percentage of non-workers among males was only 4.6% while for the females it was as much as 86.8.

Non-Workers

According to the 1971 Census, the term non-workers included: full-time students as well as persons engaged in unpaid household duties, such as housewives, other adult females, dependents, including children not attending school, disabled persons including the aged, rentiers, persons living on agricultural or non-agricultural royalties, beggars, vagrants, inmates of jails, mental hospitals and charitable institutions, persons not employed earlier but currently seeking employment for the first time, person employed earlier but currently out of employment and seeking employment. The data furnished by Census gave a total of 366 million persons as non-workers. These included 232 million females and 134 million males. They were further classified into 7 categories. The maximum number included full time students, dependents and infants. The number of beggars was 7 lakh, including 4.6 lakh males and 2.8 lakh females. The percentage of illiterate males among non-workers was about 50.8% both in the rural and urban areas. The percentage of illiterate non-worker female was 50 in the urban areas and 7.14 in rural areas. A striking fact was the differentials evident in the type of activity according to rural-urban residence as well as sex. It was found that in urban areas there were more full time students both among male and female non-workers than in rural areas.

Trends in Labour Force Participation Rates 1901-1971

According to the 1971 Census there had been a decline in the labour force participation rates both for males and females as compared to Census 1961. This decline was sharper in the case of females. However, it has been pointed out by some scholars that this is not so much due to a real decline but a change in the definition of workers. Yet generally the decline was evident. The explanations put forward for this decline included rapid increase of population, war with China and Pakistan, severe draughts, etc. The following table shows workers' participation rate by sex during the period 1901-1971:

TABLE 3.7

Workers's Participation Rate by Sex, 1901-1971[1]

Year	Male	Female	Total
1901	61.11	31.70	46.61
1911	61.90	33.73	48.07
1921	60.52	32.67	46.92
1931	58.27	27.63	43.30
1951	54.05	23.30	39.10
1961	57.12	27.96	42.98
1971	52.50	11.85	32.92

The above table shows a clear decline in workers' participation, part of which may be attributed to definitional change. However, it was clearly established by a sample survey carried out in March 1972 that 1961-71 decade did not keep pace with the rate of population growth due to the two wars and the two severe draghts, which haulted the five year plan and adversely affected employment opportunities within the country.

TRENDS IN 1971-1991

For the 1981 Census, the population was divided into main workers, marginal workers and non-workers. The figures of only these broad groups are available. In the 1971 Census, the population was divided into workers and non-workers. There were 9 categories of workers, which is shown in table below. It shows the number of workers and non-workers in rural and urban areas as on 1 March 1981 as compared to those on 1 April 1971.

TABLE 3.8

Population by Categories of Workers and Non-Workers, 1981

(In crore)

	Rural	Urban	Total
1981 Census			
Total population	52.551	15.971	68.521
Main workers[2]	17.64	4.61	22.25
Marginal workers[2]	2.09	0.12	2.21
Non-workers[2]	31.03	11.04	42.07

1. *The Population of India*, CICRED Series, New Delhi: Office of the Registrar General of India, 1974, p. 110.

TABLE 3.9

Population by Category of Workers 1991

(In crore)

	Rural	Urban	Total
1991 Census			
Total Population	63.13	21.53	83.66
Total workers[1]	24.93	6.56	31.49
Marginal workers[2]	2.77	0.17	2.95
Main workers	22.16	6.38	28.54
(*i*) Cultivators	10.74	0.32	11.06
(*ii*) Agricultural labourers	7.04	0.42	7.46
(*iii*) Household industry workers	0.68	0.36	1.04
(*iv*) Other workers	3.70	5.28	8.98

1. The figures exclude Jammu and Kashmir where the 1991 census has not been held.
2. Figures may not tally due to rounding off.

QUESTIONS FOR EXERCISE

1. Define Labour and mention its characteristics.
2. Write an essay on Labour Force in India.

4

Labour and Personnel Policy

Labour policy in India derives its philosophy and content from the Directive Principles of State Policy as enshrined in the country's Constitution. The Directive Principles enjoin equal pay for equal work, provision of just and humane conditions of work and a living wage to all workers. Government's concern for the welfare of organised sector of workers in the country, particularly after Independence, is evident from the fact that a large number of Acts in the field of social security, safety and welfare, etc., have been enacted after 1947. While in the early years of industrialisation, labour policy was preoccupied mainly with the organised sectors of the labour force, growing attention is now being paid to the interests of workers in the unorganised sector without detracting from the concern of Government for the improvement of the real earnings and working conditions of those in the organised sector. Some Acts and rules have also been framed for the unorganised sector. The Minimum Wages Act, 1948, has been made applicable to many categories of workers in this sector.

FACTORY AND WORKER

Under the Factories Act, 1948, a factory is defined as any premises including precincts thereof where 10 or more workers are working or were working on any day of the preceding twelve months and in any part of which power is used for the manufacture. Where power is not used, the number of workers should be 20 or more.

A worker is defined in the Act as a person, employed directly or through any agency including a contractor whether for wages or not, to any manufacturing process, or in cleaning any part of the machinery or premises used for a manufacturing process or in any other kind of work incidental to or connected with the manufacturing process or the subject of the manufacturing process.

WAGES, ALLOWANCES AND BONUS

The average per capita annual earnings of factory workers in different states and union territories are given in table below.

Earnings

The variation in money earnings is shown on next page and applies to persons employed in any factory including the establishments declared as factories under the Factories Act, 1948 and in any railway and in industrial establishments such as tramway or motor transport service, air transport service, dock, inland vessel, mine, quarry or oil-field, plantations, workshops in which articles are produced, and establishment in which any work relating to the construction, development or maintenance of buildings, roads, bridges or canals, etc., is being carried on.

Regulation of Wages

The payment of wages is governed by the Payment of Wages Act, 1936 and the Minimum Wages Act, 1948, as amended from time to time.

Average Per Capita Annual Earnings of Factory Workers

(In ₹)

State/Union Territory	1975	1976	1978	1979	1980[1]	1981[1]
Andhra Pradesh	2,824	3,731	3,625	4,884	3,635	3,481
Assam	2,627	3,504	4,673	4,717	4,505	5,899
Bihar	2,158	5,262	5,527	5,480	5,481	5,761
Gujarat	2,149	4,793	5,645	6,437	8,803	7,447
Haryana	3,371	4,931	5,664	6,248	5,320	8,098
Himachal Pradesh	2,745	4,395	3,636	4,691	4,745	4,745
Jammu and Kashmir	2,843	2,087	3,400	3,186	3,176	3,178
Karnataka	2,893	3,042	NA	4,936	4,936	4,936
Kerala	2,947	5,253	5,436	5,696	5,696	6,948
Madhya Pradesh	3,942	6,378	7,391	7,065	7,964	8,295
Maharashtra	3,459	5,680	7,210	7,165	7,154	8,762
Orissa	4,194	5.417	6,119	7,414	6,128	7,497
Punjab	3,089	3,675	4,285	5,069	5,149	5,643
Rajasthan	3,325	4,954	5,811	6,382	5,811	5,811
Tamil Nadu	2,543	4,817	5,388	4,305	4,205	6,845
Tripura	2,453	2,251	3,630	5,007	3,001	3,630
Uttar Pradesh	3,054	4,486	5,418	5,983	5,418	5,418
West Bengal	3,966.	5,840	6,970	7,283	7,967	8,304
Andaman & Nicobar Islands	3,300	2,831	3,620	4,602	2,827	2,187
Delhi	3,239	5,092	5,528	5,491	5,892	6,035
Goa, Daman & Diu	3,792	5,965	5,715	5,853	10,587	11,523
Pondicherry	2,615	4,879	5,473	5,978	7,945	8,694
All India	3,158	5,125	6,068	6,144	6,387	7,049

Notes:

1. Provisional.
2. The data given in the table relate to workers earning less than ₹ 400 per month upto 1975 and from 1976 onwards relate to workers earning less than ₹ 1,000 per month.
3. The figures relating to factory workers exclude those for railway workshops and groups of industries seasonal in character consisting of food, beverages, tobacco and construction but include defence installations.
4. NA means not available.

The Act applies only to those who are in receipt of wages which average below ₹ 1,600 per month.

Employers cannot withhold the wages earned by workers nor can they make any unauthorised deductions. Payments must be made before the expiry of a specified day after the last day of the wage period. Fines can be imposed for only those acts of omission which have been approved by the appropriate government and must not exceed an amount equal to three per cent of the wages payable. If the payment of wages is delayed or wrongful deductions are made, the workers or their trade unions can file a claim. The payment of overtime in scheduled employment is governed by the Minimum Wages Act, 1948.

Minimum Wages Act

The Minimum Wages Act, 1948, empowers the Government to fix minimum wages of employees working in specified employments. It provides for review and revision of minimum wages already fixed after suitable intervals not exceeding five years. However, the Labour Ministers' Conference in July 1980 recommended that the revision of minimum wages should be made within two years or on a rise of 50 points in the Consumer Price Index, whichever is earlier.

Working Journalists Act

The Working Journalists and other Newspaper Employees (Conditions of Service) and Miscellaneous Provisions Act, 1955, regulates the conditions of service of working journalists and other persons employed in newspaper establishments. By a specific provision of this Act, the provisions of the Industrial Disputes Act with certain modifications have been applied to working journalists. The Act was amended by an ordinance on 26 July, 1981 to provide for amplification of the definition of the term 'working journalist', so as to include part-time correspondents; and prevention of dismissal discharge retrenchment of newspaper employees (including part-time correspondents) by newspaper establishments in order to avoid payment of wages as revised by Central Government.

The amendment was given retrospective effect from 13 August 1980. The ordinance was subsequently replaced by an Act of Parliament which received President's assent on 18 September 1981.

Palekar Tribunals

Government appointed two tribunals under the provisions of the Working Journalists and other Newspaper Employees (Conditions of Service) and Miscellaneous Provisions Act, 1955 to recommend rates of wages in respect of working journalists and non-journalist newspaper employees in February 1979 headed by D.G. Palekar, retired judge of the Supreme Court. The tribunals submitted their recommendations to the Government on 13 August, 1980.

Government had accepted the recommendations of the tribunals except those relating to the dearness allowance. A formula, with minor modifications and orders to this effect, was published. The dearness allowance formula recommended by the tribunals, was finally modified by the Government after giving the opportunity to everyone concerned to present their opinion. Orders notifying the revised rates of dearness allowance were published on 20 July, 1981.

A Committee of Ministers was appointed to oversee the progress of implementation of recommendations and problem relating to implementation. The Committee had several meetings and gave necessary directions to the concerned authorities. The Committee has now been replaced by a tripartite committee. The state governments have also been requested to consider the setting up of similar tripartite committees at state levels.

Contract Labour

The Contract Labour (Regulation and Abolition) Act, 1970, which became applicable to the whole of India in February 1971, provides for the regulation of employment of contract labour in certain establishments and for its abolition in certain circumstances. It fixes responsibility on the principal employer for payment of wages in case of defaults.

Equal Remuneration

With a view to giving effect to the Constitutional provisions as well as to ratify the ILO Convention No. 100, the Equal Remuneration Ordinance, 1975 was promulgated on 26 September, 1975. The Ordinance was replaced by the Equal Remuneration Act, 1976. The Act provides for the payment of equal remuneration to men and women workers for the same work or work of similar nature and for the prevention of discrimination against women in matters of employment.

The Act has been enforced throughout India and has been extended to various trades and establishments including plantations (as covered under the Plantations Labour Act, 1951), local authorities, Central and State governments, banks, educational institutions, mines, hospitals, manufacture of textile products, wholesale and retail trade, construction, agriculture, air transport, industry, community, social and personal services, etc.

Bonded Labour

The bonded labour system has been abolished all over the country with effect from 25 October, 1975 through the Bonded Labour System (Abolition)

Act, 1976. On the enforcement of the Act all bonded labourers stood freed and discharged from any obligation to render any bonded labour and their debts liquidated. Rehabilitation of bonded labourers so released form part of the 20-Point Programme.

The Act is being implemented by the state governments concerned. The incidence of bonded labour system has been reported from 11 states *viz.* Andhra Pradesh, Bihar, Gujarat, Karnataka, Kerala. Madhya Pradesh, Maharashtra, Orissa, Rajasthan, Tamil Nadu and Uttar Pradesh. Upto February 1984, 1,62,637 bonded labourers had been identified and freed; of them, 1,23,194 have been rehabilitated either under the Centrally sponsored scheme or under the ongoing schemes of the state governments.

Implementation of rehabilitation schemes is being continuously monitored and reviewed by the Ministry of Labour.

Bonus

The right to a share in the profits of a concern was conferred on the workers under the Payment of Bonus Act, 1965. The Payment of Bonus (Second Amendment) Act, 1980 provides for payment of a minimum bonus of 8.33 per cent or ₹ 100 whichever is higher, irrespective of whether there is allocable surplus or not. Bonus up to a maximum of 20 per cent of the annual wages is payable under this law in accordance with a prescribed formula. Bonus may be paid under a different formula linked to production productivity in lieu of allocable surplus by mutual agreement between employers and the workers. Payment under any other formula would, however, be contrary to the law. The Act is not applicable to public sector enterprises except those operating in competition with similar undertakings in the private sector; it is also not applicable to institutions not working for profit like the Reserve Bank of India, Life Insurance Corporation of India and departmentally managed undertakings. All banks are, however, covered.

Under Section 32 (iv) of the Payment of Bonus Act, 1965, the employees employed by an establishment engaged in any industry carried on by or under the authority of any department of the Central Government or a State government or a local authority stand excluded from the purview of the Act. However, it has been decided to pay productivity linked bonus to the employees of the Railways, Post and Telegraph Department, certain defence establishments, and a few other such organisations. While schemes for payment of productivity linked bonus have been drawn up in the case of the Railways and Post and Telegraph Department, in other cases schemes are yet to be evolved.

Occupational Wage Surveys

Occupational wage surveys are conducted by the Labour Bureau at periodic intervals to collect occupational data on wage rates and earnings in important manufacturing, mining and plantation industries in the country. The first and second surveys (both covering 44 industries) were conducted during 1958-59 and 1963-65 respectively. The third survey covering 81 industries, including all the 44 industries covered by the first two surveys, was conducted in four phases spread over the period 1974-79. Brochures on dearness allowance and statutory bonus in respect of all the 81 industries have been released. As regards main reports giving occupational wage rates and earnings, the reports on 3 plantation industries, 9 mining industries, mica factories, tea factories and 4 textile industries covered during the first two phases of the survey (1974-75) have been released. Seven analytical notes on workers' earnings in 67 manufacturing industries covered during the second, third and fourth phases of the survey have been released for limited official use.

INDUSTRIAL RELATIONS

Industrial Employment Standing Orders

The Industrial Disputes Act, 1947 is the principal central legislation which provides a machinery for the settlement of industrial disputes. In addition, the Code of Discipline (1958) and the Industrial Truce Resolution (1962) also help in the promotion and maintenance of good industrial relations.

Model rules were framed by the Government under the Industrial Employment (Standing Orders) Act, 1946 for adoption by the industrial establishments employing one hundred or more workers to ensure industrial peace. An amendment of the Act in 1961 empowered the appropriate Government to extend it to establishments employing less than hundred workers.

Another amendment in 1963 made the model standing orders, framed by the appropriate Government, operative in all industrial establishments covered by them until the standing orders framed by the industrial establishments are certified. The Government by notification on 19 May, 1982 extended the Industrial Employment (Standing Orders) Act to all industrial establishments under the control of the Central Government for which it is the appropriate Government and all mines, wherein fifty or more but less than hundred workers are employed.

The Act now applies to all establishments in Andhra Pradesh, Gujarat, Maharashtra and West Bengal employing fifty workers or more. In Assam, it covers establishments (except mines, quarries, oil-fields and Railways) which employ ten workers or more. In Tamil Nadu all factories under the Factories Act, 1948 are covered.

Works Committees

Works Committees have been set up in industrial establishments employing one hundred or more workers. They comprise equal number of representatives of employers and workmen and aim at promoting measures for securing and preserving amity and good relations between the two parties. On 31 December, 1983 Works Committees were functioning in 583 establishments.

Management

Workers' participation in management has been in vogue in this country for the last over thirty years in one form or the other. There is a provision for statutory bipartite Works Committees at the plant level under the Industrial Disputes Act. The scheme for voluntary joint management council at the plant level was tried for some years but it did not meet with much success. There is a provision for the appointment of worker-directors in the nationalised banks and a voluntary scheme for worker-directors in selected public undertakings where there is a duly recognised union and the labour-management relations are cordial.

In October 1975, Government introduced a voluntary scheme for workers' participation in management in manufacturing and mining industries employing 500 or more workers. This scheme was followed in January 1977 by another scheme for workers' participation in commercial and service organisations employing at least 100 persons, the latter scheme was, however, confined to public sector. The scheme provided for the establishment of shop councils and plant councils with distinct functions to them.

The Government have since reviewed the working of the earlier schemes on workers' participation and in the light of the review and experience gained so far, introduced on 30 December, 1983 a new comprehensive scheme for workers' participation in Central public sector undertakings.

Code of Discipline

The Code of Discipline, requiring employers and workers to utilise the existing machinery for the settlement of disputes and avoiding direct action was evolved at the Indian Labour Conference in 1958. It has been accepted by all the central organisations employers and workers and several others.

The implementation organisations, at the Centre and in the States, assist in settling disputes. The central organisations of employers and workers and public sector undertakings, except the All India Trade Union Congress have set up committees or cells to screen cases for dissuading their affiliate members from filing appeals in higher courts against the judgments of lower courts like industrial tribunal, labour courts, etc., in keeping with the letter and spirit of the code. A similar procedure for screening cases of appeals proposed to be filed by central undertakings has been in operation since 1964.

The Code is also applicable to public sector undertakings run as companies and corporations except those under the Ministry of Defence and Railways and also Ports and Docks. The Department of Defence Production has agreed to apply the Code, with some clarifications, to its public sector undertakings run as companies and corporations. The Code has also been applied, with certain modifications to the insurance industry, the State Bank of India and the Reserve Bank of India.

Industrial Truce

To ensure industrial truce during emergency in the country, an Industrial Truce Resolution was adopted by the central organisations of employers and workers in 1962. It laid down that there would be no interruption or slowing down of production, on the other hand, the production will be maximised and defence effort promoted in all possible ways. A standing committee, set up in August 1963 to review the working of the Truce Resolution, has since been merged with the Central Implementation Evaluation Committee.

National Arbitration Promotion Board

Both the Code of Discipline and Industrial Truce Resolution lay particular emphasis on the settlement of disputes through voluntary arbitration. Almost all the State governments and Union Territory administrations have either set up Arbitration Promotion Boards or made some other institutional arrangements to popularise voluntary arbitration.

Grievance Procedure

Under the Code of Discipline, managements have to establish a procedure to ensure full investigation of disputes to help in their settlement. The central industrial relations machinery persuade managements to set up grievance procedure in undertakings falling in the central sphere.

Lay off and Retrenchment

In order to prevent avoidable hardships to the employees and to maintain higher tempo of production and productivity, the Industrial Disputes Act, 1947, has been amended to prevent layoffs and retrenchments. Under the new Act, known as the Industrial Disputes (Amendment) Act, 1976, reasonable restrictions have been put on an employer's right to lay-off, retrenchment and closure. Now the employer has to seek prior approval of a specified authority or the appropriate government stating clearly in the application the reasons for laying off, retrenchment and closing of industrial establishment where 300 or more workers are employed. The provisions with regard to closure in the amendment Act are not operative as a result of the Supreme Court judgment in Excel Wear *versus* Union of India case 1978.

The position has now been set right by the Industrial Disputes (Amendment) Act, 1982, in which the relevant section has been redefined. The amendment Act is yet to come into force.

Conciliation and Adjudication

The central industrial relations machinery, known as the Central Chief Labour Commissioner's Organisation, is responsible for the prevention, investigation and settlement of industrial disputes under the Industrial Disputes Act, 1947. It also enforces some labour laws in the central sphere.

When industrial disputes cannot be resolved by mutual negotiations the conciliation machinery steps in. It is compulsory for the conciliation officer to hold conciliation proceedings when an industrial dispute exists or is apprehended in a public utility service and a notice under Section 22 of the Industrial Disputes Act, 1947 has been received, but it is optional in the case of other industrial establishments.

The Industrial Disputes Act also provides for voluntary or compulsory adjudication of industrial disputes. Nine Industrial Tribunals-*cum*-Labour Courts have been set up to adjudicate disputes in the central sphere. Of these, three are at Dhanbad, two at Bombay and one each at Calcutta, Jabalpur, Delhi and Chandigarh. The states have their own tribunals and labour courts. The Tribunal-*cum*-Labour Court at Calcutta and one of the Industrial Tribunai-*cum*-Labour Courts at Bombay are functioning as national tribunals.

National Labour Institute

The National Labour Institute was set up by the Government on 11 February, 1972 under the Societies Registration Act. It became operative on 1 July, 1974 as an autonomous institute. The education and training programmes of the institute are primarily designed to benefit labour administrators of Central and State governments engaged in the field of conciliation, labour welfare, enforcement of labour laws, etc., leaders and office bearers of trade unions, organisers of rural poor, leaders of the agrarian workers' unions and managers and supervisors of public and private sector industries.

The National Labour Institute has been engaged in carrying out certain designed educational activities for different categories of rural poor/labour since 1975. One of these activities is to organise rural labour education training camps. Fortyfive such camps have been held in different parts of the country covering approximately 2,500 participants. These camps have helped them to grapple with the problems confronting their day-to-day life in a better way.

WORKERS' EDUCATION

The Central Board for Workers' Education was set up in 1958 with the main object of organising educational programmes designed to provide instructions to the workers in trade union consciousness and in the management of trade union and allied matters. On a review of the working of the programme, the objectives of the Board have now been broadened. The present objects are mainly to equip all sections of workers for their intelligent participation in social and economic development of nation, to develop among them a greater understanding of the problems of their social and economic environment, to promote leadership from the rank and file of workers, to enable trade unions themselves to take over ultimately the functions of workers' education.

The Board is a society registered under the Societies Registration Act, 1860. It is a tripartite body comprising representatives of workers, employers and Government both Central and States. The Board has its headquarters at Nagpur with 43 regional centres and 18 sub-regional centres spread all over the country. The Board is financed entirely by the Government.

The programmes of the Board are conducted at national, regional and unit levels. At the national level the training is parted to candidates selected after a countrywide advertisement for employment as education officers under the Board. The refresher courses are held for the officers of the Board and the trade union leaders. At the regional level the workers from different establishments sponsored by trade unions and released by employers are trained by the education officers at the regional centres. At the unit level the worker-teachers conduct classes for the rank and file of workers. Residential facilities have also been provided at 14 regional centres for worker-teacher trainees and rural worker educators.

The Board started the programme of training workers from small-scale industries/unorganised sector from September 1980. It also expanded its activities for spreading functional adult literacy among the workers.

Leadership development programme of one month duration which aims at training leadership qualities among the participants has been started. In order that the courses at the unit level are need-based and are of short duration, subject-based short-term courses of 15 days have been evolved.

In keeping with the Revised 20-Point Programme, the Board has evolved educational programmes to cater to the needs of the weaker sections of the community. These programmes are being conducted vigorously. The scheduled caste and scheduled tribe workers have been participating in various training programmes of the Board. Women have also been participating enthusiastically in the rural workers' education programmes.

PERSONNEL POLICIES

Definition

1. *Edwin B. Flippo*: "A policy is a man-made rule or predetermined course of action that is established to guide the performance of work towards the organisation. It is a type of standing plan that serves to guide subordinates in the execution of their task."

2. *Richard P. Calhoon*: "Personnel policies constitute guide to action. They furnish the general standards or bases on which decisions are reached. Their genesis lies in an organisation's values, philosophy, concepts and principles."

3. *James B. Bom*: "Policies are statements of the organisation's overall purposes and its objectives in the various areas with which its operations are concerned—personnel, finance, production, marketing and so on."

4. *Dale Yoder*: "A policy is a predetermined and accepted course of thought and action that is defined and established as a guide towards accepted goals and objectives."

5. *Industrial Relations Glossary*: Labour policy is "the principle of objective established by a company for the guidance of the management in its relations with employees."

Characteristics

1. Personnel policy is a statement of objectives for the guidance of management in its relations with employees.
2. Personnel policy is a predetermined course of action.
3. Personnel policy is the recognized intention of the top management and guide to the subordinates in the execution of their task.
4. Personnel policy provides general standards or bases on which decisions are taken.

Policies, Procedures and Practice

Explaining the difference between policies and procedures says Ernest C. Miller, "Policies are general instructions-procedures and specific applications." Policies respond to 'what' and 'why' whereas practices explain the way of executing the policies. They transform the policy into action, 'practices', on the other hand, "are what is actually done in the organisation."

Need of Personnel Policies

1. To achieve the objectives of the organisation: Policies are guide to action towards the objectives of the organisation. Hence, they must be known and well understood by every one in order to concentrate efforts on the objectives.

2. To achieve uniformity in decisions: Personnel policies furnish the general standard on which decisions are taken. Various line authorities take decisions in an organisation keeping in view the personnel policies. Thus, uniformity of action is maintained in similar cases. There is the least possibility of worker's exploitation through biased decision. If the person in authority is transferred and the other person takes charge of the office the decisions to be taken by the new authority are similar to those which have already been taken in similar circumstances by the former authorities due to the predetermined policies of the organisation. This brings simplicity and uniformity in action.

3. To delegate authority: Personnel policies make delegation of authority possible, which means assigning the work to others and give them authority to do it. Personnel policies help executives at various levels of decision centres to act with confidence without consulting the superiors every time. Personnel policies give a manager liberty to choose the alternatives provided and to decide upon the action.

4. To achieve better control: Personnel policies specify relationship among organisation, management and workers. Therefore, each group works for the achievement of the large objectives of the organisation without any policy conflicts. Thus, personnel policies provide better control.

5. To evaluate efficiency: Personnel policies serve as standards in execution of work. Efficiency of a group may be evaluated by its performance in the light of the policy. After assessing whether organisation has achieved the desired results set in the policy, personnel policy may be amended or a new policy may be formulated in the light of the actual performance.

6. To create confidence among employees: Personnel policy provides the workers a security against exploitation and creates confidence in employees who may know where they stand in the organisation.

7. To motivate: Personnel policy introduces the employees to the objectives of the organisation. It guides the workers in achieving the objectives. They work enthusiastically and with loyalty to get those objectives.

8. To guide the management: Personnel policy provides guidance to management in relation to the personnel problems. Personnel policy decides how to get the work done by the people or how to behave with them.

Formulation of Personnel Policies

1. Due to day-to-day problems: Formulation of personnel policies and their development is the sole responsibility of top management. Their main purpose is to assist the top executives in reaching the decision in a given situation. If the policy fails to suggest a solution to the problem in a new situation it may be amended suitably or a new policy may be formulated to cope with the arising situation. Thus, the development of personnel policies depends upon the day-to-day problems arising in an organisation.

2. Role of Personnel Manager: In a position of staff officer the personnel manager assists the line authorities in formulating and developing the personnel policies. While developing the personnel policy we must have in mind the needs, goals and objectives of the organisation. The personnel policies should be flexible enough to offer sufficient scope for the department administrator to meet different situations.

3. Factors in policy formulation: A company having operations in various parts of the country or having global operations must adjust its policies in such a fashion as to enable the regional manager to develop specific principles to meet the requirements of their areas. Personnel policies should not contravene the basic policies of the organisation. Each group must be represented in the formulation and development of the personnel policy, otherwise it will be very difficult to bring the policy into action.

The laws of the country, social values and customs and employees aspirations should be taken into account in designing the personnel policies. These should be integrated in such a manner that these could not purport the economic and social objectives of the organisation.

4. To communicate policy: Personnel policy is a total commitment of the organisation for carrying out the work in a specified way. It should be communicated to all concerned. Any amendment and change in it should be brought to the knowledge of all employees and executives so that they may have full knowledge of the intentions of the organisation. If such policies adversely affect their interests they should be given full liberty to raise objectives. Cooperation from all sections may be sought in reviewing and finalising the policy.

Objectives of Personnel Policies

1. To achieve maximum individual development: The main objective of personnel policy is the maximum individual development. It should be designed in such a way that a healthy competition and effective co-operation among workers may be promoted and better results may be achieved.

2. To achieve maximum use of human resources: Personnel policy aims at the best and the maximum use of available human resources. Individual development of workers is not much advantageous to the organisation unless they are used in the best manner possible. There should be a direct relationship between man and the job. Right man should be placed on the right job. The job should be assigned to the man most interested in that work and has sound knowledge of working. He should be so developed that he may be able to accept the challenge of any eventuality of job. Maximum individual development and the maximum use of human resources should be a continuous process.

3. To develop good industrial relations: Personnel policy aims at good employer-employee relations. The promotion of good industrial relations requires co-operation between the management and workers. Nothing is possible unless there are good industrial relations. Taylor emphasised the principle of Mental Revolution which aims at the conciliation of the antagonistic views.

4. To achieve individual satisfaction: Personnel policies aim at individual satisfaction. The management should consider social values, customs and employees aspirations in formulating and developing personnel policies. Individual satisfaction is linked to the monetary and non-monetary incentives provided by the organisation to its workers. This ensures good wage and salary administration. The general attitude of the management towards labour should be reflected by personnel policies. Due recognition given to the work will promote cooperation and loyalty.

5. For protection of workers interest: Personnel policies should protect the interest of workers and recognise the trade union activities.

6. To provide opportunities: Personnel policies provide the opportunities for promotion to workers within the organisation.

7. To motivate people: Personnel policies seek to motivate the people at work and increase their morale.

8. To provide job-security: Personnel policies seek to provide security to job.

9. To promote loyalty: Personnel policies promote and develop among the workers a sense of loyalty to the organisation so that a sense of common interest may develop.

10. To develop sense of responsibility: Finally, personnel policies develop a sense of responsibility in executives.

Contents of a Personnel Policy

1. Name of the company: This includes a complete historical review of the development of the company and full details regarding persons in management.

2. Mode of selection: This includes sources of recruitment and methods, procedure and techniques for selection.

3. Working conditions: Working conditions such as working hours, leave Rules, top most authority-levels, channels for promotions and rules regarding suspensions and retirement etc. should be clearly mentioned in personnel policy.

4. Training programmes: Full details regarding training programmes, planning and objectives of training programmes for existing and new employees are included in personnel policy,

5. Procedure for handling grievances: Procedure for handling grievances should be mentioned in detail, *i.e.* to whom should they contact in case of any grievance and when, where and how?

6. Rules and regulations: Rules and regulations governing accidents, unfair termination, maintenance of discipline and standing orders should be clearly defined in the personnel policy.

7. Description of offices: Full information regarding numbers and positions of various offices in the organisation, their grades, wages, allowances and perquisities attached to their bonus and incentive wage plans, methods of payments and priorities should be given in the personnel policy.

8. Provision for labour welfare: Provision for labour welfare and service activities such as education, entertainment, canteen facilities, financial assistance, profit sharing, benefits of provident fund, compensation for accidents etc. should be made, is a personnel policy.

9. Industrial relations: Full details regarding maintenance of industrial relations, *i.e.*, notice period for strikes and lock-out rules for declaring strike illegal, monetary and other losses of strikes and lock-outs to workers etc.

10. Representation in collective bargaining: Personnel policy should include full particulars regarding representation in collective bargaining.

11. Line of communication: Line of communication and authority relationship should be ascertained in personnel policy.

12. Methods of consultation: The personnel policy should clearly mention the methods and procedures of joint consultation.

13. Fulfilment of needs: The items to be incorporated in the personnel policy may be more or less according to the needs of the organisation.

PRINCIPLES OF PERSONNEL POLICY

1. Common interest: The principle of common interest must be given due recognition in designing personnel policies. Economic success of the enterprises, the interest of the employer and the employees. It benefits all the concerned parties—employees, employer and the Government. Employees must have a chance for a better standard of living, better security and opportunity for living a fuller and better life. In return the employer must be able to get the maximum possible return. A successful business enterprise contributes substantially to the national exchequer and creates propriety all around.

2. Development: The organisation must provide ample opportunities for the growth of employee's personality. People want to improve their status, to earn more, to shoulder higher responsibility. Personnel Policies should lay down rules for the opportunities for development to those who are willing to contribute something to the prosperity of the organisation and to sacrifice their time and efforts for undergoing training to improve themselves on the job.

3. Recognition of work and Accomplishment: There must be direct relationship between work and accomplishment. A job should provide for sufficient wages and benefits that will enable an employee to buy his bare necessities. The personnel policies should take into consideration the employee's expectations such as reasonable security on the job against accidents, sickness and old age.

4. Recognition of Trade Unions: As the trade unions play an important role in the development of industrial relations, therefore, the management must recognise them. The personnel policies, should incorporate the clause for amicable settlement of the dispute with the trade unions through negotiations and collective bargaining.

5. Participation in management: Employees' representatives should be given participation in decision-making bodies of the organisation so that they may realise their responsibilities towards the management and workers. The success of any programme or policy depends considerably upon its willing acceptance by the employees. If the decisions regarding personnel affairs are taken in the presence of workers' representatives, there shall be better employees' satisfaction and morale. It will also minimize resistance to change.

6. Face the change: Employees always resist change which may be pleasant or unpleasant one. An assignment to an Indian technician abroad on company's expense may be a welcome change. But unwelcome change may relate to loss of income, loss of status, reassignment or retraining activities and broken friendship. Therefore, the employees should be prepared by the management well in advance to face the change as and when warranted. This may be done through bulletin boards, company magazines and newspapers, committee meetings, union-management meeting, broadcasting system and so forth. In this regard management viewpoint should be reflected in personnel policies.

To conclude, personnel policies be designed to promote common interest, create safe and healthy working conditions, give proper recognition for work and accomplishment, recognise impact of change on people, encourage employees participation and recognise the functions and responsibilities of the trade unions.

AN IDEAL PERSONNEL POLICY

1. Protecting interests: An ideal personnel policy must protect the interests of all parties associated with the enterprise, *i.e.*, workers, entrepreneurs, consumers, government and community. All concerned parties must get their due share in the total production of the enterprise.

2. Precise and certain: Ideal personnel policy should be precise and clear to the point and complete in every respect. It should not lead to varying and conflicting interpretations otherwise unnecessary disputes would arise in the organisation.

3. Flexible: An ideal personnel policy should be flexible enough to adjust and adapt any change in economic, social, legal and technological factors from time to time without disturbing the present norms and ideals.

4. Stable: An ideal personnel policy should be reasonably stable and permanent. Frequent changes should not be allowed as it would lead to confusion. It should be a long-term policy.

5. Framed within overall policies: An ideal personnel policy should be framed within the overall policies of the enterprise with the objective to achieve the organisational targets through better personnel planning and organisation.

6. Integrative: The ideal personnel policy must integrate characteristics of all people. It must fully take into account the differing capacities, capabilities, interests, aspirations, beliefs and temperamental make-up of the people for whom it is meant.

7. Uniform: An ideal personnel policy should be applicable to all members and all units of the enterprise although variations are possible keeping in view the nature of work and regional variations.

8. Acceptable: An ideal personnel policy must possess acceptability among the people for whom it has been formulated. This will reduce the number of disputes and will help maintain the discipline in the organisation.

9. Properly communicated: An ideal policy should be properly communicated to all those for whom it is intended so that all employees could know their rights, liabilities, duties and obligations in advance and could behave likewise.

10. Responsive to prevailing trends: An ideal personnel policy should be capable of being adjusted to the prevailing norms and trends of the business society. It should not be against the prevailing trends. For example, if the current thinking is in favour of workers' participation in management the personnel policy should not be against it.

QUESTIONS FOR EXERCISE

1. Discuss Labour Policy in India.
2. "A policy is a man-made rule or predetermined course of action that is established to guide the performance of work towards the organisational objectives"—Edwin B. Flippo. Discuss and explain the meaning of Personnel Policy.
3. "A policy is predetermined course of thought and action that is defined and established as a guide towards accepted goals and objectives." Explain the above statement and discuss the principles of Personnel Policies.
4. What is Personnel Policy? Why is it required? How is it developed?
5. What are the principles of personnel policy? Describe an ideal Personnel Policy.

5

Industrial Organisation and Human Relations

If two or more persons establish among them co-operative relations and make concerted efforts, the state of these co-operative relations and concerted effort is called organisation. The organisations can perform simple or complex tasks. All individuals within an organisation try to work for a common aim. The word organization is a derivative of the word *organ*. The word *organ* means a part or limb of an animal or man. Thus brain, heart, liver, arms, legs etc. are the various organs of man. The man or an animal as a whole is said to be a structure and organization. He is an organisation because his various limbs, parts or organs are mutually and co-operatively related. A group of individuals together working for a definite common aim is called an organization. The mutuality and togetherness found in a group of persons engaged in industrial production is called industrial organization.

Basic Elements of Organization

An organization may be industrial or formed for the attainment of some social or political aim. Every organization has some common basic elements. The basic elements constitute structure of an organization. Generally three elements are considered basic for any organization. Firstly, an organization must have numerous components. As a living organism consists of numerous organs and millions of cells, in the same manner an industrial organization has many wings or components and hundreds of units. These components perform their respective roles. The second element basic to an organization is the adjustment between various components. In respect of adjustment also, living organism provides best illustration. As an organism lives and functions only as long as its various organs function harmoniously, similarly, an industrial organization retains its character only as long as its various components work in a complementary manner. It is true of course, that there cannot be such ideal adjustment among the industrial components as in the case of human organism. Nonetheless without a minimum amount of adjustment there can be no industrial organization. It is not possible for workers to do any work if raw material is not supplied or the supervisory staff is missing to supervise the work. The third basic element of an organization is that it should be suited to purposive activity. This means that all elements of an industrial organization should be such as will contribute to the aim specified for it. For the attainment of different aims different types of organizations are required.

KINDS OF ORGANIZATIONS

Organizations are of two kinds: spontaneous or informal organization and formal organization. The spontaneous organizations are natural and these are not formed for any particular purpose. The organizations in the human, animal and vegetable kingdom are the examples of spontaneous or informal organizations. A sudden voluntary get together of human beings is another example of informal organization.

A formal organization is a result of deliberate efforts and is brought together for some specific purpose. Compared to informal organization, a formal organization is more systematic and works under specific rules. It is only within the framework of law and rules which brought it together that an organization remains an organization. In the event of violation of rules it is liable to break down.

The industrial organizations are always the outcome of deliberate efforts and are established with a specific aim. In an industrial organization we find both kinds of organization, that is, an industrial organization contains within it both formal and informal associations. In fact wherever men get together both formal and informal associations come into being. A deliberately organized structure brings together a lot of men. This togetherness, in turn, give rise to certain informal organizations. Besides, in as much as each industrial organization is organized to achieve certain specific aims, it has a formal character. With expansion and diversification of an industrial organization several sub-organizations under it come into being. For example, in every huge industrial complex, several organizations of workers and managerial staff come into being. These sub-organizations can be either formal or informal. However, these sub-organizations have their role and importance within the framework of the parent organization. It is however possible that sub-organizations may be in revolt against the parent organization.

In order to understand the industrial organization, it is essential that the nature of formal and informal organizations be discussed in detail.

Formal Organization

As it is clear from the above discussion, formal organization in industry is that human group which deliberately comes together for the achievement of a specific purpose or aim. According to C.L. Barnard following are the chief features of a formal organization.

The formal organizations are not concerned with nor do they revolve around a person or persons in particular. It is not the name or heredity of the person but his status and work that are important in a formal organization. An organization requires a man to perform according to his or her status. A formal organization has a hierarchy of status. On relinquishing of a post by one person another person assumes his office and the work of the organization goes on. The members of a formal organization bear to each other impersonal and not personal relations. Their relations depend upon the plan of the organization. For example, if in an industry an *x* makes a component of a machinery and *y* makes another component and *z* fits them together, the relation between *x, y, z* is purely formal and is limited to certain processes in an industry. However, this does not mean that there are no personal relations among *x, y, z.* Indeed, in an organization, it is but natural that various members should spontaneously develop various types of relations, social, economic, religious etc., among themselves. However, these relations are informal and are not strictly essential for the maintenance and sustenance of the industry. Within the framework of an industrial organization the relations between members are formal but outside of its framework these are informal.

Another characteristic feature of formal industrial organization is that it is formal and functional, it is nonetheless in the background of vast social organization or system. The social atmosphere affects it much. The socio-economic-ethical conditions of a society affect the industrial organization directly or indirectly.

Another characteristic of industrial organization is that it is scientific and systematic. Under the formal organization the role, status and importance of all jobs is well determined. The structure of formal organization is quite explicit and these are tractable of easy investigation.

Departments of Formal Organization

Whenever an industrial organization develops and becomes vast it becomes complex and the functions within it become quite intricate.

Under these conditions the organization gets split up in various departments for its smooth functions. The departments are generally considered to be parts of the organization. Normally there are three such departments in an organization. These are:

(1) Linear Organization
(2) Functional Organization
(3) Staff Organization.

(1) Linear Organization: Once an industry assumes gigantic proportions it requires a hierarchical system which can effectively control and manage the whole organization. This hierarchy directs the entire organization towards its pre-determined ends. This system is known as linear organization.

(2) Functional Organization: The industrial organizations have a variety of functions. For convenience each of these functions is entrusted to one department. This system of departmentalising of functions is known as 'Functional Organizations'.

(3) Staff Organization: In modern industry technological changes and inventions are taking place daily. New devices and sophisticated methods of work are being discovered daily in the fields of technology, economics, law and social sciences. The discoveries in all these fields have their direct or indirect application to industry. As a result of these there is a conceptual and practical revolution in every aspect of business management, production, marketing etc. It is not possible for everyone to be fully posted with latest developments in various fields of socio-economic and techno-legal developments. Besides, the scientific research is snowballing and requires special cadre to imbibe and absorb its impact. As the industry requires successful application of various new techniques to maintain progress, every industry keeps a team of specialists to keep track of development in science, technology, social research and law. Thus, a successful industrial organization would have experts in engineering, sociology, science and legal studies etc. This organization of experts is known as staff organization.

VARIOUS LEVELS OF INDUSTRIAL ORGANIZATION

Besides the classification described above, there are some other kinds of classification in an industrial organization. This classification is hierarchical and is according to status and position. This is also known as vertical organization. According to this classification there are different levels of posts and positions starting from labour and going upto the highest executive.

In any industrial organization, the wrung positions are occupied by those who are the founders of that organization. The capitalists themselves appoint the Board of Directors. The Board of Directors appointed by the capitalists elects the Chairman of the company. The Chairman in turn entrusts to each director one department according to his ability and capability. There is some difference of opinion with regard to the number of top managerial posts. But generally top positions are as follows: (1) Chairman; (2) Managing Director; (3) Executive Director; (4) General Manager; (5) Works Managers; and (6) Regional Sales Managers. In India Tata Oil Mills Co. Ltd. has the above described arrangement of posts.

Next to top wrung officials are middle wrung officials. This set of officials comes between the topmost and the low wrung officers and workers. The middle wrung officials are concerned with the implementation of policies and directions laid down or given by topmost officials. This set of officials must have plenty of practical knowledge. These officials are usually the specialists in the fields. The staff organization described above is the organization of these officials.

The third wrung of the industrial managers is occupied by supervisory staff. They occupy a position just above the clerical staff. Their job is to supervise work and report to the higher officials from time to time.

Thus, in an industrial organization we find hierarchy of status. The persons occupying different places in this hierarchy have their respective privileges and obligations.

Principles of Industrial Organization

In regard to industrial organization and business management new principles are being continuously established. However, certain principles laid down by relatively old experts still have their significance. Some of these experts are: E.W. Taylor, H. Fayol, C.I. Barnard, L. Urwick and P. Sargent. The laws and principles discovered and established by them have not only historic significance but have certain validity and practicability even today. These principles are based on actual experience of industrial management. Henri Fayol has laid down fourteen principles for efficient industrial management. These are:

(1) Division of Work
(2) Authority & Responsibility
(3) Discipline
(4) Unity of Command
(5) Unity of Direction

(6) Subordination of Individual Interests to General Interests
(7) Remuneration to Personnel
(8) Centralization
(9) Scales Chain
(10) Order
(11) Equity
(12) Stability of Tenure of Personnel
(13) Initiative
(14) *Espirit de corps.*

The above mentioned principles are crucial to every industry. By following these principles one can conveniently obtain the desired goals.

INFORMAL ORGANIZATION

Besides formal organization certain informal organizations spontaneously spring up in every industry. These informal organizations are generally complementary in nature and play a supporting role in respect of main formal organization. The informal organizations are based upon personal as against the impersonal relations of formal organizations. Wherever some persons get together there is exchange of social and personal human relations and this forms the basis of informal organizations. Many such informal organizations are found in industries. The informal organizations are neither deliberate nor do they possess neat well-defined structure. Yet there are certain preconditions for the formation of such organizations:

(1) The first type of informal organization is the totality of members of the organization bearing with each other certain relations at personal level. In the terminology of sociology this informal group is derivative or secondary group. In the secondary group members have interpersonal relations remaining within the primary group.

(2) The second type of informal organizations are those which spring upon on account of common tastes, interests or hobbies of some person. The members of trade unions, for example come together on account of commonness of interest or purpose. Certain clubs or societies develop, for example, we find dramatic clubs in many an industry. This is a clear example for an informal organization. We also have informal societies based on religion, region and language. There are also sports clubs which again an example of informal organization.

(3) The third type of informal organizations are represented by persons doing similar jobs in an industry.

(4) The fourth type of informal organizations are of very few and limited persons. There may be half a dozen poets in an industrial organization and they may form a poetry club. Again, there may be more than two persons in an industry hailing from same family. Their association will be an example of informal organization. Besides family relations, such organization may be based on friendship or intimacy.

It is imperative that there should be informal organization within an industry. The informal organizations are generally complementary to formal organization. They are not contrary to it. If care is taken to nourish the informal organizations they prove beneficial to the industry. If there is sufficient co-ordination and co-operation between industry and informal organization within it, the chances of strikes and lock-outs are minimised. Any work connected with industry can be done easily through the heads of informal organizations. The efficient managers try to maintain support with these heads.

Now the question is why is an informal organization necessary and how it comes to be established. The answer lies in human nature. Basically man is gregarious and has an instinct for establishing informal relations with his fellow beings. It is on account of this instinct that informal organizations come into being. Secondly, industrial workers are in the habit of avoiding work. They need some or other things to fill their empty hours. The informal organizations fill this bill. The habit of gossiping, smoking etc. are symbolic of this. Another reason for coming into being of informal organizations is that every worker knows well that he can be shunted from work, therefore he feels comparatively insecure. Besides informal organizations give emotional security.

HUMAN RELATIONS IN INDUSTRY

In the olden days, the workers in factories were regarded as objects no better than the machines and tools used in it. Behaviour towards them was not humane. And in many cases, the workers were no better off than slaves. In the days of British India, in the margarine blue factories of the country, many national leaders had to raise their voices in protest against the cruelty meted out to workers under the owners of the factories. In the South, too, owners of factories and mines did not treat their employees at all well. The worker was coerced into submission, and in many occupations the worker was often turned out without prior notice or any compensation. In cases of accident, fatal or incapacitating, the worker and his family were reduced to abject misery and impecunious poverty. When machines were invented, women and children were also added to the labour force, no concessions were made to their delicate condition and ideally exalted position in life. Even when leave was absolutely necessary for women, it was not permitted and pregnant women were often turned out of work. The system in the factory and working conditions were deplorable. The owner was concerned solely with his own profit, and the conditions in which work was carried on was not regarded to be his concern. It bothered him least to worry about air, light, sanitation, water, etc. There was no legal bar to the extent of work to be forced out of the labourer, the owners forced the poor workers to work long hours on very small remuneration. Promotion was a term unheared of in those days. Incentives to workers were not required, and were not tendered. Thus, exploitation was the rule of the day.

Call for Human Behaviour and Decent Conditions

Propagation of socialist and democratic principles caused people to revolt against such conditions. Labour unions were formed at most places. Different professions made their own organizations. In progressive countries labourers and other workers in different professions combined together to voice their desire for better working conditions, and for workers in industries to be treated as human beings. Democratic and socialist government also turned their attention to this problem. Besides this, thinkers and scientists came forward with the suggestion that because of absence of proper human relations in industry, workers were not the only losers, the government and the owners also suffered. This led to the propagation of the thought that efforts should be made to improve working conditions and human relations in industry.

Human Relations in Industrial Administration

In industry, human relations are in evidence in two spheres, in that of administration, and that of welfare. In the field of administration, it is the relations between the authority and the worker which are important. A labourer is not a machine, nor a cog in a wheel. He is human and has elements as motives, feelings, hopes, desires and aspirations. He wants as much as any other person that his good work be praised and that his efforts should bring him additional gain. Love and respect are things for which he yearns. Treated like a human being by those above him, his work becomes easier and pleasurable for him. Various incidents of labour strikes and lock-outs were mainly of administrative origin. Administration of a factory involves proper and systematic organization of the factory, besides human treatment of the workers. It is desirable that a feeling of security be induced in the worker by making precise and definite rules regarding appointment, promotion, etc. within the factory. The position entrusted to the worker should be made permanent. He should be made to know that the road to progress is straight and narrow, and that honesty is the best policy. Absence of these conditions is reason enough for a worker to feel dissatisfied and to lose his concentration in the work. A worker should be praised for any extraordinary effort that he may put in. He should also be made to benefit in some manner or the other if he does something unusually good. His salaries should be increased, so should his bonus, and he should be given a higher position. Conditions of work should be improved and the workers of a high calibre be transferred to good places. Such factors being existent, the worker's inspiration in his work continues and so does his enthusiasm. Without these incentives no industry can achieve much good results.

Misunderstandings and differences of opinion between workers and authority are nothing to cause extraordinary worry as they are part and parcel of life, all of them being human and capable of harbouring various kinds of emotions regarding each other. Hence, occasions of conflict are only too natural. Such problems of human relations require careful and tactful handling. If those in authority show laxity, unscrupulous individuals may take undue advantages and turn in bad performances. If, on the other hand, the authorities decide to make it too difficult for the workers, maltreat them for every little thing, interfere constantly, offend their respect and threaten them every off and on, it would be difficult for the poor workers to maintain their equanimity and work enthusiastically. Actually, the attitude and nature of every worker differs from one to another, but, nevertheless, efforts must be made to maintain cordial relations between them.

Welfare in Industry

At earlier stage in the development of human thought, the responsibility of an owner was supposed to end once the worker had been remunerated for his efforts on behalf of the owner. Economics as it stands today is more interested in welfare than in financial disposal of obligations. Governments of today are haunted with dreams of the ideal of welfare state. Consequently, it is now conceded that besides paying wages to the worker, it is essential to attend to his welfare also. Human services, conveniences and pleasures should be available to the worker as to any other individual. Atmosphere at home and in the office or factory should be congenial. They should get adequate opportunities of intellectual, material, moral and economic progress. Factors in their welfare would be the provision of such conveniences as convenient housing, educational and health service facilities, good food and adequate provision for rest and recreation. For female workers it is essential to provide more holidays and rest. Creches and maternity homes should be provided near the working premises for mothers. Special help should be forthcoming to workers when they are ill. Maternity benefit programmes are essential for women workers. Educational facilities should be provided for the children of workers. The future of the workers should also be made secure so that they should be able to concentrate upon their work wholeheartedly. Provident fund benefits, pensions and life insurance schemes are some of the ways in which this can be assured. In this way, it is now believed that the owners should do their best to provide for the integral development of the workers entrusted to their care by society.

Advantages of Welfare Activity

In fact, the mill-owners and industrialists get a certain percentage or returns on the money that they spend in labour welfare, as this money improves the efficiency, skill and cooperation of the worker. And if in the process of working in a factory, a worker loses his life, or at least his capacity to earn money, it becomes the moral duty of the owner to arrange for the upkeep of his helpless family. Actually, money spent on labour welfare is more in the nature of investment than that of expenditure since whatever is spent ultimately influences the owner favourably. Increase in the labourer's skill means an economy in raw material and increase in production. Scientific selection of workers helps to eliminate the improper exploitation at the hands of middlemen, and this improves the peace and enthusiasm of the workers who work better. In the same manner, technical training of individuals involves an initial expenditure of huge sums of money, but finally it also means considerable additions to their income and profits because a trained individual works better than his untrained counterpart and reduces overall damage. He stands to gain because the trained labourer does better both in quantity and quality of work. An employer does not have to spend much in improving light, ventilation and other facilities on the factory premises, but they have a very great influence upon the health and performance of the workers, with the result that production improves in quality; and quantity percentage of absentees falls, workers do not complain of fatigue and they less often fall a prey to disease. Healthy conditions of work encourage workers to attain a peaceful frame of mind and think more kindly and favourably of their employers as they are conscious of the latter's concern for them. This improves their mutual relations, and the workers do not tend to migrate to other jobs very often. Welfare work in respect of prevention of accidents has obviously a very direct advantage for the employer, since he stands to lose just as much as the worker does. He is compelled by law to make some compensation in case of accident, beside which such occurrences lead to unrest among the other workers. If it is a trained worker who is involved in any serious accident, the employer is quite directly hit. Prevention of fire breaking out on the premises is a form of labour welfare that should be right after the employer's own heart, and should concur with his way of thinking. But it also leads to the welfare of the workers' minds. Efficiency of workers can be increased by providing means and opportunity of rest and refreshment in the factory. Organisation of canteens helps them in getting food at the right time, and they can return to work shortly. It is in such ways as these that the employer stands to derive direct and indirect benefits from schemes of labour welfare.

QUESTIONS FOR EXERCISE

1. What are the basic elements of Industrial organisation? Describe its kinds.
2. Explain levels and principles of industrial organisation.
3. Write short note on (*i*) Informal Organisation; (*ii*) Human Relations in Industry.

6

Personnel Selection, Recruitment and Placement

Definition of Recruitment

1. ***Dales S. Beach***: "Recruitment is the development and maintenance of adequate manpower resources. It involves the creation of a pool of available labour upon whom the organisation can depend when it needs additional employees."

2. ***Edwin B. Flippo***: "Recruitment is the process of searching for prospective employees and stimulating them to apply for jobs in the organisation."

IMPORTANCE OF RECRUITMENT METHOD

The method of recruitment that an origination uses directly affects the efficiency of its selection and placement programme in at least three ways:

1. It determines the number of qualified applicants applying for a particular position.

2. It influences how well the organization meets its obligation to hire minority group members and women. This usually entails advertising in minority newspapers, sending recruitment to minority colleges and high schools, and cooperating with such agencies as the Urban League that specialize in working with the minority community. It also involves actively searching for qualified women when filling positions not traditionally held by women.

3. It can sometimes affect the subsequent turnover, rates of employees. Several studies have shown that when recruiters give applicants realistic expectations about a particular job by pointing out both the positive and negative aspects of it, lower turnover rates result. This is particularly true when the job is fairly complex in terms of the psychical and mental demands placed on the incumbents, as in the case of managerial and

sales positions. Often recruiters give applicants unrealistic expectations regarding the company and their future jobs, thereby resulting in frustration, dissatisfaction, and early termination. One possible solution to this problem used by several companies is a work sample preview, which gives the prospective employee a realistic picture of what will be expected of him or her. This involves providing films, videotapes, printed booklets, or job visit to realistically depict training and work.

Sources of Recruitment

Sometimes organisations recruit internally by using computerized data banks that store information about the skills, knowledge and abilities of each employee. When a new position becomes available, the computer can survey the entire work force in a matter of minutes. Quit rates (number of hired persons who subsequently quit) by recruitment sources has been investigated. If an organisation limits its recruiting to its best sources, it can reduce its quit rates—thereby resulting in substantial cost savings. In general, employee referrals have been found to be among the best sources of applicants.

Among the many external sources that organizations use to actively recruit new employees are the following: (1) advertising in newspapers, radio, professional magazines and local television; (2) visits to the college and high school campuses; (3) government and private employment agencies; (4) word-of-mouth recruiting by current employees, who are given incentives for doing this; (5) labour unions; and (6) professional organizations and societies.

A. Internal sources of recruitment: Internal sources of recruitment means promotion of workers from the lower rank to the upper rank. Most of the companies have a policy of promotion from within. Vacancies other than at the lowest level are filled up by promoting the personnel to the higher office. Thus, there is a chain of promotions that can be filled from those lowest in ranks by giving them training to make them eligible for higher position in the organisation. Practice of internal recruitment leads to a healthy and progressive atmosphere, lower cost of training and a high rate labour turnover. This source of recruitment is generally adopted to fill vacancies of middle and top personnel. Lowest recruitment is generally from external sources.

B. External sources of recruitment: Vacancies at lowest level or recruitment of the time of expansion of the firm or where job specification cannot be met by the present employees, require external sources of manpower supply. Following are amongst the most commonly used outside sources.

1. Recruitment of present employees: Sometimes, the present employees recommend their friends and relatives to the organisation. It is expected that the present employees will command only such candidated who have the potential and qualification to meet the company's standard of expectation. However, in order to avoid nepotism a great care should be taken in selecting a person among those recommended by the present staff.

2. Recruitment of former employees: Former employees are persons who have ever worked in the enterprise and have been laid off or have left the organisation for personnel reasons and now wish to return. These former employees having good record on their credit may be prepared for filling up new vacancies. These will require less initial training to bring them up to the standard of production than strangers to the enterprise.

3. Contracts of intermediaries: This system of recruitment is most current in Indian industries. Intermediaries are generally known as jobbers, Mukaddams, Choudhary or contractors. Management consult intermediaries at the time of their requirements. This system of recruitment has many disadvantages.

4. Recruitment at the gate: Direct recruitment of unskilled and semi-skilled workers is generally made at the gate of the factory or office. The number of vacancies, nature of work and time of interview are notified by the personnel department on the blackboard at gate. Prospective candidated attend the interview at the appointed time and get the appointment.

5. Use of unsolicited applications: Now-a-days an organisation of repute draws many unsolicited applications at the company's office. These applications are examined off and on whenever needed to locate suitable candidates for the job.

6. Advertisement in newspapers and journals: This is the most popular source of recruiting staff. Though employers resort to advertising for all types of vacancies, but it is the most suitable source for filling the vacancies of technical and senior personnel. Particulars regarding the job and the qualifications of the prospective candidate are given in the advertisement in newspapers, journals and magazines. Candidates possessing the requisite qualifications apply for the job in reference to the advertisement. This system attracts the applicants of requisite calibre.

7. Visit to schools, colleges, universities and technical institutions: These are a very useful source of recruitment for a full range of jobs. The employment managers of the enterprises maintain a close liaison with the universities and schools of technology particularly for recruiting officer Apprentices or Management Trainees. Universities and technical institutions also empanel the promising young talents for employment and refer their names to the prospective employers as and when asked for.

8. Notification to Employment Exchanges: Employment Exchanges are the most popular source of recruitment for unskilled, skilled, or semi-skilled operative jobs. The job seekers get their names registered with employment exchanges, managed and operated by the Central and State Governments. The employers notify the vacancies to such exchanges and the exchanges refer the names of prospective candidates to the employers.

9. Recruitment through private agencies: Some private agencies also do recruit the technical and professional personnel for a company. They provide a nation-wide service in attempting to match the demand and supply of personnel. Many private agencies tend to specialise in a particular type of work like sales, office, engineers, etc.

10. Recommendation from professional bodies: Some professional institutions like Institute of Charted Accountant, ICWA, Institute of Company Secretary etc. maintain a register of qualified persons from which they recommend the names of the job seekers to the employers when asked for.

11. Assistance by personnel consultants: Now-a-days consultants who specialise in the recruitment of managers and other senior officials are also called upon to assist the management in filling of these posts. At the time of recruitment of the senior officials companies hire the services of these consultants. On receiving requisition from the client companies, these consultant agencies advertise job descriptions in leading newspapers and periodicals without disclosing the names of the employers. The applications received are passed on to the concerned employers. If asked by the company these firms may screen, interview and select the candidates for the company.

12. Assistance of trade unions: Trade unions assist in recruiting the staff in some companies. This cooperation helps in developing better labour relations. However, this source of labour supply is not reliable since sometimes trade unions support a candidate who is not fit for the job and is not acceptable to management. This worsens the labour relations.

13. Missing part-time employees full time: Sometimes, persons are employed to dispose off heavy seasonal work or the arrears of work temporarily on part-time basis. These part-time employees are a good source of labour supply as and when vacancies occur. If they fulfil the requisite qualifications to suit the jobs, vacancies are filled up among them.

14. Leasing of personnel: Short-term fluctuations in personnel needs are sometimes stabilised through leasing of personnel for some specified period from other industries, offices and units. This system of leasing is well adopted by the public sector organisations. The acute shortage of managerial personnel, particularly at higher levels in public sector leads them to borrow the personnel of requisite calibre from the Government departments. They are given an option to choose either their parent services or the present organisation at the end of their term.

Concluding Recruitment

No source is good or bad in itself in all circumstances and for all employees. No single source of recruitment can suit all the companies for filling up the posts of different nature and at different times. Fore recruiting the unskilled workers, direct recruitment at gate of friends and relatives of existing employees or casual workers may be the best sources of recruitment. For the recruitment of managers and high officials at various levels, consultants, professional bodies, universities and technical colleges may be the good sources of recruitment for skilled or semi-skilled operative personnel. Finally, the suitability of the source of labour supply depends upon the size of the company, nature of job and the supply of qualified personnel.

PROCESS OF SELECTION

Meaning

In the words of Dale Yoder, "Selection is the process in which candidates for employment are divided into two classes—those who are to be offered employment and those who are not." Selection means a process by which the qualified personnel may be chosen from the applicants offering their services to the organisation for employment. Thus, selection process is a tool in the hands of the management to differentiate the qualified and unqualified applicants by applying various techniques such as interviews, tests, etc. Thus, selection is a negative process of employment in which only a few qualify for the job and offered employment while all others are denied the opportunities. It is a decision-making process where the management decides certain norms and principles to adhere to standards on the basis of which, a discrimination between qualified and unqualified candidates may be made. A sound selection policy ensures the selection of a suitable candidate.

Procedure

1. Scrutiny of application forms: Selection procedure starts only after the applications are received by a concern. Considering the standards set out by the organisation these applications are scrutinised. The applicants are screened out at each step.

2. Priliminary interview: Its purpose is to eliminate the unqualified or unsuitable candidate. It should be brief to have an idea of general education, experience, training, appearance, personality and salary requirements of the candidate etc.

3. Application Blank: A Blank Application Form or Application Blank is a weeding out device in the selection procedure. It is supplied to the successful candidates in preliminary interviews. Application Blanks give a written record of the following informations:

(*i*) *Identification*: Such as family background, date and place of birth, age, sex, height, citizenship, marital status etc.

(*ii*) *Education*: It includes information about academic career, subjects taken at various school certificate and degree levels, grade, division or place awarded in school and college, technical qualification etc.

(*iii*) *Experience*: Giving full details of past jobs such as nature of work, job responsibilities, periods involved, designations, salaries with allowances, reasons for leaving the present assignment etc.

(iv) *Expected salaries*: Allowances and other fringe benefits.

(*v*) *Community activities*: These consist of details regarding extra-curricular activities, hobbies, position held in social organisation such as clubs, management association etc.

(*vi*) *References*: These may be gathered from reliable persons.

4. Employment Tests: These days psychological and other tests are becoming increasingly popular, as a part of the selection process. The personnel department may guide and help in the selection of types of tests appropriate for a particular position.

(*a*) *Trade Tests*: Technical jobs require trade test. The purpose of trade test is to assess the capabilities of the candidates for the type of job which is being offered to them. For example, for recruitment of a stenographer in an office, a test can be taken to check his speed at dictation and typing.

(*a*) *Psychological Tests*: As the individual differ from one another the industrial psychologists have devised certain tests to assist the management in evaluation the expected performance on the task relative to that of the other candidates. Some of these tests are the following:

(*i*) *Aptitude Tests*: These are designed to measure the aptitude of applicants and their capacity to learn the skills required on a particular job. These are more useful for clerical and trade positions.

(*ii*) *Intelligence Tests*: These aim at testing the mental capacity of a person with respect to various things. It measures the individual learning ability to grasp or understand instructions and also ability to reason and make judgement. There are verbal and non-verbal individual and group intelligence tests.

(*iii*) *Interest Tests*: These determine the preference of the applicants for occupations of different kinds.

(*iv*) *Knowledge Tests*: These are devised to measure the depth of the knowledge and proficiency in certain skills already achieved by the applicants such as engineering, accounting etc.

(*v*) *Projective Tests*: In Projective techniques the applicant projects his personality into free responses about pictures shown to him which are ambiguous.

(*vi*) *Personality Tests*: These determine personality traits of the candidate such as co-operativeness against dominance or the emotional balance the temperamental qualities of a person.

(*vii*) *Judgement Tests*: These are used for evaluating the ability to apply knowledge judiciously in solving a problem.

(*viii*) *Dexterity Tests*: These are used to discover the ability to use the different parts of body in a coordinated manner. These are useful in identifying accident prone candidates for certain manufacturing jobs. Psychological tests are simply a step and not a replacement for the other phases of the selection process.

5. Employment interview: It must be conducted in a friendly atmosphere. The candidate must be made to feel at easy. The questions should better be asked on the basis of job specifications. Unwarranted questions should be avoided. A verification of the information furnished by the candidate in Application Blank may be made. An additional information may be sought for future record. The candidate should be given a chance to ask questions to satisfy himself regarding the history of the concern, future prospects, salary offered and nature of job, etc.

6. Reference check: If the applicant crosses all the above hurdles, an investigation may be made on the references supplied by the applicant regarding his past employment, education, character, personnel reputation etc. Referees may be called upon on telephones. They may be contacted through mail or personal visit. Additional material may also be recorded by asking the question from referees.

7. Medical examination: It is a part of selection process for all suitable applicants. It is conducted after the final decision has been made to select the candidate. A thorough physical examination is also essential to ensure that the candidate is able to handle the job efficiently.

8. Final selection: If a candidate successfully passes through an appointment letter may be given to him mentioning the post on which selected, the terms of appointment, pay scales, etc. When he joins the organisation, the personnel manager should introduce him to the company and his job.

Whatever may be the procedure the personnel department play an important role in the selection of a candidate. Though the decision to recruit the personnel is not taken in the personnel department but it assist the top executives in selecting the candidate by devising the form of Application Blank and preparing job description and setting the job specifications.

RECRUITMENT THROUGH INTERMEDIARIES

Most of the recruitment in Indian industry is done through intermediaries or brokers. These intermediaries or brokers are either in the pay of the industrialists or work as commission agents. To gather and recruit workers according to the needs and specifications of the industrialists is the job of these intermediaries or brokers. The brokers go around the villages and residential quarters of workers and offer them opportunities of employment. At times these intermediaries bring the workers to cities by enticement and offer of illusory hopes. The industrialists pay the travel and other expenses incurred by the intermediaries. They are also paid in advance under certain circumstances the rail fare and other expanses incurred by them in transporting the workers from villages to cities. All over India these brokers recruit quite a good number of workers. In different regions of India these intermediates are known by different names. The chief local names for brokers are: Dalal, Jobber, Sardar, Mistry, Thekedar, Chaudhary, Mukaddam etc. These days even lady brokers are meant for the recruitment of girls and women for various kinds of job. The packing departments have majority of women as workers. The lady brokers are known by various names in different regions. Some of these names are: Chaudharani. Mukaddamin, Thekadarni and Naikin. The functional importance of brokers have been clearly brought out by Labour Investigation Committee: "He is almost an ubiquitous feature of recruitment and labour administration in India and usually combines in himself a formidable array of functions. Thus, he is not only a recruiting agent but very often a supervisor or a foreman, even a subemployer and a worker sharing the income with other workers." This observation makes it plain that usually these brokers are the agents of the industrialists. Generally they function as go-between the worker and the employer and are the agency or instrument whereby workers represent their grievances to employers. Besides, these brokers act as informers: they pass on to the industrialists advance information about strikes and other confabulations of the workers. The workers who get employment through brokers generally have to pay some commission to the brokers.

These brokers have sometimes the right to dismiss them from service At certain places these brokers, besides performing their usual functions; also do the job of money-lending. By this means they are able to exploit workers.

Advantages of Recruitment though Intermediaries

1. Easy availability of workers: These are certain times when workers are not easily available. Besides in certain industries environmental and working conditions are such that an average worker is repelled by them and does not want to work under those conditions at any cost whatsoever. The industrialists are unable to find sufficient workers for the running of their industries. Under the circumstances where workers are not easy to come by the industrialists feel constrained to rely upon brokers for the recruitment. These brokers go around places to persuade, entice and entangle workers. They bring workers to the industries under many pretexts and gradually gain such hold over them that the workers can ill-afford to belly them. In India the coal mines and tea gardens are the two industries where the recruitment of workers is done almost exclusively by brokers.

2. Facility in industrial management: The brokers in industries know everything about workers. They are well-informed about their background, their adaptability and above all their problems regarding word. Therefore, they are able to give to the employers from time to time correct assessment about them. Based on this assessment they are able to take advance action to rectify the genuine problems of the workers and also check the building up of frustration in workers. Thus, the brokers play a useful role in keeping the wheels of industry moving by aiding in successful management of the problems of workers. The brokers are useful to the employers in another way. They know everything about the activities of workers and are able to give advance information about strike, sabotage etc.

3. Lessening of employer's responsibility: As it is clear from the above discussion the brokers perform many functions of the employers. The overseeing of workers problems, maintenance of their attendance record and settlement of inter-factional rivalries of workers are some of the tasks which the brokers competently look after. In some places the brokers impart general training to workers. On account of all these factors the responsibility of the employers is much reduced.

Disadvantages of Recruitment through Intermediaries

1. Exploitation of workers: The majority of industrial workers in India are illiterate and poor. Moreover India is a populous country and the supply of workers for jobs far exceeds the demand. Under these circumstances it is rather difficult to find any suitable job. Taking advantage of this situation the brokers exploit the workers and charge commission for getting them jobs. Sometimes the workers are forced to make regular monthly payments to brokers. The brokers also charge money for condoning inefficient work, granting leaves and for recommending promotions. Thus, brokers exploit the workers in every possible way.

2. Recruitment of incompetent workers: It is quite apparent from the above discussion that the real criterion of recruitment of workers is commission, graft or bribe. As can be easily appreciated, payment of commission means that preference in recruitment will be given to those who are able to give maximum bribe. Under these conditions the necessary conditions of getting employment is not efficiency of work but the ability to pay. Thus, in broker-recruitment system many an incompetent worker get entry into industry. This gradually undermines the morale in industry. Besides, the work shy workers do not put in regular hours of work but get away with their truancy by silencing the broker by greasing his palm. In this connection Textile Enquiry Committee has this to say, "It would not be out of place to say that whereas hundreds of efficient and competent workers are roaming about in the city for want of employment a large number of fresh and incompetent workers are seen working in the mills on job for which they have no qualification except their willingness to pay a price for that job to the jobber."

3. Increase in industrial conflicts: The broker, as a rule are extremely hard-hearted. In order to remain in the good books of industrialists they keep back-biting the workers and give exaggerated or false accounts about the activities of workers. Their game is not one-sided; it is dual. They not only report assist workers to the industrialist but also incite the workers against employers. Thus, they keep workers and employers in dark about the real situation and try to exploit both to their personal advantage. Thus, while acting as go-between or contract between workers and employers, they normally are instrumental to increasing of industrial conflicts.

4. Non-availability of permanent workers: By employing various forms of enticement, persuasion etc., brokers bring the innocent persons from far off villages and primitive tribal belts to cities for industrial jobs. These innocent persons are unable to adjust with the urban climate and the complexities of urban life terrify them. Therefore, they do not like to stay in the cities for any length of time and rush back to villages at the first available opportunity. Thus, the recruitment by brokers fails to get the industrialists permanent workers. The transient labour, as can be well appreciated, is a great liability.

5. Immoral exploitation of female workers: Under the system of recruitment by brokers there is immoral exploitation of female workers. The majority of jobbery in industry is in the hands of men and they indulge in immoral exploitation of the female workers. Whenever a woman needs some job, she has to approach some or the other jobber. This jobber usually demands physical satisfaction from her for getting her a job. Thus, it is difficult for ladies to get jobs without making a moral compromise. In big industries where there are female jobbers, they are of low moral caliber as a rule and they do not shirk from immoral exploitation of female workers and make money out of it.

From the above discussion the merits and demerits of the broker recruitment system become quite apparent. If we think seriously about the relative balance between merits and demerits we shall find that demerits outweigh the merits. In spite of the preponderance of faults of the system is fairly popular in industry. Even today broker-recruitment system is very much prevalent in Sholapur, Kanpur and Bombay. Indeed the Indian worker is not fully awakened and is unable to make successful effort for job in his own. Besides, the task of the employer is made much easier by this. For all these reasons this system is quite popular.

RECRUITMENT THROUGH CONTRACTORS

In India a large number of workers are recruited to industry through the medium of contractors. The industrialists make arrangement for getting any job done against a specified amount with the contractors. Now it becomes the duty of the contractor to complete the job in specified time: otherwise they could not get any payment. Once a contract is made, it becomes an exclusive responsibility of the contractor who not only engages the labour force but also provides for the raw materials, machinery, an equipment needed for the completion of the job. In Public Works Department most of the jobs are done on contract. In textile mills of Ahmedabad and Cement and Paper industry 10 to 15% of the labour force is recruited through contractors. In coal mines also a substantial percentage of worker are recruited through this method. In Kolar mines where gold is dugged, about 33% of workers are engaged on contract basis. Besides, in other industries some percentage of workers are engaged on contract.

Advantages of Recruitment through Contracts

1. Short notice: The contract work can be got done at short notice. With the help of contractors a every large number of workers can be arranged at very short notice. Moreover, whenever there is extreme urgency of time in the completion of any job the services of contractor prove very helpful indeed.

2. Contractor's responsibility: In contract work, the completion of a job within a specified period, becomes the responsibility of the contractor and the headache of the industrialist is off. As a rule, it is made a term of contract that if a job is completed within the specified period the contractor would compensate for the loss suffered on account of non-completion of the job. Because of this condition of the contract the industrialist becomes free from all anxiety.

3. Less cost: It is generally believed that the work done on contract is less costly. These days there is a system of inviting tenders for all big jobs. Whosoever asks for the least amount and promises to do good job gets the contract. As a result of competition among contractors the job done on contract proves to be relatively cheap.

4. Contractor's control: If a job is done on contract, the entire labour force is recruited by the contractor. These workers are the employees of the contractor. They have no concern with the industrialist. Therefore, the industrialist does not bother about the government regulation pertaining labour welfare in the case of employees of the contractor. If the recruitment of the labour is made by the industrialist himself he has to make provision for various type of facilities for these workers. Thus, the industrialist saves himself the botheration of spending money and looking after the workers if he gets a job done through the contractors. Moreover, the industrialist does not have to engage supervisors to oversee the work done by the labourers.

Disadvantages of Recruitment through Contracts

1. Denial of benefits: The workers recruited by contractors are denied various compulsory benefits available to their counterparts in the industry. Now-a-days, the industrial workers' wages, leaves, pension, maternity benefits are regulated by definite labour laws enacted by government of India and state government. Any violation of these is liable to be punished suitably. Thus, the interests of industrial workers are protected by government legislation. On the other hand, there is no such legal protection of the interest of contract labour. They are completely at the mercy of contractors.

2. Arbitrary treatment: The contractors give arbitrary treatment to the workers. They exploit the workers freely. The needy workers are engaged at very low rates and their working hours also determined by the contractor. Generally, these workers are not regularly paid. Besides, the contractor always withholds certain part of the salary of the workers so that they are constrained to work the contractor in adverse conditions and much against their will.

3. Moral exploitation: Besides monetary exploitation, the poor workers are also subjected to moral exploitation.

From the above discussion about the system of contract labour it is clear that while this system is quite advantageous to the industrialists, it is equally harmful to the workers. From time to time labour welfare associations have recommended the abolition of this system. According to the recommendations of these associations it is best to do away with this system. But under special circumstances where its abolition is not feasible, the recruitment through contractors should be governed by definite rules and regulations. From time to time the government should review the conditions of workers under contractors. In order to remove these defects U.P. Government set up 'Labour Depots' in 1951. These depots were set up with the view that the contractors would recruit all the workers they need through these depots. These labour depots impart preliminary training to the workers. However, in practice these labour depots have not proved to be very effective in solving the problems of workers.

DIRECT RECRUITMENT

Besides the methods of recruitment outlined above, the industrialists employ another method for the recruitment of workers. This is known as Direct Recruitment. Under this system recruitment is not made either through brokers or though contractors. In direct recruitment a list of type of vacancies, their number and the expected qualifications in each type is pasted on the main entrance door of the mill or factory. Sometimes a copy of this list is given to newspaper for advertisement. On the appointed day and the appointed hour numerous workers throng to the main entrance gate. From this crowd of workers those who fulfil the requirements are chosen according to the availability of vacancies. The election of suitable candidates is made by the manager or labour superintendent. These officers put some questions to the workers and if need be ask them to complete certain preliminary tasks. Besides, these officers give due consideration to the health and general efficiency of those selected.

Merits of Direct Recruitment

1. Relief from exploitation by brokers: In direct recruitment the jobber has no role and importance. Therefore, the workers recruited directly are not in any way under his shadow and are free from possible exploitation by him. The workers who are fortunate to find direct recruitment do not have to pay anything for getting the job nor are they under any pressure to pay monthly commission to the jobber.

2. Recruitment of able and efficient workers: In direct recruitment there is a possibility of finding able and efficient workers. The reason for this is that in direct recruitment the recruitment is made by the representatives of the industrialists and they see to it that able and efficient workers are recruited.

3. Increase in the productivity: In direct recruitment able and efficient workers are recruited. These workers put in their best and work with great zeal and dedication. This naturally helps to boost the production.

4. Saving of funds: In direct recruitment the industrialist does not have to make any payment to the jobbers. In recruitment through brokers the employers have to spend a lot of money. Thus, in direct recruitment there is saving of funds.

Demerits of Direct Recruitment

From the above discussion one gets the impression that the method of direct recruitment is highly meritorious but, in fact, it is not the case. This system also has its defects. As a matter of fact this method is not suitable for all types of recruitment. This method is suitable for the recruitment of unskilled and semi-skilled workers but this does not work effectively in case of skilled workers. Another defect of this system is that there is no adequate provision for the publicity of various vacancies. Many workers are unable to get the information about the vacancies.

Thus, many suitable candidates are deprived the chance to be present for selection. Sometimes the defects of broker recruitment system creep in this system also. Many managers and labour superintendents are liable to accept bribe and are otherwise influenced by various pressure and recommendations. Thus, many undeserving candidates gain entry into the factories.

SELECTION IN TRAINING

"Selection in training" emphasises the selection of the qualified personnel. If there is a sound policy and procedure; there is the least possibility of being biased. If abilities, aptitudes, character and individual differences are considered the skilled and qualified personnel would be able to get the appointment in the enterprise. This will reduce the cost of placement and training. The period of training will also be reduced considerably as the person selected after proper screening shows a better performance on the job. A person placed on the job most suited to his qualifications, aptitude and interest, will be the most satisfied person in the organisation. His morale will be high and he will try to understand the work better. He will perform his duties efficiently and quickly, imparting training to person who is selected after proper screening require less efforts, cost and time.

While selecting a candidate for the job appraisal should be made not for the present job for which he is being considered but also future promises for higher job so that he may be prepared for higher positions in the organisation at little cost.

Now-a-days most of the concerns select the personnel from within on the basis of their proficiency on the present job. Promotion motivates employees for better performance. It is a mode of training for higher job.

Each individual differs in nature and quality and such qualities must be developed to suit the job. A well designed selection policy will help the management train the worker. Training aims at development of individuals.

Importance of Selection

1. Procurement of skilled workers: Selection is the process in which candidates are divided into two classes—those who are to be offered employment and those who are not. Thus, the candidates fit for the job are selected from among the prospective candidates for employment. Thus, selection is a process by which only desirable candidates are hired and others are denied the opportunities.

2. Reduction of the cost of training: Proper selection of candidates reduces the cost of training because (1) qualified personnel have better grasping power. They may understand the technique of the work better and in no time; (2) the organisation may develop different training programmes for different persons on the basis of their individual differences, thus reducing the time and cost of training considerably.

3. Solution of personnel problems: Proper selection of personnel reduces personnel problems in the organisation, such as labour turnover, absenteeism and monotony etc. Labour relations are better because workers are more satisfied by their work.

Problems of Proper Selection in India

1. Defective recruitment practices: The main sources of recruitment in Indian industries is jobbers or Mukaddam or contractors who recommend or select the operative staff. This has encouraged the exploitation of workers. It has led to many abuses. Hence, several new sources of recruitment have been developed since independence such as recruitment through employment exchanges or through labour officers. However, the old method of recruiting the workers through intermediaries is still alive in some private industries.

2. Obsolete selection techniques: Obsolete selection techniques are employed in Indian industries except a few public sector undertakings. Interview is regarded as the most modern techniques of selection. Use of psychological tests is made only to select the personnel at management levels and that too in some industries of repute.

3. Untrained selectors: Selectors in Indian industries are not aware of the modern techniques of selection. They are not trained even in the techniques of interview. Their behaviour with the prospective candidates is generally unwarranted and in some cases even inhuman.

4. Prejudicial preferences: Generally no scientific procedure of selection is adopted for hiring the worker at lower levels. No emphasis is laid on the future development of the personnel. Candidates who are recommended by the relatives of the existing employees are preferred whether they are fit for the job or not. Preference, not the quality, is the basis of selection of workers in industries. Sometimes unqualified workers got appointment and suitable persons are left.

5. Lack of planning: India has no manpower planning, persons are recruited as and when the posts are vacant. Therefore, there is always a dearth of skilled workers.

6. Unfavourable attitude of employers: The attitude of Indian employers towards employees is not favourable. They recruit the workers for a short time only and deprive them of the statutory benefits. They do not select good personnel, not develop new techniques of selection or training for the development of personnel in the industry. They consider the cost of development as wastage and not an investment.

Principles of Recruitment

1. Centralisation: Recruitment of personnel for the whole organisation should be centralised. Personnel Department may be charged with this responsibility.

2. Clear policy: Both the internal and external sources of recruitment should be given due importance. It should have clearly spelt out in the policy whether the existing employees would be given any preference in filling up the higher vacant posts and if so at what basis.

3. Comparative policy: In establishing the recruitment policy for the organisation, the recruitment policies followed in similar organisations and in Government undertakings should be considered.

4. Statutory provisions: Statutory provisions regarding recruitment of personnel should also be given proper consideration.

5. Flexibile policy: The recruitment policy should be flexible so that it may be amended suitably to achieve the organisation policy.

6. Consistent policy: Recruitment policy should be within the framework of personnel policy and organisation policy.

7. Clear rules: Rules regarding recruitment of existing employees' words should be very clear.

8. Proper qualifications: The qualifications of the applicants should be commensurate with the job specification as worked out through job analysis.

9. Merit: Merit should be the basis of recruitment of other consideration like friendship, relations etc. should be ignored.

Principles of Selection Policies

1. Selection Board: The responsibility for the selection of employees should be assigned to an efficient and qualified selection board so that only the right man can be selected.

2. Job first, man next: This should be the basis and fundamental principle for selection.

3. Proper services: Selection should be from internal as well as external sources and the management should not rely much on one single source.

4. Proper standards: Selection should be based on standards set out by job analysis. If suitable candidates is not available, the post should be allowed to remain vacant for the time being till such a right man is made available.

5. Different selection methods: The different selection methods for different levels of posts should be followed.

6. Consistency: The selection policy should not surpass the organisation's general policy. It should be within that framework.

7. Commensurate: The selection policy of the organisation should be commensurate to the employment policy of the state.

8. Flexibility: Selection policy should be flexible, not rigid so that necessary amendments may be made whenever necessary.

9. Vocational guidance: The selection policy should provide the vocational guidance for the prospective candidates.

10. Unbiased: The selection policy should be unbiased and employment-oriented.

PLACEMENT OF WORKERS

Importance of Placement

According to Pigors and Myres, "Placement has an experimental element. But for most employees it is a decisive step and should consist in matching what the job demands (job requirement), imposes (in stray, working, conditions etc,), and offers (if the form of pay rate interest, companionship with others, promotional possibilities etc.)". Placement is the act of offering the job to a finally selected candidate. With the placement of worker to the job, the selection procedure ends. Personnel department evaluates the various factors required for a job. It is difficult to match all these factors for a new employee, quite unknown to the job and the environment. Therefore, the first placement generally carries with it the status of probationer. The probation period is trial period, extended from 3 months to 12 months. If the employee shows a good performance he is confirmed as a regular employee of the organisation at the end of the probation period. If the worker does not work well, the management may take a decision to discharge him. But once a worker has achieved the status of regular employee he may be discharged only for sufficient reason. Thus, the trial period is a transition period at the end of which the management has to take a decision whether the employee should be made regular or discharged from the job.

Principles of Placement

1. Job Requirements: Man should be placed on the job according to the requirements of the job. The job should not be adjusted according to the qualifications or requirements of the man. 'Job First, Man Next' should be the principle of placement,

2. Qualifications: The job should be offered to the man according to his qualifications, neither higher, not lower, except in case of interview placement.

3. Information: The employee should be made conversant with the working conditions relating to the job prevailing in the industry. He should also know the penalties if he commits a wrong.

4. Loyalty and co-operation: While introducing the job to the new employee, an effort should be made to develop a sense of loyalty and cooperation in him so that he may realise his responsibilities better towards the job and the organisation.

INDUCTION OR ORIENTATION OF EMPLOYEE

Meaning of Induction of Employee

When a candidate is finally selected, he is issued the appointment letter asking to join the organisation on or up to a specified date. Induction is a follow-up action of hiring. It is concerned with the problem of introducting or orienting a new employee to the organisation.

When a new employee reports for duty, he should be welcomed as a new member of organisation. He must be helped to get acquainted and adjusted with his fellow employees and work environment. The first day of employment is long remembered by most of the people. Initial impression counts much in the later attitude of the employee towards the job and the company.

If he has not already been introduced at the time of occupational test the new employees should be introduced to the fellow employees and to the working conditions, rules and regulations. It is a first step in the proper communication of the personnel policy. It seeks to build a two-way channel of information between management and employees.

Elements of Good Induction Programme

1. Introductory information: Introductory information regarding the history of the company and company's products, its organisational structure, personnel policies, rules and regulations of the company relating to leaves, attendance, pay etc. should be given informally or in group sessions in the personnel. It helps the candidates to understand the company and its organisational policies and standards.

2. On the job information: The department supervisor should give further information to the new employee in the department concerned where he is placed on the job about departmental facilities and requirements such as nature of the job, the extent of his liability, and employee's activities such as recreational facilities, association, safety measures, job routine etc.

3. Follow-up interviews: Several weeks after the employee has been on the job a follow-up interview should be arranged by the supervisor or a representative of the personnel department to answer the problems that a new employee may face on the job and to supplement some of the information given earlier.

Objectives of Induction

1. To promote loyalty: To promote a feeling of belonging and loyalty to the organisation among newcomers so that they may not form false impression regarding the company because first impression is the last impression.

2. To make agreement: To make an agreement between the organisation goals and the personnel goals of the newcomers.

3. To build up confidence: To build up the new employee's confidence in the organisation and in himself so that he may become an efficient worker.

4. To give information: To give the new employees information regarding company, its structure, product, policies, rules and regulations and facilities provided by the company such as cafeterias, locker room, time to break off, leave rules etc.

5. To introduce the new worker: To introduce the new worker to the supervisor and the fellow-workers with whom he has to work.

6. To create a sense of security: To create a sense of security for the worker in his job by impressing the idea that fairness to the worker is the inherent policy of the organisation.

7. To lessen cost of replacement: To lessen or avoid the cost of replacing the worker in the early impressionable period because of lack of information or incorrect business impression.

Induction Practices

1. Induction guide: Induction guide books are prepared by the personnel department with information on what induction steps have been taken and what are still to be covered. The guide book lists various steps to be taken and by whom and when the instruction are to be given. Guide book containing the informations regarding the company and its various personnel activities is distributed among the newcomers is some large concerns.

2. Counselling: The supervisor may induct the new employees working under him by introducing and counselling them by reassuring and reinforcing the confidence and guarding against false impression.

3. Follow-up interview: On the basis of follow up interview, personnel department can take action to readjust conditions, reassure the worker dispel fears, gain their confidence and promote their efficiency.

The best method of induction training includes lecture plus visuals followed by printed materials. A tour of the plant and the department should be arranged to acquaint the new employee with the overall operations of the company.

QUESTIONS FOR EXERCISE

1. Define recruitment and the importance of recruitment method. Explain main sources of recruitment.
2. Explain the process of selection of employees which is generally followed in a large-scale business concern.
3. Discuss the advantages and disadvantages of recruitment through Contractors.
4. Assess the merits and demerits of direct recruitment of industrial workers.
5. "Selection is one of the most important of all functions in the management of personnel." Comment. What are the major problems in the way of proper selection in India?
6. Describe the main principles of recruitment.
7. Explain basic principles of selection policies.
8. Describe the importance and principles of placement of workers.
9. What do you mean by Induction or Orientation of Employee? Explain elements of a good induction programme. Discuss objectives and practices of induction.

7

Personnel Management

DEFINITION OF PERSONNEL MANAGEMENT

1. *Edison*: "Personnel Management is the service of human engineering."

2. *Michael J. Jucius*: Personnel Management is "the field of management which has to do with planning, organising and controlling various operating functions of procuring, developing, maintaining and utilising a labour force, such that the (*a*) objectives for which the company is established are attained economically and effectively; (*b*) objective of all levels of personnel are served to the highest possible degree; and (*c*) objectives of the community are duly considered and served."

3. *Thomas G. Spates*: "Personnel administration is a code of the ways of organising and treating individuals at work so that they will get the greatest possible realisation of their intensive abilities, thus attaining maximum efficiency."

4. *E. Dale Yoder*: "Personnel Management is that phase of management which deals with the effective control and use of manpower as distinguished from other sources of power."

5. *E.M.C. Cumming*: "Personnel Management is concerned with obtaining the best possible staff for an organisation and having got them, looking after them so that they will want to stay and give their best to the jobs."

6. *E.F.L. Breach*: "Personnel Management is that part of management's process which is primarily concerned with the human constituents of an organisation."

7. *E. Paul G. Hastings*: "Personnel Management is that aspect of management which has its goal effective utilisation of the labour resources of an organisation."

8. *E.B. Flippo*: "The personnel function is concerned with the procurement, development, compensation, integration and maintenance of the

personnel of an organisation for the purpose of contributing towards the accomplishment of the major goals or objectives of organising, directing and controlling of performance of those operative functions,"

9. *Society for Personnel Administration of America*: "Personnel administration is the art of acquiring, developing and maintaining a competent work force in such a manner as to accomplish with maximum efficiency and economy the functions and objectives of the organisation."

10. *Indian Institute of Personnel Management*: "Personnel management is that part of management function which is primarily concerned with human relationship in an organisation, its objective is the maintenance of those relationships which enable all those engaged in the undertaking to make their maximum contribution to the effective working of the undertaking."

CHARACTERISTICS OF PERSONNEL MANAGEMENT

1. Specialised branch of general management: Personnel Management is a specialised branch of General Management. Therefore all the principles of general management apply to this branch of management.

2. Definite principles and policies: Over and above the general principles of management, there are definite principles and policies of personnel management which help overall development of human force.

3. Management of human resources: Personnel Management is the management of human resources in the industry. Best possible results are secured by managing this source of power in an effective manner.

4. Defines inter-personnel relationships: Personnel Management defines the relationship between (*a*) employer and employee, and (*b*) employee and employee. The word employee includes not only the workers at the lowest level but the employees at all levels and types of management such as craftsmen, foremen, operators (low level), department managers (middle level) and general manager or chief executive (top level) are also included in it.

5. Considers development as individual and as member of a group: Personnel Management considers the development of individuals at work, as an individual and as a member of the group. Therefore, in formulating personnel policies and solving the human problems of an organisation intelligently their individual character and the entity as a member of the group are considered so that the intrinsic abilities of the workers may be developed to the best use of the organisation and the goal of the organisation is attained to the maximum possible extent.

6. Considers labourer as a human being: The whole philosophy of personnel management is based on the assumption that labourer is a human being. Humanly treatment should be given to him so that he can recognise his intrinsic abilities and these may be developed and motivated towards the best interest of the organisation.

Thus, Personnel Management is an approach, a point of view, a technique of thinking and philosophy of management concerned with the overall development of men at work.

FUNCTIONS OF PERSONNEL MANAGEMENT

The function of personnel management may be divided into two parts —Managerial functions and Operative functions. These are as follows:

FUNCTIONS OF PERSONNEL MANAGEMENT

Managerial Functions	Operative Functions
1. Planning	1. Procurement of Personnel
2. Organising	2. Development of Personnel
3. Directing	3. Compensation to Personnel
4. Controlling	4. Employees' Benefits Schemes
	5. Maintaining Good Industrial Relations
	6. Record Keeping
	7. Personnel Planning and Evaluation
	8. Personnel Research and Audit.

1. Managerial Functions

(*i*) Planning: It is the main function of management. It is concerned with manpower planning; studying labour turnover rate, forecasting the future requirements of personnel and planning for selection and training procedures, etc.

(*ii*) Organisation: It involves the establishment of inter-relationships within organisation. By identifying the various sub-groups headed by individuals in managerial jobs as well as operative jobs, it provides a structure for the company.

(*iii*) Direction: It includes issuing instruction to the workers, developing communication network, interpreting various industrial laws and integrating workers.

(*iv*) Control: It provides basic data for establishing standards, makes job analysis and performance appraisal, etc. All these techniques assist in effective control of the qualities, time and efforts of workers.

Operative Functions about Personnel

***(i)* Procurement:** It is concerned with the obtaining to the proper kind and number of personnel necessary to accomplish organisation goals. It deals specifically with such subjects as the determination of manpower requirements, their recruitment, selecting, placement and orientation, etc.

***(ii)* Development:** Development has to do with the increase through training, skill that is necessary for proper job performance. In this process various techniques of training are used to develop the employees. Framing a sound promotion policy, determination of the basis of promotion and making performance appraisal are the elements of personnel development function.

***(iii)* Compensation:** Compensation means determination of adequate and equitable remuneration of personnel for their contribution to organisation objectives. To determine the monetary compensation for various jobs is one of the most difficult and important function of the personnel management. A number of decisions are taken into the function, *viz.*, job-evaluation, remuneration policy, incentive and premium plans, bonus policy and co-partnership, etc. It also assists the organisation for adopting the suitable wages and salaries, policy and payment of wages and salaries in right time.

***(iv)* Good industrial relations:** It covers a wide field. It is intended to reduce strifes, promote industrial peace, provide fair deal to workers and establish industrial democracy. If the personnel manager is unable to make harmonious relations between management and labour industrial unrest will take place and millions of man-days will be lost. If labour-management relations are not good the moral and physical condition of the employee will suffer, and it will be a loss to an organisation *vis-a-vis* a nation. Hence, the personnel manager must create harmonious relations with the help of sufficient communication system and co-partnership.

***(v)* Record keeping:** In Record-keeping the personnel manager collects and maintains information concerned with the staff of the organisation. It is essential for every organisation because it assists the management in decision-making such as in promotions.

***(vi)* Planning and evaluation:** Under this system different type of activities are evaluated such as evaluation of performance, personnel policy on an organisation and its practices, personnel audit, morale, survey and performance appraisal, etc.

(*vii*) **Research and audit:** It is concerned with the research in newer motivational techniques and auditing, its effect on the workers of the organisation.

IMPORTANCE OF PERSONNEL MANAGEMENT

1. Harmony in management-employees relationship: The personnel function is concerned with the relationship of management and the employees. The management has to get the work done through the employees who implement the plans. Despite tremendous technical development the man still remains the main factor of production. He plans, thinks, produces and sells the products. Thus, production, marketing, finance, accounting, products research and development, all the functions are performed by human beings. As Peter Drucker says, "The proper or improper use of different factors of production depends upon the wishes of the human resource. Hence, besides other resources, human resources need more development." If employees are satisfied and motivated they will contribute their best towards the attainment of organisational goals. Without this no object of organisation can be realised. Apply has aptly said, "Management is the development of the people and not the direction of things." Management and personnel administration cannot be separated, though in a relatively large organisation, personnel management activities are characteristically carried out by a separate department having a title such as Personnel Department or Personnel Management, Industrial Relations Department and so on. The specific designation may vary from company to company. Personnel department is primarily interested in the selection, training, development and motivation of employees. The activities involved in personnel management affect the entire organisation. As every manager has to deal with his subordinate, he must know the techniques to deal with them successfully.

2. Wide Scope: Thus, the scope of personnel function is very wide. It is concerned with the maintenance of the organisation. It aims to achieve both efficiency and fairpiay. It seeks to bring together and develop into an effective organisation the men and women who make up an enterprise enabling each to make his own best contribution to its success. It seeks to provide fair terms and conditions of those who are employed. To conclude with an apt observation of M.W. Cumming: "The personnel function is basically concerned with the relationship of management with the employees and employees in all matters other than actual work itself."

3. Duty of Manager: In a large enterprise, the various functions in the personnel division are grouped into departments. The major divisions usually contained in the personnel department are employment, record keeping, job evaluation, performance appraisal, safety and health, education and collective bargaining, etc. Though these are operative responsibilities of personnel department but the personnel function is the duty of each manager. It is so because each manager has to deal with the people and his main responsibility is to get the work done through and with the people. His main duty is to deal with his subordinates and co-workers fairly and nicely. The importance of proper personnel management has been summed up by Mayer in these words, "Those industries who care not for the needs and feelings of human resources, they are only a heap of machinery. They could not be called industrial organisation at all."

4. Development of people: L.A. Apply says that "Management is the development of people and not the direction of things, Management and Personnel Administration are one and the same. They should never be separated." Personnel function is to achieve both efficiency and justice. It seeks to bring together and develop into an effective organisation the men and women who make up an enterprise enabling each to make his own best contribution to its success both as an individual and as a member of a working group. It seeks to provide fair terms and conditions of employment and satisfying those employed in an organisation. It is not concerned with the effective utilisation of manpower only but equally with the organisational maintenance also.

Summary

The importance of personnel management may be summed up in the words of Glean Gardiner as follows: "By centralizing the personnel function in a personnel department, too many people have assumed that you can centralise human relations, it was perhaps the error in thinking of the production, people and general manager who felt that it would be very helpful if we could just put all our personnel headaches into one that left somebody else worry about them for all of us. The personnel function is by no means a one man function or a one man department." Thus, each manager is essentially a personnel manager.

SUBJECT MATTER OF PERSONNEL MANAGEMENT

The subject matter of Personnel Management is human being *i.e.* employees of the organisation. It is that part of management process which is concerned with the effective utilisation of the labour resources of an organisation. Human labour has always been a significant factor of production. The proper or improper use of the different physical factors of production depends upon the wishes of the human resource of the organisation.

SCOPE OF PERSONNEL MANAGEMENT

Earlier, the business organisations were mainly one man show. The proprietor, manager and even worker was the one and the same person. With the development of modern industries and management techniques, the organisation structure became complex. The increase in the size of the industrial units, their development and importance has led to indirect management, *i.e.*, indirect relationship among workers and management. Besides, a significant change in the viewpoints and attitudes of the workers as well as management has come about. Therefore, the scope of personnel function has become wide. The major divisions usually contained in the personnel department of a modern industrial organisation are employed record keeping, job-evaluation, performance appraisal, health and safety, education and training, wage surveys, wage determination and administration, redressal of grievances and in some organisations, collective bargaining also. Following are two descriptions of scope of personnel management.

1. Indian Institute of Personnel Management:

(*i*) Labour requirement, selection, test and their best utilisation.

(*ii*) Conditions of working, remuneration system, management of working condition and labour services and convenience.

(*iii*) Amicable settlement of the industrial disputes and maintenance of good industrial relations.

2. Strauss and Salyes:

(*i*) Recruitment of labour, selection and placement,

(*ii*) Analysis, description and evaluation of the work,

(*iii*) Compensation and schemes of appraisal work,

(*iv*) Keeping records of the personnel,

(*v*) Welfare programmes,

(*vi*) Special services like safety, inspection and control,

(*vii*) Training and educational programmes,

(*viii*) Labour relations,

(*ix*) Public relations, and

(*x*) Personnel Appraisal and development.

Thus, the scope of personnel management is very wide. It is not limited to industrial and business field only. Its importance is extended to every type of organisation whether commercial, religious, social or political wherein people work in groups. The basic concept of management is the art of getting the work done through and with the people. Hence, the use of personnel management extends to all kinds of enterprise, big or small, efficient or inefficient, commercial or non-commercial, private or public enterprises.

NATURE OF PERSONNEL MANAGEMENT

According to Scott, Clothier and Spriegel, "Viewed from the standpoint of the enterprise as a whole the personnel division is a staff unit." Personnel department enjoys both the ranks-line department as well as of a staff department. Personnel function is both a staff activity as well as a line function.

1. Line function: Personnel function is said to be a line function because all the functions co-operative in the process of earning profits for the organisation. All activities are carried out by persons and personnel management department, controls the functions of these persons. It plans, organises and channelises their efforts of the common goal of the organisation. The personnel manager motivates them, creates an atmosphere of sound human relations, industrial peace and so on. Thus, personnel department can rightly be said to be a line department. As an activity or function the personnel function is a line responsibility because each manager whether a production manager or a marketing manager has to deal with persons. Hence, he must have sufficient knowledge how to deal with them.

2. Staff Function: Personnel function is also a staff function. In business organisations, the main function of a personnel manager is generally to advise the Board of Directors or General Manager in personnel matters. He helps in formation of sound personnel policies and maintaining good industrial relations between the management and the workers. He assists and serves the workers and other departments too. He provides efficient workers to different departments through proper recruitment and training, etc. He keeps necessary personnel records, makes job evaluation, makes performance appraisal and chalks out the programme of executive development, workers' training, etc. He acts as mediator between the management and workers' union in case of industrial dispute.

OBJECTS OF PERSONNEL MANAGEMENT

(A) *General Objectives*: General objectives express the basic philosophy of top management towards the labour force engaged on the work and its deep underlying conviction as to the importance of the people in the organisation. Therefore personnel management must formulate and adopt a basic creed and make it known to its employees and the public. The statement of basic objectives should include the following as the most important objectives:

1. Maximum Individual Development: The employer should develop the personality of each individual. If an act of the employer adversely affects the personality of the individual, he should avoid it. He should establish and support such human values that may have social recognition and importance. Employees should always be regarded as co-owners or partners of the organisation and given a due importance in the organisation. As each individual differs in nature therefore the management should recognise his individual ability and make use of such ability in an effective manner.

2. Defining relationship of employer and employees: Personnel management seeks to have a desirable working relationship between the employer and employees so that they may co-operate with the management. This is possible only when there is complete mental revolution. The top management should realise that labourer is a human being and humanly treatment should be given to him. The workers should co-operate with the management in accomplishing the goals of the management.

3. Efficient moulding of human resources: A man is the only active agent of production who engages the other factors of production to work the management should emphasise the effective utilisation of human resources as contrasted to physical resources so that maximum production at minimum cost is possible. Without effective moulding of human resources, other factors of production will be ineffective.

(B) *Specific Objects*: These refer to the various activities of the personnel department such as the following:

1. Selection: Personnel management selects type and number of persons required to the organisation concerned.

2. Orientation: Personnel Management ensures proper orientation and introduction of new employees of the organisation to their jobs.

3. Training: Personnel management seeks organisation of suitable training facilities for better job performance and to prepare a man to accept the challenge of higher job.

4. Better working conditions: Personnel management aims at provision of better working conditions and other facilities such as medical facilities, facilities of provident fund, gratuity, leave with pay etc. so as to help to hold the competent and qualified personnel in the service of the organisation.

5. Incentives: The objective of personnel management is the provision of sound or fair and effective wages and salary administration and other incentives which will result in the highest possible productivity of workers.

6. Retirement: An objective of the personnel management is that a full and fair consideration should be given to an employee when his services are terminated or he leaves the organisation. He should hold a good impression of the management at the time of retirement.

7. Trade Unions: Trade unions today play an important role in the industrial life. Personnel management seeks to maintain good relations with representatives of trade unions on mutual confidence and respect.

8. Personnel Research: Personnel research keeps the management equipped with recent development and trends essential to take sound decisions without any further delay as regards personnel matters.

To conclude, the objective of personnel management is to satisfy the men at work. The management should be aware of the problems faced by the workers and try to solve them effectively with the least controversy.

TRAITS OF PERSONNEL MANAGER

According to survey made in U.S.A. in the year 1958, in 60% companies personnel manager was called Personnel Director, in 10% as Personnel Officer; in 10% companies as Personnel Manager; in 10% companies Public Relations Officer and Personnel Manager and in 10% companies he was termed as Employees Officer. In India, Personnel Manager is treated as a member of the top management team of the organisation. He is an executive requiring essentially the same executive qualities as other executives. He needs technical competence in the areas of his division's specialities. He need not be a specialist in all the areas of the personnel division, yet he should have a high degree of skill and competence in at least one of the areas.

1. Philosophy of social justice: Personnel management should have a keen sense of social justice and be fully appreciative of the rights and interests of the men and women as well as of the economic necessities of management. His philosophy of social justice should include two fundamental concepts:

(*i*) Industry is a partnership between management, men and owners whose objective is profits through service.

(*ii*) Industry can profit greatly by developing and co-ordinating the capacities, the interest and the opportunities of each worker and of each member of management.

2. Interest and common sense: Personnel Manager should take interest in people and possess a wealth of common sense which will protect him from sentimentality on one side and from coldness on the other.

3. Sound advice: He must be qualified to advise management on matters of personnel and capable of talking without fear of favour with any executive in the organisation.

4. Qualities of head and heart: He should possess legal, social, human and managerial qualities of head and heart as well.

5. Responsibilities—

1. *Geoge Henon*:

   (*i*) Responsibilities towards Personnel System.

   (*ii*) Responsibilities towards the Top Management.

   (*iii*) Wage and Salary Administration.

   (*iv*) Protection of Physical Resources.

   (*v*) Assistance in Cost in Expenditure Control.

   (*vi*) Maintenance of Records.

   (*vii*) Maintenance of Industrial Peace.

2. *Scott, Clothier and Spriegal*: "The chief personnel officer should be a specialist in organisation theory and as such be an effective adviser to top management in organisational matters, as well as being able to organise his own division (department) in such a manner as to minimise frictions, promote goodwill and release the latent energies of his own people and associates to be expanded on their primary assignments."

3. *M.W. Gumming*: "Top personnel manager aims to achieve both efficiency and justice, neither of which can be pursued successfully without the other. It seeks to bring together and develop into an effective organisation of the men and women who make up an enterprise enabling each to make his own best contribution to its success both as an individual and as a member of a working group. It seeks to provide fair terms and conditions of employment and satisfying work for those employed."

SEQUENTIAL METHOD OF CLASSIFYING PERSONNEL FUNCTIONS

Procurement	Retention	Development	Relations	Administration
1. Recruitment	1. Promotion	1. Training	1. Govt. Rules & Regulations	1. Application & co-ordination of Personnel policies and programmes.
2. Selection	2. Transfer	2. Appraisal	2. Policies	2. Personnel Records and Reports.
3. Introduction	3. Wages & Salary Administration.	3. Rating	3. Union relations	3. Personnel Research and Statistics.
4. Placement	4. Management of Fringe benefits: (*a*) Financial (*b*) Education (*c*) Housing (*d*) Health (*e*) Recreation (*f*) Other Welfare Activities.	4. Develop ment Programmes.	4. Community Relations	4. Evaluation of Personnel Administration
			5. Relations with Govt. industrial machinery.	5. Personnel Audit
			6. Collective Bargaining	
			7. Grievance Procedure.	

POLICIES OF PERSONNEL MANAGEMENT

According to George D. Hasley, following principles of sound personnel management are useful in building good worker morale:

1. Care and skill should be exercised in the selection of employees.
2. Introduction to the job should be friendly skilful and adequate.
3. Each employee should be made to feel that his efforts are really appreciated.
4. Careful and thoughtful consideration should be given to the probable effect each rule, each notice, and each practice will have on the feelings of all concerned.

5. Employees should have a part in planning those things which affect their working conditions (whenever it is practical to do so).
6. There should be a sense of security and reasonable freedom from worry.
7. There should be constant and intelligent effort on the part of management to be absolutely fair in every policy and every practice.
8. Each employee should have a feeling of pride in the worthwhileness of his work and his company.
9. The organisational set up be such that there is no confusion in any one's mind as to his duties or responsibilities.
10. Conditions should be such that working proves to be satisfying social experience as well as means of making a livelihood.

NEED FOR A SEPARATE DEPARTMENT OF PERSONNEL MANAGEMENT

1. Job Analysis: The personnel administration must have information about the job specifications describing details of the duties involved for long job. The information will help to fill vacancies. It will also enable assignment of substitutes from among employees of the same or other organisation units, in case of temporary absences due to sickness, vacations, or other reasons. The personnel administrator must be currently informed about all conditions and charges in manpower. He should use books and tables to record all requirement and changes pertinent to his field of responsibility. Many personnel administrators use visual charts containing slots for every employee that is needed, and names and other data for jobs currently filled. These visual instruments permit quick orientation just like a balance sheet in an account book. Hence, it is essential to have a separate department of Personnel Management.

2. Reduction in the cost of production: There are a number of techniques to bring about reduction in the cost of production. A proper control over the wastages and leakage caused by labour is the most important. Hence, it is desirable to have an independent department of personnel administration.

3. Contented Manpower: A satisfied labour force is a *sine qua non* of personnel administration. It requires the provision of welfare amenities, implementation of social security measures and such other activities that may bring labour and capital closer to each other. The successful working of such activities necessitates the existence of a separate department of personnel administration looking after the problems of labour, trying to meet its demands, chalking out schemes of social security, providing welfare amenities, etc.

4. Trained and efficient labour force: This is the age of scientific technology and automation. If any country aspires to keep abreast with the march of time and come out with flying colours the modern cut-throat competition, it is all the more necessary to provide the most up-to-date training to those who have to handle the machines. Efficiency can also be achieved by means of proper training. Training within industry is a popular feature in most of the American concerns. Thus, there should be an independent department of personnel administration having a training sub-division for a careful appraisal of the above problem.

5. Scientific Recruitment: Recruitment is the most important function of the employment department, a part and parcel of the department of personnel administration and management. The recruitment process is largely responsible for the disposition and allocation of manpower. Unskilled or thoughtless recruitment may occasion the misuse, misapplication and underutilization of labour. It may direct manpower into positions in which participants will not utilize their highest talents, where they will not secure the training or experience essential to their maximum contribution or where they may face long periods of idleness or numerous changes from one inappropriate job to another equally inappropriate. Scientific selection seeks to separate the most likely and promising from among those made available by recruitment. This necessity of scientific recruitment of manpower further emphasizes the need of having a separate department of personnel administration and management.

6. Scientific promotion, demotion and transfer: Promotion of deserving employees from the lower to the higher cadre, demotion of the guilty and inefficient and suspension of the indisciplined workers requires scientific treatment. Promotion, demotion, inter-departmental transfers, suspension, etc., should be based on certain scientific principles. A strict observance of these rules requires the establishment of an independent department of personnel administration and management.

7. Cordial Employer-Employee Relations: Cordial relations between the superior and the subordinates is the key to the maintenance of industrial peace. Industrial production is bound to suffer without peaceful atmosphere. This can be achieved only when industrial relations is scientifically and properly tackled. There must be a department of industrial relations as a wing of the major department—the department of personnel administration and management—whose primary function should be to link the top management with the working people. If both, labour and capital, surrender a little and proceed hand-in-hand with a feeling of goodwill and co-operation there is no power on the earth that may hinder production.

The department of personnel administration and management should be under the charge of a capable and experienced senior officer of the concern. He may be designated as the Deputy Manager or Director of the Department of personnel administration and management. There may be several Deputy Directors under him for his assistance, who may be entrusted with different activities and functions which may be undertaken by the department of personnel administration and management.

FUNCTIONS OF A PERSONNEL MANAGER

In promoting the optimum utilization of the abundant human resources by providing expert professional and competent advice to management resources by providing expert professional and competent advice to management in the areas of selection of employees, training and development, job evaluation, wage and salary administration, men-boss relations, human relations, etc. Personnel Manager have a great responsibility. In the words of Shri V.V. Giri, "They (Personnel Managers) should assist employers not only in formulating proper, humane and progressive personnel policies and procedures, but also in implementing them effectively in an industrial organisation. Personnel managers should command respect of both sides of the industry-labour and management and they must follow an independent attitude and must have in view the promotion of the organisation's health as well as the health and prosperity of the individual employee." Following are the functions of a Personnel Manager:

1. To select personnel: Personnel Director (or Manager) in industries carries on sound policy of recruitment. Proper selection of personnel is the first task which confronts him. To the old methods of recruitment such as interviews and recommendations, modern method adds psychological testing used in addition to normal trade tests or recruitment tests and interviews.

2. To carry on scientific placement of recruits: After proper selection of personnel, the personnel manager should do the judicious and scientific placement of the recruits. This requires the skill of matching the man, the job and the supervisor so that the department where he is put, can work with optimum efficiency.

3. Induction and training of new recruits: This is another fundamental assignment of the personnel manager. Induction and training should start immediately on personnel's appointment as they are important for orientating an employee and training him up for his job. These help the department to avoid some accidents which could happen if the employee is completely unacquainted with the working conditions. A brief idea of the organisation and a detailed training of the department where he is scheduled to work will help the employee as well as the department.

4. To establish good industrial relations: An important function of the personnel manager is to establish industrial relations. Industrial peace is of vital importance for the peace and prosperity of an organisation. The bigger the organisation the greater is the task of the personnel manager.

QUESTIONS FOR EXERCISE

1. Explain the salient characteristics of Personnel Management.
2. Define Personnel Management and explain its importance.
3. "The activities involved in personnel management pervade the entire organisation." Comment on this statement and discuss the importance of Personnel Management.
4. "Personnel Management involves two categories of functions—managerial and operative." Describe these functions in detail.
5. "Management is Personnel Administration." Comment.
6. "Personnel Management is a basic management function pertains to all levels and types of management," Discuss.
7. "Personnel Management is a way of approach, a point of view, a technique of thinking and a philosophy of management." Elucide the statement by describing the main characteristics and importance of personnel management.
8. "Personnel Management is clearly a management function and not a 'third force' as practised in some industries." In this context discuss the various functions of a Personnel Department.
9. "Personnel Management is a basic management function pertaining to all levels and types of management." Discuss.
10. "The activities involved in personnel management pervade the entire organisation. They are not performed solely by those in the personnel department." Explain this statement and bring out the importance of personnel function in a business enterprise.

11. "Management and Personnel Management are one and the same." Explain this statement.
12. "Personnel administration is a line responsibility, but it is also a staff function," Examine this statement carefully.
13. "The objective of Personnel Management, Personnel Administration or Industrial Relations in an organisation is to attain maximum individual development, desirable working relationship between employers and employees and effective moulding of human resources as contrasted with physical resources." Discuss the objectives of Personnel Management.
14. "Managers are not born but made". Discuss.
15. What are the traits required in a personnel manager? Explain the responsibilities of a Personnel Manager in large-sized business organisation.
16. What arc the policies and principles of Personnel Management?
17. What is the need of a separate personnel department in business enterprises?

8

Development of Personnel Management

DEVELOPMENT OF PERSONNEL MANAGEMENT IN INDIA

The development of personnel management in India can be studied under two heads: (A) Development before independence, and (B) Development in post-independence era.

(A) Development before independence

1. Appointment of labour welfare officers: Before independence nothing commendable was done either on the part of employers or on the part of Government for the development of industrial relations. The development of personnel management in India was as late as in 1920 when labour welfare activities were initiated by some Indian business enterprises like Tata Group, British India Corporation, Calico Mills, Empress Mill, etc. who appointed labour welfare officers to look after the interest of the working people and of the enterprise in relation to the human problems.

2. Industrial unrest: The year 1920 was the year of industrial unrest. Employers and the Government took various steps to resolve better industrial relation including the recognition of trade unions. But satisfactory progress in industrial relations could not be seen on the whole.

3. Governmental efforts: Before and during World War II, the Government (Central and States) were the leading agencies in India to develop and improve the labour relation in Indian industries. In 1934 with the efforts of Bombay Government, the appointment of the labour welfare officers was made compulsory in industries employing 500 or more workers throughout the State of Bombay to resolve the labour disputes with labour commissioner as the chief conciliation officer. Industries in other states also appointed the labour officers.

4. Royal Commission on Labour: In 1939, Royal Commission on Labour recommended the appointment of labour officers so that the labour problems might be reconciled amicably. The Union Government convened a tripartite labour conference to discuss the extent of labour laws in Indian industries, to evolve a system of grievance handling and to establish conciliation system in industrial matters.

A. Development in Post-Independence Period

1. Labour legislations: Government of India did commendable work in this direction. On the recommendations of the Central Labour Investigation Committee 1946, several labour legislations were enacted such as, Labour Disputes Act, 1947, Industrial Employment Act, 1946, Factories Act, 1948 etc. The Factories Act, 1948 provided the appointment of a labour welfare officer in every industry employing 500 or more workers for the purpose of helping the management in providing welfare measures to the workers as enunciated in the Act. Now the urgency of appointing personnel or labour officer is being felt even in such industries where there is no legal compulsion to appoint welfare officer as there is a need of such agency to guide the management in tackling the ticklish labour problems by providing the specialised services. The services of these labour welfare officers are not up to the mark even now because of their taking a biased view. While dealing with the workers, they consider themselves as an agent of management.

2. Training: The Government arranged for the training of workers and management personnel in India and started several training centres and institutes for imparting training in industrial relations. In 1949, for the first time in independent India 'Xavier Institute of Labour Relations' was established. Several other institutions were started later on such as Indian Institute of Personnel Administration, Calcutta, Indian Labour Management Institute, Bombay, Institute of Industrial Relations, Bangalore, Federation of All India Labour Welfare Officers, and Indian Productivity Councils, Shri Ram Centre for Industrial Relations and Human Resources at Delhi.

3. Reforms during emergency: In the middle of 1975, the government proclaimed the state of emergency in India and took several administrative steps to eradicate the system of bonded labour, to give momentum to the scheme of workers' participation in management in Indian industries and to extend the scheme of apprenticeship.

4. Post-emergency labour legislation: In 1978, a comprehensive Industrial Relation Bill was introduced in Parliament in order to improve the labour relations in industries through collective bargaining by consolidating Trade Union Act, 1926; Industrial Employment (Standing Order) Act, 1946 and the Industrial Disputes Act, 1947. But due to dissolution of Lok Sabha in 1979 the bill could not be passed. In 1981 the President promulgated an ordinance giving powers to the Government to ban strikes in essential services for six months. The essential services include Railways, Post and Telegraph, Telephone, Docks, Airports, Banks. Petroleum, Water and Sewer Disposal, Defence and Hospitals. The Government was empowered to declare any service as an essential service. In 1982, Government amended several labour laws, including Industrial Disputes Act, Industrial Employment (Standing Order) Act, 1946. The Government also amended the Employees State Insurance Act in 1984.

EVOLUTION OF PERSONNEL MANAGEMENT

1. Early Philosophy (Before 1900): The history of modern personnel management began with the name of Robert Owen. Owen is called the founder of Personnel Management. In 1813, he wrote a book, 'A New View of Society'. In it he propounded the need of better industrial relations and improvements in the service conditions. His attitude towards workers was very cordial, liberal and patternalistic. He got good houses constructed for his workers by the side of his factory. He eliminated child labour and provided healthy conditions. Mr. J.S. Mill, Andrew Yule and Charles Bewarage contemporaries of Robert Owen, developed personnel management as a science and supported the idea of wage incentives, profit sharing and labour welfare, etc.

2. Efficiency and Productivity Movement (1900-1920): During the last year or 19th century arrived the age of efficiency and productivity movement. The two decades of 1900-1920 were the years of scientific management movement. Taylor's Scientific Management thought was accepted during this period. Taylor opposed the idea of trade unionism and workers' organisation. The main contribution of these two decades has been the increase in the size of units, introduction of scientific thinking into actions, job analysis, standards costing, scientific selection and training of workers and the idea of mental revolution.

3. Period of Welfare-ism and Industrial Psychology (1920-1930): Upto 1925, the personnel management had taken a definite form. Staff line organisation became the basis of personnel management. The opposition of scientific management movement by workers introduced the need of industrial psychology. Industrial psychologist developed many new techniques like psychological testing, interviewing, workers training and non-financial incentives. They helped to give a professional form to personnel management. The personnel management began to be realised as a profession and a specialist's function.

4. Period of Human Relations (1930-1950): Prof. Elton Mayo and his companions conducted Hawthorn experiments as the beginning of human resources having greater influence on production than that of other psychical resources. Worker must be treated as a human being. His social, psychological and moral instincts should be fully recognised by the management. Due to these experiments the commodity concept of labour changed to social concept. The decade of 1940-1950 was very important for the development of personnel management. During the decade, many new techniques were developed for the selection, training and induction of workers. The personnel philosophy became people-oriented. Trade unions flourished and provision of fringe benefits for the workers became common.

5. Modern Times (After 1950): The history of personnel management since 1950 upto current times is the age of modern developments. It is the period of the citizenship concept of labour where the workers have full right to be consulted in determining the rules and regulations under which they work. The concept of industrial democracy has imposed many new responsibilities upon the personnel managers of industrial houses. In modern times, the personnel management is widely accepted as an independent discipline. One finds two important developments during this period: After 1960, the personnel management began to be realised as a behavioural science which centred completely on human elements with the study of organisational behaviour as its main crux. After 1970s the belief of 'open social and industrial system' became very popular for business organisations. In modern times, personnel management is fully recognised as a profession dealing with the management of human resources. Some authors call it manpower management. These developments widened the scope of personnel management.

APPROACHES TO PERSONNEL MANAGEMENT

1. Commodity approach: This was the first or traditional approach towards workers which took birth from the factory system of production. It is also known as a Factor of Production Approach or Mechanical Concept of Labour. The observation that wages are high when labour is scarce in relation to demand and wages are low when labour is in excess of demand gave rise to the idea that affected by the law of supply and demand, labour is like a commodity and it may be bought like other commodities. The approach was supported by the proponents of scientific management movement. It developed the idea of economic concept of man. Money was accepted as the only and most effective motivator for more work. The absence of government intervention and lack of labour laws created the situations of labour exploitation. The factory owners took them as a cog in the machinery of production. It led to the machinery labourer concept of labour. The employer regarded his employees as operating organisms or machines, capable of a certain amount of output. Thus, philosophy led to an impersonal attitude towards workers. Hence, the worker's mind was diverted to protection rather than to production. With the growing knowledge that neither the commodity nor the machinery conception of labour was complete, the resulting inefficiency led to the beginning of the welfare protective movement.

Evaluation: The commodity approach of labour prevailed upto the end of 19th century. It made the condition of workers worst. They were loaded with more work, low wages, unhealthy working conditions and other types of exploitation. It led to class-struggle. Eventually, the trade unions came into existence to protect the rights of the workers.

2. The protective approach: After First World War, employers began to realise that the welfare of their employees had a direct effect upon their productivity. Hence, were introduced safety measures, lunch rooms, rest rooms, bulletin boards visiting nurses and a horde of ameliorating movements. The provision of housing, labour welfare measures, recreational and medicinal facilities were considered to be the duty of the employer. The employer without a welfare movement was considered backward. Robert Owen, the famous British industrialist, was an ardent proponent of this viewpoint. He used to say that an employer should treat his employees like his wards. But labour organisations attacked these welfare efforts of the employers. The visiting nurse was looked upon as spy, bulletin boards were interpreted as devices of propaganda, the costs of safety devices were sometimes objected to on the grounds of lowering wages. According to Scott, Clotheir and Spriegel: in many instances labourers took the attitude: "Put the money in our pay envelops, and we will take care of ourselves."

Evaluation: However, this attitude of workers towards labour welfare measures could not last for a long time. Today labourers claim these provisions as a matter of right. Various labour legislations have made them obligatory on the part of the employees.

3. The humanitarian approach or social approach: The period of human relations approach stressed the human use of human assets. The experiments of Prof. Elton and their associates asserted that the factory is a social system and its employees are human beings having their mind, heart and human values. Management should behave with them with dignity respect so that they would like to put their hearts with the work. The human approach maintained that the workers had certain 'inalienable' rights as human beings. These rights were as important as the right of other persons, and it was industry's duty to recognise them. All men are equal in the sense that they have many of the same impulses and reactions. The industry has a moral obligations not only to permit its workers to enjoy their rights, but to encourage and help them to make as much of themselves as possible. Psychologists stressed labour-management relations. They pointed out that men differ from one another in mental abilities, emotional stabilities, traditions and sentiments more than physically differences. These differences should be recognised. The worker cannot be separated from his job. A reciprocal relationship exists between the job and the market. The worker influences the nature and volume of performance, his job in turn influences the attitudes of the worker.

Evaluation: These developments led to an emergence of social approach to labour. The workers movement became more organised. It demanded more and more share in the prosperity and development of the business. This led to the development of the citizenship concept of labour. This mooted the idea of industrial democracy. As in a democracy a citizen has certain fundamental rights and a voice in determining and exercising these rights so do workers as industrial citizens have a right to be consulted in determining the rules and regulations under which they work. The legal recognition of this concept of labour is relatively recent in origin. More and more participation of workers in management is in offing. Industrial democracy is self-government by the workers, determining the mutual relationships of employer and employee, terms of employment, conditions of labour, rules and regulations affecting employees and the relationship of employees to each other. It accepts that 'the employee is both a social and economic entity, possessing different characteristics in various work situations'.

LOWER STATUS OF PERSONNEL MANAGEMENT IN INDIA

1. Insufficient Appreciation: In India personnel managers have been viewed as contributing little to the essential functioning of an organisation due to the fact that they were entrusted with such tasks as did not offer challenges. They generally prepared routine plans, programmes and procedures, handled employment details, did wage and salary surveys, and handled employee welfare programmes. Other executives were involved in many challenging tasks such as financing and looking after complex production problems. This lack of involvement on the part of personnel managers often led to frustration among them. The personnel function itself was placed at a lower level in the organisational structure. Untrained persons, who were not needed anywhere else, were employed in this department with the resulting low status and prestige of the personnel manager and his department.

2. Low position in the organisation: The personnel function was given a low status in the organisational structure. Line manager were reluctant in seeking help from the personnel department, mainly because personnel executives were contacted for the solution of a single problem. There was hardly any personnel planning, personnel programme and personnel policy in the organisation.

3. Lack of expertise: Frequently, a mediocre line manager was asked to perform personnel functions. Sometimes this was done: "to kick him upstairs" or "to reward him for his good performance elsewhere." As a result, he did not command the respect of his subordinates. As incompetent managers could not anticipate the problems of an organisation; they underestimated their possible effects. Some did not have even sufficient knowledge of, or interest in broader organisational personnel matters.

4. Poor self-image: As personnel managers found that they held low level positions, or were not fairly treated by other executives, they did not take any lively interest in their work, and often performed a static role.

Present Rising Status

These weaknesses influenced the status of personnel managers. But today the top executives have begun to realise that in order to meet the changing needs, there should be "human resources experts" well versed in the diverse aspects of personnel management. These experts must be knowledgeable, competent and committed personnel specialists capable of making meaningful contributions to their organisations and utilizing human resources very effectively.

Today, the Personnel Department is enjoying good status in the overall organisational structure. High sounding designations such as Personnel Director, Senior Personnel Manager, Manager, Human

Resources are being used for them. The personnel manager, very often serves as a key member of the top management team. In a large company, vice-presidential position is usually assigned to the top personnel man. He has ultimate responsibility for all personnel and industrial relations policies. He assists in decision-making, organisational planning, executive development and community relations policy.

GENESIS OF PERSONNEL MANAGEMENT IN INDIA

The Royal Commission on Labour (1931) recommended the appointment of labour officer in order to "protect the workers from the evils of jobbery and indebtedness, to act as a spokesman of labour and to promote an amicable settlement between the workers and the management." The Commission made following observations:

1. Exclusion of labour: The jobber should be excluded from the engagement and dismissal of labour and that, instead, a Labour Officer should be appointed for this purpose.

2. Traits of Labour Officer: The traits required of a Labour Officer should be integrity, personality, energy and the gift of understanding individuals. He should have a linguistic facility. If he is of the right type workers will rapidly learn to place confidence in him and regard him as a friend.

3. Powers: All labour should be engaged by him and none should be dismissed without consulting him.

4. Duties: The Labour Officer should fulfil many duties and should particularly initiate and administer welfare measures.

REASONS FOR RECENT HIGHER STATUS

1. Technical factors: (*i*) *Industrial Revolution*: Industrial Revolution brought in revolutionary changes in the method and techniques of industrial production. The industries were shifted from the former workshop to new mills and factories. Steam and power supplemented or substituted the efforts and energy of people. Production processes were simplified by the use of new machineries and techniques. On the other hand emerged other problems relating to men, materials and machines. The existing principles of management were suitably changed or amended or new principles were developed in order to reconcile the situation.

(*ii*) *Experiments in social sciences*: New experiments and research in social sciences contributed to the growth of personnel management. For example, Hawthorn experiment in the field of psychology affected the attitudes of the employers to a great extent. Researches in behavioural science also subscribed to the development of personnel management. New techniques and methods were developed which are not being used in selecting the right person on the right job and developing them scientifically by introducing new methods of training.

(*iii*) *Use of science in industries*: With the advent of science new and newer products, methods, techniques and processes were developed in the fields of production, communication and marketing, affecting the industrial development and the personnel relations. New offices were created to cope with the problems of industrial development, such as engineers, production manager etc.

2. Awakening among workers: After World War I, workers started to unite. A new industrial labour movement soon became an important element in this structure. In the early stages of industrialisation the unions emerged as means of protecting the careers, levels of wages, stability of employment and status in the new industrial society of work. Some other factors also subscribed to their cause at later stages. These were: (*i*) Economic hardship to workers due to inflation after World War I; (*ii*) Political movements and success of Russian Revolution in 1917; (*iii*) Emergence of International Labour Organisation in 1919. The union movement succeeded in improving the labour relations in industries. The concept of industrial democracy is the outcome of the labour movement.

3. Change in Government Attitude: The change in Government attitude towards labour, management and business was mainly due to the following reasons:

(*i*) *Laissez faire:* Widespread acceptance of *laissez faire* viewpoint was popularised by Rousseau, Bentham and Hobbes and was further advanced by Malthus, Adam Smith and others so-called classical school of economists. It proposed a minimum of public intervention in economic activities. As the political interests of the countries could not safeguarded by this policy in World War I hence the protection policy was introduced by nearly all the countries in the world. As businessmen could get an opportunity to earn huge profits at the cost of employees the Government come to the rescue of the employees in getting them rid of exploitation by the employers.

(*ii*) *Change in the concept of labour*: The change in the concept of labour from the commodity concept to other human concept was given a wide recognition. Labourer is now regarded as a human being and master of all the industrial activities. The idea of workers' participation in management has been recognised by almost all the Governments of the world.

(*iii*) *Labour Legislation*: Establishment of welfare states in most of the countries led to the enactment of various labour laws for the welfare of the industrial force. International Labour Organisations and other national labour agencies recommended several countries to introduce numerous labour statutes to reconcile the viewpoint of the labour and management.

Thus, the Government attitude was one of the factors in the development of personnel management or industrial relations.

4. Cultural and Social Changes: (*i*) *Education*: Education brought the change in the attitude of labour towards their word. They realised that work is worship and they would be more benefited if they worked hard. They could understand what was favourable and what was against their interest. Hence, they could no longer be exploited.

(*ii*) *Population problem*: Population problem also had its impact upon the problem of personnel management. The problem of active utilisation of men arose in the countries having a vast population like China and India. Problems of unemployment and wage fixation had direct link with the population. The other population problem is the migratory character of the labour causing absenteeism and labour turnover. These problems could be overcome by motivating the people in the right direction.

(*ii*) *Change in social values of the labour*: Social values of workers affect the efficiency of worker on the job. If a worker is given due regard in the society or by his fellow workers, he will be the most contented man in the society and his efficiency will be increased thereby. Large-scale production and advanced means of transportation and communication increased the social value of labour. Personnel problems increased and new personnel principles developed.

5. Change in the size of the business: Industrial Revolution and technical changes in methods and machines led to large-scale production. The use of technically-developed machines, simplification of methods and large-scale production led to development division of labour and specialisation functions requiring a large number of technical and non-technical workers. The need of personnel management was felt in order to get the work done by these people efficiently.

6. Change in the attitude of management: Some of the factors which compelled the management to make a change in its attitude towards labour were the development of scientific management, Industrial Revolution, awakening of workers, favourable attitude of Government towards labour and change in the social value of workers.

7. Change in the form of business organisation: In earlier years business was carried on under sole proprietorship. With the advent of joint stock companies as a form of business organisation, the size of the business increased exorbitantly. New management techniques developed to cope with the problems of personnel in large industrial houses.

8. Problem of co-ordination and control: Large-scale production created the problem of control over the thousands of persons working in unit. The need of co-ordination between personnel objectives, developed methods and techniques and overall objectives of the organisation was realised. New structural relationships were developed. The problems of control and coordination required an intensified study if made in the nature of working personnel.

FUTURE OF PERSONNEL MANAGEMENT IN INDIA

In future there are possibilities for the development of personnel management in India. Industrial development in India is progressing very fast. In order to solve many problems of industrial development, it has become necessary to develop the science of personnel management. This shall be possible only when there is a revolution in the minds of Indian industrialists and they feel that workers are human beings and humanly treatment must be given to them. They should not undermine the importance of labour as compared to other factors of production. Labourers should be induced to work hard so that other factors of production may be exploited in a better way to achieve the primary goal of maximum output at minimum cost. As partners in the industry, workers can contribute much to the national prosperity. Thus, the future of personnel management in India depends upon the change in the attitude of the industrialists towards labour. The Government has announced certain steps for the development of healthy industrial relations such as effective implementation of workers' participation in management scheme and enforcement of labour laws.

QUESTIONS FOR EXERCISE

1. Trace development of Personnel Management in India.
2. Describe the evolution of Personnel Management in modern times.

3. Explain important approaches to Personnel Management.
4. Account for the lower status of Personnel Management in Indian business houses. Trace reasons for their recent higher status.
5. Highlight the future of Personnel Management in India.

9

Manpower Planning

MEANING OF MANPOWER PLANNING

1. *Vetter*: "The process by which management determines how the organisation should move from its current manpower position to its desired manpower position. Through planning management strives to have the right number and the right kind of people, at the right places, at the right time, doing things which result in both the organisation and the individual receiving maximum long run benefit."

2. *Flippo*: "A manpower planning programme can be defined as an appraisal of an organisation's ability to perpetuate itself with respect to its management as determined necessary to provide the essential executive talent."

3. *Dale S. Beach*: "It is a process for determining and assuring the organisation to have an adequate number of qualified persons, available at the proper times, performing jobs which meet the needs of the enterprise and which provide satisfaction for the individual involved."

4. *Coleman Bruce P*: "Manpower planning is the process of determining manpower requirements and the means for meeting these requirements in order to carry out the integrated plans of the organisation."

5. *Macbeth*: "Manpower planning involves two stages. The first stage is concerned with the detailed planning of manpower requirements for all types of levels of employees throughout the period of the plan. The second stage is concerned with planning of manpower supplies to provide the organisation with the right type of people from all sources to meet the planned requirements."

CHARACTERISTICS OF MANPOWER PLANNING

1. A continuous and never ending process: As the manpower needs of an organisation change from time to time, it is a continuous and never ending process.

2. A comprehensive process: Manpower planning includes various aspects of manpower management which ensure the availability of right type of people in sufficient number in the organisation.

3. Determination of future needs: Determination of future needs of manpower in the organisation includes forecasting of demand for and supply of human resources. Determination of manpower needs in advance helps management to take up further actions. Suitable actions can be taken to make the existing manpower suitable for the future positions.

4. Utilisation of manpower: By indicating the various factors which should be considered like working environment, suitable performance appraisal, promotion etc, manpower planning helps in utilisation of manpower.

5. Fixing responsibility of management: Manpower planning is the responsibility of management as a whole and not only of the personnel department. The personnel department only guides and assists operating managers in framing manpower plans.

BASES OF MANPOWER PLANNING

1. Existing stock of manpower: The first basis of manpower planning and the starting point of all planning processes is the existing stock of manpower. Analysis of the existing stock of manpower requires studying the position of total stock of manpower by dividing it into groups on the basis of function, occupation, level of skill or qualification. A group-wise detailed statement is prepared giving the number of workers in the group, their age, qualification date of retirement and chances for promotion, etc.

2. Checking wastage: For a good manpower planning, appropriate adjustment in the existing stock of manpower should be made for the possible wastage of manpower caused by any foreseeable changes in the organisation. Rate of labour turnover and the period of active management etc., should be studied in order to analyse the wastage of manpower. Other reasons of wastage may be expansion and modernisation of plant, retirement, promotion, transfer and training of workers etc. These factors should be taken into consideration to make the necessary adjustment in the requirement of personnel.

3. Future manpower requirement: After evaluating the existing stock of manpower and analysing the various factors of wastage caused by any foreseeable change in the organisation, one may easily assess the future requirement of manpower in an industry taking into account the future plans of the company, government plans and programmes, employment policy, demand and supply of manpower in future, productivity of labour and other factors of production and replacement needs. Care should be taken of the possible changes in the techniques and methods of production in the near future.

OBJECTIVES OF MANPOWER PLANNING

1. To increase the size of the business: A number of workers are required to be recruited in expansion of the plant. A stock of the existing manpower should be taken and future needs of the personnel should be assessed at the time of taking the decision. It is essential to know whether new responsibilities should be assigned from among existing personnel or they should be recruited afresh from outside to meet the challenges of the new responsibilities. It should be decided whether persons are to be trained within the organisation to take charge of the new responsibilities or fresh well qualified personnel should be recruited. All this requires manpower planning.

2. To achieve effective recruitment and selection policy: Future needs may be predicted by manpower planning for which only right man on the right job at the right time may be recruited and selected. An enterprise has not to invest much amount on the training of workers who are recruited and placed after proper scrutiny. Effective manpower planning reduces the rate of labour turnover.

3. To reduce cost of labour: To maintain the supremacy over the other competitive firms, it is necessary for any organisation to control the cost of labour by effective use of manpower and thus reducing the wastage. This may be well done by manpower planning.

4. To avoid disruption in production: Manpower planning may help the organisation in producing the skilled and qualified workers. Through manpower planning future needs of personnel may be estimated and they are recruited and trained on the basis of a well-developed recruitment and training policy thus lowering the amount of expenditure on training. This production is carried on uninterrupted.

5. To follow national policy on employment: National policy on employment does not permit any employer to dismiss the worker once recruited by the organisation. Therefore, care should be taken in recruiting the worker according to the needs of the enterprise and to develop a recruitment policy of the organisation to avoid any unnecessary hardship in the near future. Here manpower planning alone can help the organisation.

6. To provide effective employee development programme: No effective employee development programme can be worked out without linking it with the manpower requirements of the organisation. While executing the employee development the talents, abilities and motives of the individuals as well as the organisational objectives in relation to the manpower should be taken into consideration thus making employee development programmes effective.

7. To maintain good industrial relations: An effective manpower planning helps the management in developing the good employer-employee relationship. For example, redundancies of workers caused by automation or any other technical change in methods and machines may be estimated well in advance with an effective manpower planning. It will help management consider the ways and means to avoid the anticipated untoward situation. Management may plan to absorb the redundant workers to some new job after proper training. Thus, good industrial relations may be maintained by an effective manpower planning.

FACTORS IN MANPOWER PLANNING

A. Quantity of Personnel or Workforce Analysis

In many companies, steps are taken to find replacement only after vacancies occur or are likely to occur. This method aggravates interruptions to production and tends to result in hurried and hence poorly evaluated selection of replacements. The effectiveness of hiring can be increased by forecasting manpower requirement of different categories of personnel, operative, technical and executive on the basis of the following factors:

1. Economic forecasting: The economic forecasting relating to national economy, international economic scene and future perspectives are made to determine future manpower requirements. If prospects of future economic situation are good, the future sales and production prospects will also be good resulting into more hands to obtain that level of activities. Hence, inflation, deflation, increase in costs of inputs and raw materials are the economic contingencies which influence the short-term and long-range plans of all business organisations.

2. Production estimates: Manpower requirements in some cases change with fluctuations in production. Hence, production forecast depends upon sales forecast. Thus, sales forecast are the basis upon which the estimates of manpower requirements are built. How much manpower is needed in a given department of a company depends upon factory and storage policies.

3. Departmental schedules: Most companies do not produce strictly to the sales curve. In its place a production schedule is prepared which levels out somewhat the peaks and valleys of sales estimates. The degree to which the production schedule is stabilized in comparison with sales curve is largely dependent upon the storability of the products and their non-susceptibility to the style factor. Departmental workloads can be established after factory schedules are computed. These department schedules provide the basis for determining future manpower needs of the department.

4. Expansion programmes: If expansion programmes are on the anvil, it will create needs of different types of personnel. Therefore, expansion programme should also be taken into account while calculating future manpower requirements.

5. Work standards: A change in work standards due to a negotiation between trade unions and management also creates demand for labour. For example, if standard production per worker is at present 50 units per day and it is reduced to 40 per worker under a settlement it will require 25% more workforce in order to maintain the same level of production.

6. Manpower inventory: After making economic forecasts and production estimates, total manpower requirements may be determined keeping in view the work standards. It is necessary to ascertain how much manpower of various kinds is available to produce the output scheduled for the period of time in question. These two classes of information can be compared to compute the manpower to be added to or removed from the payroll. It may be put as following:

Total manpower requirements existing or available manpower
= Manpower to be added or to be removed from the payroll.

7. Labour turnover rate: An old device of estimating future manpower requirements in any company is through the computation of labour turnover in the company, it is wise to estimate statistically how many are likely to leave. It may be possible to learn about the number of job vacancies, even though it cannot be ascertained as to who will specifically leave. Such estimates are best made in terms of past turnover. Labour turnover rates may be calculated either by separation method, replacement approach or flux method. In every case knowing the trends of turnover is an excellent means of calculating how many vacancies are likely to occur in the future.

8. Estimate of retirement and resignations: In estimating future manpower requirements, the expected losses should also be taken into account which are likely to occur through retirement, deaths, transfers, promotions, demotions, dismissals, disability, resignations, lay off etc. Changes in the human quality resulting from the experience gained in the jobs during the period and the training achieved should also be considered. The real shortage or surplus may be found out after making adjustments for wastages, anticipated and expected losses and separations.

9. Estimates changes in management: Changes in the quality or quantity of productive services require a change in the organisation structure. Changes in management philosophies and leadership styles, the use of mechanical technology such as the introduction of automatic controls or the mechanisation of materials handling functions necessitate changes in the skills of workers as well as a change in the number of employees needed.

B. Quality of Personnel or Work-load Analysis

Work-load analysis is the technical aspect of human resources planning which involves the study to nature and composition of existing workforce, *i.e.* auditing of human resources, study of work standards, demand analysis etc.

1. Auditing of human resources: Auditing initiates the preparation of a skill inventory. A skill inventory contains data about each employee's skills, abilities, work preferences and other items of information. It assists in examining the nature and composition of existing workforce and estimating the future type of requirements of different categories of personnel. Some organisations prepare organisation charts for it while others compile and maintain Employee Information Card for this purpose.

2. Study of work standards: The study of work standards is essential for determining the quality and type of personnel required. It is necessary to prepare a job analysis which records details of training skills, qualifications, norms, abilities, experience and responsibilities, etc., needed for a job. Job analysis includes the preparation of job description and job specifications. Study of work standards also removes the possibilities of underestimation of the quality and number of employees required leading to shortfalls in performance.

Importance of Manpower Planning

According to Dr. Ram Tarneja, "Management can ensure control of labours costs by avoiding both shortages and surpluses of manpower through proper manpower planning." Failure in planning and in developing personnel proves a limiting factor in achieving the organisational objectives. There will be disruptions in the flow of work and the pace of production will also be low if the number of persons in an organisation is less than the number of persons required to carry out the organisational plans. On the other hand, if some persons are surplus in the organisation, they will have to be paid remuneration if they are retained or compensation if their services are terminated. A sound personnel policy requires that there should be adequate number of persons of the right type to attain the organisational objectives. For this the manpower planner should be concerned with the timing and the scheduling of planning of personnel and persuading the management to use the result of manpower planning studies in the conduct of the business. Manpower planning can prove to be important to frame the training and development programmes for the personnel because it takes into account the effects of anticipated changes in technology, markets and products on manpower requirements and educational and training programme requirements.

FORMS OF MANPOWER PLANNING

A Short-Term Manpower Planning: It involves the matching of present employees with their present jobs so that they may perform their functions efficiently. It is wrong to expect a perfect match between jobs and individuals. In the short-run, only jobs can be adjusted or modified to adjust with the individuals due to many constraints—legal, organisation and social. It is very difficult to throw an employee out of job. Hence, some adjustments have to be made in the job itself in the short-run. Short-term manpower planning is influenced by the following factors:

1. Employees less qualified than the requirements: The following steps should be taken:

(*i*) Providing training, (*ii*) Change in the job, (*iii*) Providing assistant to the man, (*iv*) Change of incumbent such as transfer or demotion, (*v*) Separation of the incumbent.

2. Employees more qualified than the requirement of job: The following adjustments may be made:

(*i*) Job enlargement, (*ii*) Additional charge, (*iii*) Promotion of higher position (if vacant), (*iv*) Seeking council and advice from him. (*v*) Temporary assignments.

B. Long-term manpower planning: In this management has sufficient time gap to take necessary steps and making this matching process a calculated exercise. It is a planning for 10-15 or more years in respect of manpower requirement for the organisation. In the long-run the management may take the following steps in the direction:

1. Projecting manpower requirements: This is required to meet future needs of the organisation. As environment in which an organisation operates is constantly changing, the whole job structure should keep pace with such changes. The present organisation structure may continue to be the best. The management must predict as accurately as possible what jobs will be needed in future. However, such prediction is neither easy nor always possible. As Flippo has observed 'that some firms claim that executive manpower needs are too intangible to forecast, that management cannot be defined or planned for in any constructive manner'. Three problems can be identified under projecting manpower needs :

(*i*) Can one predict a rate of loss of manpower, and thus predict the need for its replacement?

(*ii*) Can one predict the need for new manpower over and above the need for replacement?

(*iii*) Can one determine the abilities necessary to man these jobs so that requirement and training processes can be facilitated? An analysis of these problems may help in protecting the manpower needs.

2. Manpower inventory and analysis: It involves the appraising of present key personnel and cataloguing their characteristics without reference to specification to a particular position. Inventory in a term used in relation to the counting of tangible objects such as raw materials, goods in progress, or finished product. In manpower inventory, however, the items involved are intangible. It is not simply the counting of number of persons available presently, but it includes a cataloguing of present and potential abilities and aptitudes. The inventory should include young men who have good potential, as well as present executives, because a good deal of shifting from position to position will undoubtedly occur in future. The manpower inventory requires the following:

(*i*) Determination of personnel to be inventoried.

(*ii*) Cataloguing of factual background information on each individual.

(*iii*) Systematic and detailed appraisal of those individuals.

(*iv*) Detailed study of those individuals deemed to possess potential for development.

Thus, manpower inventory provides information about present and future executives in the organisation. It may be more complete and accurate than any unsystematic impression of the general status of the organisation. The existing and future gap in number of managerial personnel and their ability may be ascertained through this inventory. It will form the basis for recruitment, selection and training process.

3. Recruitment and selection of suitable persons: After making manpower inventory, the next step in the direction is the recruitment and selection of suitable persons. These activities involve various functions of long-term nature.

4. Training and development: Training and development is the process of developing men to cope with the new responsibilities. The efficiency of any organisation depends on how well its members are trained and developed.

STEPS IN MANPOWER PLANNING

1. To Prepare manpower inventory (current manpower position): Manpower planning seeks to avoid the situation of over—and understaffing. The stock of existing manpower is to be assessed for this purpose. It requires a critical assessment of present manpower. Manpower inventory refers to the assessment of the potential capabilities of present employees—qualitatively and quantitatively. Not simply a head count of existing staff it is cataloguing of their present and potential talent. It reveals the degree to which these capabilities are employed optimally. It helps to reveal the undeveloped potential, if any, and also the gap that exists or that is likely to arise in the firm's human resources. Preparation of manpower inventory involves the determination of personnel to be inventoried, cataloguing of factual background information such as level, skill, work experience, number, job history, date of recruitment etc., of each individual, systematic appraisal of each individual and listing the present and potential abilities and aptitudes of each. It helps in designing the selection and training programmes for the future. Present manpower should be evaluated according to age groups, skill groups, level groups, potential-wise and cost effectiveness.

2. To Forecast manpower needs: Manpower planning determines the future manpower needs of the organisation. These can be projected on the basis of production and sales budgets, workload analysis and workforce analysis, taking into account the objectives, size, area of operations, expansion schemes, technology of production processes, future changes in organisation etc. Absenteeism and rate of loss of personnel on account of retirement, discharge, resignation, death, disability, etc., should also be estimated. Again, the future manpower requirements should be estimated qualitatively and quantitatively. The quality of manpower is determined with the help of job description and job specification on the basis of information collected from job analysis.

(*i*) *Job description*: Job description describes the details about the title of the job. It involves nature of the job to be performed, duties involved, authority, relationship, working conditions, tools and techniques, responsibilities etc. The details of the job are required, not only for selection of personnel but also for preparing training and development programmes.

(*ii*) *Job specification*: Job specification summarises the man specification *i.e.* the characteristics of man required to perform the job. It lays down the educational qualification, technical qualification, experience, mental ability, skills, aptitude etc. required to perform the job efficiently. The contents and requirements of a job provide an objective guide for determining the quality of personnel needed in future. While job description describes the details of the job, job specification describes the quality of the person required to perform the job.

3. To identify manpower gaps: A comparison of future needs of personnel and the person's manpower inventory reveals the gap in terms of number and quality of personnel which points out the additional personnel required in future. It also identifies the improvement to be made in the present personnel to prepare them for the jobs in future.

4. Manpower programme: Programmes and strategies are developed for recruitment, selection, training, transfer, promotion and appraisal. If the net requirement reveals the need of additional staff, development plans are designed to ensure a continuing supply of trained people to take over job as they fall vacant either by promotions or by recruitment or through training. On the other hand, if the existing staff is in excess of future needs, plans must be prepared to absorb them in the organisation against future vacancies as it is now-a-days not easy to discharge or lay off a person due to trade union pressure. Thus, persons may be trained to fill the future vacancy so that the shortage and redundancies can be avoided in the long-run.

TURNOVER

Meaning of Turnover

To quote Flippo, "Turnover refers to the movement into and out of an organisation by the workforce. This movement is an index of the stability of the workforce." Turnover is an important aspect of manpower planning. Workers sometimes leave a firm or industry at their own instance. Occasionally they are ousted from a firm or industry. New workers are employed in their places. Thus, the composition of labour force changes from time to time. Turnover is the rate of displacement of the personnel employed in an organisation due to resignation, retirement or retrenchment. If the rate of labour turnover is high this is a sign of instability. It adversely affects their efficiency as well as the profitability of the firm.

Causes of Turnover

1. Unavoidable factors: (*i*) personal betterment; (*ii*) illness or accident; (*iii*) death or retirement; (*iv*) discharged due to insubordination; (*v*) marriage (in case of female workers).

2. Avoidable factors: (*i*) Lacks of congenial and healthy atmosphere in the factory, (*ii*) Lack of proper facilities and amenities; (*iii*) Low wages, ill-treatment, etc., (*iv*) Redundancy, *i.e.*, lack of planning and foresight of higher management.

It is not a matter of anxiety if the persons leave the organisation due to personnel reasons. Otherwise, they should be provided opportunity for promotion within the organisation according to their seniority and merit. It will motivate them and the organisation will be benefited by their experience, sincerity and loyalty. Thus, if workers leave the organisation due to lack of good working conditions and harmonious industrial relations, it is a matter of great anxiety. The management should look into the causes and try to improve physical and mental environment of the organisation so that people may like to in it and contribute their maximum for the attainment of its objectives.

Measurement of Turnover

1. Separation Rate Method: According to this method, turnover rate is measured by dividing the usual number of separations during a periods by average numbers of workers on the pay-roll during the same period.

$$\text{Turnover rate} = \frac{\text{Turnover of separations in a period}}{\text{Average number of workers in the period}} \times 100$$

2. Replacement Method: This method is based upon the actual replacement of the employees irrespective of number of persons leaving. If new workers are employed on account of expansion of the business, they should not be included in replacements.

$$\text{Turnover rate} = \frac{\text{Number of replacement in a period}}{\text{Average number of workers in the period}} \times 100$$

3. Flux Rate Method: The method is based both upon the number of replacements as well as number of separations.

$$\text{Turnover rate} = \frac{\text{Number of separation + Replacements}}{\text{Average number of workers in the period}} \times 100$$

It should be noted that turnover cannot be completely avoided nor is it desirable. However, its rate can be kept at a considerable low level by taking such steps which improve employee morale and create a congenial atmosphere in the organisation power inventory sheet for future, in determining the type and number of workers required in future, in proper recruitment, selection, training, etc.

QUESTIONS FOR EXERCISE

1. What is the meaning of manpower planning? Describe its characteristics and bases.
2. What are the objectives of manpower planning? Discuss the nature of short-term and long-term manpower planning in business enterprises.
3. Describe various factors in manpower planning. What is its importance?
4. Distinguish between various forms as manpower planning.
5. Explain the steps in the process of manpower planning in industry. Describe the meaning and causes of Training.

10

Industrial Leadership and Supervision

DEFINITIONS OF LEADERSHIP

1. *Peter F. Drucker*: "Leadership is a human characteristics which lifts man's vision to higher sights; raises man's performance to higher standards and builds man's personality beyond its normal limits."

2. *Hersey and Blanchard*: "Leadership is as the process of influencing the activities of an individual in efforts towards goal achievement in a given situation. This process as Hersey and Blanchard has explained in the form of following equation:

$$L = f(l, f, s)$$

That is leadership is a function of the leader (1), the followers (f) and other situational variables (s) are who exercises this influence is leader whether he is a manager in a formal organisation or an informal leader in an informal group or the head of the family."

3. *Robert Tannenbaum*: "Leadership is inter-personal influence exercised in a situation and directed through communication process, towards the attainment of a specialised goal or goals."

4. *Ordway Tead*: "Leadership is that combination of qualities by the possession of which one is able to get something done by others, chiefly because through his influence they become willing to do so."

5. *Alford and Beatty*: "Leadership is the ability to secure desirable actions from a group of followers voluntarily without the use of coercion."

6. *Haimam Theo*: "Leadership can be defined as the process by which an executive imaginatively directs, guides and influences the work of others in choosing and attaining specific goals by mediating between the individual and the organisation in such a manner that both will obtain maximum satisfaction."

Characteristic of Leadership

1. Personal quality: Leadership is basically a personal quality of character in a man that influences the behaviour of others. This quality motivates the people to be with the leaders.

2. Followers: There must be a group of followers, because leadership cannot flourish in vacuum. Leadership cannot be imagined without followers. The followers suspend their decision in specific situations. The leader exerts influence only on followers.

3. Reciprocal: Leadership is a reciprocal relationship between the leader and the led (followers). Both influence the behaviour of each other.

4. Continuous: Leadership is essentially a continuous process of influencing behaviour. It is not a one time shot. A leader breathes life into the group and motivates it to do acts in a desired way.

5. Relative: Leadership is related to a particular situation at a given point of time and under the specific set of circumstances. However, its style may differ from time to time.

6. Guide: Leadership guides the individual and the group to achieve a common goal and unifies and motivates the followers for this purpose.

7. Process: Leadership is something a person does and not something he has. It is something that emerges, grows and is achieved.

8. Function: Leadership is a function of the leader, the followers, and other situational variables. It removes barriers in a situation so that followers may function with freedom and independence.

LEADERSHIP QUALITIES—TRAITS OF A LEADER

The various thinkers have given different traits of a leader to be successful and there is lack of agreement between them.

Authority	Qualities
1. F.M. Viscount Shim	1. Courage, 2. will powers, 3. Judgement, 4. Flexibility, 5. Knowledge, 6. Integrity.
2. Ordway Tead	1. Physical and nervous energy, 2. Enthusiasm, 3. Sense of purpose and direction, 4. Technical Mastery, 5. Integrity, 6. Technical skill, 7. Friendliness and affection, 8. Decisiveness, 9. Intelligence, and 10. Faith.
3. Henry Fayol	1. Health and physical fitness, 2. Intelligence and natural vigour, 3. Moral qualities, 4. Knowledge, and 5. Managerial ability.
4. Chester I Bernard	1. Vitality and education, 2. Decisiveness, 3. Persuasiveness, 4. Stability, 5. Intellectual capacity, and 6. Knowledge.

Broad Categories of Leadership Traits

1. Physical qualities: These include (*i*) Sound health, (*ii*) Vitality and endurance.

2. Psychological qualities: These include: (*i*) Personal magnetism, (*ii*) Enthusiasm, (*iii*) Cooperation, (*iv*) Ability to inspire, (*v*) Forcefulness, (*vi*) Tact.

3. Intellectual traits: These include: (*i*) High degree of intelligence (*ii*) Open mind, (*iii*) Capacity for sound judgement, (*iv*) Ability to teach, (*v*) Scientific approach.

4. Qualities of character: These include: (*i*) Integrity, (*ii*) Self-discipline, (*iii*) Fair play, (*iv*) Willingness to accept responsibility, (*v*) Physical and moral courage, (*vi*) Humanism.

ARE TRAITS COMMON TO ALL LEADERS?

Various thinkers have identified various leadership traits but there are hardly any two leaders who have common traits. Personnel traits play significant role in leadership but trait and leadership have no relations. The studies of past successful leader's life indicate that though certain useful traits made them leaders it was the environment or situation which made the traits active on that they emerged as leaders. As each leader has different traits therefore, analysis of traits in different leaders made the list of traits longer and larger. The traits found in two leaders are not common. There was very little consensus over common traits among researchers. It is not easy to identify which and how many traits a leader must possess. For example, good health is desirable in many leadership situation but history is witness to the fact that there have been so many leaders who did not possess good health.

LEADERSHIP AND MANAGEMENT

Berris once commented, "There are many institutions, I know, are very well managed but very poorly led." This statement clearly demonstrates that managing and leading are not the same. Leadership and managership are not synonymous though effective management requires effective leadership.

Points of Differences

1. Organisation relationship: Managerial behaviour implies the existence of a manager-managed relationship which exists in the context of organisation, on the other hand, leadership may occur anywhere it and not necessarily in the organisational context. There may be a leader in a completely unorganised group. For example, a mob may have a leader but cannot have a manager. Informal groups in an organisation have leaders but not managers.

2. Sources of influence: Leader and a manager differ in their source of influence. A manager gets authority from the organisation. The organisation gives the manager authority to get the work done by his subordinates. On the other hand a leader may not have authority but may receive power from his followers.

3. Sanctions: A manager commands over the allocation and distribution of sanctions. He has control over positive sanctions such as promotions and awards for better task performance and contribution to organisational objectives. He is in a position to exercise negative sanctions such as imposing fine for defaults for withholding promotions or increments, etc. On the other hand, a leader has different types of sanctions to exercise and grant. He may withhold access to satisfying the very purpose of joining the group such as social satisfaction and related task rewards. These informal sanctions are relevant for individuals in respect of their ego needs or a feeling of belongingness. Organisational sanctions exercised or granted by a manager are geared to psychological and needs of individuals like the feeling of the security and communality.

4. Role continuance: A manager may continue in the office till he performs his duties satisfactorily in line with the organisational objectives or till his continuance in office is acceptable to the organisation. On the other hand, a leader can maintain his position only through day-to-day wish of the followers.

5. Reasons for following: People follow managers because they are a part of the system in which they work. They have been allotted the positions having job description and are governed by rules and regulations framed by the organisation. To the contrary, people follow their leaders on voluntary basis. They may snap ties with the leader as soon as they realise that he cannot give them what they want.

6. Need of followers: A manager may continue in office even if there is no subordinate (follower) but leader will he redundant if there is no follower.

7. Accountability: Managers are accountable both for their own behaviour and also for the behaviour of their subordinates. On the other hand, leaders are not accountable to the followers or to the organisation for their own behaviour or for the behaviour of their followers.

8. Scope of functions: A manager has to perform all the five functions of management *i.e.*, planning, organising, staffing, directing and controlling. Leadership function is directing to get maximum use of subordinates ability. Subordinates are guided by rules and regulations framed by the organisation and enforced by managerial authority. In this process, they may work about 60 to 65 per cent of their capacity, just enough to satisfy the requirement of holding their jobs. In such circumstances, managers must invoke zealous response in them to raise efforts towards total capacity on their part by exercising leadership. Thus, leadership is a part of manager's directing function but not all of it. A strong leader may be a weak manager because he may be weak in any other function of management, say planning. A manager may be a weak leader though he may be acceptable as manager. Thus, management is not a part of leadership whereas leadership is a part of management.

DIFFICULT SEGREGATION OF FUNCTIONS

Though management and leadership are not synonymous, however, it is always not possible to segregate the behavioural functions of managership and leadership. As Katz and Kahn, say "Every act of influence on a matter of organisational relevance is in some degree an act of leadership." The implication is that every instance of managerial behaviour has a leadership component in it and it is difficult to determine how much of this represents leadership. It is better to concentrate on the concept of managerial leadership instead of indulging in separating and determining what behaviour is associated with leadership and what with managership. The term managerial leadership itself suggests the necessity of bringing together the managerial and leadership roles for the more effective task performance, organisational effectiveness and human satisfactions.

MAIN FUNCTIONS OF LEADERSHIP

1. Team work: Three vital determinantes of team work are the leader, the followers and the environment. These factors are independent. The leader's duty is to make the environment conducive to work. He studies the followers individually. He instill in them the interest to work. He creates hygienic environment encouraging the inquisitive employees and by prohibiting insidious elements. He inculcates a sense of collectivity in employees to work as a team.

2. Integration of team work and organisational objective: Leadership or a leader integrates the efforts of the followers and the organisational objectives. He directs the efforts of the group towards the attainment of objectives of the organisation of which he is a part. As each individual performs a part of the total work an interaction of those parts of the whole is of paramount importance towards the attainment of goal.

3. Representative of subordinates: A leader is the representative of management and also the representative of subordinates. Thus, he is an intermediary between the top management and the work group. Rensis Likert calls them linking pins. As linking pins leaders integrate the whole organisation. They represent the work group before the top executives and also represent management before the work group. The effectiveness of an organisation depends upon the strength of these linking pins.

4. An appropriate counsellor: Sometimes, an emotional disequilibrium is created among workers. The leader provides them counselling to eliminate the disequilibrium created in the organisation. He removes all barriers and stumbling blocks to effective performance. He releases the emotional tension of the subordinates and thus restores equilibrium.

5. Domination or use of power: A leader must dominate his followers by using organisational power and authority to effectively achieve the goals of the organisation expected of him. He must use power and authority in a manner that will stimulate a positive response from the subordinates. Depending upon the situation a leader uses different types of power *viz.* reward power, coercive power, legitimate power, referent power and expert power. Besides formal basis, sometimes informal basis of power also have a powerful impact on organisational effectiveness. A leader may be effective only when his subordinates obey him winningly. So, he must use the power in the best interest of the group he leads.

6. Striving for effectiveness: Sometimes managers are too busy in petty things to address to major details of effectiveness. In this situation the leader makes concerted efforts to bring effectiveness in the organisation by encouraging and nurturing team work, by better time management and by the proper use of power. He provides an adequate reward structure to encourage performance of employees. He delegates authority wherever necessary . He invites participation to achieve the better results. He brings effectiveness to the organisation by providing workers the necessary resources, and by communicating them what is expected of them.

7. Managing of time: Time is precious and vital but often overlooked by the management. The leader has thorough knowledge of the principles of the time management. He can monitor the time in the interest of the organisation.

8. Fraternity: Fraternity implies cooperation among the subordinates to achieve a common goal. Leadership style and its approaches play an important role in developing industrial harmony. Leader should develop a climate of cooperation among workers to achieve the success.

9. Communication: A leader must communicate the organisational policies, procedures and programmes, to the members of the organisation group. He must communicate authority and responsibility of each individual in the group so that he may know what he has to do and what not and how to do it. He must also communicate the results of his performance good or bad, so that he may improve his effectiveness.

IMPORTANCE OF LEADERSHIP

1. Indispensable: Leadership is indispensable in managing the affairs of an organisation successfully and effectively. An organisation, howsoever good it is, cannot be run effective without effective leadership. It must be led by an effective leader in order to achieve the organisational objectives by directing the efforts of the subordinates in that direction. An effective leader alone can pull out the organisation from darkness to light and push it to the path of development by resolving the various genuine difficulties. Organisation without an effective leadership, is nothing but a muddle of man, machines and materials. Unless they are engaged in a coordinated manner to produce more towards the accomplishment of organisational goal all of these elements of production are useless and inactive.

2. Source of motivation: Efficient leadership motivates the subordinates in the work place. It influences the performance of the workers. Higher the motivation better would be the performance. By exercising his leadership a leader motivates the employees at work for high performance. He must apply an appropriate leadership style which is most suited to the organisation a given situation.

3. Directing group activities: The main responsibility of the leader is to get the work done effectively by engaging fruitfully. For this purpose, he promotes sincerity of action among the workers. By his personal conduct and behaviour a good leader infuses confidence in his followers by directing them to work; giving them advice and getting good results in the organisation through them. If a subordinate attains high performance, the leader and also the subordinate try to maintain it as he is fully confident of his capacity.

A good leadership consolidates the efforts of the organised group. He diverts them towards the goals. But an unorganised group cannot attain the goal, however efficient its members may be. Good leadership directs the efforts of a group towards the goal.

4. Building morale: Morale is an internal feeling of the members towards the organisation. It is a state of mind and emotions affecting willingness to work. It represents the attitude of the employees towards management. It offers voluntary cooperation. High morale leads to high productivity and organisational stability. Employees morale can be raised through leadership.

5. Better utilisation of manpower: Effective leadership mobilises the workforce and engages it fruitfully to get higher performance. Leadership coordinates its efforts, makes plans, policies and programmes to develop it all to utilise the available manpower effectively so as to get highest output without minimum human cost. It is possible only through effective leadership.

6. Developing good industrial relations: Industrial relations represent the relations between the management and the workers. An efficient leader develops the talents of the individuals. He motivates them to work. He promotes self-confidence in them. He provides an opportunity to demonstrate their ability. He seeks cooperation of the workforce and thus creates an environment of good industrial relations.

7. Fulfilling social responsibility: A good leadership strives for fulfilling its social responsibility towards various social groups such as employees, organisation, consumers, society, investors etc., it is concerned with the need satisfaction of all these groups such as more wages to workers to improve their standard of living, higher productivity and production to the organisation, lower price to consumers, higher national product and increased revenue to the nation and a fair return to the investors. Through dynamic leadership all this is possible.

8. All round development: Thus, an all-round development of the organisation including the development of its workforce is possible only through dynamic leadership.

THEORIES OF LEADERSHIP

1. TRAIT THEORY OR APPROACH

Meaning and Method

Trait theory of leadership is a classical theory. It is based on the assumption that there are certain distinguished characteristics, qualities or trait that make an individual a leader. On the basis of which he may be distinguished from other persons (non-leaders). Trait approach leadership studies were very common between 1930 to 1950. These researches were based on the hypothesis that the persons having certain traits could become successful leaders. There were two methods for identifying traits:

(*i*) *Interview*: To ask the successful leader himself to explain the distinguished characteristics he possessed or how he considered himself different from his followers.

(*ii*) *Analysis*: To analyse the past and the present of eminent leaders in terms of their family background, education, social life, career events, character etc. and enlist the traits which the leaders possess.

Trait Theory Studies

Various research studies have identified various traits for successful leadership and emphasised various aspects of intelligence, attitudes, personality and biological factors. F.M. Viscount Shim identified only six basic qualities of a leader. Ordway Tead enlisted ten qualities of a good leader. Irwin H. Paul insisted only on three qualities. Henry Fayol gave five and Bernard six qualities. Thus, different theorists identified different number of traits which a good leader must possess. There are no universal traits which a leader should possess. A review of various studies and Stogdill presented the following identified traits: (*i*) Physical and constitutional factors (height, weight, physique, energy, health, appearance), (*ii*) intelligence, (*iii*) self-confidence, (*iv*) sociability, (*v*) will (initiative, persistence, ambition) (*vi*) dominance, and (*vii*) surgency (talkative, cheerfulness, gentility, enthusiasm, expressiveness, alertness and originality).

Ivaneevich and others have grouped the leadership traits, identified by various researchers, as follows:

1. **Physical characteristics:** Age, appearance and height.
2. **Social background:** Education, social status and mobility.
3. **Intelligence:** Judgement, knowledge, decisiveness and fluency of speech.
4. **Personality:** Alertness, dominance, extroversion, independence, creativity and self-confidence.
5. **Task-related characteristics:** Achievement drive, initiative, persistence, enterprise, and task-orientation.
6. **Social characteristics:** Attractiveness, popularity, sociability and interpersonal skills.

The various traits can be classified as innate and acquired traits. Earlier trait theories maintained that leadership qualities are innate *i.e.*, they are inherited and are inborn natural and god given. On the basis of these traits became popular the concept of 'born leadership', or concept of 'Leaders are born and not made. Later theorists conceded that many of these traits could be acquired and developed through experience or training. Thus, traits are not only inborn or inherited but they may be acquired as well.

Critical Evaluation

The trait theories are very simple. These failed to produce a clear-cut result. It could not produce one personality traits or a set of trait that may be used to distinguish a leader from a non-leader. It does not consider the whole environment in which leadership develops. There is a lack of generalisation about various traits as there were great variations in traits established by various researchers who agreed that the use of traits had not proved useful for selecting leaders. Byrd analysed over hundred studies and found that only 5 per cent of the traits appeared in four or more studies. Trait theory fails to explain why some persons who possessed some of the traits of a leader, could not become a leader.

Grounds of Criticism

1. No exhaustive list of traits: Various thinkers have presented different lists of traits of successful leaders. Rarely do two lists agree on the essential characteristics of a successful leader. Great variations may be observed in traits enlisted by several researchers. No exhaustive list of traits has been prepared. No thinker has enlisted the traits in order of preference or importance. Thus, lists of traits are confusing to the readers.

2. No universal traits: None of the thinkers has presented any list of traits which is universally acceptable. Hence, it is very difficult to indicate what mix of traits is necessary to make an effective leader.

3. No consideration for situational factors: Traitists did not consider the situational factors which are important in making a person leader of the group. Traits come to light only when a situation arises and they are helpful in facing a particular situation.

4. Different Roles require different traits: Even in the same organisation different traits appear necessary for different roles. Technical knowledge is of paramount importance at lower managerial levels where there is direct contact between workers and the supervisor. Human relation skill is of more important of middle level managerial positions where policies are interpreted and elaborated. Conceptual skill gains pre-eminent position at top level, where policies are framed, ideas are generated, strategic and long-term planning is undertaken. Organisations compete with people not products. Hence, the demand for uniformity of traits across all levels is questionable.

Leadership in a large organisation has a limited role to play because jobs are highly specialised. In small organisations on the other hand, it demands multiplicity of roles because one person has to do many jobs at a time. Hence, different combinations of traits are required in different organisations and at different organisational levels.

5. No room for developing future leaders: Trait theory stresses that leader possesses certain inborn qualities which cannot be developed or acquired later, however, it was later accepted that such basic traits can be developed or acquired through experience or training. Training programmes desired to develop traits may be futile if we accept the version that leaders are born and not made. Training may help improve a person if he possesses the basic traits. This will leave no scope for developing future leaders.

6. Separation of people: Trait theory requires an initial classification of leaders into 'leaders' and 'non-leaders' or 'good-leaders' and 'not so good leaders'. But there is no particular correlation between a man's ethics and morale and his power to attract people.

7. Problem of defining and measuring traits: It is very difficult to define trait. Executives often come out with bewildering variety of explanations, making a mockery of trait theory. Moreover, the measurement tools to quantify traits are open to doubt. For example, some psychological attributes such as intelligence, initiative etc. can be only inferred from the behaviour. There are some tools to measure personality traits but no definite conclusion can be drawn. Leaders have various traits in different degrees, but such degree cannot be measured. There are no personality traits that always distinguish the leader from his followers. Trait approach, however indicates that a leader should have certain personal characteristics. This theory helps management to develop such skills through training and development programmes.

2. BEHAVIOURAL APPROACH OR THEORY

The trait theory seeks to explain leadership on the basis of what leaders are and not what leaders do. In contrast to traitists, the behaviourist attempt to explain effective leadership in terms of what the leaders do. They emphasise that strong leadership is the result of effective role behaviour. Leadership is shown by a person's acts rather than by his traits. The basis of this approach lies in how the management views the workers.

Under classical management approach a man or worker was regarded not more than a commodity or an appendage to machine. Management used to coerce, direct and motivate them through the offer of economic awards. To increase efficiency and productivity management wanted to reduce wastes of time and materials. Management thought that men, by nature, are lazy, uncreative and irresponsible and therefore, the manager should be directive. Classical management was concerned only with high production and productivity. It considered people as machine having no feeling. Man was not an asset who should be developed in the interest of the organisation. The myth of management thinking was exploded by Hawthorne Experiments, conducted by Eltan Mayo and his associates. They discovered informal groups and informal leaders and stressed on inter-personal relationship as a significant factor in productivity. Therefore, they advocated to ignore human behaviour and expressed sole concern for output, whereas the human relations movement showed an overriding concern for people.

Behavioural approach gave birth to many leadership styles such as autocratic and democratic which produced different and conflicting results due to different behaviour of leaders and followers in different situations.

Behavioural theory attempted to explain the leadership phenomenon in terms of behaviour of the leader. There are four basic elements determining suitable behaviour: leaders, followers, goal and environment. Leadership acts may be viewed in two ways—functional favourable and dysfunctional unfavourable. Dysfunctional acts dismotivate employees to work together. The functional behaviour for a successful leader includes setting goals, motivating employees, raising the level of morale, developing team work, effective communication etc.

Traitist *Vs.* Behavioural Approach

The basic difference between trait is approach and behavioural approach is that while the former emphasises some particular trait to be possessed by a leader the behavioural approach emphasises particular behaviour by him. It is true that favourable behaviour is more effective and gives more satisfaction to followers and the person may be recognised as a leader.

Weaknesses of Behavioural Approach

(*i*) *Neglect of situational factors*: It ignores situational factors and favours a particular behaviour for all times. A particular behaviour may be effective at one time but may be quite ineffective at other times. This shows that time factor becomes an important element. A particular behaviour may not be effective in different situations at different times.

(*ii*) *Lack of scientific measurement*: Behaviour cannot be measured scientifically. Various methodologies such as questionnaires interviews or observations have their limitations. Therefore, these not are universally accepted by behaviourists. This is, however, an unavoidable limitation.

3. SITUATIONAL APPROACH

On the other hand, behavioural approach attempted to explain the various practices or styles available to a leader to discharge his leadership functions but it failed to indicate which style is the best which a leader should follow to be an effective leader in all circumstances. Both traitist and behavioural important variable *i.e.* the situations which greatly influence the trait or behaviour. During 1970 various researches established that it was not the trait or behaviour of a leader that mattered but it was a particular situation in which a particular trait or behaviour (style) is effective or ineffective. A leader may prove effective in one situation may be quite ineffective when situation changes. For example, Winston Churchill who was very successful Prime Minister during World War II proved quite ineffective in peace period. According to situational it is a particular situation that helps developing leadership and from which leaders emerge. Traits for behaviour may be elements supportive to situation.

Situational Varieties

Ohio State University research has given four situational variables that affect the performance of behaviour:

(*i*) *Cultural environment*: Culture is a man-made social system of beliefs, faith and values. Persons coming from different cultures behave differently. Any understanding of employee behaviour requires understanding of culture in which he lives. The leadership should be directed to influence behaviour of followers in the context of culture.

(*ii*) *Individual differences*: Individuals differ in behaviour which is a combination of antecedent factors. There are a variety of factors that affect behaviour in different ways such as attitudes, personality, characteristics, physical, sex, education, experience etc. Within this framework, individuals are classified as leaders and followers. Individual characteristics affect the leadership process. Thus, while some perceive a particular leadership style others may perceive a different style.

(*iii*) *Job differences*: People perform different types of jobs in an organisation. Different job conditions influence leadership differently. Demands of job almost inevitably force a leader into certain kinds of activities. This limits the leadership options available to the individual.

(*iv*) *Organisational differences*: Organisations differ on the basis of size, age, ownership pattern, objectives, complexity, managerial pattern, cultural environment etc. A different type of leadership is required in different type of organisations. For example, as compared to business organisation in government organisation, leadership behaviour is quite different.

Situational theory of leadership gives the analysis how leadership differs with situational variables or why a person in a particular situation is successful or unsuccessful.

Limitations of Situational Approach

1. Overemphasis on situation: Situational theory overemphasises the situational aspect of leadership. It ignores the traits or behaviour of a leader which also play important role in the emergence of a particular leader. Situation may affect the leadership decision but other variables should also be considered.

2. Emphasis on ability: Situational theory emphasises leadership ability of an individual in a given situation. It measures his present leadership potentialities. It does not show whether this leader will be fit in another situation.

3. Constraint over leadership development: Situational theory also puts a constraint over leadership development process as it neglects the process by which good leaders may be made in an organisation.

4. THE FOLLOWERS ACCEPTANCE THEORY

This theory asserts that the followers are important in deciding whether an individual is or is not their leader. If they recognise or accept him as their leader irrespective of his traits and behaviour. If they discard him or do not accept him as a leader, he is not their leader no matter how strong he may be. The followers must form groups because leader represents the group and not individuals. The groups have certain basic needs. A person who is successful in satisfying their needs is assumed to be their leader. On the contrary, if he fails to do so will not be accepted as good leader, nor can he be allowed to function as such. Thus, satisfaction of needs of the followers is the most crucial and guiding factor in the leadership phenomena.

The major weakness of this theory is that it completely ignores the qualities of the leader.

5. ECLECTIC APPROACH

No approach to leadership is complete in all respects and no single theory has been universally accepted. Stamford has developed eclectic approach to leadership. He contends that leadership depends upon traits of leader, situational variables, and types of followers. These three variables should be integrated to study leadership pattern.

SUPERVISION

Meaning

1. *Literal meaning*: Supervision is a Latin word in which 'Super' denotes 'from the above' and 'vision' is to 'see'. In ordinary sense of the term supervision is called overseeing activity. But overseeing alone does not convey anything worth taking note of. In management supervision means 'overseeing the subordinates at work with authority and with an aim to correct the employee if he is going wrong'. The real purport of supervision is to oversee the employees at work.

2. *Viteles*: "Supervision refers to the direct and immediate guidance and control of subordinates in the performance of their task."

3. *Davis*: "Supervision is the function of assuming that the work is being done in accordance with the plan and instruction."

4. *G.R. Terry*: "Supervision is the task of achieving the desired results by means of intelligent utilisation of human talents and utilising resources in a manner that provides a challenge to human talent. It is concerned with initiating action, putting into effect the plan and decisions by stimulation of the human resources of the enterprise."

To conclude, supervision is direction, guidance and control of working force with a view:

(*i*) to see they are working according to plan, policy, programme, instruction and keeping up the time schedule, and

(*ii*) to help them in their working if they are in need of help of any kind in accomplishing their assigned tasks.

Who is a Supervisor?

America's Fort Hartley Labour Act of 1947 defines supervisors as those having authority to exercise independent judgement in hiring, discharging, disciplining, recording and taking other actions of a similar nature with respect to employees. Therefore, supervisors are those persons in authority who have direct control over their working force. According to Allen, a supervisor is an authority who is responsible to get the work done. He is to see that directions are being followed, instructions and orders are being carried out, the plans, policies and programmes are being executed and deviations, if any, are being corrected and reported on to the authority to whom one is answerable.

Essential Qualities of a Supervisor

1. Knowledge of techniques of supervision. A supervisor should have knowledge of different techniques of supervision. This will enable him to know his men and he can make use of them according to requirement.

Supervisory techniques are usually divided into the following three categories:

(*i*) *Autocratic Technique*: In it there is a concentration of power in the hands of the supervisor. He uses 'rule of thumb' as weapon indiscriminately. He is a hard task master. He imposes his will upon the workers who are to carry it out without 'its and buts'. Workers have no say in the management decisions. The supervisor commands fear and has full control over his men.

(*ii*) *Democratic technique*: In it the democratic principles are followed. Workers have full say in the management decisions. They are taken into confidence by the management. They are allowed to participate in the decision-making process. Debates precede the decision. Supervisor is also responsible for getting the work done. He is not allowed to rule by thumb. He is to rule by consent. He seeks cooperation. He motivates their skill, knowledge, training, working capacity and wisdom and helps them in increasing their abilities and efficiency.

(*iii*) *Free reign technique*: In it the policies, programmes, the time schedule and objectives etc. are fully explained to workers. The workers are left free to work as satisfactorily as possible for them within the framework of the instructions, methodology and other allied things already explained to them. They have to follow the explained path and procedure and are responsible and answerable for deviations. The supervisor only guides the workers. He leaves the supervision part of his functions to the sound judgement of the workers themselves.

It is the individual trait, the working force, the work and the requirement which decide as to which of the three techniques are best to an organisation or in a given situation. It may differ from one situation to another, one individual to another, one group to another and one organisation to another.

2. Leadership qualities: The supervisor leads a group of personnel who look to him for guidance and direction. Unless he possesses the leader's qualities he will lack the rythm of supervision and thus the desired discipline, loyalty and efficiency in the group cannot be expected.

3. Managerial skill: The supervisor is part of the management. He must therefore possess the knowledge of managerial skill. The management functions require him to encourage team spirit in his men and solicit all types of cooperation. He must command respect and unquestioned loyalty to him by the use of managerial skill and technique.

4. Unbiased and fair: The supervisor should behave in an unbiased manner. He should be fair to all. He should not be prejudiced to any one of his men. Bias leads to troubles and vitiates the atmosphere. Therefore, it should be avoided at all costs.

5. Know and let know: The supervisor's duty is to know all his men their work, conduct, skill, training, knowledge, wisdom, success, failures, habits temperament, likings and disliking, social status, domestic problems, and all which he could possibly know. He should understand the spirit of his men. And his behaviour should be adjusted accordingly. On the other hand he should let his men know about him. This will remove suspicion, develop friendly attitude and create oneness.

Thus, a supervisor is required to play a very significant role in an industrial organisation. He is in constant and direct touch with the operating staff, that is the real working force. He is responsible for getting the work done from the force of which he is the supervisor and who are under his direct control. Because of his peculiar but significant position in the organisational structure the supervisor:

(*i*) influences the work environment;
(*ii*) influences the support of workers; and
(*iii*) influences the (*a*) attitude, (*b*) behaviour, (*c*) conduct, and even (*d*) co-operative efforts of the workers under his charge.

He is a morale booster. He influences the wholesome attitude of the whole lot. To quote Peter F. Drucker, "Even the best supervisor is no substitute for poor principles and practices in managing workers."

TYPES OF SUPERVISION

Scholars have classified the types of leadership and supervision in identical terms. The types of leadership and supervision are similar or parallel. The supervisory role in industry is the same as that of leadership. But industrial leadership and political leadership are quite distinct affairs.

An industrial leader *ex hypothesi* must be a supervisor. There are the following types of industrial leaders:

1. Authoritative supervisor: An authoritative supervisor exercises control and direction over his subordinates by virtue of the authority vested in him. In authoriative leadership there are the two following types of supervisors:

(*i*) *The hard-boiled autocrat*: An autocrat believes in unflagging discipline and firm control over the workers. He rarely appreciates the role of work of his subordinates. Rather he looks upon them with slight and mild contempt. He keeps himself aloof from the workers and does not give them a chance to get near him. He wants automatic obedience of his orders and can brook no criticism of his directions and orders. Such autocrats are apt to give credence to backbiting and this leads to tension and conflict in industry. As the autocrats show no respect for the feelings of their subordinates the subordinates also harbour a spirit of vindictiveness against such persons. At times this flares up and finds expression in violence against supervisors. In fact, a hard boiled autocrat does not deserve to be called a leader. He lacks all the qualities of leadership. The obedience which he is able to claim is due purely to the authority vested in him.

(*ii*) *The Benevolent autocrat*: The benevolent autocrat gives guidance and direction in all matters. He seeks to maintain discipline. He is annoyed by any infringement of the discipline. But unlike the hard-boiled autocrat, he is not averse to saying a word of praise to the workers who perform their duties well. The workers carry out the orders of such supervisors though they do not really fell inspired by them. In certain cases such a leader comes to symbolize the father and this helps to bring forth easy and free allegiance of workers and smooth functioning of the factory or mill. The authoritative leader is impressed by the quality of his decision but his decision cannot become an effective instrument unless it is accepted by the whole group.

2. *Laissez faire* leadership: The *laissez faire* leadership is exact reverse of the autocratic leadership.

(*i*) *Freedom of workers*: While in autocratic leadership there is no place for the personal freedom of workers, in *laissez faire* leadership the personal freedom of workers is respected.

(*ii*) *Responsibility*: Whereas in autocratic leadership the leader is considered responsible for everything, in *laissez faire* leadership the responsibility is distributed among various persons.

(*iii*) *Autocracy of democracy*: The *laissez faire* leaders neither do to impose any decision nor do they coerce them to any type of action. These leaders act democratically. They try to seek the voluntary cooperation of workers. These leaders do not project any fixed goals. *Laissez faire* leadership gives rise to indiscipline and discontent among workers. It also promotes a sense of insecurity among them. There is loss in production also. That is why one rarely finds such type of leadership in industry.

3. Democratic supervision: The most prevalent form of leadership and supervision in industry is democratic supervision. According to Bradford, a democratic leader believes in the following things:

1. Problems should be allowed to crop up.
2. For the sake of collective action and thinking, assemblies and conferences are a must.
3. There should be fixed collective ideals.
4. The criteria of action should be fixed.
5. The reasons for decisions should be known.
6. With progress freedom and responsibility increases.

The above-mentioned characteristics of democratic supervision are correspondent to and congruent with modern democratic ideals. However, everyone cannot be led democratically. Some workers misunderstand the democratic attitude of the supervisor and take it to be a symptom of weakness. They try to exploit this weakness and shirk work. This results in loss of production.

CONDITIONS OF EFFECTIVE SUPERVISION

1. Favourable social environs: Creation of an atmosphere of mutual trust and confidence is an essential condition of an effective leadership. It must be able to associate workers in decision-making and feeling of responsibility. The directives of the leader are easily accepted and carried out by the workers under such an atmosphere.

2. Knowledge of company's policy: The leader must know the fundamental tenets which govern the functioning of the company. He must acquaint the workers with the policy and the rules of the company. He must explain his status and role in the company in clear and frank terms. This would enable him to feel secure because he knows what he has to do and what he must avoid doing.

3. Gaining confidence of workers: A good leader should win the confidence of workers. Before effecting any change in the technique of production, they should consult the workers even if the change has been finally decided upon. This helps to induce a sense of well-being and confidence among the workers and they highly appreciate the fact that workers have been considered worthy for consultation by authorities.

4. Strict discipline: Whatever rules and regulations are framed once, these should be strictly adhered to. If a worker violates them he should be penalized without let or hindrance. Similarly, if the performance of a worker is noteworthy and deserves reward, he must be rewarded ungrudgingly.

5. Participation in decision-making: Finally, it is very necessary for good leadership that workers should be given a chance to participate in the decision and policy making of the company. This will enthuse them to toil hard and work with grit and determination.

PRINCIPLES OF EFFECTIVE SUPERVISION

The psychologist Blum has suggested the following principles for good leadership:

1. Don't be an autocrat: Autocratic leadership is self-defeating because the workers feel alienated and do not obey the leader willingly.

2. Listen carefully: The leader should be a good listener. He must listen carefully to everything told to him by subordinates. He must accord full opportunity to the worker to present his case, only after it should the leader express his opinion.

3. Don't decide hurriedly: It is rash to form an opinion about some person hurriedly after a casual glance or brief hearing as most of the complains are not genuine. But some are certainly so and if these are not removed the morale in the company would suffer.

4. Don't argue with subordinates: Under no circumstances supervisor should indulge in argument with his subordinate, because if he fails to persuade or convince by his arguments, he is liable to issue orders to vindicate his point of view. This creates frustration and sense of insecurity among the workers. A good leader should not argue but listen carefully and issue orders only after careful listening.

5. Don't criticize publicly: If a worker is rebuked publicly he feels insulted. The workers are usually rash and they tend to retaliate if they are wounded emotionally. Therefore, a good leader avoids discussing the faults of workers in public. He points them out to him in private and in a direct manner.

SUPERVISION TECHNIQUES

The following are the important supervision techniques:

1. Autocratic technique.
2. Democratic technique.
3. Free-reign technique. Success of this technique depends on:
   (*i*) Unrestricted supervision,
   (*ii*) Free delegation of authority, and
   (*iii*) Efficient and effective communication.

According to R. Lickert, "There is no one best way to supervise. Supervisory practices that are effective in some situations yield unsatisfactory results in others." Indeed supervision is individual trait and wisdom. Techniques are developed by the supervisor himself in a given situation. His technique differs from situation to situation, from work to work, from individual to individual, from group to group and from organisation to organisation. Under these circumstances it is difficult to adjudge one of the three as 'best'.

FACTORS AFFECTING A SUPERVISION

1. Human relations skill: Supervision assimilates in itself the following functions:

(*i*) Guiding the working force,
(*ii*) Instructing them, and
(*iii*) Inspiring them for better performance.

The supervisor has to depend on the decisions of top and middle order management for the following:

(*i*) Leadership,
(*ii*) Counselling,
(*iii*) Communication,
(*iv*) Determinants of human relations.

Without their guidelines the supervisor remains handicapped. In modern set up he can take routine decisions within the framework provide for the purpose. But he cannot take a major decision without consulting superiors in middle order and top management. He is the person to toe the lines as suggested by his superior though he is directly responsible to get the work done. But he is the person who is in direct touch with his men. He watches them working. He knows their emotions, feelings and sentiments, notes them and shares them. He is on the spot.

Therefore, in these matters he is left with no alternative but to take quick decision before any sparking situation arises. He is the best judge of human relations. He has to apply his skill, use his training, draw lessons from his experiences and handle the situation accordingly. So far as human relation is concerned he is a master of skill.

2. Technical and managerial knowledge: The guidance and instructions are largely based on the technical knowledge and the managerial acumen. These help the supervisor in serving his organisation well. His supervision capabilities are increased by adequate training and sufficient technical and managerial skill.

3. Leadership position: The supervisor's ability of supervising his workmen depends on his position and status in the organisation. This position may either be delegated or may be acquired. The supervisor can improve his position provided a status worth his responsibilities is given to him. This is fundamentally important and no organisation can afford to ignore it.

4. Improved upward relations: A supervisor is well heard and responded to by his superiors at all levels of the management. His suggestions are received with appreciation and due attention paid to it. His adverse reports as well as appreciations are equally responded to and action taken accordingly. He must have good relations with his superiors by way of encouragement. This helps him in establishing good relations with his workmen.

5. Relief from non-supervisory duties: A supervisor must be free from all duties except supervision and its related functions. Submission of reports, returns etc. is not his job. If he is free from all these then he may devote more time with his workmen. Job training too is not his duty. Instead it should be given by instructional staff. The supervisor should be allowed to concentrate on directing functions for which he should be given sufficient authority under the basic norm of management—'power with people'. This would ensure the maximum supervision from which results can be generally expected.

QUESTIONS FOR EXERCISE

1. Define leadership. Are there any traits which seem to be common to all successful leaders?
2. What qualities (traits) are necessary for a successful leader?
3. "Without leadership an organisation is but a muddle of men, machines and materials" Comment. Explain the importance of leadership in present industrial and business organisation.

4. Critically examine the different theories of leadership.
5. "Supervisor should be people-minded rather than production-minded." Discuss and analyse the statement.
6. "Supervision is overseeing employees at work." Discuss this statement.
7. What are the various types of supervision? Mention conditions and principles of effective supervision.
8. What do you mean by supervision technique? Which is the best one? Enumerate the factors that affect supervision.

11

Theories of Motivation in Industry

DEFINITION OF MOTIVATION

Motivation is derived from 'motive', which means an idea, need emotion or organic state which prompts a man to an action. Motive is an internal factor that integrates a man's behaviour. As the motive is within the individual, it is necessary to study needs, emotions, etc. in order to motivate him to work. There are so many inducing factors which induce a person for the best performance to meet his needs and emotions. This motivation is a process of getting the needs of the people realised to induce them to work for the accomplishment of organisation objectives. Hence, motivation is nothing but an act of inducement. Following are some definitions of motivation:

1. *Edwin B. Flippo*: "Motivation is the process of attempting to influence others to do their work through the possibility of gain or reward."

2. *Michael J. Jucious*: "Motivation is the act of stimulating someone or oneself to get a desired course of action, to push the right button to get the desired action."

3. *Caroll Shartle*: "Motivation is the reported urge or tension to move in a given direction or to achieve a certain goal."

4. *Delton E. McFarland*: "The concept of motivation is mainly psychological. It relates to those forces operating within the individual employee or subordinate which impel him to act or not to act in certain ways."

5. *Beralson and Steiner*: A motive "is an inner state that energises, activates or moves (hence motivation) and that directs or channels behaviour towards goals."

6. *Koontz and O'Donnell*: "Motivation is a general term applying to the entire class of drives, desires, needs, wishes and similar forces that induce an individual or a group of people to work."

7. *Lillis*: "It is the stimulation of any emotion or desire operating upon one's will and promoting or driving it to action."

8. *The Encyclopaedia of Management*: "Motivation refers to degree of readiness of an organism to pursue some designated goal, and implies the determination of the nature and locus of the forces, including the degree of readiness."

9. *Dubin*: "Motivation implies any emotion or desire which so conditions one's will that the individual is properly led into action."

10. *Viteles*: "Motivation represents an unsatisfied need which creates a state of tension or disequilibrium, causing the individual to make it a goal directed pattern towards restoring a state of equilibrium by satisfying the need."

NATURE OF MOTIVATION

1. An unending process: Man is a social animal. He has innumerable wants to satisfy. These induce him to work. All the wants cannot be satisfied at one time. Where one want is satisfied the other may emerge. Satisfaction of wants is an unending process. Hence, motivation is also an unending process.

2. A phychological concept: Motivation is a psychological concept. It arises from inside the individual. The inner feeling balances the perception of an individual and satisfaction of his needs that influence that direction, volume, behaviour, limitations and efforts of an individual. Hence, motivation is an inducement of inner feeling of an individual. It cannot be forced upon from outside.

3. Concerned with individual: Each individual is an integrated organised whole. A part of him alone cannot be motivated because motivation is a psychological fact concerned with the whole individual. A man's basic needs are determined and cannot be separated from each other.

4. Hampered by frustration: A man becomes frosted if he fails in satisfying any of his basic needs in spite of his best efforts. Such a frosted man cannot be further motivated until his basic need is fulfilled.

5. Goals and motivation: Goals and motives are inseparable. A man works to achieve some individual goals. After the goal is achieved he is no longer interested in work. Goal means satisfaction of needs. Therefore, it is very essential for the management to know the goals or motives or needs of each individual, so that they may be pushed to work by directing them towards achievement of their goals.

6. The self-concept as a unifying force: Unifying forces run through each individual's history. Unifying force means drive to actualise his own image. The outline of a person's self-image is fairly well realised in his early childhood while in his later age he acts accordingly. For example, a child who thinks himself as a leader, will try to behave the way in later life if possible. Thus, an individual is always trying to do two things: (*i*) to act like a person, he thinks he is, and (*ii*) to get what he thinks he can. Thus self-concept is an important motivating force.

7. Insurance of group motivation: Motivation is due to an inter-play among three groups of factors:

(*i*) Influences operating within an individual *i.e.* his goals, needs and values.

(*ii*) Influences operating within the organisation, *i.e.* organisation structure, technology, physical facilities, nature of jobs etc.

(*iii*) Forces operating in the external environment *i.e.* culture, customs, norms etc. of the society.

8. Positive and negative motivation: Positive motivation implies use of incentive such as increase in pay, reward, promotion etc. for better work. Negative motivation means to emphasise penalties such as reprimands, threat of demotion, fear of loss of job etc.

9. Different from job satisfaction: Motivation and job satisfaction are related though not synonymous. Motivation is a drive to satisfy a want. It is goal-oriented behaviour. On the other hand, satisfaction refers to contentment experienced after the satisfaction of want. Motivation is a process whereas job satisfaction is the outcome or consequence.

Importance of Motivation in an Organisation

According to E.F.L. Brech: "The problem of motivation is the key to management actions and in its executive for it is among chief tasks of the General Manager. We may safely lay it down that the tone of an organisation is the reflection of the motivation from the top." Following is the importance of motivation in an organisation:

1. Utilisation of human resources: Motivation induces men to work. It results in increased production and productivity. Same men try to put their efforts to produce more and more for the benefit of the organisation. Thus their efficiency increases. The inherent qualities of workers are developed by employing different techniques in the interest of the organisation so that they are able to use the methods, systems and technology effectively.

2. Utilisation of other resources: All resources except human resource can produce no results, unless men try to put them in action. By utilising the other resources to the best of their efforts men should be motivated to carry out plans, policies and programmes laid down by the organisation. Unless the men are induced to contribute their efforts towards attaining the organisation goals utilisation of resources is not possible to their fullest extent.

3. Willingness to work: Motivation influences the willingness of people to work and willingness comes from within. A man may have a capacity to work and he may be physically, mentally and technically fit for work but he may not be willing to work. Motivation creates a need and desire on the part of the workman to present his better performance.

4. Good labour relations: In an organisation all the members of the staff connect rate their efforts to achieve the objectives of the organisation and carry out the plans in accordance with the policies and programmes laid down by the organisation if the management introduces motivational plans. Both workers and management, are benefited by such plans. While efficiency and wages of operating force increase, productivity of the organisation increases due to consolidated efforts of the motivated people. The labour problems such as absenteeism, labour turnover, indiscipline, grievances, etc. are considerably reduced by proper motivation. Thus, motivation helps build good labour relations.

5. Basis of co-operation: In their zeal to produce more the members work as a team to pull the weight effectively, to get their loyalty to the group and to the organisation, to carry out properly the activities allocated and generally to play an efficient part in achieving the goals which the organisation has undertaken. Thus motivation is the basis of co-operation to get the best results out of the efforts of the men on the job.

6. Improvement of skill and knowledge: All the members of an organisation try to be as efficient as possible and to improve upon their skill and knowledge so that they may be able to contribute to the progress of the organisation as much as possible because they know that they will get what have been promised and ultimately they will be able to satisfy their personal as well as social needs.

7. Building human relations: As the human concept of labour has changed and now labour is treated as human being, motivation builds human relations. He is treated as a man and not a commodity. This attitude contributes towards motivating the people at work. Workers are invited to participate in the decision-making function of the management. Thus, motivation builds human relations.

8. Tool of management: Motivation is an important tool in the hands of management to direct the behaviour of subordinates in the desired and appropriate direction and thus minimising the wastage of human and other resources. It is the best way to achieve the organisational and individuals goals in an economical and efficient manner.

VROOM'S EXPECTANCY THEORY

As an alternative to various content theories such as Herzberg's two-factor theory, Maslow's need theory, etc. Vroom has proposed a new theory of motivation. According to Vrooms's theory, people are motivated to achieve certain goals which they expect from their actions. If People have their own needs and expectations of what they desire from their work. They use rewards to decide on which company to join and how hard to work on the job. Expectancy theory assumes that people are decision-makers. They have many alternatives out of which they choose one which seems to be most desirable at the time. Thus, motivation depends upon the situation facing people and how it satisfies their desires. Both the individual and situation differences are considered is Vroom's model. It is built concept of Valence, Expectancy and Force. Its concept of force is equivalent to motivation and also equivalent to the product of valence and expectancy. Algebraically, it may be shown as follows:

$$\text{Motivation (Force)} = \text{Valence} \times \text{Expectancy}$$

1. Valences: Valence means preferences that people have for various outcomes or incentives that are potentially available to them. It is an individual's preference for a particular outcome. It refers to the personnel value which workers place on the rewards they believe they will receive for performing. It is the individual's importance to the potential outcome or reward that can be achieved on the job. It is preference of an individual to one particular outcome in relations to others. It is the subjective value attached to an incentive or reward. It is zero when an individual is indifferent to the outcome. It is negative, when an individual prefers not attending the outcome in comparison to attaining it. It is positive when an individual prefers attaining the outcome in comparison to not attaining it.

2. Instrumentality: A major input valence is the instrumentality of the first level outcome in obtaining a derived second level outcome. Instrumentality refers to the degree to which the first level outcome will lead to a desired second level outcome. Hunt and Hill have explained the instrumentality of the first level outcome by promotion motive. For example, suppose, an individual desires promotion and feels that outstanding performance is necessary for achieving the goal. Then his first level outcome is superior performance. His second level outcome is the promotion. By virtue of the expected relationship to the preferred second level outcome of promotion his first level outcome of superior performance thus acquires a positive valence. The person would be motivated for superior performance to achieve the desired second level outcome of promotion. Thus, superior performance or first level outcome is instrumental in obtaining promotion or the second level outcome.

3. Expectancy: Expectancy is another factor in the model in determining motivation. Expectancy is the probability that a particular action will lead to a particular outcome. It refers to the perceived relationship between a given level of effort and a given level of performance. It refers to the extent to which a person believes that his efforts will lead to the first level outcome or performance.

Thus, Expectancy = Efforts to first level outcome (The belief that efforts lead to performance).

People usually have certain expectation about whether their behaviour will be successful or not. If they see that they will not succeed, they do not even try. Expectancy is subjective and depends upon individual's perception. By matching people to jobs managers may influence people's expectancies positively.

Expectancy is different from instrumentality input into valence. It relates to efforts to first level outcome whereas instrumentality relates to first and second level outcomes. Thus, expectancy is the probability that a particular action will lead to a particular first level outcome.

Implications of Vrooms Expectancy Theory

Vroom's theory' recognises the individual differences in work motivation. As compared to Maslow's or Herzberg's simplistic models it suggests that motivation is a complex process. It tries to integrate individual goals and organisational goals. In content theories it is assumed that satisfaction of a particular need is likely to influence the organisation objectives in a certain way. In this theory one finds out how important is the second level outcome to the employees workers' goals the instrumentality of various first level outcomes or organisation objectives for their attainment and the expectancies that are held with respect to the employee's ability' to influence the first level outcomes. Thus, Vroom's theory implies that a manager's job is to design an environment for performance, taking into account the differences in various situations. This theory is consistent with management by objectives.

Criticism of Vroom's Theory

Vroom's theory has been criticised on the following grounds:

(*i*) *Not Empirically*: The theory complex and its validity cannot be fully tested. There are only a few research studies designed to test the theory.

(*ii*) *Impractical*: The theory cannot be applied in practice. From the theoretical standpoint, its model seems to be a step in the right direction but it does not give the manager any practical help in solving the motivational problems.

(*iii*) *Overtly rational*: Not everyone is wiping to spend him energy to calculate the probabilities. 'People rarely sit down and list their expected outcomes for a contemplated behaviour. They do not estimate expectancies and valences, multiply and add up the total unless, of course, they are asked to do so by a researcher.

(*iv*) *Less Predictive accuracy*: The predictive accuracy of the theory leaves much to be desired. The amount of efforts which individual puts on the job is influenced by many factors other than those mentioned in the theory.

(*v*) *Methodological problems*: There are so many technical and methodological problems to make a research on the theory. Valence cannot be measured on ratio scales. Each valence is explained in the terms of all other valences.

The Vroom's Expectancy theory holds great promises for predicting behaviour in organisation in spite of these limitations.

PORTER AND LAWLER MODELS OF EXPECTANCY THEORY

Conditions of Performance

Early human relationship theorists believed that there is a close relationship between satisfaction and performance. All content theories implicitly assume that contented employee will certainly show a better performance. However, Porter and Lawler presented a more complete model of motivation. They promoted the thesis that performance causes satisfaction and *vice versa*. They tried to explore the relationship between motivation, satisfaction and performance. They pointed out that effort does not directly lead to performance, which is a function of three important factors:

(*a*) One must be motivated if he is willing to perform the assigned task;

(*b*) For this purpose, he must have necessary skill and traits; and

(*c*) He must have an accurate knowledge of the job requirement.

Porter and Lawler explain their choice for the expectancy' approach in these words: "The emphasis in expectancy theory on rationality and expectation seems to us to describe best the kinds of cognition that influence managerial performance. We assume that managers operate on the basis of some sort of expectancies which, though based upon previous experience, are forward-oriented in a way that does not seem to be easily handled by the concept of habit strength."

Elements of Porter-Lowler Model: The variouse elements of the model are:

(*i*) *Satisfaction variables motivation*: Satisfaction and Performance are separate variables.

(*ii*) *Effort*: Effort refers to the amount of energy exerted by an individual on a given task. It is a result of the attraction of the reward and the way in which the individual perceives the link between reward and payoffs. Perceived-reward-probability refers to the individual's perception of the probability that different rewards depend upon differential amount of effort. Value of reward and perception of effort-reward-probability, these two factors determine the amount of efforts that an employee will put in. Motivation is a force on the employee to make effort.

(*iii*) *Performance*: Effort leads to performance, but the two are not equal. Performance results from the combination of effort that an employee must put forth and the ability and role perception of an individual. Thus, if an individual has ability and/or inaccurate role perception, his performance may be ineffective in spite of his putting great efforts.

(*iv*) *Rewards*: Performance leads to intrinsic rewards such as sense of accomplishment and self-actualisation as well as extrinsic rewards such as pay, status, promotion, job security etc. Porter and Lawler believe that intrinsic rewards are much more likely to produce attitudes about satisfaction. That are directly related lo performance. Extrinsic rewards given by the organisation are imperfectly related to performance. In addition, perceived equitable rewards vitally affect the performance-satisfaction relationship. These reflect the fair level of rewards that the individual feels should be given to a given level of performance.

(*v*) *Satisfaction*: Satisfaction is derived from the extent to which the actual award falls short or meets or exceeds the perceived reward. If actual reward meets or exceeds the perceived reward, the employee will feel satisfied. If it falls short of perceived reward, he will feel dissatisfied. This provides the following two implications:

(*a*) The satisfaction is only in part determined by actual rewards; and (*b*) Satisfaction is more dependent on performance than performance is on satisfaction. This is a marked departure of this theory from the traditional satisfaction-performance relationship.

Implications of Porter-Lawler Theory

On the results of their study Porter and Lawler point out that variables presumed to affect performance turned to show relations to performance and the variables presumed to result from performance were also typically related to performance. Researches support this theory. The model is complex. It fully explains the variables underlying in motivation. In practice too, motivation is a complex phenomenon and not a simple cause-effect relationship. The model suggests that management should carefully assess its reward structure. Through careful planning and clearly define role requirements, the effort-performance-reward-satisfaction system should be integrated into a whole system.

McGREGOR'S THEORY 'X' AND THEORY 'Y'

McGregor propounded two theories of human behaviour in management philosophy on the theme of dual nature of human being best known as theory 'X' and theory 'Y' McGregor believes that nearly all management actions flow from these two theories and they (actions) reflect their philosophy controls practice. Management assumptions about human behaviour influence the personnel practices, decision-making, operating practices and even organisation design. McGregor observed that people appear to have a capacity for tenderness, sympathy and love, while they also possess tendencies towards cruelty, callousness, hate and malicious aggression. These two different philosophies are two different theories of McGregor Theory 'X' and Theory 'X'.

THEORY 'X'

Theory 'X': It is the traditional theory of management philosophy. 'Power is supreme' is the main theme of the theory where the people at work-level have no authority to suggest or object anything except to carry out the orders of the supervise. The line of authority or chain or command traditionally goes direct from the top, down through various layers of organisation with some delegation of authority but full and detailed accountability is up the line. People at work-level have no option except to obey the directives or order of the authority.

Assumptions of Theory 'X'

(*i*) Most people inherently dislike work and always try to shirk their responsibility.

(*ii*) Therefore, people must be coerced, controlled, directed and threatened with punishment, rebuffed or rebuked so as to get them to put forth adequate efforts towards the achievement of organisational goals.

(*iii*) The average human being prefers to be directed, wishes to avoid responsibility and puts off the work till it is necessary.

(*iv*) Most people at work have little ambition as to the improvement of work. They do not work with interest but wait for direction and act according to it.

(*v*) The average human being wants security and safety above all, hence, he tends to work slowly.

(*vi*) Most people have little capacity to contribute something towards solving the organisational problems as their importance in the management is always undermined by the authority and they are treated as an instrument of a machine.

(*vii*) Working method of the people is generally tractional and hence, there is little scope for the development and research.

(*viii*) People can be motivated at money and, on the basis of financial greed, they can do whatever management wants.

Propositions of Theory 'X'

(*i*) Management is responsible for organising the elements of production—money, material, machine, man and methods—in the interest of economic gain.

(*ii*) Management is responsible for directing the efforts of the people, motivating them, controlling their actions and modifying their behaviour to fit the needs of the organisation.

(*iii*) People would be passive unless management intervenes. Even they are resistant to organisational needs. They must be persuaded, rewarded, punished and controlled.

Importance of Theory 'X'

1. Authoritarian: The theory 'X' quite unwarranted to the modern times. It supports the authoritarian view which is not warranted in the present day economy. The man at work is not a machine, he is a human being. He is not only to execute the orders of the top line executives but he should also think over the order on its merits before its execution. Management may get results by coercion or throughout pressure tactics only in short run till people respond to pressures and controls partly out of fear of consequences of not following the orders of the top line executives.

Himself condemning the theory, McGregor says, "The conventional approach of Theory 'X' is based on mistaken notions of what is cause and what is effect. An organisation built upon theory 'X' notions will be one in which there is clear supervision and control of subordinates and high centralisation of authority. Leadership will tend to be autocratic and workers will have very little to say in decisions affecting them."

2. Wrong assumption of human nature: The assumptions contained in Theory 'X' do not reveal the true nature of human beings. Recent behavioural science researches does not support the traditional view. It concludes that the most effective way to get better results in an organisation is to work with people rather than through them.

3. Against labour welfare: In modern times, the governments of most of the countries have stressed that the worker should be given an honourable partnership in management. In this way, the theory has now become out of date.

THEORY 'Y'

On the basis of the results of many psychological and social researches, McGregor an opposing theory—Theory 'Y', as a more realistic assessment of the capabilities of the people. This theory 'Y' presents an alternative management approach which does not involve abdication of managerial responsibility. Management is still responsible for achieving the organisational objectives, but on different assumptions about human behaviour and motivation. The workers are fully aware of the organisational objectives, which is directly related to the satisfaction of employees' needs. McGregor recognised certain needs that Theory 'X' fails to take into account. For example, self-fiilfilment, ego satisfaction and social needs of individual workers. Thus, it pleads for a humanistic and supportive approach to managing people. Management tries to provide an atmosphere of peace and discipline within the organisation, without the oppressive measures. Hence, people work with interest and simultaneously enjoy the benefits of congenial relationship.

Assumptions of Theory 'Y'

(*i*) Work is natural: The average human being does not dislike work. Work is as natural as play or rest. Work may be a source of satisfaction or punishment depending upon the controllable conditions.

(*ii*) Positive means of motivation: External control and the threat of punishment are not the only means for accomplishing the organisational objectives. Workers are committed to objective and exercise self-control and self-direction to achieve them. They are fully conscious to their job.

***(iii)* Value of responsibility:** The average man works under proper conditions, not only to accept but seek responsibilities. Avoidance of responsibility, lack of ambition and emphasis on security are not the inherent qualities of the man but they are all consequences of experience.

***(iv)* Reward for work:** The reward for the execution of work is that it should be properly recognised. Satisfaction of ego and actualisation needs can be product of efforts directed towards organisational objectives.

***(v)* Co-operation:** The capacity to exercise a relatively high degree of imagination, ingenuity and creativity in the solution of organisational problems is widely distributed in the population, *i.e.*, labour co-operates the management in solving the problems of the organisation.

***(vi)* Development of abilities:** Human abilities and capabilities are not fully developed till now with reference to modern industrial system. Management has ample scope to develop the intellectual potentialities of the average human being.

***(vii)* Democratic theory:** The theory is based on democratic principles wherein all persons are given equal chance to develop their skill.

Postulates of Theory 'Y'

(*i*) Management is responsible for organising the elements of productive enterprise in the interest of economic and social ends.

(*ii*) People are not passive but they become so as a result of experience.

(*iii*) Motivation, potential for development, capacity for assuming responsibility and readiness to direct behaviour towards organisational goal are inherent in the people. It is the responsibility of management to recognise and develop these characteristics.

(*iv*) The management should arrange for organisational conditions and methods of operation so that workers may achieve their goal through self-direction.

Applicability of Theory 'Y' in India

Thus, Y theory establishes co-operation in achieving the objectives of the organisation between the man in authority and the man at work. The fact of inter-dependence in human organisation is widely recognised. The theory is participative in the sense that supervisors consult their subordinates about proposed course of action before taking any decision. However, management still takes decision for the organisation as a whole.

Development of management in India is slow. Due to the unchanging attitude of the employer and employee, relationship of master and servant still persists between them. The development of trade unions is still in its infancy. Organisational behaviour is mainly based on the assumptions of theory X. Recently, some statutory provisions regarding participative management, minimum wages, hours of work etc, have been made by the government in order to improve the working conditions and bring about change in the mentality of the employers and the employees. Government have provided training institutes for workers and managers so that they can be conversant with the modern management approaches. Profession managers have begun to accept the human values for the better management. They response their faith in workers' participation and profit sharing techniques. But some managements still hesitate to accept the theory in full. Inefficient and uneducated workers are indifferent towards sharing the responsibility. Thus, the assumptions of theory Y have not been fully recognised in India.

Distinction between Theory X and Theory Y

1. Value of work: Theory X assumes that the human beings are inherently distasteful to work, whereas Theory Y assumes that for human beings work is as natural as rest or play. They become distasteful to work only as a result of experience.

2. Ambitions and responsibilities: Theory X assumes that people are unambitious and prefer to be directed and they try to avoid responsibilites in jobs. Theory Y, on the other hand assumes that workers are ambitious and are capable of directing their own behaviour. They are ready to accept responsibilities if proper working conditions are provided.

3. Creativity and change: According to Theory X most people lack capacity and they always resist change while according to Theory Y, the capacity for creativity is widespread in the population. Most people are creative nature and they accept any change.

4. Need levels: The motivation factors in Theory X are lower level physiological and safety needs. Theory Y, on the other hand, recognises both lower level and higher order needs like social esteem and self-esteem and self-actualisation for motivation. However, emphasis is laid on higher order needs.

5. Control and supervision: Theory X proposes external control close supervision to achieve organisational objectives, They lack self-motivation, whereas Theory Y proposes self-direction and self-control.

6. Levels of authority: Theory X emphasises scalar, chain of command, centralisation of authority and autocratic leadership, whereas theory Y emphasise decentralisation of authority and greater participation in decision-making process.

Criticism of McGregor's Theory

McGregor's theory of motivation helped crystalise and put into right perspective the findings of the Hawthorne Experiments. However, it has been widely criticised on many counts:

(*i*) Oversimplification: It tends to overgeneralise and oversimplify people as being one way or the other. People cannot be put on two extremes. No enterprising man belongs either to Theory X or Theory Y.

(*ii*) Two extremes: McGregor's theory squeezes managerial styles and philosophies into two extremes of conduct which is devoid of reality.

(*iii*) Job and motivation: MgGregor suggests that job itself is the key to motivation. But all People do not see motivation in the job. The management has to motivate people to work.

(*iv*) Value of direction and control: People who follow theory Y still find that they have to behave in a very directive and controlling manner.

Most people believe Theory Y to be more appropriate but not in all situations. In some routine and formalised situations, Theory Y is more suitable. In underdeveloped countries like India, Theory X is more suitable. Neither theory is best in situations. An amalgam of both the theories may be more useful than either of the two alone as the best approach to motivation is one which is appropriate to the situation.

MASLOW'S NEEDS PRIORITY MODEL

Propositions about Human Behaviour

1. Innumerable wants: Wants of man are innumerable and never ending. As soon as one of his wants is satisfied, another appears in it place. This keeps a man engaged on the work. Human needs are multiple, complex and interrelated.

2. A Satisfied need is no more a motivator: As soon as a need is satisfied, it loses its capacity to induce the man to work. Hence, only unsatisfied needs or fresh needs can motivate people to work.

3. Hierarchy of importance in needs: Maslow is of the opinion that needs are satisfied in an order. As soon as the lower needs are satisfied those on the next higher level emerge and demand satisfaction.

Types of Needs

1. Primary needs: There are two types of needs—basic or primary or innate or physiological needs and secondary or acquired needs. Primary needs are those needs which are very important for the survival and preservation of life. These needs are universal and are felt by every one in the universe, but their intensity may differ from man to man or from society to society. Food, water, shelter, sex, air to breathe, sleep, clothing are examples of such needs. This theory has also been supported by McGregor and the state, "Man is a wanting animal, as soon as one of his needs is satisfied, another appears in its place. This process is unending."

2. Secondary needs: These are those needs which are related to mind and spirit rather than psychological of like. These needs develop as one gets maturity or education. These include rivalry, self-esteem, sense of duty, self-assertion etc. These are acquired needs.

Hierarchy of Needs

Man has both these types of needs. A.H. Maslow was the pioneer in contribution a systematic approach to this problem. He arranged the needs of a person in order of priority. Maslow's need-priority model was accepted widely. According to this theory, human needs tend to follow the pattern given below, presented in the sequence in which individuals usually become concerned with them.

1. Basic physiological needs: The physiological needs include the needs of human body such as food, shelter, clothing, sex etc. They are basic to preserve human life and are more or less universal. These are at the lowest level in the hierarchy of needs. Therefore, these must be satisfied first of all. These are a powerful motivating force when thwarted. Man lives by bread alone when there is no bread.

2. Safety and security needs: These needs are concerned with the physical and financial security. These include job security, physical security of income, old age provision, security from risks, etc. Management can influence these needs by providing security against such uncertainties *i.e.*, by implementing pension scheme, insurance plans, fear of dismissal etc.

3. Social or love needs: Being a social animal man is always interested to live in a society or group which loves him most. He wants to give or receive love. These needs include the needs of conversation, sociability, exchange of feelings and grievances, recognition and belongingness.

4. Esteem and status needs: These needs are: (*i*) self-esteem or (*ii*) public esteem. Self-esteem means esteem in the eyes of self *i.e.*, a feeling that he is doing something worthwhile. Public esteem means esteem or image in the eyes of public such as praise, admiration, public appreciation, etc.

5. Self-actualisation or self-realisation needs: There are individual's needs for realising his own potentialities, opportunity for creativity and for continuous development of the individual power and skill. Thus, these are where a person considers to be his mission in life.

Lower order and Higher order Needs

Maslow has further classified the five needs into two categories:

(*i*) *Lower order needs*: Basic physiological and safety and security needs are labelled by Maslow as lower-level needs. These needs are finite. These are to be satisfied in priority to others because they are the first order needs. A man cannot survive without them and he will be ready to do anything to satisfy these needs. A hungry man can do anything to get the bread. His secondary needs of security and safety get priority as soon as he satisfied his basic needs. Hence, a man collects grain for further use or tries to save money for his old age.

(*ii*) *Higher-order needs*: Belongingness, social or love needs, esteem and status needs, and self-actualisation needs are categorised as higher-order needs. They are secondary needs. They relate to the society and are external needs. They are infinite or unlimited. They are satisfied only after lower level needs are satisfied. All the needs under this category should be satisfied in order of priority. Lower level needs effect the higher order needs and *vice versa*. Higher order needs are dominant factors in motivating people at higher level in the management.

Advantages of Maslow's Model

Maslow's needs priority model presenting nature and priority order of needs is a landmark in the field of motivation helping the management in understanding the human behaviour of people at work. It is very simple, direct and practical. Everybody, except few, has some priority of needs, not necessarily in the priority order as described by Maslow. Maslow himself has admitted that his hierarchy is not rigid.

Criticisms

1. It is conditional: If the model may not apply at all times, in all places and in all circumstances, it may not follow the sequences as postulated by Maslow. Following are some examples:

(*i*) *More self-esteem than love*: There are some people in whom self-esteem seems to be more important than love. This reversal in hierarchy is possible where a strong or powerful person seeks self-assertion as a means to love.

(*ii*) *Absence of ambition and initiative*: In certain people the level of aspiration may be permanently dead because of prolonged experience of life at a very low level. Such people lack ambition and initiative.

(*iii*) *Absence of love needs*: Some people do not have love needs because they have lost love in their early childhood.

2. Other determinants of behaviour: There are many determinants of behaviour other than needs and desire such as perceptions, expectations, experience etc. Thus, the behaviour of a man is now a result of his needs or desires only.

3. Neglect of interaction of needs: This approach overlook the interaction of needs. Motivation is caused by several needs at a time. A person is hardly motivated by a single need.

4. Difference in expectations: People differ in their expectations significantly. The same need does not lead to the same response in all individuals. For example, people who have been satisfying their basic needs throughout their lives, may not be very keen to satisfy higher order needs.

5. Gives only general impression: Maslow's model gives a general impression. Hierarchical order is not very much rigid as Maslow himself accepted.

Application in Organisation

While designing a plan for people's motivation the management must keep in mind the above weakness of Maslow's need priority model.

1. Conditioned by environment: The need priority model of Maslow applies to people in general. It does not always apply even to employees working in organisation because people satisfy most of their needs outside their organisations. Needs are conditioned by environment. Importance of different needs is determined by environment of their social system.

2. No general applicability: The Maslow's model seems to apply to managers and professionals in developed countries. Several studies have tested the model that show that they meet their physiological and security needs and seek higher order needs. Researches show that in some developed countries like Japan and Continental European countries, the model does not apply even to managers. The order in developed countries too differs because of their cultural influences.

3. Applicable in underdeveloped countries: The model seems to apply even in underdeveloped countries like India, where economic conditions of worker do not seem to be satisfactory. They prefer to satisfy their lower order needs, physiological as well as security needs. A survey of 200 factory workers in India in sixties showed that they gave top priority to lower order needs, job security, earnings and personal benefits.

4. Applicable in substantive conditions: This model is tightly fit in case of managers and professionals in some of the developed countries and in under-developed countries, where none live under subsistence conditions. In other cases, the model is less reliable.

HERZBERG'S MOTIVATION-MAINTENANCE MODEL

In the late 1950s, Frederick Herzsberg made interesting studies that concentrated on self-esteem and self-actualisation. Out of these studies developed a theory of work-motivation. It has broad implication for management and its efforts towards effective utilisation of human resources. The theory is known as Herzberg Motivation Maintenance Theory or Motivation Hygience Theory or Two-Factor Theory of Motivation.

Herzberg's Problem

In his studies, Herzberg tried to understand the motivation problem. He felt that knowledge about human behaviour, nature, motivation and needs could be invaluable to organisation and individual. In his efforts to uncover the circumstances where a person felt satisfied or dissatisfied with his work, Herzberg conducted a study and interviewed about 200 engineers and accountants from 11 industries in the Pittsburgh area. These engineers and accountants were asked to think of time when they felt especially good about their jobs and the time when they felt particularly bad about it and then to describe the conditions that led to those feelings. Employees named different types of conditions for good and bad feelings. The study revealed that the factors responsible for job satisfaction are different not obverse from the factors that led to dissatisfaction. If a person was satisfied with his job in particular condition, the absence of such condition would not mean job dissatisfaction but it might be called no-job satisfaction. In this way this theory is based on a two-factor hypothesis, *i.e.,* factors leading to job satisfaction and factors leading to job dissatisfaction. These factors were classified into two categories:

(*i*) Motivational factors, and

(*ii*) Hygienic or Maintenance factors.

1. Motivational Factors: Certain factors are related directly to the job itself. Their presence creates a highly motivating situation, though their absence does not cause dissatisfaction. With the presence of such factors people always respond positively. Herzberg mentions six such motivational factors: (*i*) achievement, (*ii*) recognition, (*iii*) advancement, (*iv*) work itself, (*v*) possibility of growth, and (*vi*) responsibility. While achievement and responsibility are related to job itself others are secured from it. This set of factors has been designed as motivators or satisfiers. They are job-centred factors related to job contents.

2. Maintenance Factors: There were other factors, the presence of which did not significantly motivate them but the absence of such factors caused serious dissatisfaction. The presence of such factors prevented dissatisfaction and maintained a certain level of motivation, but any reduction in the availability of these factors was likely to affect motivation and bring down the level of performance. For example, an increase of ₹ 10 in the salary of a person does not mean much but a reduction of ₹ 10 from salary may upset him and is likely to cause dissatisfaction. Maintenance factors are mostly related to environment outside the job. Herzberg called these factors hygiene or maintenance factors because they produce nothing to the worker's capacity but they help maintain or prevent losses to the worker's performance due to work restriction. Herzberg named 10 maintenance factors as: (*i*) company policy and administration, (*ii*) technical supervision, (*iii*) inter-personal relations with subordinates, (*iv*) salary, (*v*) job security, (*vi*) personal life, (*vii*) working conditions, (*viii*) status, (*ix*) inter-personal relations with supervisors, and (*x*) inter-personal relations with peers.

Intrinsic and Extrinsic Factors

Intrinsic motivations are internal rewards that occur at the time of performance of work. Due to them there is a direct motivation to perform work because the act of performance is itself rewarding. The employee is self-motivated in this situation. Extrinsic motivators are external rewards which are not directly related to the performance of work. These occur after or away from the work such as retirement plans, leaves, health, insurance etc.

Prior to Herzsberg's research, organisational manager generally paid attention to extrinsic maintenance factors. Now with better understanding they insist more on intrinsic motivational factors, due to their superior possibilities for the worker's society and organisation.

Implications of Herzberg's Research

Herzberg's findings were in sharp contrast to the existing policies. The management used to emphasise Hygienic needs because non-satisfaction of these needs means dissatisfaction among workers and the organisation might have faced the resultant consequences. This, in itself was not wrong but it was based on wrong assumption that prevention would have positive health and the return of increased productivity, lowered absenteeism, turnover etc. They did not consider that the effect of improved hygiene lasts only for a short time. In fact, man's avoidance needs are recurrent. They will continue to occupy management's attention. Besides, understanding human needs in totally hygienic terms is fundamentally wrong. It has affected the self-concept of the employee very seriously.

Thus, Herzberg reaches a conclusion on the basis of these factors that people felt motivated if the job is challenging and investing, with the possibility of growth in it; authority to use their desecration; and ability to advance in the profession and receive recognition for the task they did.

1. Based on opposite points: Herzberg-model is based on two-factor theory of motivation *i.e.,* factors leading to job dissatisfaction and factors leading to job satisfaction. It suggests job satisfies and dissatisfies as two different qualitative factors. This was objected by others on the ground that job satisfaction and dissatisfaction are two opposite points.

2. Method bound: It is easier to get results favourable to the model by using the Herzberg method, while other methods failed to produce similar results. Thus, the model is 'method bound' which limits its applicability for general use.

3. Neglect of pay, status and relations: This model does not lay sufficient emphasis upon the motivation qualities of pay, status and inter-personal relations, while these are important employee-motivators, the model gives credit primarily to their maintenance capabilities.

4. Lack of clarity and distinction: The terminology used in this model is confusing. The difference between motivational and maintenance factors is very thin. Items designated as maintenance factors may serve as motivational factors to some and *vice-versa.* There is no absolute distinction among factors, neither factor is wholly unidimensional in its influence.

5. Limited Sample: The theory is based on a small sample of 200 accountants and engineers which cannot be said to be a representative sample. It has no universal application.

In spite of the above criticisms Herzberg's theory is useful in distinguishing factors that motivate people on the job and factors that primarily employees ready to be motivated. The model provides new insight in organisational behaviour.

QUESTIONS FOR EXERCISE

1. "Motivation is the core of management". Discuss what can management do to motivate the staff in an industrial organisation.

2. What is meant by motivation? Discuss the nature of motivation in the context of a business organisation.
3. Indicate how management can successfully motivate people taking clue from Vroom's Valence Expectancy Model. How does this theory differ from Porter and Lawler's model?
4. How do McGregor's Theory X and Theory Y of human behaviour, help motivation of employees? Do you think an integrated approach, an amalgamation of these theories may be more effective in our culture?
5. Explain Maslow's Need Priority Model and the extent to which it applies in organisation.
6. "A more complete theory of motivation recognises that individual works to fulfil a variety of needs". Critically examine.
7. Discuss Herzberg's Two-Factor Theory of Motivation.

12

Industrial Morale

DEFINITION AND APPROACHES

1. Classical approach: According to classical approach, the satisfaction of basic needs is symbolic of morale. If the basic needs of the employees are satisfied, their morale will be, to quote Robert M. Guion, "The extent to which individual needs are satisfied and the extent to which the individual perceives that satisfaction stemming from his total job satisfaction is morale."

2. Psychological approach: Psychological approach emphasises that not only the basic needs but psychological needs also influence the morale of the people. Psychological needs are the main motives of morale. Morale is the attitude and willingness to work. The following definitions support this approach.

(*i*) *Edwin B. Flippo*: "Morale is mental conditions or attitude of individuals and groups which determines their willingness to co-operate."

(*ii*) *Jucius and Slender*: "Morale is a state of mind and emotions affecting willingness to work which in turn affects individual and organisational objectives."

(*iii*) *Dale Yonder*: "For a group of workers morale refers to the tone climate and atmosphere of work, if workers appear to feel enthusiastic and optimistic about the group activities and mission and friendly to each other, they are described as having good or high morale. On the contrary, if they seem dissatisfied, irritated, crank, critical, restless and pessimistic, these reactions are described as an evidence of poor or low morale."

(*iv*) *Morris S. Vitales*: "To define morale primarily in terms of attitudes and behaviour traits associated with or derived from the activity of the individual as a member of a group, an important element in high morale is the feeling on the part of the individual that he shares the basic purpose of the group of which he is member."

1. Social approach: For a social scientist, the morale is a social phenomenon which pulls the men to live in society or groups in pursuit of a common goal. The following definition support this view:

(*i*) *Alexender Leighton*: "Morale is the capacity of a group of people to pull together persistently and consistently in pursuit of a common goal."

(*ii*) *Blackmanship*: "Morale is the feeling of togetherness. There is a sense of indemnification with an interest in the elements of one's job, working conditions, fellow workers, supervisor, employer and the company."

To conclude, the morale indeed, is 'willingness to work'. Keith Davis has summed up different views in the following words, "Morale can be defined as the attitude of individuals and groups towards their work environment and towards voluntary co-operation to the full extent of their ability in the best interest of the organisation."

CHARACTERISTICS OF MORALE

1. State of mental health: Morale is related to the state of mental health which is closely associated with loyalty, egoism, enthusiasm etc.

2. Identification of group interest: Morale is an identification of group interest and that of the interest of the enterprise, fellow workers and requirements of the job.

3. Subjective feeling: Morale is the subjective feeling of the employees. The morale of a group is said to be high when the group shows an attitude of satisfaction.

4. Affects behaviour, performance and discipline: Morale affects human behaviour, performance and discipline. It cannot be measured directly but is reflected in productivity, employee discipline, absenteeism, turnover etc.

IMPORTANCE OF MORALE

1. Higher production: Higher production and productivity of workers are the direct result of high morale. If the management is genuinely interested in high production and higher productivity of workers to achieve the desired results, it should know the impact of its policies and practices and on the attitude of the workers about work and be ready in promoting the good feeling about the work, policies, practices and about the organisation, among the workers to stimulate them to get the predetermined objectives willingly. Higher productivity is the direct result of the attitude of the workers about work, *i.e.*, high morale will yield more production and better quality at lower cost.

2. Harmonious relationship: Morale is an index of good feelings about the fellow workers and the organisation. According to Dale Yonder, "If workers appear to feel enthusiastic and optimistic about the group activities and mission, and friendly to each other, they are described as having good or high morale. If they seem dissatisfied, irritated, crank, critical, restless and pessimistic, these reactions are described as evidence of poor or low morale." Therefore the managers consistently and persistently make efforts for stimulating a feeling of togetherness, a sense of identification with the elements of one's job, working conditions, fellow workers, supervisors, and the company which is conducive to the achievement of the company's goals. It is an index of good industrial relations.

3. Success: High morale leads to success and low morale brings defeat in its wake. The success or failure of the industry very much depends upon the morale of its employees. To quote Keith Davis, "Never underestimate the power of a woman and the same certainly must be said about morale, never underestimate the power of morale."

4. Solution of labour problems: High morale assists the management to solve several labour problems such as labour turnover, absenteeism, indiscipline, grievances etc. It helps seek co-operation of the workers in the running of the organisation and thus getting higher production at minimum possible cost by reducing the wastage of time, man, machine and materials.

5. Utilisation of psychological factors: In modern times the psychological researches have increased the importance of the morale in the industrial field. Remarkable progress in industrial output may be secured by improving morale among the industrial workers. Taking interest in this direction the Government have introduced several labour welfare and social security measures to improve the morale of the industrial workers. The management has recognised the importance of high morale. It has realised that low morale has long-range effects damaging to the organisation.

MOTIVATION AND MORALE

According to Mrityunjay Banerjee, "Motivation is intimately connected with the morale. Good motivation leads to high morale. Poor morale is the manifestation of defective motivating process." Thus, morale is a state of mental health which is closely related to motivation. Morale is 'willingness to work'. Job satisfaction and dissatisfaction create the problem of morale among the employees. If an employee is satisfied with his work, his morale will be high. If he is dissatisfied, his morale will be low. Motivation and morale differ in the following aspects:

1. Composition: Motivation is something that moves a person to action. It is a process of inspiring people at work in order to achieve the desired goals. Morale is a composite of feelings, attitudes and sentiments that contribute to general feeling of satisfaction at the work place.

2. Scope: Motivation is basically an individual's willingness to work, while morale is a group phenomenon.

3. Sources: While motivation is a function of drives and needs, morale is a function of freedom or restraint towards some goals.

4. Nature: While motivation is basically a predisposition towards the job itself, While morale indicates predisposition towards all aspects of.

5. Concern: While Motivation is concerned with mobilisation of energy, morale is concerned with mobilisation of sentiments.

APPRAISAL OR MEASUREMENT OF MORALE

John M. Pfiffner has suggested two ways of measuring morale: (1) Direct method, and (2) Indirect method.

1. Direct Method: In direct method persons at work are contracted to express their feelings. Morale is measured in terms of the extent of increase or decrease in the profitability, productivity and other direct benefits which indicate of high or low morale. If profitability, productivity, etc. are increasing, it is an index of high morale. If they are decreasing, it is sign of low morale. Following techniques are employed in measuring the morale under this method:

(*i*) *Observation technique*: In observation the evaluator observes the employees on work and records their behaviour, attitude, sentiments and feelings towards the organisation, supervisor or his fellow workers. Comparing the observations of two periods, any change in the behaviour and attitude of the employees will indicate high or low morale.

(*ii*) *Interview technique*: Under this technique, the interviewer calls upon the employees and ask questions which may be guided or unguided.

(*a*) *Guided interview*: It emphasises mainly the questions set out beforehand in the form of a questionnaire in consultation with the higher management. Interviewer goes to the employees, with his printed questionnaire form, explains them the general object and supplies information if any asked for by the employees. He asks a set question with simple choice responses, included in the questionnaire which are answered orally.

(*b*) *Unguided interview*: In it the employees are encouraged to talk freely what they think about the organisation and its people. There are no formal questions. Interviewer listens to and encourages them to be free with an assurance that their talks wall remain secret and confidential. He may ask questions of general interest individually or in groups.

(*iii*) *Attitude survey technique*: Under this technique, detailed questionnaires are prepared by the organisation with the help of psychologists and distributed among workers to return duly filled in forms. The surveyor then steps further to analyse them and measure the general attitude of the workers. The answers to the questions are in Yes/No or True/False items. Check-list sometimes provide space for comments.

(*iv*) *Productive techniques*: These include a series of devices involving the use of written as well as verbal materials in the measurement of attitudes. 'The word-association', the sentence competition, the short story competition tests are some of the devices generally employed. Under this technique, the persons are allowed to express their feelings in detail with arguments which are later on analysed and projected by the analysts.

2. Indirect Method: In this method the men at work are not directly approached but the in-depth study is made of variations in output, profitability, rate of labour turnover, absenteeism and accidents, number of grievances and accidents and their severity. These are analysed with the help of the records and reports maintained by the personnel department regarding each employee of the organisation. The results are compared with the results of earlier study or budget targets or any other standard fixed for the purpose. The extent of increase or decrease in profitability or productivity may result in increase or decrease in the morale.

Indirect method should be used very carefully because productivity or profitability are not always affected by the morale. There may be several other factors which affect the productivity and profitability. Output may decrease not because the morale of the employees is low but morale may be low because of which affect the productivity and profitability. Output may decrease not because the morale of the employees is low but morale may be low because of use of low quality materials or defective machines or methods. Similarly various factors leading to absenteeism, labour turnover, accidents, grievances, and complaints should be studied carefully while analysing the morale. Unavoidable circumstances be ignored.

The above appraisal methods show the tendencies or attitudes of the employees. Statistical measurement of morale is not possible because it relates to the inner feelings of human beings.

MORALE AND PRODUCTIVITY

Productivity will also increase where morale is high because workers put their heart and soul to achieve the organisation's goal. A direct morale productivity relationship is widely assumed. High morale and high productivity are positively correlated. High morale contributes to the organisation. Contrarily, the low morale affects the production and productivity adversely because they feel lack of identification with the company due to which there cannot be an interrogation of efforts and productivity and the result cannot be encouraging. Recent researches show that the relationship between the morale and productivity is not so direct and positive. Production level may be lower in spite of high level morale or higher production is possible even if there is low morale. Thus, morale and productivity may be related to each other in the following four possible ways:

(*i*) High morale, high productivity.

(*ii*) Low morale, low productivity.

(*iii*) High morale, low productivity.

(*iv*) Low morale, high productivity.

1. High morale, high productivity: In most of the cases results in high productivity but only when the workers are motivated in the right spirit and supervision is of right type. There is a circular relationship between morale and productivity . High morale pushes up the productivity and high productivity in turn, pushes up morale and so on. This requires motivation.

2. Low morale, low productivity: Morale and productivity both will be lower, in the absence of proper motivation. Here also circular relationship exists between the two. Low morale pulls down the productivity and low productivity shrinks the morale of the employees.

3. High morale, low productivity: This is found in circumstances where the men are not fully trained and supervisors are not fully competent in getting the work done. This is also seen in organisations where supervisors are of the view that workers should not be unhappy, whatsoever be the effect on organisation, goal. In such circumstances, morale of the workers may be high at the cost of productivity.

4. Low morale and high productivity: Low morale and high productivity go together when the management does not co-operate with the workers and maligns the feelings of the men at work or where management uses penalties and punishments and provides better machines and equipments to carry on the production. Thus low morale with high productivity exists only when management is highly production-oriented. This cannot be sustained for long because a major work-group will be affected and industrial peace will be disturbed which it will further lower down the morale leading to lower productivity.

Thus, there is no certain correlation between morale and productivity. Therefore, it is not correct to say that high morale leads to high productivity because there are so many other factors which affect morale and productivity. But high morale is one of the several factors of high productivity. It is the function of the management to try to maintain the high level of morale because it is directly related to the favourable attitudes of the workforce. In the long-run high morale certainly adds to the productivity provided proper motivation of workers is there.

FACTORS CONTRIBUTING TO HIGH MORALE

Alexandar Leighton enumerates the following five major determinants morale:

1. Confidence of individual members in the purpose of the group.
2. Confidence of members of the group in the leadership.
3. Confidence of individual members in their fellow workers.
4. Organisational efficiency.
5. Conditions in the group and working conditions.

1. Confidence of the individual members in the purpose of the group: An individual works whole-heartedly only when he feels inspired by the purpose of group for which has is required to make efforts along with the other members of the group. It is, therefore, imperative to impress upon the worker, the importance of the product they produce. Once they begin to link their endeavour to the communal or national beings they work with a crusading spirit and this is precisely what we meant by good or high morale. The workers feel that they are doing something worthwhile for the nation or community.

2. Confidence in leadership: If leadership is of right type, the leader will win the confidence of his subordinates or followers and it will definitely raise their morale. A leader should be fair to all, helpful, friendly, honest industrious, capable and have the full knowledge of the job. In order to win the confidence only then, he shall lead the followers in the right perspective workers pose their confidence in a leader who can inspire the workers for united actions, make them realise their responsibilities, and also have sympathies for their problems. The morale of the worker will be high if their leader is capable, fair minded and impartial in dealing with the cases relating to promotions, penalties, rewards, etc. and is sympathetic towards them. In the absence of these, workers confidence in him will be loosened and their morale will be low. Thus, high or low morale is correlated to the capability of the leader in handling the affairs amicably.

3. Confidence in fellow workers: Every worker seeks full co-operation and guidance from his fellow worker at the time when a problem crops up in the group. Everyone in the group must be confident of getting such type of co-operation from other members of the group. Everyone should feel secure in expressing his point of view and grievances. He must have faith in the loyalty of his fellow workers.

4. Organisational efficiency: Organisational efficiency leads to the high morale. This requires:

(*i*) *Definiteness of responsibility*: The line of authority and responsibility should be distinctly and firmly clear so that there is no confusion in the mind of workers as to whom they are responsible for their work and whose order they are to follow. Lack of clarity here will disgruntle the workers and it will have an adverse affect on the morale.

(*ii*) *Adequate and effective communication*: An adequate and effective communication channel between workers and the management leads to high morale of the workers. If they think that the management listens to them, consults them in matters concerning job and organisation, informs to them as and when their interests are affected and makes them feel that they are the real participants in the organisation, their morale will climb at the top. A system of joint consultation should be evolved to consider the matters of mutual in the organisation. The suggestion scheme may also be introduced in the organisation to heighten the morale.

5. Working conditions and allied factors: Morale is an index of job satisfaction. A worker can be happy and contented at his job if the organisation shows a good measure of care for him and takes all possible steps to make the work place congenial for works. The following factors relating to work conditions help in raising the morale:

(*i*) *Fair wages*: Workers feel contented if they have the satisfaction of having equitable compensation for their labour and skill put in their respective job. If they are low paid or their wages are inequitable, their morale will be low because they are not in position to meet even their lower needs satisfactorily. On the other hand, if they are allowed a better wage and incentives to work, they will be free from worries and may devote themselves to the organisation and to the work, which will chance the productivity. Therefore, fair wage is necessary to build up morale.

(*ii*) *Security and opportunity*: Job security is an essential factor in raising the morale. If the organisation provides security to its workers, they will get their hearts into the work and will not think of leaving the organisation unless it becomes necessary. Likewise, availability of promotional avenues will raise the morale of the workers because they will work with renewed zeal and vigour, if they know that there are ample opportunities to rise.

(*iii*) *Work environment*: The building and its appearance, conditions of work and work place, machine and the location of the factory, safety measures, medical care etc. are some of the determinants of the work environment which are directly related to worker's morale.

SUGGESTIONS TO PROMOTE MORALE

1. Sound wage structure: Workers expect a just and fair wage corresponding to their qualifications and efficiency. This should for the workers and their families a reasonable level of subsistence including entertainment and medium of savings. A sound wage structure based upon sound and fair incentive plans coupled with bonus earnings is conducive to high morale wage structure which provides a systematic procedure for the fixing up of just and fair wage rates for different categories of employees, taking into consideration the job contents, is an ideal wage structure. It may help boosting up the morale and encourage greater productivity.

2. Security of job: The management should consistently follow a personnel policy ensuring the security of job to the competent employees so that they may devote their time fully with their heart and soul. A person under a constant fear of losing the job cannot work with devotion. His efficiency will be adversely affected and his morale will be low. Thus, security of job leads to high morale.

3. Delegation of authority: Delegation of authority to subordinates at different levels is desirable in order to boost the morale of the employees.

It is advantageous to employees as well as to the organisation. They feel a sense of importance and realise the responsibility. This improves the quality of work and efficiency of the workers on the job.

4. Grievance procedure: The management must establish a sound grievance procedure to ensure the employees of the impartiality and fairness of the various decisions taken by it about them. It creates confidence in leadership among the workers and promotes a sense of loyalty to the organisation. This confidence in leadership raises the morale of the workers.

5. Suggestion scheme: The management should invite suggestions from the workers for the improvement in the job contents, leadership behaviour and the general environment of the organisation. If any suggestion is considered advantageous to the organisation, it should be properly rewarded and recognised. This will improve the morale of the employees.

6. Joint consultation: To improve industrial relations and reduce the labour unrest, the management should establish joint consultation committees in the organisation consisting of the representatives of workers and the management in an agreed number to consider the matters affecting their participation in management and other matters incidental thereto.

7. Sound promotion policy: A sound promotion policy ensures the workers their promotion to the superior position without any hue and cry. It may be based on seniority or merit or both. The prospects, the advance to the higher position according to a consistent policy, heightens the morale of the workers.

8. Employees counselling: The executives in the organisation should sit together with the workers, discuss and exchange views on the burning problems of the organisation and the industry. They should listen to the grievances and complaints of the workers. Regular meetings may be arranged with the workers to invite or give suggestions on the problems generally faced by the employees at their work and guide them wherever required. Thus, will develop a sense of togetherness and increase morale.

9. Recognition: Every worker desires that his achievements in the organisation should be recognised by the superiors and he expects credit for his work. Even mere word from the boss may boost his morale.

10. Sound communication: The management should maintain a sound communication system with the employees so that any information concerning them may be passed on to them. Some progressive managements publish regular bulletins containing the latest news, views and developments about the working and the workers of the organisation and circulate them among the employees. It satisfies their ego and helps maintaining high morale.

11. Inspiring credos and mottos: These have positive effect in boosting the morale of the workers. Credos and mottos inspire the employees and give them a sense of importance. To give the workers a feeling of importance and credit for having taken part in the production of quality products some organisation organise exhibitions etc.

The above mentioned administrative steps pave the way to higher morale. It is a continuous but very slow process. The management should take various favourable measures to reduce the tension in order to develop the morale of the employees.

QUESTIONS FOR EXERCISE

1. What do you understand by morale? Discuss the measurement of morale. What steps can be taken to raise (or to build) the morale of employees?
2. Is 'morale' related to 'motivation'? What measures would you take as a manager-leader to build the morale of your men?
3. What is meant by employee morale? Why should managers be concerned with employee morale?
4. Distinguish between motivation and morale.
5. Write short note on 'Appraisal of Morale'.
6. Explain the relationship of Morale and Productivity. "A motivated employee with high morale is always more productive." Do you fully agree with this statement?
7. Discuss the various factors that contribute to high morale among workers of an industrial undertaking.
8. Make constructive suggestions for the promotion of morale in an industrial organisation.

13

Wage Administration and Policies

MEANING OF WAGES

1. *Benham*: "Wage means the amount paid to the labour for his services by the employer."

2. *Yoder and Heneman*: "Wages are the compensation of wage earners, the numerous employees who use the tools and equipments for their employers to produce goods and services that are sold by their employers."

3. *P.M. Stohank*: "Wages is that labour's remuneration which creates the utility."

Types of Wages

1. Money Wages: Money wages refer to the monetary form of wage payment. Normally the wages earned by employees are expressed in terms of money. Money wages, however, do not express real or intrinsic price of any work unless we know what the wages can buy. Thus, they do not express the real worth of job. They only express the amount in terms of currency. The real wages give the actual worth of the amount.

2. Real Wages: Real wages refer to the purchasing power of money wages. It represents the actual exchange value of wage rates. It reflects an adjustment to changes in the price level based on price indices.

3. Minimum Wages: The concept of minimum wage has developed due to different standards in different countries. In Indian reference minimum wages means the minimum amount which an employer thinks necessary for the sustenance of life and preservation of the efficiency of the worker. According to Fair Wage Committee, the minimum wages must also provide for some measure of education—medical requirements and amenities.

4. The Living Wages: According to the Committee on Fair Wages, the living wages represent the highest level of the wages and include all amenities which a citizen living in a modern civilized society is to expect when the economy of the country is sufficiently advanced and the employer is able to meet the expanding aspirations of his workers. Traditionally, the living wage is "a will-of-the wisp" which floats a little further ahead, an arm's length out of reach. It belongs to the same category as "squaring the circle". After considering various observations made by Indian and foreign authorities, the Committee observed that "the living wage should enable the male earner to provide for himself and his family not merely the basic essential of food, clothing and shelter but a measure of frugal comfort including education for the children, protection against ill-health, requirements of essential social needs, and a measure of insurance against the more important misfortunes including old age." It was felt that when such a wage is to be determined, the considerations of national income and capacity to pay of industry concerned has to be taken into account. The committee was of the opinion that although living wage standard should be made the ultimate goal, "it is generally recognized that the present level of our national income does not permit the payment of a living wage on standards prevalent in more advanced countries."

5. Fair Wages: In order to bring about improved relations between labour and management an effort has been made in modern times that the labour gets a fair deal at the hands of owners and managers of industries. Various proposals were undertaken at the Industries Conference in 1947 and a resolution known as the Industrial Truce Resolution was passed. It provided for the payment of fair wages to labour. The Government of India appointed a Fair Wages Committee in 1948 to determine the principles on which fair wages should be based and to suggest the lines on which those principles should be applied. According to the report of this Committee, Fair Wages is that wages which the labourer gets for his work just near to minimum wages and living wages. Generally, the current rate of wages being paid in the enterprise are known as fair wages.

COMPENSATION

Definition

According to Wendell French, compensation is a comprehensive term which includes wages, salaries, all other allowances and benefits. Wages are the remuneration paid for skilled, semi-skilled and unskilled operative workforce. Salary is the remuneration of those employees who provide mental labour to the employer such as jobber, supervisor, office staff, executives, etc. While salaries are paid on monthly basis, wages may be paid on daily basis or even hourly basis. However, the same problems are involved in the administration of wages and salary policies. The process of compensation is a complex network of sub-process directed towards remunerating people for the service rendered and motivating them to attain a desired level of performance. The intermediate components of this process are wage and salary payment, the awarding of other cost items such as allowance, leave facilities, housing, travel, leave travel concession, house travel concessions and also the provision of essential non-cost rewards such as recognition, privileges and symbols of status.

In brief, compensation may involve the following three payments:

(*i*) Primary compensation such as basic wages and salaries.

(*ii*) Incentive compensation such as premium or bonus.

(*iii*) Supplementary compensation such as D.A.; C.C.A.; H.R.A., L.T.C., G.T.C., annual bonus, etc.

Problems in Compensation Planning

1. Wide area: The area of compensation planning is very wide. It requires the study of wage theories, job evaluation, job pricing, individual pay determination, introduction of incentive plans, introduction and implementation, of supplementary compensation, evolution of sound system of wage/salaries recording and their timely payment, etc. Wages are the root cause of industrial disputes, hence, they should be dealt with seriously and timely. The personnel manager should develop ample time for employees' compensation planning.

2. Industrial Disputes: The question of wages assumes paramount importance in India due to acute poverty, large-scale unemployment and a rising population. Most of the industrial disputes relate to the question of wages in one form or the other. This underlines the need for a uniform and rational wage policy. However, no serious and determined effort has been made in this direction so far and the situation remains uncertain. There are fixed norms and indices in wage administration. In spite of the use of modern techniques like job evaluation and job pricing, there is no definite and exact means of determining the correct wage. Ad hocism and expediency are used liberally for wage fixation leading to many knotty industrial problems crying for a solution. Hence, the need and importance of sound salary and wage administration in Indian context.

THEORIES OF WAGES

1. Subsistence Theory: The English economist Ricardo (1772-1823) developed his subsistence theory of wages in the 18th and early 19th century. He took his inspiration from the population theory of Malthus, He maintained that the total amount available for wages is fixed and its distribution provides a subsistence wage to all the workers employed in the industry. If real wages rise above the subsistence level, there is increase in population to exert pressure on wages and force them to come down to the subsistence level.

2. Wage Fund Theory: The weaknesses of subsistence theory led to the emergence of the Wage Fund theory having an element of supply and demand. According to this theory, a fixed amount of wage fund is available for distribution at any one time and the level of wages depends on its equitable distribution according to the price of labour. If the wages of workers rise above the available amount of fund in any one industry other workers would be attracted to it and as the supply of workers grows, the wages come down. Thus, wages are maintained at a uniform level. Criticising wage fund theory, Prof. J. R. Higgs says in his book *Theory of Wages*, "The theory of the determination of wages in a free market is simply a special case of general theory of value. Wages are the price of labour; and thus, in absence of control, they are determined, like all prices by supply and demand." All the classical theories tend to emphasise conditions of a central equilibrium of wage rates which emerges when supply and demand are quoted. The term equilibrium is appropriate because if wages are fixed above this level and if they fall below this figure, similar forces drive them up to that level again. However, these theories proceed on an assumption that the available supply of labour and the number of potential employers is fixed for the time being. Thus, the term 'equilibrium' appears appropriate.

3. Marginal Productivity Theory: In pursuance of the approach based on equilibrium rates of wages another theory was formulated in the beginning of this century known as the marginal productivity theory. It takes into account demand, supply and competition as the main regulators of wages. It postulates that any industry would go on employing additional labour so long as it pays to employ them. The addition of labour must result in increase of production. Thus, additional employment will become counter-productive after a certain point.

4. Modern Theories of Wages: Modern theories are an improvement over the classical theories. Having taken note of the shortcomings of the previous classical and neo-classical theories of wages, a few modern theories postulate that wages are governed by the laws of demand and supply on the one hand and by the various external factors and constraints on the other. The traditional theories were essentially individualistic. They did not take note of workers' organisations and collective bargaining. Modern theories take note of the emergence of new factors such as the bargaining power of the parties involved in wage negotiations. Increase in wages can be secured by the workers irrespective of other limiting circumstances referred to earlier due to the influence and bargaining power of institutions like the modern trade unions. The pressure of trade unions makes it obligatory on the industry to introduce modern technology and improved methods of operation to earn higher margins and to cope with higher wage costs. The financial position of the industry and other factors also impinge on the rates and levels of wages.

GUIDELINES OF WAGE POLICY

1. Formulate carefully: The wage policy should be carefully formulated.

2. Communicate to managed staff: The wage policy must be communicated to the managerial staff and to the workers and their trade unions.

3. Decide according to requirement: Wage decisions should conform to the basic requirements of the wage policy. If any anomalies or mistakes come to the light corrective measures must be taken.

4. Evaluate periodically: The wage policy should be examined, evaluated and reviewed periodically so that it meets the changing needs of the organisation.

5. Base on job description, specification and analysis: Wherever possible, job evaluation should be done on the basis of job description, job specification and job analysis.

6. Encourage production: In the Indian environment it is necessary to reorient wage policy in order to encourage production and productivity, the micro level in each industrial unit. The role of personnel management in this regard is both educative and administrative.

ASPECTS OF EMPLOYEE COMPENSATION

1. Economic: The problem of wage determination is an economic, social, behavioural as well as psychological problem. The rates of wages determine how hard a person will work for the compensation received or what pressure he will exert to get his compensation increased. The economic compulsion is based on the physiological needs of the man. If a man is hard pressed, unemployed and suffering from hunger, he will be ready to work at lower rates of wages or less salary. If he is satisfying his physiological needs comfortably, he will bargain for better compensation.

2. Behavioural: From behavioural point of view the problem of wage determination is based on need-motivation and reward model.

3. Psychological: Psychologically, a person perceives the level of wages as a measure of success in life; *i.e.* higher wages/salaries, more satisfaction. Such people may feel secure, have a superiority complex, esteemed and high social status or may feel the reverse of all these. They may or may not take pride in their work, or in the wages they get. These things should be remembered by the management in establishing wage rates.

4. Sociological and Moral: Sociologically and ethnically people feel that, "equal work should carry equal pay" or "the wages should be commensurate with their efforts" and "they should not be exploited". They feel that no distinction should be made on the basis of caste, colour, sex or religion fixing the wage rates. The management should take into consideration the principle of equity, fairness and justice while fixing wage rates and devising wage and salary structure.

CHARACTERISTICS OF SOUND POLICY OF COMPENSATION

1. Adequate: Economically reasonable and adequate wages for a reasonable standard of living of the family of the worker.

2. Equality: There should be equally pay for equal work.

3. Recognition of differences: There should be proper recognition of individual differences in ability and contribution.

4. Clear procedure: There should be clearly established procedure, plan for fixing, revising and adjusting wage rates.

5. No discrimination: There should be no discrimination on the basis of caste, creed, colour and sex.

6. Removal of complaints: There should be a proper system for hearing and removing wage complaints.

7. Flexibility: The wage and salary structure should be flexible enough to cope with the changing economic and social environment.

8. Promptness: The payment of wages should be prompt, "Justice delayed is justice denied" should always be remembered.

TYPES OF WAGE VARIATIONS

1. Time variations: According to the economic conditions of the country wages may vary from time to time. In slump period, the wage rates may be cut whereas the inflationary pressures may hike wage rates. Price and wage indices are prepared for the two periods to measure the variations in prices and wages and adjust accordingly.

2. Regional variations: There are different wage rates in different regions for the same work in the same industry. For example, Cotton textile mills in U.P. pay lower wages to their workers in comparison to the wages paid in cotton textile mills in Maharashtra or Gujrat. This may be due to the several reasons such as economic development of the region, demand and supply of the workers, cost of living index and standard of living etc.

3. Industrial variations: Wage rates differ from industry to industry. An industry may pay more to its workers in the same region for similar work. Various factors influence the wage rates such as demand and supply of skilled labour, nature of work and working conditions in the industry, place of industry in the national economy etc.

FACTORS AFFECTING WAGE RATES

1. Demand and supply: The wage rates are fixed by the demand and supply position of the workers in the labour market. If labour is in short supply, the workers will offer their services only if they are paid well. If their supply is in plenty labour will be available at cheaper rates.

2. Bargaining power: To a considerable extent wages also depend on the relative bargaining power of the labour unions and the employers. If the labour unions are strong enough to force the employers, the wages are determined at a higher level in comparison to other units where unions are weak.

3. Cost of living: Progressive employers do not work with the blind forces of demand and supply. They take due notice of the cost of living for the workers at a place and try to fix the wages to ensure a decent living wage to the workers. Cost of living varies under inflationary and deflationary pressures. Labour unions come out with a demand of wage adjustment according to the cost of living index number.

4. Conditions of product market: The wage levels are influenced by the degree of competition prevailing in the market for the product of the industry. If it is a keen competitive market the wage level may be at par with the value of the net additions made by the workers to the total output. But if imperfect competition exists in the product market wages may not reach this level.

5. Comparative wages: Wage rates must be consistent with the wages paid by other firms in the same industry. The comparative wages will increase the job satisfaction among the workers.

6. Ability to pay: Wage rates are influenced by the ability of industry or a firm to pay its workers. Firms earning huge profits may naturally afford much better wage rates and more facilities to its workers in comparison to those firms which are earning only marginal profits.

7. Productivity of labour: Productivity is the main basis of wage determination. Higher wages are paid in firms, where productivity of labour is high, as compared to other firms where it is low.

8. Job requirements: If a job requires higher skill, greater responsibility and risk, the worker placed on that job will naturally get higher wages in comparison to other jobs which do not require the same degree of skill, responsibility or risk.

9. Government policy: As the bargaining power of the worker is not enough to ensure fair wages in all industries, the Government has to interfere in regulating wage rates to guarantee minimum wage rates in order to cover the essentials of a decent living.

10. Goodwill of the company: Employers who want to establish themselves as good employees in the society fix higher wages for their workers. It also attracts qualified employees.

Objectives of a Sound Wage and Salary Policy

An essential ingredient of wage and salary administration in an organisation a sound wage policy should be carefully developed to safeguard the interests of (*a*) management, (*b*) the employees, (*c*) the consumers, and (*d*) the community. Following objectives must be borne in mind while formulating the wage policy.

1. To Link with productivity: In some way or the other wage plan must be linked with the productivity of the workers otherwise it will not be fair for either the management or the workers or both.

2. To Link with job requirement and skill: A satisfactory wage plan should correlate the job classification and skill in terms of job requirements. Due consideration should be given to factors such as skill, length of time required in learning, versatility required and working conditions.

3. To lower cost of production: To cater the interest of the plan should usually result in the reduction of per unit of production. It makes possible lowered prices and higher profits so that a share of higher efficiency should be passed on to the society by way of lower price. Thus, a good wage and salary plan ensures the gains of higher productivity to the workers, management and consumers:

(*i*) Workers by way of higher wages and incentives;
(*ii*) Management by way of lower and higher profits; and
(*iii*) Consumers by way of better quality and lower price.

4. To provide incentive system: A satisfactory wage plan must include an incentive system of wage payment to the efficient workers to produce more and to increase the efficiency of the low efficiency of the low efficient work.

5. To provide proper wage differentials: The wage plan should have proper wage differentials based on proper 'Job Evaluation' so that wages earned by different categories of workers have a proper relation to the content and its worth. Moreover, difference in wage rates at different jobs must be justified.

6. To guarantee minimum wage: The wage plan must guarantee a minimum wage to protect the interest of the workers against conditions over which they have no control. It should take care of the minimum essential needs of the workers in a given environment to maintain his working efficiency.

7. To provide flexibility: Wage plan should be flexible enough to meet the changing conditions without involving much administrative cost.

8. To evolve good industrial relations: Wage is the centre of all disputes. It should be fair so that good industrial relations be maintained and improved. For this purpose, it is necessary that the employees and the union must be informed about the procedure used to establish the wage rates. Every employee should be informed of his position in the wage structure.

9. To provide rationale: The wages should be comparable to the wages being paid in other firms in the same locality and of the same industry. It will reduce the labour turnover.

10. To give sound selection and placement: A wage plan should attract able persons to the organisation. It should reduce the recruitment training and development cost. Introduction of performance appraisal studies as a regular feature will help the management in transfers, promotions etc.

11. To hedge against inflation: Inflation is today a regular feature of economy. A sound wage system must have a provision to prevent erosion of real wages by binding it with the cost of living index. Workers must be paid dearness allowance for the increased cost of living. It is necessary for the present though it is not a permanent solution of the eroded money value.

QUESTIONS FOR EXERCISE

1. What is the meaning of wages? Explain its different types.
2. Define compensation. What problems involved in compensation planning?

3. Explain the main theories of wages. Give guidelines.
4. What are the aspects of Employee Compensation? Describe the characteristics of a sound policy of compensation.
5. Describe types of wage variations. What factors affect wage rates? Explain objectives of a sound wage policy.
6. "One basic problem in personnel management is that of prescribing a satisfactory wage structure." Explain the above statement.

14

Systems of Wage Payment

SYSTEMS OF WAGE PAYMENT

Different systems of wage payment are prevalent in the different industries in various countries. The type of system used depends upon the needs and circumstances of different units, following are the important wage systems:

1. Time Rate System
2. Piece Rate System
3. Payment by Results.

TIME RATE SYSTEM

It is the oldest method of wage payment. In it a rate pre-determined for a particular time unit spent for the organisation, say, an hour, a day, a week or a month, etc. Wages are calculated on the basis of attendance. It is computed by multiplying the time units spent by the determined time.

As per formulae:

Wages = No. of days worked × Rate per day.

or

Wages = No. of hours worked × Rate per hour.

Advantages of Time Rate System

1. Suitable for quality work: For example, if in a particular organisation, a daily wage rate of ₹ 50 is determined, the wages of 30 days will be ₹ 1500, for 20 days ₹ 1000 and so on. The System is very suitable where quality of work is more important than the quantity when work cannot be measured in terms of merit systems.

This is done as follows:

(*i*) *Time Rate at high levels*: In the case of 'Time Rate At High Levels' the wages are paid at a rate higher than one which is in vogue in the same area or industry. This attracts better workers and decrease labour turnover.

(*ii*) *Graduate time rate*: The 'Graduate Time Rate' may be used when the prices are rising. In this case, the daily wage rates may be increased according to the ease of living index numbers.

2. Simple method: It is the most simple method. Wages may be easily calculated by workers as well as by the management. The workers are satisfied as the system is very simple to understand.

3. Useful for artistic jobs: As there is no hurry to the workers for completing the work, he handles work with his ability and cares for the job. Hence, this system as the system is very simple to understand.

4. Economy in costs: As labour and procedure are in no hurry for the work, it is done properly and accurately with care. There is no need of control, hence there is economy in administration costs.

5. Eliminates standardization: Time wage system eliminates the necessity for standardization.

6. Appropriate use of factors of production: As there is no rush of work and haste, machines, instruments and materials are properly handled and wastes are avoided.

7. Easy calculation: Workers may calculate their wages easily. Working for a certain period gives them the knowledge as to what they have earned as wages.

8. Safety of salary: The timely prescription of wages or salaries is safe. Sickness, accident or less work have no effect on the wages.

9. Sense of unity: Workers engaged in the same kind of work with equal wages have a feeling of unity which makes their union strong.

10. Security of health: As no hurry exists, the work is done slowly and ably and thus his health remains in good form.

11. Possibility of job efficiency: Workers perform the job with care and ably, hence, there is enough chance to show job efficiency.

Disadvantages of Time System

(*i*) Need of more inspection: Time wages make the labour costly. They do not care for time and consume time wastefully. Hence, they need more control and inspection.

(*ii*) Slack production: As the worker is no hurry to work, hence production slackens.

(iii) Uncertainty of labour cost: As work and wages are not directly related in production labour cost is uncertain. Hence, cost per unit is uncertain which affects the production cost.

(iv) Fatal to efficiency: Efforts and rewards are not correlated. This works as distinctive to efficient and skilled workers. They feel frustrated. It leaves a bad moral influence on them in the long run.

(v) Dissatisfaction among labourers: As both the inefficient and efficient persons get equal wages, hence, efficient workers loose their enthusiasm for work. They are dissatisfied because of less wages and they find other outlets for working.

(vi) Fall in morality: Workers lose in morality also. They prefer staying away from work and demand more wages. They work on the principle 'Do that much work to save the service'.

(vii) Uninteresting work: Many persons have no interest in the work. Due to standardization of work, they are not relieved from the services while this mars their chances to work elsewhere. To quote Franklin: "Under daily wages many workers work, who are neither interested nor have ability to do."

(viii) Employer's complaints: The employer is dissatisfied with the work of labour even if he may do much work. He always seeks more work from them.

(ix) Higher cost of production: As there is no check on the quantity of production by workers, more supervision is required. Thus, the additional cost of supervision increase the labour cost per unit. Moreover, workers try to make work last for a longer time, thus increasing the cost per unit.

PIECE RATE SYSTEM

Under this system, the wages are paid on the basis of output of workers without considering the time taken in performing the work. They are paid on the basis of quantity of work which is expressed in terms of units, such as per meter, per yard, per tonne, per piece and so on.

Wage = Number of units produced × Rate per unit

For example, if per unit rate is ₹ 10 p.u. if a worker produces 10 units he will get ₹ 100; if another worker produces 12 units, he will get ₹ 120.

Thus, per unit rate of wage is fixed with the help of time and motion studies. Sometimes, differential piece rates are also used.

Advantages of Piece Rate System

(1) More incentive: This system works as an incentive to workers to produce more. The efficiency of workers has a tendency to increase. Thus, it maximises output and minimises the per unit cost.

(2) Reward related to effort: The reward is related to effort and this can be regarded as more equitable than the time rate system.

(3) Known cost: As the cost per unit can be known exactly the quotations can be made confidently and accurately.

(4) Low cost: As compared to the time rate system, under this system the supervision costs are not high, because the the workers are to be paid on the basis of performance.

(5) Minimum cost: The loss of breakage is minimised because the workers handle the machines, tools and implements with great care. They know that breakage will reduce their output which means reduced wages.

(6) Minimum leisure: The quantum of leisure is minimised. Workers know that they will not be paid for leisure time. Thus, it persuades them not to waste their time.

(7) Trial of new techniques: The workers always try to discover new techniques for efficient production resulting in some production and more wages for them.

Disadvantages of Piece Rate System

1. Low quality: As more output means more wages, the workers are always in a hurry to produce more. They are encouraged to have quantity at the cost of quality. Low quality means a wastage of material and other resources on the same goods.

2. More breakage: The workers always attempt to maximise their output and in doing so they use the machines and tools recklessly and thus, the breakage cost may increase.

3. Insecurity: If the workers are not able to do the work because of machine breakdown or failure of electricity or any other reasons, they lose their wages. Thus, they always feel insecure.

4. Ill-health: The workers may be tempted to have quantity even at the cost of his health.

5. Inefficiency: The system will frustrate the less efficient worker. The efficiency may further decrease because of discontent.

6. Overproduction: If there is no good and ready market for production, the problem of overproduction may arise.

7. More disputes: Determination of the piece rate is a difficult task and generally disputes take place between the employer and the employees due to it.

WAGE PAYMENT BY RESULTS

In wage payment by results the basis of measurement of wages is the quantity of work done by the worker. The per unit rate of wages is predetermined. As wages are calculated on the basis of work done, it increases the efficiency of worker due to reward being directly related to the efforts and efficiency.

Types of Payment by Results

1. Straight piece rate: This is purely result based system. Worker's wages tend to more or less in the ratio of the quantity of work. The rates are prescribed for the work beforehand. For example, if a worker is a paid for a unit of work @ ₹ 4 if he makes 20 units, he will get ₹ 80 and if he turns out 10 units he will get ₹ 40. As there is no assurance to minimum wages the workers oppose this system.

2. Increasing piece rate: Under this method per unit increase as the production increases. It is assessed as undermentioned. For the first 10 units, wages will be ₹ 4 per unit, from 10 to 20 units wages go to ₹ 5, over 20 units wages go to ₹ 6 per units. This system is more encouraging to workers.

3. Decreasing piece rate: As the production grows, the rates of wages for increasing production goes down. As for the first 10 units the rates are ₹ 4 per unit, for 10-20 units production rate is ₹ 3 per unit. In the same way if more is produced, the rate may again go down. This system goes in favour of employers.

4. Straight piece rate system with minimum wages: Here minimum wages are assessed for the used time ratio. This will be provided when he will do less than the standardized work. If he works more than the standardized work he will be paid wages on the basis of straight piece rate. For example, if standardized time is hours and the standard work in 10 units and minimum wages in ₹ 4 per hour, *i.e.*, ₹ 32, but if he makes 10 units or more he will get wages according to work.

5. Balance and debt system of wages: Here after less work being performed, he is paid minimum wages so that he makes up the deficiency of work in future by doing more work. Whatever shortage is there, it is just like a credit to him which is adjusted with more wages earned by him in future by doing more work.

PREMIUM OR BONUS PLANS

Meaning of Premium or Bonus Plans

Any wage system which induces a worker to produce more is called 'Incentive Wage System'. Incentive wage plans adjust earning to output or production, thus providing a special financial incentive for increasing effort. The incentive wages are given in the form of 'premium' or 'bonus' calculated on the basis of efficiency of workers, time saved or any other variable. Thus, output-based system is a broad or general type of incentive plan. It has many ramifications suggested by different experts. These plans are meant both for the 'individual' as well as 'group of workers'.

Classification of Plans

1. **Individual Incentive Plans:**

   (A) *Different piece rate plans*:

   (*i*) Taylor's differential piece rate plan, (*ii*) Merrick multiple piece rate plan, (*iii*) Gantt task bonus plan.

   (B) *Premium bonus plans or bonus-sharing plans*:

   (*i*) Halsey premium plan, (*ii*) Halsey Weir plan, (*iii*) Rowan premium plan, (*iv*) Bedaux point premium plan, (*v*) Emerson's efficiency bonus plan, (*vi*) Barth's variable sharing plan, (*vii*) Accelerating premium plan, (*viii*) Diemer system.

2. **Group/Collective Bonus:**

   (*i*) Priestman Bonus Plan, (*ii*) Profit-sharing and labour co-partnership plan, (*iii*) Budgeted expense Bonus, (*iv*) Cost efficiency (Cost Premium plan), (*v*) Towne Gain Sharing Plan, (*vi*) Waste Reduction Bonus.

INDIVIDUAL INCENTIVE PLANS

A. Differential Piece Rate Plans: In these plans different piece rates are set for different amounts of output which may be recognised either by actual number or pieces or as percentages to tasks. There are the following three important plans of this type:

1. Taylor's Differential Piece Rate Plan: Originated by F.W. Taylor the father of scientific management, this plan has the following main features:

(*i*) There are only piece rates namely, high rate and a low (or ordinary) rate for each job or task.

(*ii*) For each job standard output (or tasks) and time is stipulated.

(*iii*) If the output of a worker during the time or task is less than the task, he gets his wages at the lower rate. If the output of a worker during the time is equal to or exceeds the task, he receives his wages at the higher rate.

(*iv*) There is no system of paying guaranteed wage to a worker. F.W. Taylor deliberately proposed that,

(*a*) the task point for a job should be sufficiently high so that only that worker who is really efficient can reach the point during the task time and, if he does so, he should earn at least 50% more than the worker whose output is 'below task';

(*b*) the lower rate ought to be so low that a worker whose output is below task would be able to earn just an ordinary day's pay. An illustration is given below to appreciate Taylor's plan.

Illustration

The following values are given:

(*a*) Task (standard output) = 20 units

(*b*) Actual output = 16 units

(*c*) Rates:

(*i*) High rate = ₹ 6 per unit

(*ii*) Low (ordinary) rate = ₹ 5 per unit

Give these values, the following calculations are necessary to make so as to understand this plan properly.

Calculation of Earning (E)

(*a*) In case actual output equals or exceeds standard output:

E = 20 units × ₹ 6.00

= ₹ 120.00

(*b*) In case actual output falls short of standard output:

E = 16 units × s.5

= ₹ 80.00

Thus, difference in earnings is equal to ₹ 120, ₹ 80 = ₹ 40 and difference in output 20 units –16 units = 4 units. There exists a wide gap between the two piece rates as well as the high task point. Taylor suggested this gap mainly for two:

(*i*) The saving effected by paying low piece rates can be utilised for the payment of high wages rates to efficient workers.

(*ii*) The high piece rates being considerable higher than the low rates, should urge every worker to put forth his minimum efforts and ability to his job to make the task.

Merits of the Plan

Taylor's plan is suitable under the following conditions:

(*i*) *No variation*: Where there is little or no variation in the nature of work and where the work is of respective nature.

(*ii*) *Standardisation*: Where production methods and machines have been standardized.

(*iii*) *No delay*: Where there is little or no possibility of the workers being hampered or delayed in their work.

(*iv*) *Accurate task time*: Where the task time can be accurately set according to the amount of work to be done.

(*v*) *More fixed expenses*: Where the fixed expenses are more than the variable expenses.

(*vi*) *Regulation*: Where production control and supervision are well regulated.

Demerits of the Plan

(*i*) *Attracts only best workers*: As the low rate is a sort of punishment to less efficient workers, it attracts only the best workers.

(*ii*) *Unrealistic*: Taylor has advocated the existence of the wide gap between the two piece rates as well as the high point in his incentive plan. The argument that the establishment of high piece rates should urge every worker to put forth his maximum efforts and ability is unrealistic and backed by the assumption that worker will always contribute maximum without impairing his health. It is not possible for any worker to work day after day at his maximum speed impairing his health.

(*iii*) *No minimum wages*: One of the important essentials of incentive wage plan is missing in Taylor's plan. It does not provide for a guaranteed minimum wages and is, therefore, vehemently opposed by workers who cannot produce with exceptional pace.

(*iv*) *Negative incentive*: The existence of low piece rate in Taylor plan does not act as effective incentive force, but provides a sort of negative incentive to workers. In general, workers consider the low rate below task as harsh and unacceptable.

(*v*) *No incentive to time rate employees*: This plan fails to attract workers who are accustomed to receiving time rate wages backed by a guaranteed wage.

Thus, the employers who introduced Taylor Plan without modification in their establishment had to alter it considerably. Subsequently two associates to Taylor, Mr. Dwight V. Merrick and Mr. H.L. Gantt, introduced the system of 'Basic Piece Rates' with a view to mitigating or removing the punitive nature of the low rate proposed by Taylor.

2. Merrick Multiple Piece Rate Plan: Mr. Dwight V. Merrick realised that it was unreasonable and unrealistic to classify all workers into two categories only, *viz.*, workers of high efficiency and those of low efficiency because there were various degrees of efficiency and there were many workers and apprentices who actually worked in their efforts to produce more and for their own progress and who deserved to be encouraged. Therefore, Merrick introduced three piece rates and made the lowest piece rate equally to the ordinary piece rate which became the 'Base Piece Rate'. The rates introduced by Merrick are usually as follows:

Output (% of task)	Piece Rate Wage
1. Less than 83%	Basic Piece Rate
2. From 84% to 100%	110% of Basic Piece Rate
3. Over 100%	120% of Basic Piece Rate

To the workers who are potentially high producers, Merrick plan is a good incentive system. It seems reasonable to pay production bonus at 11% of the basic piece rate to the workers when they reach 83% task with a little extra effort and when they do so they will be encouraged to reach the 100% task.

By introducing the basic rate for low output, Merrick has removed the punitive wage rate originated by Taylor. Thus, Merrick plan in only a modified form of Taylor plan. It is quite possible that in some industrial units Merrick plan is being followed under the name of Taylor plan.

3. Gantt Task Bonus Plan: It is a mixture of the time rate and piece rate and piece rate plans. Mr. Henry L. Gantt brought out his plan in 1901 when he was working with Mr. Taylor. He considered as one of the pioneers of scientific management. Though he followed Taylor plan to some extent, he modified it considerably and introduced a better plan of which one notable modification is the substitution of Taylor's punitive wage rate by a guaranteed basic wage. Under this plan, if a worker's output in a task time is equal to or more than the stipulated task he is paid a bonus at a certain percentage of this guaranteed basic wage which is always a time rate wage. The basic wage rate and the task or the task standards have to be determined with care. The tasks set should be reasonable and practical.

Higher the guaranteed wages the less is its incentive influence, because there are many workers who would prefer to remain satisfied with the guaranteed wage rather than work hard to produce more and earn more. On the other hand, only the more efficient workers will be benefited if the task is very high and it may not possible for the less efficient workers to reach the high task point.

Workers Wages

Under Gantt Task Bonus Plan a workers's wage basically consists of two parts, namely:

(*i*) *Basic Wage*: A guaranteed minimum wage (or guaranteed basic wage) on time rate which is usually an hourly rate. This time rate is the basic wage rate of the worker under this plan;

(*ii*) *Bonus*: A bonus which is paid to the workers when output is equal to or more than the task. This bonus is a percentage of the guaranteed wage.

Bonus Percentage under Gantt Plan

Gantt recommended that according to the nature of the work the bonus may vary from 10% to 100% of the guaranteed wages as shown below:

Nature of Work	Bonus (%)
1. Work not involving much physical labour combined with close and constant attention *e.g.*, the work machine attendants.	10% to 15%
2. Work in general machine shop or tool room.	35%
3. Work involving constant use of eyes.	30% to 40%
4. Heavy work including skill work.	60% to 70%
5. Work requiring his skill much physical labour or strain, ability to work under unpleasant conditions and involving acceptance of responsibility.	100%

Thus, every reduction in time means progressive increase in earnings. Hence, Gantt system is also known as 'Progressive Rate System'.

Merits of the Plan

(1) Incentive to efficient workers: Generally speaking, this plan may encourage efficient workers not only to reach the task point but even to go beyond the point. The guaranteed minimum wage ensures the workers of their minimum daily earnings.

(2) Increase in efficiency: This plan is likely to help workers to increase their efficiency. The plan has a strong incentive force. With the co-operation of the employer it is not difficult for the workers either to work under this system or to understand it.

(3) Overheads higher than wage cost: This plan may be found suitable for those industrial units where the Fixed overhead and other expenses for maintaining and running the factory and machines are higher than the total wage cost.

(4) Emphasise better condition of works: Apart from providing financial incentive in his plan Gantt has put much emphasis on (*a*) improving the efficiency of workers, (*b*) the training of workers, and (*c*) making all possible arrangements so that the workers can always execute their tasks without excessive exertion. This means that the workers should be well-trained. The employer should help them, and the working conditions and facilities should be well managed so that the workers are habitually inclined to perform their work efficiently and diligently.

Demerits of the Plan

Gantt Task Bonus Plan is not all an easy task. It is not practical. For example, an employer to make all the arrangements as perfect as recommended in the plan in order to train the workers or to control the production in such a manner that the workers should always be able to work without the least hindrance or set back is no joke and is virtually academic. However, this difficulty is inherent in all systems of payment by results.

B. Premium or Bonus Plan or Bonus Sharing Plans: In a straight time rate system of wage payment the employer takes all gains or suffers all losses resulting from the labour of an employee on any job while the wage or the wage rate or the employee is not affected. In a straight piece rate system the employee receives the full amount of his earning and the employer has no share in it.

Objectives of Premium Bonus Plans

(*i*) Unification of time rate and piece rate system.

(*ii*) Provision of suitable monetary incentives to employees and the employer, for the wage saved by the worker in completing his task.

VARIOUS BONUS SHARING PLANS

1. THE HALSEY PLAN

Halsey plan may be called a 'Constant Bonus Sharing Plan'. In it bonus is shared by the worker and the employer in some definite fixed proportion of sharing bonus. In this plan task time on the basis of past experience, time study or other suitable method and task point are set. It provides for the establishment of standardised conditions by preliminary investigations. It is based on careful time study. Task point means the amount of work a worker is expected to complete in or within the task time set. The 'guaranteed base rate' is assured for each worker. If the actual hours taken by a worker to complete his task are less than its stipulated standard hours, the total wage for the time saved, calculated on the basis of the guaranteed base rate of workers, is shared by the workers and the employer. The share of the 'wage' as shared by the worker is premium-bonus. In addition, the worker will get his usual guaranteed wage for the time he has spent on his work. Premium-bonus is given to foremen or supervisors who succeed in increasing the productivity of the workers under them. Usually 10 to 40% of the employer's share of bonus is distributed among such foremen or supervisors. Saved time may be utilized by the workers by working on the other jobs. The formulae is as follows:

$$\text{Time wage} = \text{Time taken} \times \text{Time rate} + \tfrac{1}{2}\,(\text{Time saved} \times \text{Time rate})$$

Merits of Halsey Plan

1. Positive incentive: Under Halsey plan every worker is guaranteed a minimum hourly wage which creates a sense of security and brings a positive incentive for the workers.

2. Benefits of saved time: The wages of time saved are divided equally between the employer and the worker. Since division of profits of saved time benefits both the parties, therefore, it makes for the permanence of the bonus rate.

3. Leisure for other jobs: Workers do not reject Halsey plan particularly on the question of earnings it fetches to the workers who save time and can utilise the time saved in doing other jobs and earn more.

4. Easy: This plan is easy to introduce as in this plan task time and task point are set on past experience or time study. This saves a lot of time required to introduce the system. The workers can easily follow the method of calculating bonus and compare it with the previous method.

Demerits of Halsey Plan

1. Inconsistency in standards: Inconsistency in the matter of setting standards for tasks and task time for jobs of different nature may cause disagreement over the question of some jobs or tasks, being easier or lighter than others.

2. Uneconomic: If the guaranteed wage rate is unreasonably high, the plan may not be economically workable. On the other hand, if the wage rate is low the incentive value may be low.

3. Complicated: As compared either to a straight time rate plan or to a straight piece rate plan, the work involved is more complicated in keeping a correct account of performance, time saved, wages and bonus earned, determination of standard hours worked, etc.

4. Require more supervision: Careful supervision is necessary to ensure that the workers in their eagerness to work fast, do not waste materials unduly or damage machines and tools carelessly. Since Workers are overinduced, they may take no care of the quality standards.

5. Little incentive: The plan does not provide full benefit to the worker. This may provide little incentive to work hard if the bonus is exclusively the result of worker's own efforts and ability.

6. No protection against bad-rate setting: It does not give the employer full protection against bad-rate setting.

2. HALSEY-WEIR PLAN

This is just another form of Halsey premium-bonus plan. It was introduced by Messrs. G. & J. Weir Ltd. of Glasgow in the year 1900. In it a worker receives 30% of the time saved *(i.e.,* standard hours-actual hours), while under Halsey plan the percentage varies from 25% to 75% and it is usually 50%. A minimum wage is guaranteed under Halsey-Weir bonus system as in Halsey system.

3. THE ROWAN PLAN

In 1898, Mr. James Rowan of the David Rowan and Company Ltd. of Glasgow brought out a premium bonus plan in which he kept in view the guideline of Halsey plan. In this plan also premium time rate is guaranteed to each worker. This plan exhibits features like amount of bonus earned by a worker which depends on the ratio of time saved/ task time. Like Halsey plan task and time (task time) are set on the basis of past experience and records making provision for time required in machine setting, collecting raw materials, etc. The total time spent on the job till the beginning of the next job is included in calculating actual time.

Unlike Halsey plan in Rowan plan the proportion of bonus a worker earns varies if time saved by the worker varies. The time saved by worker depends on his efficiency, which in turn depends on the nature of the task and circumstances prevailing the organisation. Hence, the proportion of the bonus to be paid to a worker is a variable quantity. Therefore Rowan plan is a 'Variable Bonus Sharing Plan'. The formula is as follows:

$$\text{Total Wages} = \text{Time Taken} \times \text{Time Rate} + \left(\frac{\text{Time Saved}}{\text{Std. Time}}\right) \times \text{Time Rate} \times \text{Time Taken}$$

Rowan plan may be understood by an illustration given below:

(*a*) Task time (std. Time) = 20 hours
Actual time taken = 10 hours
Hourly rate = ₹ 2

Calculation of Bonus or Premium

$$\text{Bonus} = \text{Time Saved} \times \left(\frac{\text{Actual time}}{\text{Task Time}} \times \frac{\text{Hourly}}{\text{Rate}}\right)$$

By substitution different values in the formulae, we get

Time saved = Standard hour = Actual hours

10 hours = hours (20 – 10).

$$\text{Bonus} = 10 \left(\frac{10}{20}\right) \times \text{Re. } 1.0$$

= ₹ 10; hence total wages = ₹ 10 + 10
= ₹ 20

Merits of Rown Plan

(1) Incentive to learners: It provides good incentive for comparatively slow workers and learners.

(2) Protection against loose rate setting: It protects the employer against loose rate setting.

3. Employer's benefit: It enables the employer to share in the benefit of increased output and encourages him to increase working facilities.

Demerits of Rown Plan

1. Complex and expensive: The system is more complex and expensive than the Halsey system.

2. Low incentive: Its incentive value is low at high production levels and thus sharing system is not popular.

3. Easy excuse: It provides easy excuse for loose rate-fixing.

4. BEDAUX POINT PREMIUM PLAN

Introduced by Mr. Charles E. Bedaux the main purpose of this system is to measure human effort through time study. Thus, it is not a wage of incentive wage plan.

According to Bedaux, all human effort may be measured in terms of common unit composed partly of actual work or operation and partly of compensation relaxation. Bedaux stresses that human labour and relaxation are closely associated. Thus, energy and time is the basis of Bedaux system. In determining the task time or operation time for a job it is necessary to take into account the actual time of operation and the time of rest. Depending on the nature of the work, Bedaux point for a work may contain 5% effort and 25% rest or other promotions. Bedaux called his unit 'Bedaux Unit of Human Power Measurement' called 'B' in short. B has been defined as "a fraction of a minute of effort plus a fraction of minute of compensation relaxation, always aggregating unit but a varying in proportion the nature of the strain."

The difficulty of a job is measured in terms of B's assigned to it and the task time (or standard time) for the job would mean a minute for each B.

For example if,

Standard time	=	10 hours
Actual time	=	8 hours
or Standard time	=	60 × 10 = 600 B's
Actual time	=	60 × 8 = 480
Saving in terms of B's	=	120 B's

Under Bedaux plan, the rate of pay is also reduced to the minutes basis. The profit of the saved time is divided between the worker and Supervisor (75% respectively) because worker shows good results due to co-operation.

Merits of Bedaux Plan

(1) Scientific production control: Bedaux plan can be useful as a basis for scientific production control particularly for estimating, planning and controlling machine capabilities and for determining standard production costs in industrial units where conditions are standardised and where facilities exist for measuring the task and output with a fair degree of accuracy, rough time and motion study.

(2) Effective in some plans: The Bedaux premium plan is mostly used in those units where the performance by individual machines or workers has to be constantly watched and kept under control by comparing the numbers of B's actually produced with the number of B's standard.

Demerits of Bedaux Plan

1. Costlier: Much clerical work is involved in maintaining records and in preparing wage accounts, etc. Thus, Bedaux plan is costlier than many other incentive wages.

2. Increment in a straight piece rate plan: Though the earnings of a worker increase as his efficiency rises, the rate of increment in the earning is in a straight piece rate plan.

3. Not easily intelligible: Some employees consider that this plan is not easily intelligible to many workers.

4. Modification necessary: Like all other incentive plans, the success of this plan depends on the reaction of the workers to the plan. Therefore, before adoption, this plan may need a certain amount of modifications.

5. EMERSON'S EFFICIENCY BONES PLAN

In 1919 Mr. Harrington Emerson of U.S.A. brought out his efficiency bonus plan. He tried to remove the deficiencies faced by workers in Taylor, Gantt, Merrick, Halsey and Rowan Plans. In all these plans, a worker has to reach or cross a constant barrier in the high task point before his wage rate is increased or before he can earn a premium or a bonus. Under Taylor and Gantt plans if the actual output of a worker is either equal to or more than the task his piece rate increases by 1.5 and 1.2 times respectively; moreover, the task point is high. If the worker fails to make the 100% task even by a very small margin his piece rate wage does not increase. Similarly, under Merrick plan a worker's piece rate wage does not increase so long as his actual output is less than 8% of the task. In Halsey and Rowan plans a worker does not get any premium or bonus unless he can save time sought to remove these difficulties. Thus, in Emerson's plan whenever the efficiency of a worker reaches 67% he gets a bonus. Bonus increases as the efficiency increases. When a worker's efficiency varies from 67% to 99% he receives bonus at different percentages of basic wages. When the efficiency is more than 100% the worker's bonus is 20% of the basic wage. When the efficiency is more than 100% for every 1% increase in efficiency there is a 1% increase in bonus. The efficiency of a worker is determined on the basis of his monthly or weekly output. This procedure compensates the decrease in worker's efficiency on some of the days.

Merits of Emerson Plan

(*i*) *Easily understood*: The plan is easily understood by workers.

(*ii*) *Reduction in cost*: Direct labour cost reduces rapidly when the worker's efficiency is between 67% and 100% though the reduction is not so rapid when the efficiency is above 100%.

(*iii*) *Reward to workers*: Under this plan whenever the efficiency of a worker reaches 67% he gets a bonus. In this sense this plan provides an encouraging reward to workers.

Demerits of Emerson Plan

(*i*) *Careful attention required*: Wage calculations need careful attention.

(*ii*) *Less output*: The lowest efficiency percentage which enables a worker to earn bonus being very low (67%), many workers other than those who are habitually diligent or ambitious, may tend to remain satisfied with the guaranteed wage, a small amount of bonus. This may result in less output than expected from workers.

6. BARTH VARIABLE SHARING PLAN

It is a premium bonus system which does not guarantee a time rate. It is specially suitable for learners or beginners until they become proficient enough to go on to some other scheme. The payment is proportionately less than output. Earning is computed by multiplying the rate per hour by the geometric mean of standard hours and the actual hours worked, as follows:

Earning = Rate per hour × St. Hrs. × Actual hrs. worked

This plan is not popular as it is difficult to explain it to workers. It provides only an incentive to beginners and not to efficient workers.

7. ACCELERATING PREMIUM PLAN

Under this plan, bonus increases at a faster rate as output increases. It provides a powerful incentive to the workers. There is no simple formula for such a plan. One scheme of bonus, may be as follows:

x (Efficiency level)	=	1.0	1.1	1.2	1.3	1.4	1.5
y (Premium)	=	1.1	1.25	1.50	1.60	1.80	2.0

Now multiplying the values of x and y by 100, one gets percentage wages earned against percentage efficiency. For example, at 120% efficiency level, a worker will get 150% bonus of his basic wages.

8. BAUM DIFFERENTIAL PLAN

This is a combination of Taylor scheme and the Halsey scheme. It contains steps at different stages in the output range which provide strong incentives at the points where they are made. It provides good incentives to different workers. But it is complicated as the multiplicity of steps makes the system difficult and impracticable. It also requires considerable clerical works.

9. DIEMER SYSTEM

This is a premium bonus system based on the Halsey and Gantt systems. Under this system guaranteed time wages are paid at high task level. A substantial bonus step of 20% at 100% production appears as a good incentive to workers.

GROUP BONUS PLANS

The output of individual workers cannot be measured in many cases while output of a group of workers can be conveniently measured. Group incentive plans are very useful under such circumstances.

Objectives of Group Bonus Plans

1. To ensure production: The main purpose of introducing group and collective bonus system is to ensure production and obtain better productivity.

2. To create co-operation: Group work creates a sense of mutual co-operation amongst workers. Due to interdependence of work, workers and supervisors keep a watch over the work of another thereby ensuring good and speedy work.

3. To produce incentive: Group and collective bonus system prove very much beneficial to workers to whom no incentive wage can be given individually.

4. To provide bonus: In the absence of interdependence there may be differences of opinion amongst the workers over the question of distribution of bonus. Fast worker may demand larger share of bonus than that of the slower workers. Sometimes, equal apportionment of group bonus is give after thorough discussion to workers concerned.

Types of Group and Collective Bonus Plans

1. Priestman's Production Bonus Plan: This scheme was adopted by Messrs Prietman Bros. Ltd. in 1917. It is a good example of group bonus plans. Under it a committee representing the management and the workers' union sets forth the standard of performance or task standard. This task standard is usually set in advance every week or every month. It is set per unit of output either numerically or qualitatively. Bonus is payable to the department which gives results higher than the standard output. It is calculated on the basis of the ratio of excess performance to standard task according to the following formula:

Percentage of Bonus = Increased Production/Standard Production

For example, if standard production in year is 2000 units and actual output comes to 3,000 units, the workers will be given bonus equivalent to 50% of their wages:

i.e., $$\left(\frac{1,000}{2,000}\right) \times 100$$

2. Profit Sharing Plan: Under it, the workers, in addition to their normal wages, get a share in the profits of the undertaking in a predetermined ratio. It expected that the workers will be more co-operative when they get a share in the profit of the company. The share of profit of the workers may be given in cash or in the form of shares in the company. These shares are called 'bonus shares'. This form of profit sharing is also called 'labour partnership', as it gives workers permanent interest in the future of their organisation.

3. Budgeted Expense Bonus: Under it bonus is based on the saving in actual total expenditure compared with the total budgeted expenditure. Its application is not limited to direct workers. It may be applied to indirect workers and staff as well. The percentage of bonus is predetermined share of saving in budgeted expenditure.

4. Cost Premium Plan: Under it a part of the saving is distributed among the workers as bonus if the actual cost of production comes less than its standard cost of production. The standard cost of production should be determined very carefully before introducing this plan. In U.S.A. the Scanlon Plant Steel Industry adopted such a plan. Here, a 'norm' is fixed as a percentage between labour cost and production achieved at selling prices. Bonus is paid to all workers if this percentage is reduced.

5. Towne Gain Sharing: In 1896, Mt. H.T. Towne in U.S.A. introduced this group bonus system. The bonus is calculated on the reduction in costs usually the labour cost as compared with a pre-determined standards. One-half of the savings is paid to individual workers *pro-rata* with the wages earned. The supervisory staff also receives a part of this bonus. Thus, cost reduction is encouraged through their co-operation.

6. Waste Reduction Plan: It provides incentive to workers in order to reduce material waste to a minimum. It is generally used in industries where cost of material is high. It takes the form of a percentage standard.

Merits of Group Bonus Plans

(1) Fosters cooperation: It fosters cooperation and a team spirit amongst workers.

(2) Require less supervision: Each group enforces its own standards of efficiency and the production of the whole group is checked. Consequently, there is less supervision and inception work.

(3) Requires less clerical work: The calculation of wages requires less clerical work.

(4) Increases production: It increases production and reduces wastage and spoilage.

(5) Safe: It guarantees time wages and hence, it is safe from the workers point in view.

Demerits of Group Bonus Schemes

1. No distinction in efficiency: It does not distinguish between efficient and inefficient workers in the group for the purpose of distribution bonus.

2. Insignificant bonus: The amount of bonus received by an industrial worker is sometimes insignificant so it does not motivate them.

3. Difficulty in amount and basis: There is difficulty not only in the amount of bonus but also its basis of distribution.

ADVANTAGES OF INCENTIVE WAGE PLANS

1. Benefits to Workers

(*i*) *Increase in the wage*: This system increase the total wages of worker as he gets the premium or bonus besides prescribed wages. Different schemes have different premium amounts.

(*ii*) *Improvement in work capacity*: Work is to be finished in prescribed time or before time to get premium. Hence, every worker works more. One who is unable to do his prescribed work, tries to reach the standard work level so that he may also get premium.

(*iii*) *Improvement in living standard*: This system increases the wage of the worker on one side, while on the other hand the producer has to pay less for more work proportionately. This reduces the cost per unit, workers get goods cheap and their living standard improves.

2. Benefits to Procedure

(*i*) *Increase in production at less cost*: Production increases rapidly as workers work more for earning more bonus premium. Production cost per unit falls as a worker gets a single prescribed of wages, not the full amount for more production.

(*ii*) *Minimum Supervision*: Workers work themselves for their increasing wages. Hence, supervision is more needed.

(*iii*) *Good labour relations*: Workers and the employers both have same interest such as saving in time, increase in production, etc. Hence, labour disputes are minimum.

(*iv*) *Improvement in organisation*: Wages according to work and extra motivation (Premium) improve the organisation and diminishes misuse of time and other factors.

(*v*) *Standardization*: All premium schemes are based on standardization. Hence, time and job standards are standardized by time and motion studies. A determined basis is settled and the work of labour is evaluated. Standardization also improves the method of production.

3. Other Advantages

(*i*) *Encouragement to co-operation*: Group premium plans promote mutual co-operation among workers and management. Both become interested in increasing the surplus of the enterprise which leads the enterprise to its maximum.

(*ii*) *Reaction in overheads*: Premium plan bring reduction in indirect overheads.

(*iii*) *Improvement in work*: These plans improve the quality and quantity of work.

(*iv*) *Better wage policy*: The wage policies become more sound and scientific.

PRINCIPLES OF INCENTIVE WAGE POLICY

1. Thoroughly worked and explained: As many employees are sceptical of incentive plans and also because the plans must be adapted to situation in which they are used, an incentive plan must be thoroughly worked out and explained to all those who will be affected by it.

2. Provision of higher earnings: Expected earnings must be higher than provided by hourly rates. Increased ranging from 15 to 25% are widely regarded as right. A small proportion of all employees—those who are especially apt in various operations—earn as much as 50 per cent more than this average. Arrangements providing for a declining rate are not generally acceptable, possibly at very high levels where a negative approach may protect the health of the employee.

3. Establishing bases of standards of output: Establishing bases of standards of output is a matter of concern in all incentive plans. Time studies for each job represents the most satisfactory means of setting fair standards. Base rates derived from experience under unstandarized conditions are seldom reliable.

4. Inter-relation of rates on various jobs: Rates on various jobs must be properly inter-related. Job evaluation is probably the most satisfactory means of establishing such relationships.

5. Periodic review of rates: Means must be provided for periodic review of rates so that they are appropriate to each other and fair in terms of possible earnings on other jobs.

6. Prompt adjustment in rates: Means must be provided to insure prompt adjustment in rates for changes in job content.

7. Time studies: Time studies may be conducted and rates established unilaterally by the employer or jointly with unions of employees. In either case, arrangements must be made for appealing such rates. Mistakes can be and are made, and their correction must be assured.

8. Review of rates: Although rates are reviewed periodically, no change should be made merely because employees are earning "too much". This does not mean that rates can never be reduced. Newly established rates may be on the liberal or "loose" side as well as on the "right" side. If they reflect improper standards, the standards should be revised. Further, if jobs change, standards and rates must be reviewed.

W.H. Spencer has listed the following 11 basic considerations in planning incentive wages:

1. Fit the plant and its operation.
2. Have the understanding and interest of top management.
3. Have the constant attention of competent supervisors.
4. Have standard fixed and guaranteed against changes, except when there are changes in methods, material or producer.
5. Have standards directly measuring the productivity.
6. Be understandable to and accepted by the workers.
7. Be as simple as possible and still be a direct measure of the productive effort of the workers.
8. Do not appreciably increase the unit labour cost.
9. Do not pay a premium for productivity below that which should exist.

10. Do not be a subterfuge to increase pay without a corresponding increase in productivity.
11. Do not be a scheme to avoid a justifiable base hourly increase.

GROUP BONUS

What is Group Bonus?

Incentives may be paid to individual worker if a proper system of determining his individual output can be designed. Alternatively, bonus may be paid to a gang or a group of workers. The latter system is better in the jobs where the contribution of one worker cannot be distinguished from that of another. Both the systems have their own advantages. The choice of the particular system would depend upon the circumstances of the case.

Schemes of Individual Incentives

There are many schemes of individual incentives *i.e.*, Halsey Plan, Rowan Plan, Taylor's Differential Piece Rate System, etc. The choice would depend upon the circumstances of the case. Where the work of individual workers can be measured against the standards set, it would be better to pay incentives on the basis of the relative efficiency of each worker. In such a case, the reward would be linked directly with the effort involved. The worker will have a feeling that his incentive depends primarily on his own performance. However, the scheme should be early defined and easily intelligible to the individual worker. The incentive payment should not be affected by matters which are beyond the control of the worker. The scheme has to be supplemented with a sound system of inspection so that the quality of the goods produced can be maintained. The rates should be set with reference to time and motion studies properly conducted. The standards thus set should have a measure of approval from the workers.

Groups Bonus Schemes

Group bonus scheme may be employed where individual output of workers cannot be measured and the same depends on the combined efforts of the group. This is particularly so in live production system where the output of a worker depends upon what is passed on to him by his predecessor.

Advantages of Group Bonus

1. Reward for joint efforts: Group bonus schemes reward a group of workers for their joint efforts. These are particularly useful in case where the output of individual cannot be measured separately. The performance of the group as a whole is measured and payments made accordingly. Some schemes also take into account the variation in the skills required in different jobs comprising the task.

2. Team spirit: It creates a sense of team since all the workers in a group realise that their personal interests are dependent upon the group effort.

3. Healthy competition: A spirit of healthy competition is created amongst various groups doing identical jobs resulting in the elimination of excessive waste of materials.

4. More production: The operators and the supervisors also feel interested in raising the production to higher levels.

5. Easier: The scheme is usually easier to understand and entails less costing and accounting work. It is easier to set up group activity targets, since the performance unit is large.

Disadvantages of Group Bonus

1. Disincentive to efficient workers: Some workers feel that their personal incentives are low because some members of the group are lazy or inefficient. Thus, the efficiency or inefficiency of individual members of the group is spread over the whole group.

2. Complications in manpower planning: The scheme makes it more difficult to absorb new workers in the existing group. This is because the existing group members try to avoid unskilled workers. Hence, manpower planning and distribution of workers into various gangs becomes more complicated.

ESSENTIALS OF SATISFACTORY WAGE SYSTEM

1. Simple: The wage system should be simple to understand as otherwise the workers look at it with suspicion. A complex wage system leads to strikes and agitations which may be hindrances in having harmonious employer-employee relationship.

2. Satisfaction: The wage system should be satisfactory from the point of view of both employees and employers. The rewards to the employee should be fair and must give low per unit cost to the employer. The system should have the approval of the trade union.

3. Incentive to work: The wage system should provide a sufficient incentive to workers to work hard and with great care. It should enable an efficient worker to earn more.

4. Guaranteed minimum wage: The system should guarantee a minimum wage to every worker.

5. Certain: The wage system should not have any element of ambiguity or uncertainty.

6. Quality output: The wage system should encourage the worker not only to increase quantum of output but also to improve the quality of output.

7. Flexible: The wage system must be adaptable to necessary changes.

8. Common: The wage system should be common in the same locality or industry.

9. Economical: The wage system should be economical in operation. It should increase the overall efficiency of workers.

10. Distinction between skilled and unskilled worker: The wage system should distinguish between skilled and unskilled workers. Skilled workers should be rewarded for the efforts made by them for acquiring skill.

11. Practical: The wage system adopted by an organisation should be practical. Some premium or bonus plans are theoretically quite attractive but they are not fit for practical use.

What is Wage Variations?

Wage variations means difference in wages at different places, times and in different concerns for different persons. Wage variations are found to exist in different employments, occupations and localities.

Types of Wage Variations

1. On the basis of period: At time wages differ due to economic circumstances. Deflation leads to the reduction in wage rates while inflation increases the wages and other allowances. Price and wage index is prepared on this basis for mutual comparison. Changes in income are measured and compensated.

2. On the basis of region: Wage rates differ at different places at different regions. For example, cloth mills at Maharastra and Gujarat pay more than the mills in U.P. This may be due to economic development of the region, labour demand and supply, expenses and living standards.

3. On the basis of industries: Wage rates differ according to industries. Iron and Steel industry pay more than the cloth mill. Again this is influenced by different elements like skilled workers, demand and supply position, nature and conditions of work place and industry in national development.

Factors Influencing Wage Variation

The factors which create wage differences may be the existence of non-competing group in the labour market, market imperfections and different labour qualities.

Wages also vary due to the personnel qualifications of labour: educational qualification, training and experience. Hence, there is difference of wages among workers from enterprise to enterprise and place to place.

1. Demand and supply of labour: Like other things the value of labour is assessed on its demand and supply. Wage rates will rise if the demand of labour is more than the supply. If demand is less than the supply the wages will fall down.

2. Industry's ability to pay: Industry's ability to pay also counts much the determination of wages. If the industry have more profit, it can pay more as compared to other industries.

3. Comparative wages: The local labour market and the wages of other industries is noted while assessing the wage rates. Wages in other units of the same nature should be noted. This develops labour satisfaction and checks labour migration.

4. Living standard: Living standard of a place determines the wages. Labour needs the maximum amounts that may satisfy needs of their dependents.

5. Job requirements: Jobs requiring more labour, efficiency, responsibilities and risk have rates of wages. Workers in mining get more than ordinary labour.

6. Productivity: Labour's production ability influences the wage rates. If a worker does more and better work in comparison to others, he will get more wages, while those producing less and below average good will get less wages.

7. Bargaining power: Where labour unions are effective and solid, it influences the wage rates. Rates of wages will be more in such enterprises as here collective bargaining is effective.

8. Government policy: Government tries to build the wage rates and rate policies. It fixes the minimum wage rates and declares the rules for bonus, dearness allowance etc.

9. Name of good employer: Some companies wish to have a name as a good employer in the society. Naturally, they give higher wages and attract better workers which increase production and profit.

10. Incentives: Industries providing many fringe benefits and more chances of promotion, keep wage rates at lower level. The wage rates are high where such benefits are lacking.

11. Personnel qualifications: Personnel qualifications like technical education, experience, though not responsible for assessment of wage rates do lead to higher wages.

QUESTIONS FOR EXERCISE

1. Explain and evaluate various systems of wage payment.
2. What do you understand by Time or Day Wage System? Account for the piece wage system. What are its advantages and disadvantages?
3. What do you understand by collective wage payment system?
4. Explain Price Rate Method *Vs.* Time Rate Method of wage payment.
5. What are the various methods of remunerating the industrial workers? Discuss them briefly.
6. What is the meaning of "Premium or Bonus plans of payment of wages?" Explain the essential features of such plans.
7. Describe Halsey Premium Plan and Taylor's Differential Piece Rate System, Emerson's Efficiency Plan and the Gantt Bonus Plan.
8. What are the advantages of Incentive Wage Plans? Describe the principles of Incentive Wage System.
9. Why should you have incentive plans super-imposed on a carefully constructed wage structure determined by job-evaluation?
10. In what ways do the workers and employers gain economically by Incentive Wage Plans? Explain with suitable illustrations.
11. What is Group Bonus? What are its advantages and disadvantages? Mention the essentials of satisfactory wage system.
12. Discuss the relative merits of paying bonus to an individual worker according to his efficiency and a similar payment to a 'gang' or 'group' of workers.
13. What is Wage Variation? Explain the factors influencing Wage Variations.
14. What are the principal considerations which affect the determination of and changes in a firm's general level of wages?

15

Non-Wage Incentives and Fringe Benefits

MEANING OF INCENTIVES

1. *George R. Terry*: "Incentive means that which incites or has a tendency to incite action."

2. *Dr. Earnest Ditcher*: "Incentive is a stimulus or a reason for producing action. Almost all of the human motivations can serve as incentive—anxiety, worries, fear, hope, prestige, money, security and so on—are all actual or potential incentives in our daily life."

Classification of Incentives

Incentives in an industry may be classified into two main groups: (1) Financial or monetary incentives, and (2) Non-financial or non-monetary incentives.

1. Financial incentives: These induce the workers to work hard by offering them the reward for extra work in terms of money. Financial incentive is more important than non-financial incentives. It is only by virtue of these incentives that the workers can satisfy their fundamental requirements of food, clothing and shelter according to his sweet will. Financial incentive include any form of wage, bonus, salary, premium prize or return on investment etc. It may be positive or negative. If a worker is induced to do a work against money-reward, it is a positive incentive such as production of efficiency bonus given to a work for higher production. Or he may be abstained from doing an act and offered cash incentive for not doing the act is negative incentive such as financial incentives may be given for reducing absenteeism or minimising wastage of time, labour, material and machines.

2. Non-financial incentives: These include all the influences, planned or unplanned, which stimulate exertion. In order to infuse enthusiasm in a worker for greater and better work, non-monetary incentives have a distinct and significant role. If industry provides more cash to the workers to create more interest in the work, it is possible that it may not add to his efficiency, he may misuse it in vices like gambling, drinking etc. If incentives are provided other than in cash form, it may stimulate him to work and may lead him to some productive results. Such incentives include: (*i*) job-security, (*ii*) recognition, (*iii*) participation in management, (*iv*) a sincere interest in the subordinate, (*v*) pride in the job, (*vi*) delegation of authority and responsibility, (*vii*) promotion, (*viii*) training facilities, (*ix*) labour welfare and social security measures, etc.

Both financial and non-financial incentives may be positive or negative. A person may be demoted or penalised in other way for being absent from his work off and on. It is negative incentive. If he is promoted for better and higher job, it is positive non-monetary incentive. Non-financial incentives may also be individual or group incentives.

(*i*) Positive incentives: These incentives attract people and when they obtain these incentives they feel satisfied. For example, increase in wages, promotion or bonus are positive incentives. These incentives motivate as individual to work in a particular way. If, for example, it is said that the worker who works an additional hour every day will get fifty rupees extra, then this statement is an incentive.

(*ii*) Negative incentive: Negative incentives are those which motivate an individual to abstain from doing something. If, for example, a monetary fine is imposed on causing breakages, then this fine is a negative incentive which inspires the individual to avoid breaking things. Sometimes some reform measures are instituted in industries. These reforms constitute negative incentives, and although they are beneficial they are opposed by many workers.

FINANCIAL Vs NON-FINANCIAL INCENTIVES

From the management point of view it is very important to decide whether the organisation should provide financial or non-financial incentives. It is not a prudent step on the part of the management to provide only the financial incentives. Non-financial incentives too stimulate the instinct of man to work hard. The management should provide both financial and non-financial types of incentives to improve the efficiency of the worker. Sometimes a worker seeks mental satisfaction to do better work. It satisfies his 'ego'. Thus, both financial and non-financial incentives are essential to engage him fruitfully to the work.

3. Substitute incentives: As is evident from the name this class includes those incentives which are artificial and are replacements of some natural or normal incentive. For example, a worker can be given a raise in pay in lieu of promotion so that he is saved from the frustration of not having been promoted. Evidently, then, the substitute incentive should satisfy the same need which would otherwise have been satisfied by the normal incentive. In the example cited above the worker feels satisfied with the thought that the actual promotion would have resulted in an increase in wages which he has got in spite of non-promotion. And, the worker who is satisfied with a raise in salary is deliberately coming to terms with the situation. He would have been really satisfied only with promotion. And if a worker can forego the authority accruing with it, he would be satisfied with an increase in salary. However, the substitute incentive cannot satisfy all individuals. And incentive that will satisfy an individual depends upon his individual traits and his condition. For example,

TABLE 15.1

Consumer Price Index Number for Industrial Workers

Year	Bombay	Ahmedabad	Calcutta	Madras	Kanpur	Delhi	All India	
							All Items	Food
Linking Factor	5.12	4.78	4.74	5.05	4.69	4.97	4.93	4.98
1970-71	182	176	182	170	190	199	186	201
1971-72	190	181	187	182	196	211	192	205
1972-73	203	198	197	203	212	222	207	223
1973-74	233	245	228	229	251	265	250	279
1974-75	289	305	288	301	323	337	317	358
1975-76	300	293	287	314	299	333	313	342
1976-77	298	281	297	288	294	332	301	317
1977-78	318	310	320	311	330	358	324	345
1978-79	325	323	331	318	337	368	331	347
1979-80	359	348	351	350	357	389	360	373
1980-81	400	376	382	388	396	426	401	419
1981-82	460	441	414	446	439	472	451	476
1982-83	502	487	447	475	473	508	486	508
1983-84	564	544	511	550	528	551	547	581
1984-85	609	570	576	576	554	597	582	607
1985-86	654	599	610	630	614	648	620	630
1986-87	717	657	671	681	672	707	674	700
1987-88	791	724	714	756	725	788	736	767
1988-89	856[1]	763[1]	783[1]	802[1]	763[1]	852[1]	786[1]	820[1]
	171[2]	163[2]	172[2]	167[2]	172[2]	177[2]	166[2]	172[2]
1989-90	179	171	178	172	178	182	173	177
1990-91	201	196	203	189	202	201	193	199
1991-92	234	225	223	216	228	225	219	230

1. Average based on six months indices only—April-September 1988 on 1960 base.
2. Average based on six months indices only—October 1988-March 1989 on 1982 base.

Note: Old Series (1960 = 100) has been replaced by the New Series (1982 = 100) from October 1988 Linking factors between 1960 series and 1982 series are operative from October 1988.

Source: **Labour Bureau, Shimla.**

TABLE 15.2
Consumer Price Index Number for Urban Non-Manual Employees
(Base 1960 = 100)

Year	Bombay	Calcutta	Madras	Delhi/ New Delhi	India All
1970-71	168	170	175	174	174
1971-72	172	174	188	180	180
1972-73	183	180	203	190	192
1973-74	204	204	231	217	221
1974-75	241	238	291	262	270
1975-76	246	243	306	273	277
1976-77	255	251	294	274	277
1977-78	269	265	311	288	296
1978-79	285	279	321	303	306
1979-80	315	297	350	321	330
1980-81	347	331	390	352	369
1981-82	393	367	439	395	413
1982-83	440	384	470	428	446
1983-84	493	418	531	468	492
1984-85	538	451	577	508	532
1985-86	568	481	611	551	568
1986-87	612	530	671	597	613
1987-88[1]	666	562	736	645	656
1988-89[2]	130	135	141	135	136
1989-90[2]	139	146	152	143	145
1990-91[2]	154	164	168	156	161
1991-92[2]	180	181	189	177	183
1992-93	204	198	212	196	202

1. Average is based on seven indices (April 1987-October 1987).
2. A new series of Index Numbers on Base 1984-85 = 100 has been introduced from November 1987. All-India Index on New Base may be converted to Old Base by multiplying the conversion factor 5.32. Conversion factors in respect of Bombay, Calcutta, Madras, Delhi/ New Delhi are 5.38, 4.51, 5.77 and 5.08 respectively.

a person who does not have a beautiful house will feel satisfied on getting a beautiful house and may even be prepared to give up some post for it, but one who already has such a house will never be willing to give up a post for another good house. Hence, when a substitute motive or incentive is given to person, it is necessary to keep in mind his individual traits and his needs.

CONFLICT IN INCENTIVES

Sometimes a conflict occurs between incentives. For example, if all the workers in a factory are told that the worker who lives in the quarters provided by the factory will lose ten rupees a month while the one who doesn't will get an additional ten rupees, then there will be a conflict between the incentives of the house and a ten-rupees raise in salary. In such a case the worker will take some time to make up his mind. Sometimes positive and negative incentives also come into conflicts with each other. There are certain kinds of work, for example, in which the salary is fairly high but the social prestige consequent upon it is not very great. Faced with such a choice the worker finds it difficult to decide whether he should accept the job with higher pay or the one with great social prestige. Most industries which take a toll of the worker's health pay more than other industries. The detrimental effect on health is a negative incentive since there is motivation to avoid this kind of work. On the other hand, the higher salary is a positive incentive because it inspires the worker to accept the job. The actual choice made by the workers depends upon his individual needs and his economic condition. Some people would not like to earn money at the expense of their health while others may have such a great need for money, due to their physical or social needs that they may be willing to endanger their health for the money involved.

Disadvantages of Negative Incentives

1. Frustration and hostile tendency: If a worker takes some punishment to be unjust or improper then he experiences frustration and hostile tendency. This fact assumes greater importance because punishment is often given only to those workers who in the first place are obstinate and non-cooperative. If such a man is punished there traits are further intensified.

2. Increase in deceit: When provision is made for punishment on the performance of some activity then the culprits try to avoid being caught rather than avoid doing it altogether. In this way punishment also leads to increase in deceit.

3. Negative suggestion: It is believed in psychology that negative suggestion should not be given where it is possible to give a positive suggestion. For example, it is better to say 'cross this road here' rather than to say 'do not cross this road here'. In the second case the pedestrian gets a negative suggestion which does not tell him what to do. The first signal contains a positive suggestion.

4. Destructive training: Apart from the suggestions, the training implicit in the incentive should be constructive. Punishment is intended to deter a worker from doing something, a destructive training, since it creates an obstruction in the satisfaction of some tendency. On the other hand, constructive training tries to find more legitimate and acceptable means for the expression of this destructive urge.

5. Negative attitude: Punishment leads to a negative attitude towards the work as well as towards the individual giving the punishment. Individuals who are punished in some factory develop a negative attitude not only towards their work but also against the entire organisation, including the management.

6. Creation of fear: The possibility of punishment also creates fear and fear is never a good factor in the working conditions. Hence, instead of creating fear in the worker's mind it is better to create a positive tendency. Now-a-days many experiments are being conducted in industrial conditions to introduce changes through the medium of positive incentives.

FORMS OF NON-FINANCIAL INCENTIVES

1. Making work pleasant: The reason why people enjoy playing but easily become bored with work is that playing is enjoyable, although that does not make it comfortable. Something being enjoyable means simply that it is an outlet for natural instincts. This is possible in the case of work also. Hence, work can be made enjoyable and pleasant if it is so designed that it allows the workers to express his natural instinct.

2. Use of praise: Often children are praised so that they may do some work. This love of praise or the use of praise as an incentive is successful not only in children but also in adults. Human beings in general are amenable to praise and want to do that work which will win them praise. If praise is given then they are inspired to do the work with even great application. A common mistake made by many employers is that they do not praise good work although they severely criticise all mistakes, a psychological unsound principle. Studies indicate that praise is a better incentive than criticism. Whether criticism is offered privately or in public, it invariably has some consequences. In the same way abuse or blunt language are harmful. Very positive results can be obtained on the other hand, by offering praise in public. Criticism had consequences because it injures the worker's self-respect. So do abuse and blunt language. Criticism in public is even more harmful than criticism in private because in the former case the worker also feels insulted and humiliated. Hence, offering criticism in public is the worst method of giving an incentive. Briefly, a worker will be inspired to work better if he is praised in public while the other workers will also be encouraged to work better to win similar acclaim.

3. Knowledge of results: Knowledge of results implies simply that the worker is aware of how much he has done and how much work remains to be done, or the consequences of what he has done. Both interest and motivation are influenced by a knowledge of results. No individual likes to play in the dark because then he cannot gauge the results of his play. The view of results has also been established by some experiments. The experiments of S.J. Macpherson, V. Dees and G.C. Groined have shown that approximately 25 per cent progress in work is seen with a knowledge of results. At the same time the interest in the work is maintained. D.B. Lindsey has demonstrated by his experiments that skill in work deteriorates when there is ignorance about mistakes and progress. In an experiment conducted by W.F. Book and L. Norvelle two groups of students were given mental tasks of reality and the use of speed. One group was asked to put in the maximum effort of which it was capable while the other group was kept informed of the results and asked to improve upon them. A total of 120 experiments were conducted on these two groups. Finally, it was discovered that the group which was kept informed or results showed of 16.5 per cent better work than the other group. G.F. Arps conducted an experiment in which the students were asked to raise a weight with one finger and to continue to do so until completely exhausted. This experiment was repealed 11 times with an interval of 48 hours between every two experiments. These students invariably achieved better performances when they were aware of results than when they were kept in the dark about their achievements. In this experiment self-competition was noticed because each individual wanted to improve upon the grades achieved by him in the earlier experiments. Knowledge of results not only helps to make improvements in the methods of working but also provides inspiration to work harder. The importance of knowing the results in learning has already been established. N.R.F. Maine has given an example to prove the effect of knowledge of results upon motivation. In one telephone industry the mechanics suggested that they should be sent out to attend to complaints about an instrument rectified by them in the first place. They suggested this because in that case they would be able to gauge how well they had done their work earlier. They argued that just as a doctor wants to find out how far his medicine has helped the patient, in the same way they also wanted to know how well they had worked, and that their plan should be adopted. No such plan had been adopted by the company before this suggestion. And once it was adopted it was seen that cases of repeated complaints fell from seventy per cent to only four per cent.

4. Competition of individuals and groups: Another non-financial means of providing incentive is to organise competitions between different individuals or different groups. Sometimes one particular individual may make an effort to improve his earlier performance, which should be an example of self-competition. Even if competition does not lead to any economic gain it has the advantage of giving self-satisfaction to the winner. Hence, there should be some advantage attached to the winning of a competition, the advantage, for example, of increased social prestige, winning praise from others, appearing to be ahead of others, etc. But while organising competition among workers attention must also be paid to the losers because they often suffer from frustration and they may at times also have to face humiliation. Therefore, a competition must be designed in a way that it should not result in loss of cooperation and lowering of morale. There is normally healthy competition in games because it is considered unsporting to raise the question of insult or humanisation on losing their competition. If the same spirit can be introduced into industrial contest then competitions can be put to good use. In order to increase the scope of the competition, it is sometimes divided into zones. Prize has a very great importance in competitions, and it should normally be clear and obvious. Promotion of sales is done by giving prizes to the best salesman and competitions are organised for the selection of good salesman. Competitions have also been organised sometimes to reduce the incidence of accidents. In such a competition the group involved in the least number of accidents is adjudged to be the best. Because of such a contest the members of group prevent each other from causing accidents while themselves taking care to avoid them. But if, as a result of such a competition, the groups try to conceal accidents or if a worker continues to work despite injuries, these are harmful effects of such contests.

Care in introducing competition: Industrial trade unions have objected to the use of the competition method as a means of giving incentives since, according to them, this is a means of exploitation used by the employers who follow the policy of divide and rule. Hence, in encouraging a spirit of competition it is necessary to see that the workers are willing to co-operate and that they also understand the objectives of such a measure. Competition is rarely introduced artificially because at times it naturally appears among the workers. It may be a competition in doing more and better work or in avoiding work. It also has a favourable impact upon the decision of the group. Factors like regular attendance, punctuality, the quantity and quality of work, safety, avoidance of waste and damage etc., are amenable to competition and the results can be measured. Yet care must be taken to prevent competition from becoming a burden because in that case it becomes more frustrating than pleasure giving.

More value of competitive pay: As a result of research it has been seen that competition between individuals is more effective than between groups because in the latter case ego satisfaction is less since the responsibility is shared. This fact has been established by the experiment of V.M. Sims. In one of his experiments some college students were given a test of reading. After taking the test 45 students were divided into three groups having equal ability. They were then tested again. One group was not asked to compete but in comparison to the first test it showed a progress of 8,7 per cent. This was the result of practice. The other two groups were divided into two equal parts and made to compete, and an improvement of 14.5 per cent was observed. Obviously per cent progress was the result of practice while 5.8 per cent was the result of competition. Members of the third group were motivated to individually produce better results than other competitors. This group showed a progress of 34.7 per cent of which 28 per cent was the result of competition alone. Hence, it is obvious that individual competition is more productive than group competition. But it is also possible that group competition may be able to achieve the same result as individual competition if team spirit can be raised to a very high level. Team spirit has the effect of putting social pressure so that each member feels more responsible.

5. Experience of progress achieved: In many kinds of games constant notice is taken of the progress achieved. For example, the progress in a football match is measured by the number of goals scored by a particular team. On the other hand progress in a card game is measured by the points scored by each individual player. In some other games progress is measured in more ways than one. In the sphere of industry also the worker is inspired to work better if he has knowledge of the progress he is making. In that case he works better but the difficulty lies in making an accurate measurement of the progress achieved. This job is done in different ways in different industries. It is measured by the quantity of production, the quality of production, or even by the satisfaction given to the customer. In all these ways the performance of the worker can be evaluated. As has been pointed out, each individual and each group wants to know how much work it has done. Actually progress itself is the prize of work since it indicates that the worker's skill is improving. Therefore, each worker wants to feel that he is progressing but as skill continues to increase it becomes more difficult to see this progress clearly. For example, even if safety is increased to extreme limits accidents can be prevented only upto a certain extent just as the quantity and quality of production can be improved within limits. Describing some experiments on the experience of progress Viteles has pointed out that motivation improves with a knowledge of results and experience of progress and for this reason the worker should be told of his progress from time to time. One good way of doing this is to interview him. During this the weekly or terminal report of the worker's performance can be discussed. Sometimes the worker's progress can be determined by fixing a limit to the work to be done during a day because if he feels that he has completed the day's work he realizes that he is progressing towards his objective.

6. Social motives: In addition to the above mentioned kinds of non-financial incentives there are certain motives which act as incentives. Factors which increase social facilitation are among the main social motives. Social facilitation implies an increase in a feeling of co-operation and group formation. Team spirit is of particular importance in this connection. In an industry the worker should have the feeling that as a member of group he is performing some task of vital importance. Group decisions also play a vital role. Motives which prove an obstacle in progress should be continuously eliminated, examples of which are mutual hatred and jealously, conflict, unhealthy competition. In order to give motivation to goal should be clear and conspicuous. Once the goal is established efforts should be made to create a group decision in favour of it. Once the group decision is favourable the task becomes easier because no individual wants to lag behind the group and become a laughing stock, while some individuals want the work more than the others in order to reach a position of command and leadership. The workers should also have the freedom to discuss various aspects of their job because this increases a sense of participation and responsibility, thus leading to more self-satisfaction. For this purpose various committees or groups should be created which can discuss ways and means of increasing production and of finding new ways of doing the tasks more efficiently.

7. Increasing interest in the work: Increase in interest leads to an increase in motivation. Hence, efforts should be made to increase the worker's interest in his job. Human beings naturally take an interest in games because they are chosen by the individual himself and because they provide him with a means of expressing his natural instincts. If the job is also chosen by the worker himself and it gives him the opportunity of manifesting his natural talents, he will take interest in the job. But sometimes he is compelled to take up a job not preferred by him because of the possibilities of choice, the salaries available in different jobs, his educational ability, etc. Consequently, he finds it difficult to take interest in his job.

In order to create interest the worker should be made aware of the importance and value of his works because if he feels that he is doing something worthwhile and making useful contribution to the entire effort, then he will take interest in what he is doing. As F.R. Wickert has demonstrated, a worker's motivation for some work diminishes very rapidly if he does not know why he is doing something or if he does not know the value of his work in relation to the entire work. Hence, it is better to explain to the worker the various kinds of work done in the organisation and the part he himself is playing in its success Motion pictures and meeting can help in doing this. This increases the worker's self-respect. In moments of emergency the level of motivation improves even more because then the worker is actually aware of his contribution in tiding over a difficult time. It has been seen that in times of emergency in country the workers are more motivated to work.

Another way of improving interest is to reduce the monotony involved in the work. For this all those psychological measures can be adopted which are suggested for removing monotony which itself is the result of low motivation. Therefore, if it is removed, motivation improves. Variety of work and a sense of having completed some task tend to reduce monotony.

8. Consideration of the demands of industrial unions: Now-a-days it is impossible to do anything by neglecting the industrial unions. These unions take up the task of propagating and ventilating the demands and grievances of the workers. Effort should be made to increase motivation by keeping these demands in view. It is true that at times these demands are contrary to the well being of the organisation because these unions promote class consciousness when they are influenced by political parties. But the industrial unions are the actual representatives of the workers' dissatisfaction and their demands should not be neglected. If these demands can be satisfied the level of motivation improves automatically.

FRINGE BENEFITS

An employer provides several benefits and service to the employees, working in the organisation to maintain and promote the employee's favourable attitude towards the work and work environment, because maintenance of favourable attitude is an essential part of motivation and high morale. Such benefits and services include all expenditure designed to benefit employees over and above regular wages and direct monetary incentives related to output. These are generally referred to as 'fringe benefits'. The real wages of worker are increased by the benefits provided by the employer and thus they are regarded as supplement to their wages. So, fringe benefits are also labelled as 'Wage supplement.' These may include, leave with pay, pension, gratuity, medical benefits etc. Fringe benefits may be given to individuals, or to groups; they may be long-term benefits or short-term benefits, may be financial or non-financial etc.

Kinds of Fringe Benefits

1. *C.R. Terry*: He has enumerated as many as 28 benefits under fringes such as bonus for quality and attendance, contribution to group insurance plans, lay-off and termination, pay, travel expenses, suggestion awards, medical leave with pay, overtime, university and trade courses etc.

2. *The Chamber of Commerce, U.S.A.* It recommends following fringe benefits:

(*i*) Statutory payments such as old age pension, unemployment insurance, group insurance etc.;

(*ii*) Payments for pension and labour welfare;

(*iii*) Rest or leave with pay;

(*iv*) Payment for time not worked; and

(*v*) Other benefits such as profit sharing, suggestion reward, reimbursement of tuition fee, festival allowance etc.

Administration of Fringe Benefits

1. The expenditure on 'fringe benefits' should be linked to the production and productivity and returns on investment.
2. The administration of fringe benefits should be the function of an independent body in the organisation.

QUESTIONS FOR EXERCISE

1. What is the meaning of Incentives? Classify Incentives.
2. Explain Conflict Incentives and discuss the disadvantages of negative incentives.
3. Discuss the forms of Non-financial Incentives and explain their importance.
4. What is the meaning of Fringe Benefits? What are their kinds? How are they administered?

16

Specialization

Definition of Specialization

(1) *Encyclopaedia of Social Sciences*: "Specialization is a technical term for all those phenomenon, technology, social and biological as well as economic—which are usually subsumed under the phrase division of labour."

(2) *Kimbal*: Specialization is concentration of attention and effort in a limited field. Thus, in the opinion of Kimbal specialization has two characteristics: concentration and centralisation of effort and that, too, in a limited field.

(3) *Iarsolav Tuma*: Specialization consists of concentration of intellectual attention and physical efforts on specific problems.

Characteristics of Specialization

(1) Specialization is based on modern industrial technology.
(2) Specialization encourages industrial and scientific progress.
(3) Specialization is based on division of labour.
(4) Specialization is based on specialized know-how.
(5) Specialization also takes into account the results of practical experience.
(6) Specialization encourages self-reliance.
(7) Specialization aims at the maximum use of available resources.

Forms of Specialization

(1) Labour specialization: It aims at training the workers for specific jobs.

(2) Specialization of occupations: These days there is specialization of jobs everywhere. For example, in old days doctors used to treat all kinds of diseases. But these days we have opthalomologists, dentists, ENT specialists, chest and heart specialists etc.

(3) Industrial specialization: With the industrial progress, modern industrial units instead of making the whole machines make some parts only. For example, car manufacturers do not make their own tyres and tubes.

(4) Geographical specialization: These days various industries are set up in different regions depending upon the availability of natural resources. Dispersion of industry according to regional availability of resources is called geographical specialization.

(5) Technical specialization: The industry requires technical specialization. For example, in footwear industry there are 200 technical processes.

Advantages of Specialization

(1) Standardization: The first and foremost advantage of specialization is standardization. According to Kimbal and Kimbal, "By standardization is meant the reduction of any one time to fixed types, sizes and characteristics."

(2) Advantage in production: Considering the aspect of production, specialization is highly beneficial. It leads to increase in production because by specializing in a limited field of work, a worker becomes skilled and well-versed in his job. According to Adam Smith, a person who all by himself could not manufacture more than 10 awlpins could make 4800 awlpins by specializing. The specialization reduces the cost of production. Thirdly, socialization also improves the quality of product. Fourthly, specialization helps in maximizing the use of machinery.

(3) Mechanization: The specialization leads to mechanization and due to mechanization large scale production with small labour force has become possible.

(4) Increase in efficiency: The specialization increases efficiency. This is because a highly skilled person alone can perform the specialized tasks.

(5) Facility in training: Specialization facilitates training because a person has to be trained in a limited sphere.

(6) Interdependence: Due to specialization no man can work in isolation. As a worker operates in a very limited sphere he needs the aid of others in many matters. In modern world banks and industries depend upon each other. In making a cinema so many industrials like financier, director, writer, singers and actors work together. Indeed it takes hundreds of specialized hands to make a cinema.

(7) Encouragement to research: By operating in small spheres men get new ideas and devote their energy to research.

(8) Increase in employment: The specialization led to large scale production and this requires many distributors, salesmen, overseers etc. to take care of increase in production. This means more employment.

(9) Increase in trade: Specialization has led to increase in trade, because standardization of products which has resulted on account of specialization, has created goodwill for the industrial products. Besides, due to banking and transport facilities trade has flourished. Today various agencies are ready to lead a helping hand in business activity—Banks, Insurance, Transporters, to mention a few.

(10) Increase in individual responsibility: Specialization makes men responsible. As each worker is a specialist in his job he is confident of doing it well. This enhances in him his sense of responsibility.

(11) Development of trade union: When there are a number of persons doing same kind of job a sense of fellowship develops in them. This leads to the formation of trade union. And since there is great multiplicity of specialized jobs, the number of trade union also multiplies.

Disadvantages of Specialization

No change in society is wholly beneficial. Along with advantages of a change there are certain disadvantages, too, though it is possible that the advantages may outweigh the disadvantages. The increase in specialization has led to a number of disadvantages. These are:

(1) Disadvantage in production: The greatest advantage of specialization is in the field of production. It has led to a manifold increase in production. Excessive specialization leads to division of work into numerous processes. And strike even in a single unit leads to total disruption of work.

(2) Fall of cottage industries: Due to large scale production as a result of specialisation, the cottage industries have suffered. As the cost of production is far more in cottage industry, they cannot withstand the competition of big industry.

(3) Social disadvantages: Specialization has led to social disintegration. For example, industrialization has led to exploitation of women and children. The industrial strife has increased; and slums have appeared. The industrialization has led to an exodus of population from the villages to the cities and the cities have become overcrowded. This has led to social, moral and ecological pollution. The class struggle has also become intense.

(4) Psychological disadvantages: The greatest drawback of specialization is psychological. As a result of specialization the self-confidence and self-reliance of man is rudely shaken. There is so much of specialization in modern life that even in so personal affair as marriage, there is an increasing tendency to seek counsel from the marriage counsellor. Man has lost his ability to decide his affairs by himself because there exist experts on every minutia. All this has weakened the will of man to decide the issues of life by himself; he heavily leans on others. Besides, specialization stunts mental growth. The experts become so charmed by their specialties that they think nothing of matters outside their limited field. This leads to the paradox of knowing more and more about less and less. The specialization also creates ennui and boredom.

(5) Waste of money: As a result of specialization a number of highly sophisticated machines have been invented. There is need to train men in operating these machines. This involves waste of money.

(6) Increase in exploitation: The biggest disadvantage of industrial society is the miserable condition of workers. The capitalists set up industry with a profit motive; therefore he exploits the workers to the maximum. The mechanization, rationalization and automation render thousands of workers jobless overnight. The operation of certain machines is highly dangerous. In short, the poor worker is the sufferer all the way.

Limitations of Specialization

If specialization is allowed to operate within certain limits it can be helpful. These limits are:

(1) Extension of market: The specialization should be limited to extension of market, that is, it should work within the limit of the demand of goods in the market.

(2) Progress of trade and industry: The specialization is limited by the progress of trade and industry. As much trade and industry progresses the specialization is needed.

(3) Demand of commodity: Specialization can be made in production of commodity provided there is relatively permanent demand for it on a large scale.

(4) Scientific and technical progress: Obviously, specialization can be made only if the scientific and technical know-how for it is available.

(5) Amount of capital: The amount of capital available also determines the specialization. Where large amount of capital is available much specialization is possible. Where funds are lacking there can be little specialization.

(6) Availability and co-operation of labour: The specialization is possible only if skilled labour is available and it is willing to undergo training in new techniques.

(7) Efficient organization: The specialization is beneficial only in an industry, where the management is efficient and well-organized.

Method to Profit by Specialization

In order to obtain full profit from specialization certain things must be kept in mind. Firstly, the field of work and responsibility of each worker should be fixed. The sub-division of work should be in self-sufficient units and as far as possible should be entrusted to an individual or group of individuals. The work entrusted to each individual should be according to his likings. Thirdly, the managers should make effective co-ordination between various units. Fourthly, specialization can be useful in large scale industries. Fifthly, for specialization to be beneficial an industiy should have highly skilled workers. Lastly, an attempt should be made to minimize, if not completely eliminate, the evils of specialization referred to earlier. For example, music can be useful in avoiding ennui among workers. The feeling of isolation can be avoided by encouraging *espirit de corps.*

QUESTIONS FOR EXERCISE

1. Define specialisation. Describe its characteristics and forms.
2. Discuss the advantages and disadvantages of specialisation.

17

Rationalization

Meaning of Rationalization

Literally the meaning of rationalization is making things reasonable, that is, to put things in their proper forms. Putting in proper form implies making distinction between proper and improper. And since what is proper in industry is what produces benefit and profit and what is harmful and loss is improper. Therefore, in industry rationalization means maximizing the profit and minimizing drudgery. For this purpose microscopic scientific analysis of industrial processes is made with a view to simplifying them.

(1) International Labour Organization: (*a*) Rationalization, in general, is any reform tending to replace, habitual, antiquated practices by means or methods based on systematic reasoning.

(*b*) Rationalization, in the narrowest sense, is any reform of an undertaking, administration or other service, public or private, tending to replace habitual antiquated practices by means or methods based on systematic reasoning.

(*c*) Rationalization, in the wider sense, is any reform of an undertaking and tends to reduce waste and loss due to unbridled competition by concerted action based on systematic reasoning.

(*d*) Rationalization, in the widest sense, is a reform tending to use means and methods based on systematic reasoning to the collective activities of the large economic and social groups.

The definitions given above clearly highlight the fact that the most important element in rationalization is systematic thinking. And systematic thinking means that one should be prepared to deviate and depart from the habitual and traditional modes of thinking.

(2) H.C. Wells: No new term connected with modern industry and economic systems is subject to so many conflicting, inconsistent and doubtful views and interpretations. But as we have noted above the main feature of rationalization is systematic thinking.

(3) I.L. Urwict: "Rationalization is both an attitude and a process. As an attitude it records the belief that a more rational control of world of economic life through the application of scientific methods is possible and desirable. As a process it implies the application of the methods of science to all problems arising in the organisation and conduct of production, distribution and consumption."

(4) V.V. Giri: "The essence of rationalization is revolutionary change of methods which scrap obsolete and unsystematic routine methods, replacing them by principles and methods of scientific nature."

Characteristics of Rationalization

(1) Comprehensive method: The rationalization is a total process and a comprehensive method which applies to the entirety of the processes in an industry. In other words, the whole of an industrial unit is rationalized, there can be no patch work.

(2) Scientific nature: Rationalization is scientific. As it has been described earlier all the elements of rationalization process are based on scientific and systematic thinking.

(3) A process: Rationalization is a process which is not confined to the economic field but extends to other fields of activity. If rationalization is applied to industry it is bound to affect other aspects of society also.

(4) Mechanization: The application of science to industry has led to the invention of new industrial machinery. This mechanization is an essential part of rationalization.

(5) Standardization: A characteristic of rationalization is standardization. By application of scientific knowledge new sophisticated machines are developed which produce goods of a uniform standard and eliminate variety.

(6) Based on collective effort: As science is the result of cooperation among many persons, the rationalization which is based on science is also a result of collective effort.

(7) Based on logic: As it is clear from the definitions of rationalization given above, rationalization involves logical thinking. All aspects of industries are structured and understood logically.

(8) Dynamic system: The system into which rationalization rings together the various processes of industry is not static but dynamic in character.

(9) Specialization: Rationalization leads to specialization because it is only through specialization that wasteful effort can be avoided and economy of production achieved.

(10) Saving and economy: Rationalization does away with inefficiency, waste and useless expenditure. Therefore, it leads to saving and economy in industry.

(11) Simplicity: It is a scientific principle that a simple technique is to be preferred to a complex one. Rationalization being based on the scientific thinking, leads to simplicity in all the industrial, economic and administrative processes.

Aims of Rationalization

(1) Check on waste: The first and foremost aim of rationalization is avoidance of waste. As Sargent Florence says, "Rationalization is a movement to eliminate waste and insufficiency scientifically and logically, some sort of just action between all the firms within one industry."

(2) Raising the standard of living: It is the aim of rationalization to raise the standard of living of the whole society. This can be done only by producing in sufficient quantity goods of good quality and make them available at cheap rates.

(3) Use of available means: It is only by rationalization that the maximum use of the means available in a country can be made.

(4) Stability in industry: The instability in industry is dangerous. The main reason for this instability is lack of co-ordination and balance. By introducing coordination and restoring balance the rationalization helps to maintain the stability in industry.

(5) Social aim: Lastly, the aims of rationalization are not merely economic. It also has a social aim. From social point of view rationalization minimizes efforts while at the same time maximizes production. This raises the living standard of labour class and provide them with leisure.

Aspects of Rationalization

(1) Technical aspect: The technical aspect of rationalization is most important, because, as a matter of fact, the aim of rationalization is nothing but improvement of techniques. This is at times referred to as social engineering.

(2) Organizational aspect: By introducing scientific technique and thinking rationalization cements and improves organization in the industry.

(3) Financial aspects: By cutting an undue expenditure and yielding maximum at minimum cost, rationalization strengthens the financial aspect of industry.

(4) Social or human aspect: In the words of C.S. Myers, rationalization stipulates that the industrial and economic should cease to be purely selfish and narrow but bring itself in harmony with social needs.

Advantages of Rationalization

Rationalization yields comprehensive benefits to all sections of industry and society at large. These can be analyzed as follows:

(A) Advantage to Producers

The application of new scientific technique helps most the producers. It helps them in the following respects:

(1) *Increase in productivity*: With the introduction of better techniques of production it is obvious that the production will go up.

(2) *Economy in production*: Rationalization not only increases production but it also lowers the cost of production. This means economy.

(3) *Proper use of capital*: By producing more at less expense rationalization helps in the proper use of capital.

(4) *Co-operation between labourer and capitalists*: As rationalization makes the processes of industry simpler and less hazardous the labour feels a sense of satisfaction and feels well-disposed towards capitalists.

(5) *Industrial stability*: The above-mentioned benefits of rationalization make for industrial stability. It also helps to create a balance between demand and supply and this in turn helps to maintain the industrial peace.

(6) *Advantages of standardization*: An advantage of rationalization is the uniformity of quality of the goods produced. The standardization makes large scale production of goods at competitive cost possible. The problem of selection and elimination of goods is done away with and this saves money and effort.

(7) *Decrease in competition*: Rationalization leads to specialization and specialization produces interdependence among producers. This helps to minimize, if not eliminate, competition and increases mutual give and take. Thus, a spirit of co-operation comes to supervene in place of competition.

(8) *Advantage of scientific management*: As a consequence of rationalization the management becomes scientific. In scientific management the relations between labour and capitalist is marked by rule and laws and

the arbitrariness of either party is ruled out. This improved atmosphere in industry is generally beneficial.

(9) *Advantages of mechanization*: Rationalization leads to mechanization, and this, in turn, reduces the cost of production, brings about uniformity of standards.

(10) *Promotion of research*: Rationalization introduces scientific approach and the scientific approach is obviously research-oriented. Therefore, as a result of rationalization, there is greater emphasis upon industrial research.

(B) Advantages to Labourers

(1) *Improved working conditions*: As a result of rationalization the conditions of work of labourers have greatly improved. It is a scientific principle that only in a healthy and congenial atmosphere can there be raised the level of production.

(2) *Increase in labour welfare*: As a result of rationalization the managements have come to appreciate the problems of workers. This has led to provision of better facilities to the workers.

(3) *Scientific method of recruitment*: On account of rationalization proper persons are chosen for specific works. There are aptitude tests which help to gauge the suitability of a worker for a particular job.

(4) *Stability in employment*: As a result of rationalization the vacancies created in factories are more or less of permanent nature. Besides, it is realized that experience of a worker should not be allowed to go waste.

(5) *Increase in wages*: As profits of industry have gone up as a result of rationalization, the workers have also benefitted by way of increased emoluments.

(6) *Increase in working capacity*: On account of the factors enumerated above the efficiency of workers has gone up and they are now fully alive to their responsibilities. Because of scientific conditions of work the workers are able to put in their best.

(7) *Increase in mobility*: As a result of rationalization the skilled workers are able to move freely from one place to the other in search of job.

(8) *Advantages of labour unions*: The rationalization has proved that trade unions of workers can play a constructive role in the improvement of industry. These not only work for the rights of workers but can be instrumental to maintain discipline among workers.

(C) Advantages to Consumers

(1) *Standardized goods*: Due to rationalization the goods of uniform quality and precision are available and this obviates the bothersome and hazardous task of selection and elimination.

(2) *Cheap price*: The rationalization has drastically cut the cost of production. Therefore, products are much cheaper.

(3) *Rise in the standard of living*: This has put a sequel to above two points. When standard things are available at the cheap price, it is obvious that more and more people would use them. This leads to rise in the standard of living.

DISADVANTAGES AND DIFFICULTIES OF RATIONALIZATION

Though the advantages of rationalization are numerous and considerable, it has, nonetheless, some disadvantages. As a matter of fact no human device can be hundred per cent beneficial. But most of the demerits of rationalization are due to faulty implementation of policies and these can be removed by due care. However, it will be worthwhile to enumerate the main disadvantages of rationalization:

(1) *Degeneration of cottage industries*: The chief disadvantage of rationalization is the rise of large scale industries which have driven out of existence the cottage industries. The cottage industries cannot compete with large scale industries which have more funds, skill etc.

(2) *Encouragement to monopoly*: The production at massive scale made possible by mechanization and rationalization has given rise to a tendency toward monopolization of business, that is a single business house starts producing 100% or nearly 100% product in a particular field of work. The monopoly in business is harmful to labourers and consumers and ultimately to nation. Monopoly houses come to wield undesirable political influence and financial pressure upon governments and make them yield to their whims.

(3) *Centralization of capital*: A sequel to monopoly is concentration of large amount of wealth in few hands. This corrupts the body politic.

(4) *Disadvantages of capitalism*: All evils attendant upon capitalism, that is monopolization of trade, concentration of wealth, cut-throat competition and wanton display of money power result, as a consequence of rationalization, because in practice rationalization works to the advantages of big money.

(5) *Birth of cosmopolitan cities*: The rationalization has led to proliferation of industries giving rise to birth of cosmopolitan cities. In cosmopolitan cities there is overcrowding and growth of slums. Besides, there is pollution of all kinds in the big cities.

(6) *Degeneration of personality*: With the growth of big industry, the importance of machine and technology overwhelms man and the personality of man is sacrificed to machine.

(7) *Waste of machines*: As a consequence of rationalization new machines are fastly developed and old have to be discarded. This is a great waste.

(8) *Increase in unemployment*: As new machines are labour saving devices; therefore, at least, temporarily a large number of workers are regularly thrown out of employment.

(9) *Absence of co-operation*: As a consequence of rationalization the industrial processes are split into many parts and there is a difficulty in co-ordinating different parts.

(10) *Neglect of art*: Rationalization leads to standardization, whereas artistic talent can flourish if there is appreciation of difference and variation. Therefore, rationalization results in the neglect of art.

(11) *Absence of efficient managers*: The rationalization leads to development of new sophisticated machines and consequent splitting of industrial processes leaves the old managers in quandry. They are unequipped to meet the new challenges.

(12) *Difficulty in nationalization*: As nationalization is a nation-wide process and in order to yield best result, it must be extended to all fields of national activity, the logical outcome of rationalization is nationalization of industry ultimately. The apprehension of this consequence prevents private entrepreneurs from undertaking full scale rationalization.

(13) *Disadvantages to labourers*: The rationalization raises level of stress upon human personality and tends to disintegrate. This stress was felt by workers also. They suffer mentally and physically due to boredom, ennui and ecological pollution. In order to earn more to buy new gadgets and improve their living standard they forego leisure. There is strife and competition to get better of others. This has deleterious effects upon the personality of workers.

(14) *Uncertainty of nation's industrial future*: The ever rising spiral of new innovations and techniques and fierce competition to improve technology have made future highly uncertain and unpredictable. This saps the moral fabric of the society.

The defects of rationalization can be removed to large extent by wise implementation and comprehensive planning.

SUGGESTIONS FOR REFORM

Following is the list of suggestions for wise implementation of the process of rationalization, based mainly on International Conferences and Indian Conferences recommendations:

(1) All-round co-operation: For the success of rationalization a cooperation between labour, capitalist and government is essential.

(2) Equal distribution of profit: This co-operation can be meaningful only when there is equitable distribution of profit among all.

(3) Facilities of mechanical training: In order to make best use of rationalization, it is essential to increase the facilities of mechanical training.

(4) Rationalization in all directions: Rationalization, in order to be effective, must be comprehensive. The management, workers and machines all should undergo rationalization.

(5) Creation of development fund: In order to rationalize the industry much money is needed. Many industries cannot afford rationalization on account of lack of funds. In order to make this good, there is need to create a development fund.

(6) Removal of unemployment: Rationalization throws many workers out of employment. The unemployed workers must be given suitable alternative jobs.

(7) Labour participation in management: For the success of rationalization it is advisable to associate workers with management.

(8) Collective efforts of capitalists: The rationalization can be successful if it is done in the entire industry. For this, collective effort of the capitalists is called for.

(9) Government efforts: The government should aid those industries which cannot rationalize by their own resources.

(10) Gradual application of the scheme: In order that rationalization should be without tears it must be slow and gradual process. The difficulties coming in the way should be removed before proceeding further. The problem of unemployment should be solved in humane way so that rationalization does not prove a curse. The first Planning Commission has given some suggestion for the practical application of rationalization in India. These will be discussed in sequence.

RATIONALIZATION IN INDIA

In India rationalization started first in the textile industry. In 1926, E.D. Sasoon & Co. made a plan for rationalization. In 1927, Tarrif Board made a rationalization plan for Bombay Textile Industry.

In the cement industry rationalization was brought about by the Federation of Cement Producers in 1927, In 1927, an association by the name of Concrete Association of India was set up in order to bring about an awareness in public about the uses of cement. In 1930, a Cement Marketing Ltd. was set up to regulate the sale and distribution of cement in the country. In 1932, in Ahmedabad the Textile Industry decided upon a plan of rationalization whereby techniques of rationalization were agreed upon and it was also decided that the retrenched workers will be employed on a priority basis. The disputes on any matters were to be referred to a Panchayat. After Ahmedabad, rationalization was taken up in Kanpur Textile Mills and workers went on a 50 days strike against rationalization. On August 9, 1939 an agreement was arrived among workers and employers to scarp the plan of rationalization. Between 1937 and 1944 there was a stalemate in regard to rationalization and only after the Second World War in 1944 the plans of rationalization were revived.

The Suggestions of Planning Commission

In 1947, a Planning Commission was set up which decided upon following guidelines with regard to rationalization:

(1) The mill owners and workers should jointly select the team of experts.

(2) After investigation the experts should decide about the workload.

(3) The working conditions in mills should be standardized.

(4) Before installation the new machines should be thoroughly examined.

(5) Upon introduction of rationalization no new recruitment should be made.

(6) The vacancy created by death or retirement should not be filled.

(7) Before installing new machinery capital and market conditions should be thoroughly checked.

(8) The workers willing to retire voluntarily should be entitled to gratuity.

(9) As far as possible new recruits should not be retrenched.

(10) The retrenched workers should be trained for new jobs.

(11) Upon rationalization wages of workers should be increased.

(12) Unabsorbed labourer should be given government jobs.

The Causes of Slow Rate of Rationalization

In 1951, the Industrial Development Council had recommended minimal retrenchment. The rate of rationalization should be slow and the recommendations of Planning Commission should be implemented without delay. The Planning Commission has recommended a planned, well-considered scheme of rationalization. Following are the main causes of slow progress in rationalization:

(1) Paucity of capital: Being a poor country India faces lack of funds for new costly schemes. The paucity of capital comes in the way of rationalization.

(2) Dearth of technical knowledge and experience: Rationalization demands high technical skill and well-trained personnel. As yet the availability of such persons is poor and therefore the process of rationalization is slow.

(3) Dearth of machines: Most of the machines and technical equipment needed for rationalization are to be exported from abroad. Due to paucity of foreign exchange this cannot be done.

(4) Fear of unemployment: The trade unions are not well-disposed to rationalization as it leads to large scale retrenchment of workers.

(5) Ignorance of labourers: The majority of Indian labour force is illiterate and is not capable of appreciating the long-run benefits of rationalization.

(6) Defects of concerning capitalists: In India not only workers are opposed to rationalization but even the capitalists are opposed to them for a variety of reasons. First of all an average Indian capitalist is conservative and averse to change. Secondly, they are not magnanimous and do not wish to distribute widely the gains of rationalization. Rather they wish to corner the entire profit. There is a striking contrast between the attitude of American capitalists and the Indian capitalists. The American capitalist is progressive, eager to share the gains of rationalization amongst all. This is the reason for striking industrial progress in America. Moreover rationalization requires co-operation and joint effort by a number of capitalists. This is the case in America, but in India one capitalist is apprehensive of the other and does not want to co-operate. Moreover, rationalization demands a level of enterprise, venture and risk-taking which is not available in this country.

(7) Indifference of Government: Some efforts are surely under way in India toward rationalization. A look into the history of rationalization in India makes this amply clear. In 1951, councils were set up to look into the matter of rationalization. For this governmental aid was given to some industries. Industrial Development Banks also extended financial help. In 1957, All India Trade Union Conference recommended that before introducing rationalization workers' representative should be consulted. In 1940, a Scientific and Industrial Research Council, in

1948, Scientific Research Department, in 1954, a Ministry of Scientific & National Research were created. In 1958, National Productivity Council was created. In 1957, Indian Standard Institute was created. By 1972, it had granted 6864 patents.

But on the whole, the government efforts are not satisfactory.

NEED OF RATIONALISATION IN INDIA

Rationalization is imperative for India if we are to improve life in India. Following points can be mentioned in this regard:

(1) To remove poverty: If we are to remove poverty in India we must industrialize fast and shake off foreign dependence for machinery and consumer article. More industrialization means more employment. Thus, rationalization is necessary to remove poverty.

(2) To give employment: Though temporarily, rationalization may throw some workers out of job, in the long-run the job opportunities are bound to be created.

(3) To raise the standard of living: If we are to raise the standard of living in India, we must rationalize industry. By rationalization large quantity of goods are produced at cheap rates. This naturally means that more and more people will buy them. For example look at transistor. Today we find it in even most remote villages.

(4) Raises level of production: Rationalization, by definition raises the level of production because it simplifies industrial processes and makes use of machines wherever possible. Therefore, production must go up because machines obviously produce more than men.

(5) For competition with foreign countries: When the world all over is improving techniques of production, marketing and management, India will lag far behind in competing with their goods, if it does not rationalize its industries. Japan is advanced in modern business world because its industry is rationalized.

(6) To Earn foreign exchange: No country can survive without earning adequate foreign exchange to buy raw materials and machines not available in it. But the foreign exchange can be earned more if instead of exporting raw materials, finished goods are exported. This can be done only by modernizing and rationalizing our industries.

(7) To supply demand: A vast population like India cannot be at peace if goods are not produced at massive scale. Chronic shortage are our curse. This is because of lack of rationalization in industry and agriculture.

(8) Reform of economic units: A modern industrial unit cannot be economically viable without rationalization.

(9) To increase mutual co-operation: Rationalization leads to specialization and in order to produce any item we need mutual co-operation among a number of manufacturers.

(10) Suggestion by various commissions and committees: A number of Commissions have strongly recommended rationalization in sugar, cement and textile industry. In 1951, Industrial Development Committee; in 1952, Working Party of the Cotton Textile Industry; in 1953, Jute Enquiry Commission; in 1954, International Team of Ford Foundation and in 1956, Kanpur Textile Mills Rationalization Committee, all recommended rationalization in their respective industries. In 1957, Development Council of Sugar Industry recommended rationalization in this industry.

We may conclude that the advantages of rationalization are so obvious and so heavily outweigh its disadvantages that it is a matter of time before there is comprehensive rationalization in India.

QUESTIONS FOR EXERCISE

1. Define Rationalization and develop its characteristics.
2. Discuss the advantage and disadvantages of Rationalization.
3. Write short note on Rationalization in Indian Industries.

18

Automation

Definition of Automation

1. *Encyclopaedia Americana*: "Automation is an advanced technique of industrial manufacturing and scientific investigation which has evolved from the basic concepts of the machine and mass production."

2. *Goodman*: "Automation is the technology of automatic working in which the handling methods, the processes and the design of the processed material are integrated to utilize as is economically justifiable, the mechanization of thought and effort in order to achieve an automatic in some cases, a self-regulating chain of processes."

3. *John Debawld*: "Automation is a new word denoting both automatic and processes of making things automatic."

4. *A.B. Fillipo*: "In its simplest meaning the term automation is applied to machine work processes that are mechanized to the point of automatic self-regulation."

STEPS IN AUTOMATION PROCESS

(1) Selection of automation machines: First of all for automation we have to select those machines which are self-regulated and the finished or semi-finished product should be passed out to next machine without the touch of hand. For example, there are machines into which you put a coin and a coke-bottle or ticket pops out. If the product is in a semi-finished stage the next machine lifts it all by itself and does the next process on it. The entire product may be finished by a single machine or may require a dozen or more for the purpose.

(2) Control of quality: After the selection of machine the next step is to decide what product is to be manufactured and in what form. Once this is determined the machine is accordingly fitted and the products of uniform quality are produced.

(3) Use of computer: In earlier technology the automatic machines were looked after by men but now even the control and operation of machines is done by the computers.

CHARACTERISTIC OF AUTOMATION

(1) Mechanization: Automation is nothing but a highly advanced kind of mechanization. When machines are so sophisticated as not to require the aid of man, they are automata.

(2) Co-ordination of machines, materials and methods: Automation in order to be successful requires a proper co-ordination between machines and materials.

(3) Computerization: The use of computers is the culmination of automation.

(4) Rationalization: Automation is rationalization confined to the narrow field of machines. Rationalization applies not only to machines but to management, labour etc., but automation is rationalization of machines exclusively.

AUTOMATION IN INDIA

In all advanced countries automation is quite common. But India, though poor, is not lacking wholly in the field of automation. During the British period automation was almost absent but in independent India automation has made appearance. Automation is more useful in places where labour is costly. First of all automation was introduced in the textile industry in India. Now-a-days automation is being used in pharmaceutical industry, even in bottling of soft drinks. The chief hurdle in the way of automation is that it creates massive unemployment intially. It is with this point in view that Trade Unions demanded in 1957 that automation should not lead to retrenchment. In 1967, Standing Labour Committee went into the problems of computerization. In 1969, National Labour Conference presented some significant suggestions regarding automation. The automation should provide jobs to all workers already employed and the profits accruing from automation should be evenly distributed.

In 1972, the Automation Committee of the Ministry of Labour gave valuable suggestions in this regard. It said that before introducing automation the consent of Trade Unions should be sought. As regards computers, these may be used in the fields of education, science, statistics and evaluation. In 1973, an I.L.O. delegation visited India to study the problems of computers and it recommended their use in complex jobs. It also recommended Unemployment Insurance Scheme.

SLOW PACE OF AUTOMATION IN INDIA

Automation has been used in India rather sparingly. The 3rd Planning Commission bemoaned the lack of automation in India and felt that in order to make the plans successful automation should be adopted in India. First computer was installed in the Indian Satistical Institute, Calcutta. In 1961, Esso made use of computers. From then onward the use of computers is on the increase. In 1971, the total number of computers in India was 140. Now there are in Bombay 47, in Delhi 23, in Calcutta 18, in Bangalore 15, in Madras 10, in Hyderabad, Poona and Ahmedabad 6 each and in Jamshedpur and Kanpur 5 each. In the Engineering, Pharmaceutical, Electricity and Textile the number of computers respectively is 30, 17, 16 and 14. By 1980 there were 500 computers in India whereas in U.S.A. their number is nearly 1 lakh.

REASONS FOR SLOW PACE OF AUTOMATION

(1) Lack of capital: The most important reason for the small number of computers in India is lack of funds. The cheapest computer is worth more than 50 lakhs.

(2) Lack of technical ability: The automation is highly sophisticated and requires much training and a special scientific talent. India is not very rich in this matter.

(3) Unemployment: The greatest hurdle in the way of automation is the fear of unemployment on a large scale.

(4) Traditionalism: Indian society is still conservative and does not want rapid or abrupt change.

(5) Government policy: On account of the spectre on unemployment and huge financial commitment the government policy is averse to automation. Automation is not a priority issue in Indian Government policy.

QUESTIONS FOR EXERCISE

1. Define Automation and describe its characteristics and steps.
2. Write short note on Automation in India.

19

Worker's Adjustment

Kinds of Maladjustment

Workers with a nervous temperament are maladjusted because normal personality is an essential condition of proper adjustment. Before turning to proper adjustment of the maladjusted worker it is necessary to understand his main problem. The maladjustment of the worker with a nervous temperament is essentially an emotional maladjustment. It can either be mild or serious. Fisher and Hanna have pointed out six main problems in mild maladjustment and twelve main problems in the more serious manifestation of it.

(1) Mild emotional maladjustment: In this form, as is evident from the name and emotional maladjustment is mild and its symptoms are jealousy, self-pity, absence of cheerful co-operation, fault finding, strong instincts, conflict with labour, abnormal desire to attract attention, etc. A worker with this problem is jealous of the other workers over very minor issues and at times believes himself to be a victim of other's enmity. He does not co-operate with others cheerfully and is constantly engaged in finding faults of the management and other colleagues. In attaining his own interests he pays no attention to the propriety or impropriety of means and fights with others to gain all kinds of advantages. He wants to attract the attention of others towards himself for no reason and is not bothered about the propriety of the means he adopts for this purpose.

(2) Serious emotional maladjustment: The main symptoms of this are the following:

(*a*) Frequent change of jobs,

(*b*) Extreme reticence and withdrawal,

(*c*) Tired feelings,

(*d*) Spasmodic and irregular application,

(*e*) Daydreaming,
(*f*) Deficiency in power of attention,
(*g*) Extreme irritability,
(*h*) Indigestion,
(*i*) Fear,
(*j*) Feeling of being spied upon,
(*k*) Hearing voices,
(*l*) Miscellaneous symptoms.

Workers with serious emotional maladjustment are seen changing jobs frequently. They are not very social for they store many things in their minds and experience exhaustion after very little work. Their behaviour does not follow a definite pattern. They are not very practical and are inclined to be lost in the world of to imagination. They find it difficult to concentrate their attention in any work. Small things irritate them. They also suffer constantly from indigestion. They are unnecessarily afraid of many things and feel that their friends are making complaints about them. Sometimes they also hear voices which do not actually exist. There is little synthesis between their emotions and feelings. They are victims of self-pity on the one hand and jealousy on the other. They do not turn their attention to their own shortcomings, instead they blame others for their own failure. They try to hide reality but despite this they feel inferior to others.

Explanation of the Causes of Maladjustment

In the opinion of Fisher and Hanna, mild and serious emotional maladjustment is caused by the following three main factors:

1. Emotional immaturity,
2. Exaggeration or overexpression of one or more drives,
3. Abnormal expression of emotions.

Maladjustment can also have causes other than these three. Many important researches have been conducted on this subject. H.M. Adler examined one hundred patients in 1917 and pointed out the following three causes of professional maladjustment:

1. Paranoid personalities,
2. Inadequate personalities,
3. Emotional instability.

Maladjustment is a common feature in industry. In addition to its adverse effect on the quality of production, it also injures the social environment. According to E. Toulouse, industries have to suffer much damage because of emotional maladjustment. V.E. Fisher and J.V. Hanna have pointed out that in an industry employing five hundred individuals, half the expense lay in selecting and training new employees. Maladjustment is found to be a widespread phenomenon. In one study conducted by M.C. Jarrett half the number of workers suffered from emotional maladjustment but this fact seems to be untrue. The studies of H.W. Stevens appear to be more correct on this subject; Stevens studied four thousand workers working in a store over a period of six months and found that ten per cent of them had problems of emotional maladjustment. V.V. Anderson examined the twelve hundred employees of the R.H. Massey Company and concluded that 19 per cent of the sales workers and 23 per cent of the other workers suffered from emotional maladjustment. He made a list of the best and worst of the first kind of workers and after testing them demonstrated that 22 per cent of the best had personality defects while 54 per cent of the worst suffered from elementary forms of personality maladjustment while 24 per cent of the worst had acute defects of the personality. In a study of 41 maladjusted wire workers, M. Smith, M. Culpin and E. Farmer found that 31 of them had symptoms of mental diseases like anxiety, maniac depression, etc., 26 workers suffered from neural defects.

Tests of Maladjustment

While the reports furnished by the authorities are useful many scientific methods are used to test maladjustment. The more extensively used methods are ergograph test, McDougall Schuster Dotting test, Graphic Pursuit Meter, Pressure Test, Medical Examination, finding out the emotional nature and development of the worker by examining his external behaviour, etc. All these methods should be used to discover the maladjusted worker in industry.

Causes of Maladjustment

Before trying to find out the ways of removing maladjustment it is necessary to discover the causes. Briefly, the main causes are:

(1) Bad health: Physical health is directly concerned with mental health, as a result of which the adjustment begins to deteriorate if a person falls ill. As has been pointed out earlier, most of the maladjusted workers suffer from indigestion. Bad health makes a person irritable and he takes offence at the smallest things. Decrease in physical energy has an adverse effect on skill which in turn saps him of his self-confidence. All this leads to emotional maladjustment.

(2) Marital disorganisation: The worker's maladjustment is intimately related with his marital condition. If his marital adjustment is upset then he finds it difficult to be balanced in his behaviour even in the factory. That is why in modern times stress is laid on making worker's home life happy.

(3) Bad conditions at home: If the worker's domestic condition is not good, due to economic imbalance or any other cause, he suffers from anxiety, which is never good for emotional health.

(4) Bad conditions of work: Broadly speaking all the working conditions have some or the other effect on the worker's mental health but this is most susceptible to the effect of the social environment. And in this the foreman's and the manager's behaviour is a very important element. If the social atmosphere of the factory is one of sympathy and co-operation the worker can maintain a proper mental balance. If it is not of this kind, he immediately succumbs to maladjustment.

(5) Wrong methods of work: There are many methods of working which tend to increase fatigue, boredom and monotony. They also do not satisfy the worker's desire to complete his work or to learn the results of his work. Besides, he himself feels that he is of no consequence in that particular job and he reduces himself to a cog in the machine. In this way, working conditions of this kind encourage maladjustment.

(6) Painful experience of leaving other jobs: If a worker has the experience of giving up jobs at a number of places, then this painful experience spoils his mental balance and he cannot adjust himself.

(7) Low income: Poverty is at the root of all kinds of maladjustment because a poor man finds it difficult to retain balance of mind. Because of low income the worker continuously lives in a state of anxiety. His needs are not satisfied and hence his emotional adjustment is destroyed.

(8) Old age: Viteles believes that in addition to the above mentioned seven causes of maladjustment old age is another cause. According to E.D. Smith in old age an individual cannot change himself according to conditions of work and for this reason his power of adjustment is reduced. In the opinion of E.L. Thorndike, the worker's ability to learn is reduced in old age and he cannot adopt the new and more efficient ways of doing work. H.L. Hollingworth opines that maladjustment in old age is caused not by the inability to learn but by the inability to put the learnt techniques to proper use. Many psychological investigations have indicated that people suffer in old age because they cannot adopt the modern ways of doing things. Their physical vitality is reduced and the desire to learn new things also declines. According to Viteles, in old age the individual cannot adjust with his old fixed habits, ideas and mental attitudes. His balance is disturbed also because his physical and mental vitality is run down. He tends to ramble in his conversation and criticises others for no good reason. Loss of skill also induces loss of self-confidence. Smith points out that in old age the worker cannot employ the skills and methods he has learnt because more modern methods have come into use by that time, which he is unable to acquire. Hence, his adjustment is upset.

Readjustment of the Maladjusted Worker

It should not be assumed from the above description of the causes of maladjustment that it cannot be corrected. Not only in the case of maladjustment due to many causes, even maladjustment caused by old age, can be remedied. L.J. Martin made use of special experiments to establish proper adjustment in the case of a man 61 years of age. This worker was the oldest employee of the company and was receiving the highest wages. His production had declined by 39 per cent over a period of five years. On investigation it was found that he was alone at home and he had to cook his own food. When his domestic condition was changed it was found that his production increased by ten per cent in the first month, twenty two per cent in the second month, fourteen per cent in the third month, nineteen per cent in the fourth month and by twentyone per cent in the fifth month. It is evident from this that adjustment can again be established if some of the causes of maladjustment can be removed to some extent. The following measures can be adopted for this purpose:

(1) Improvement in health: If maladjustment is to be removed, the mental and physical health of the worker should be improved. If necessary, arrangements should be made for his medical treatment. If his economic condition is not satisfactory, it should be changed. He should be given proper and nourishing food at the correct time and allowed to rest as long as necessary.

(2) Marital adjustment: In modern nations personal guidance is offered to the workers to improve their marital adjustment because this helps to improve their general adjustment.

(3) Family adjustment: Now-a-days it is believed that attention should be paid to the family requirements of the worker. If he has a large number of children, the government should provide facilities for free education and medical care. As long as improvement are not made in the worker's family conditions, adjustment cannot be expected.

(4) Improvement in the working conditions: In every industry, effort should be made to study the working conditions and to improve them wherever necessary. In addition to the working hours lighting, clean air, water, correct temperature, etc., the industry must provide security of employment, proper wages, security of future, a desirable social climate, synthetic and co-operative attitude towards the worker, etc. Thus, worker's adjustment is improved if the level of morale is kept high in the industry.

(5) Improvement in working methods: Sometimes the wrong method of working can lead to maladjustment. This can be rectified by careful examination and improvement of the working method.

(6) Individual care and treatment: Many workers suffer from maladjustment which is caused by some individual factors. In such causes each worker should be examined separately and efforts should be made to solve his problems. He may benefit by personal guidance. Some people carry with them bitter experience of past jobs which they have had to give up. Old age is also an individual state. Some people suffer from some physical or mental illness. The problems of some workers have their source in their marital or general family life. If all these problems are to be solved then each worker must be guided individually and helped in his efforts at readjustment. According to E.D. Smith, one cause of the worker's maladjustment is that he may be forced to do something he does not wish to do. For this reason the doctors and the organisers should make a study of these workers.

(7) Committee for mental hygiene: E.E. Southard has suggested the establishment of a committee for mental hygiene to eliminate maladjustment in the worker. This committee should include psychologists, doctors for mental disorders and social reformers in addition to the company organisers. According to H.L. Stevens, the psychiatrist should study each worker and cure symptoms of mental disease if he finds any.

It is evident from the above description of the means of curing maladjustment that in the first place the individual should be carefully examined so that the causes of his maladjustment can be located. For this it is necessary to win his confidence. Once the causes have been discovered they can be cured by the co-operation of the organisers, the psychologist, the psychiatrist and most of all the worker himself. It is improper to neglect this problem of maladjustment because this disturbs the adjustment of other people also and creates a social climate directly injurious to work and production. Many serious industrial difficulties are caused by maladjustment now-a-days. Hence, if arrangements are made to analyse and cure this problem, the industrialists stand to benefit quite as much as the worker himself.

QUESTIONS FOR EXERCISE

1. Discuss kinds and causes of worker's maladjustment.
2. What measures may be taken for readjustment of industrial workers?

20

Unemployment and Employment

Defining unemployment, Karl Pribram has written that unemployment is a condition of the labour market in which the supply of labour is greater than the number of available openings. According to Fairchild, "Unemployment is forced and involuntary separation from remunerative work on the part of the normal working force during normal working time, at normal wages and under normal conditions." Generally speaking, unemployment means the non-availability of work even though there is desire to do it.

FORMS OF UNEMPLOYMENT

The forms of unemployment have been given different names by different scholars. Some main views in this connection are the following:

Hook's Opinion. According to Alfred Hook, unemployment is of five kinds. These are as follows:

(1) Cyclical unemployment: It is that unemployment which results from trade cycles, profit and loss and fluctuations in the price level. For example, when there is a depression in trade thousands of people are thrown out of work.

(2) Sudden unemployment: That form of unemployment which is an evidence in those businesses which engage workers periodically, for example, workers are turned out from time to time when the work in the factories decreases.

(3) Unemployment arising from failure in industry or business: Many factories close down after a short period of existence and their workers are left without works.

(4) Unemployment resulting from deterioration in industries: When many industries deteriorate due to lack of success in competition or one of the variety of causes, many people become unemployed.

(5) Unemployment arising from seasonal business: Seasonal business shops close when season comes to an end. As a result the people engaged in it are thrown out of work.

Chapman's Opinion: Chapman has mentioned the following two forms of unemployment:

(1) Subjective unemployment: This is caused by physical or mental shortcomings of the individual.

(2) Objective unemployment: This is caused by factors beyond the control of the individual and is related to objective circumstances.

OBJECTIVE UNEMPLOYMENT

Objective unemployment can have the following four forms:

(1) Seasonal unemployment: This is the unemployment caused by the shutting down of seasonal industries.

(2) Cyclic unemployment: This is due to the cyclical economic inflation and depression.

(3) Structural unemployment: This is due to the defects in the economic structure, for example, while thousands of people are unemployed in Kanpur there may be a heavy demand for labour in Delhi. In this situation the unemployment is not due to the excess of supply over demand but rather due to the defect of the economic structure.

(4) Normal unemployment: This form of unemployment prevails in almost all countries. In the complex economic organization it is difficult to provide full-time employment for everybody.

OTHER FORMS OF UNEMPLOYMENT

Besides the above mentioned forms of the unemployment, the following three forms are also accepted:

(1) Agricultural unemployment: This form includes the unemployment of the people engaged in the agricultural sphere.

(2) Technological unemployment: This includes the unemployment resulting from advances in technological techniques. For example, as the machines in any industry or factory increase they continually displace human beings.

(3) Educational unemployment: It includes the unemployment of all those people who are educated in some respect or other.

EMPLOYMENT IN INDIA

Employment in the organised sector *i.e.* in all public sector undertakings and non-agricultural establishments employing ten or more persons in private sector, increased from 259.9 lakh in March 1989 to 263.19 lakh (provisional) in March 1990, an increase of 1.3 per cent. The increase in public sector and private sector employment during 1989-90 was 1.1 per cent and 1.6 per cent respectively. Employment is a thrust area of the Eighth Five Year Plan (1992-97). The Eighth Plan Document accords priority to the objective of generation of adequate employment to achieve near full employment level by the turn of the century. The envisaged GDP growth rate of 5.6 per cent during the Eighth Plan would result in an employment growth of around 2.6 to 2.8 per cent per annum or an average of about eighty to ninety lakh additional employment opportunities per year.

The plan emphasises the need for a high rate of economic growth, combined with faster growth of sectors, sub-sectors and areas which have relatively high employment potential for enhancing the pace of employment generation. Geographically and crop-wise diversified agricultural growth, development of waste land and forestry, development of rural non-farm sector and rural infrastructure, faster growth of small and decentralised manufacturing and expansion of housing, are the basic elements of the employment-oriented growth strategy envisaged in the Plan.

National Employment Service

National Employment Service (NES) as on 31st December, 1992 comprised 77 employment exchanges and 83 university employment information and guidance bureaux (UEIGBX). The exchanges assist all employment seekers including special groups like handicapped, ex-servicemen, scheduled castes and scheduled tribes, women, etc., through placement against jobs notified by employers, NES also carries out other function such as vocational guidance and employment counselling, collection and dissemination of employment market information and conducts studies in the field of employment and occupational research with a view to generating data for framing employment and manpower policies. Programme of computerisation of exchanges is continuing to improve their working.

Under the Employment Exchanges (Compulsory Notification of Vacancies) Act, 1959, it is obligatory for all establishments in the public sector and such of those non-agricultural establishments in the private sector employing 25 or more workers, to notify their vacancies (with certain exemptions) to employment exchanges and supply periodic information as prescribed in the Act and in the rules made thereunder.

Administration

The day-to-day administrative control over employment exchanges was transferred to the state governments in November 1956. From April 1969 states were also made financially responsible for manpower and employment schemes. The role of the Central Government is limited to Policy making, coordination of procedure and standards and development of various programmes on all-India basis and training.

Vocational Guidance

Vocational guidance and employment counselling services are provided to youth (applicants without any work experience) and adults (with specific work experience). Such units functioned in 314 employment exchanges in 1992. In addition, employment information and guidance bureaux are functioning in 83 universities. These units assist applicants and youth in planning their career. A special scheme operates in 28 selected districts as a pilot basis to motivate and guide job seekers to take up self-employment.

Special Exchanges for Physically Handicapped

There are 23 special exchanges for physically handicapped. They are functioning at Bombay, Delhi, Madras, Hyderabad, Calcutta, Ahemadabad, Bangalore, Ludhiana, Kanpur, Thiruvananthapuram, Jabalpur, Patna, Chandigarh, Jaipur, Bhubaneswar, Shimla, Guwahati, Agaratala, Rajkot, Surat, Vadodara, Imphal and Visakhapatnam. Seventeen vocational rehabilitation centres for the handicapped are functioning at Ahemadabad, Agartala, Bangalore, Bombay, Calcutta, Delhi, Hyderabad, Jabalpur, Kanpur, Ludhiana, Madras, Thiruvananthapuram, Jaipur, Vadodara, Patna, Guwahati and Bhubaneswar. These Centres provide a comprehensive package of rehabilitation services to the handicapped. Centres at Patna and Vadodara have been set up exclusively to rehabilitate handicapped women.

SC/ST Job Seekers

Twenty coaching-*cum* guidance centres for scheduled castes and scheduled tribes are functioning at Delhi, Madras, Kanpur, Jaipur, Hyderabad, Thiruvananthapuram, Surat, Jabalpur, Ranchi, Calcutta, Aizawl, Bangalore, Hissar, Rourkela, Imphal, Mandi, Guwahati, Jowai and Kohima which provide confidence building training to the job seekers.

Number of Job Seekers

Number of job seekers on the live registers of employment exchanges increased from 178.38 lakh as on 31 December, 1981 to 363 lakh on 31 December, 1991. Table 20.1 gives registrations, vacancies, placements and job seekers on the 'live register for the period 1981-1990.'

National Sample Survey Organisation

National Sample Survey (NSS) was set up in 1950 with a programme of conducting large-scale surveys to provide data for estimation of national income and related aggregates especially relating to unorganised sector of the economy and for planning and policy formulation. Today, it is a major fact-finding body and occupies a unique position in the nation's statistical system. It carries out annually socio-economic surveys covering various facets of population. It also undertakes field work of Annual Survey of Industries and carries out sample checks of area and yield of crops to improve quality of estimation of agricultural production prepared by the states, besides updating the urban framework for selection of samples in urban area. Its personnel strength is now about 6,000 in 170 offices is spread over throughout the country.

It was reorganised in 1970 by bringing together all aspects of survey work into a single unified agency known as National Sample Survey Organisation (NSSO) under the Department of Statistics. The activities of NSSO are guided by a Governing Council with requisite independence and autonomy in the matter of collection, processing and publication of data. Besides the Chairman, the Council comprises five academicians, six data users in the Central ministries and state governments and six Functionaries of the Department of Statistics. It is headed by the Chief Executive Officer, who is also the member-secretary of the Council. NSSO has four functional divisions, namely: (*i*) Survey Design and Research Division, (*ii*) Field Operations Division, (*iii*) Data Processing Division, and (*iv*) Co-ordination and Publication Division. Each division is under the charge of a Director.

The subject coverage of the socio-economic surveys conforms to a well-defined cycle of the surveys extending over a period of ten years. Survey on consumer expenditure, employment and unemployment, manufacturing establishments and enterprises and trading establishments and enterprises in the unorganised sector are to be repeated once in five years, while subjects like land-holdings, livestock holdings, debt and investment are to be covered once in ten years. Thus, out of a cycle of ten years, pre-assigned subjects are allotted for seven years while three years are kept as 'open rounds' (two full-year rounds and two half-year rounds) to cover special topics of current interest to meet the demand of data users. Integrated with the main topics of a round, annual survey on consumer expenditure was reintroduced from 42nd round (July 1986—June 1987) with a relatively smaller size of one-fifth of the usual quinquennial round during the intervening period between two quinquennial rounds on the subject. From 45th round (July, 1989—June 1990) it was decided to extend the scope of annual survey to cover employment-unemployment as well.

TABLE 20.1

Registrations, Vacancies, Placements and Job-Seekers on the Live Register

(lakh)

Year	Numer of Employment exchanges[1]	Registrations	Vacancies notified	Placements	Live Register	Percentage increase in Live Register over previous year
1981	663	62.77	8.97	5.04	178.38	10.1
1982	692	58.63	8.20	4.73	197.53	10.7
1983	726	67.56	8.26	4.86	219.53	11.1
1984	745	62.20	7.08	4.07	235.47	7.3
1985	800	58.21	6.75	3.88	262.70	11.6
1986	821	55.35	6.23	3.51	301.31	14.7
1987	835	60.12	6.01	3.34	302.47	0.4
1988	840	59.63	5.43	3.28	300.50	.07
1989	849	65.76	6.00	2.89	327.76	9.1
1990	851	65.41	4.91	2.64	346.32	5.7
1991	854	62.36	4.59	2.53	363.00	4.8

Note: Total may not tally due to rounding off.
1. Including University Employment Information and Guidance Bureaus.

TABLE 20.2

Employment in the Public Sector by Industry

Lakh persons as on 31 March)

		1981	1983	1984	1985	1986	1987	1988	1989	1990	1991	1992
	1	2	3	4	5	6	7	8	9	10	11	12
A. By Branch												
1.	Central Government	31.95	32.66	33.11	33.29	33.46	33.50	33.81	33.95	33.97	34.10	34.28
2.	State Governments	56.76	60.38	61.54	62.80	64.73	66.66	67.81	68.29	69.79	71.12	71.90
3.	Quasi-Governments	45.76	50.40	52.74	54.96	56.74	57.95	59.48	59.99	61.73	62.22	63.93
4.	Local bodies	20.37	21.11	21.30	21.64	21.90	22.14	22.11	22.38	22.23	23.13	21.98
	Total	154.84	164.55	168.69	172.69	176.83	180.25	183.21	184.44	187.72	190.72	192.10
B.	**By Industry**											
0.	Agriculture, hunting etc.	4.63	4.76	4.89	4.98	5.26	5.57	5.54	5.55	5.49	5.56	5.73
1.	Mining and quarrying	8.18	8.84	9.27	9.74	9.66	9.42	9.56	9.56	9.66	9.99	9.87
2&3.	Manufacturing	15.02	16.34	17.17	17.61	18.15	18.62	18.67	18.63	18.70	18.52	18.61
4.	Electricity, gas and water	6.83	7.21	7.33	7.60	7.85	7.89	8.49	8.69	8.97	9.05	9.16
5.	Construction	10.89	11.20	11.20	11.46	11.81	11.85	12.14	11.46	11.34	11.49	11.51
6.	Wholesale and retail trade	1.17	1.18	1.24	1.31	1.31	1.34	1.39	1.50	1.50	1.50	1.57
7.	Transport, storage & communications	27.09	28.26	28.64	28.94	29.29	29.70	30.11	29.74	30.23	30.26	30.64
8.	Finance, insurance, real estate etc.	7.48	8.72	9.14	9.83	10.30	10.56	10.95	11.23	11.54	11.94	12.14
9.	Community, social & personal services	73.55	78.06	79.81	81.23	83.21	85.29	86.35	88.11	90.19	92.27	92.87
	Total	154.84	164.57	168.69	172.70	176.84	180.24	183.20	184.47	187.62	190.58	192.10

Note: Total in A and B differ due to rounding off.

Source: Ministry of Labour.

TABLE 20.3

Employment in the Private Sector by Industry

(Lakh persons as on 31, March, 1992)

	1981	1983	1984	1985	1986	1987	1988	1989	1990	1991	1992
1	2	3	4	5	6	7	8	9	10	11	12
0. Agriculture, hunting etc.	8.58	8.47	8.19	8.07	8.22	8.48	8.44	8.68	8.76	8.91	9.12
1. Mining and quarrying	1.30	1.20	1.13	1.13	1.11	0.91	0.93	0.96	0.99	1.00	1.07
2. & 3. Manufacturing	45.45	46.56	44.73	44.21	44.48	44.10	43.95	43.83	44.57	44.81	45.66
4. Electricity, gas and water	0.35	0.37	0.39	0.39	0.40	0.40	0.41	0.39	0.40	0.40	0.40
5. Construction	0.72	0.68	0.66	0.70	0.69	0.58	0.50	0.69	0.68	0.73	0.78
6. Wholesale and retail Trade	2.77	2.75	2.76	2.77	2.77	2.77	2.83	2.86	2.91	3.00	2.96
7. Transport, storage and communications	0.60	0.59	0.57	0.54	0.54	0.52	0.51	0.51	0.52	0.53	0.54
8. Finance, insurance, real estate etc.	1.96	2.07	2.14	2.19	2.21	2.29	2.38	2.34	2.39	2.54	2.66
9. Community, social and personal services	12.22	12.83	12.89	13.09	13.32	13.59	13.97	14.29	14.60	14.85	15.27
Total	73.95	75.52	73.46	73.09	73.74	73.64	73.92	74.53	75.82	76.77	78.46

Relates to non-agricultural establisments in the private sector employing 10 or more persons

Note: Coverage in construction, particularly on private account, is known to be inadequate.

Source: Ministry of Labour.

TABLE 20.4

Estimates of Employment in Organised Public and Private Sectors

(Lakh persons as on 31 March)

Years	Public Sector			Private Sector			Public and Private Sectors (Total)		
	Male	Female	Total	Male	Female	Total	Male	Female	Total
1990	165.22	22.50	187.72	61.88	13.94	75.82	227.09	36.44	263.5
1991	167.10	23.47	190.57	62.42	14.34	76.76	229.52	37.81	267.3
1992	167.81	24.29	192.10	63.67	14.79	78.46	231.48	39.08	270.56
1993*	169.01	24.86	193.87	62.80	15.51	78.31	231.81	40.37	272.18

* Quick estimates.

Notes: (*i*) Includes all establishments in the Public Sector irrespective of size of employment and non-agricultural establishments in the Private Sector employing 10 or more persons.

(*ii*) Excludes Sikkim, Arunachal Pradesh, Dadra & Nagar Haveli and Lakshadweep as these are not yet covered under the programme.

Source: Ministry of Labour, DGE&T.

QUESTION FOR EXERCISE

1. Discuss the problem of industrial unemployment in India, Suggest remedies.

21

Problems of Housing

The problem of housing in India is a complex one requiring finances on a huge scale and is dependent for its solution on the concerted efforts of individuals, co-operatives and central and state governments to be planned and executed over a number of years. There is acute shortage of housing in urban and rural areas and much of the available accommodation is qualitatively of sub-substandard variety. The shortage in urban areas has been largely on account of considerable increase in population since 1921, the steady shift of population from the rural to the urban areas, the haphazard growth of towns owing to lack of proper town planning and the comparative inability of private enterprise to keep pace with the growing demand.

Size of the Problem

According to the 1971 census, some 5.79 lakh human settlements accommodate India's population. Nearly 80 per cent live in 5.76 lakh villages. The remaining 20 per cent live in 3,119 urban settlements.

The problem of housing in India is a complex one, requiring finances on a large scale, and is dependent for its solution on the concerted efforts of individuals, co-operatives and central and state governments, to be planned and executed over a number of years. There is an acute shortage of housing in urban and rural areas and much of the available accommodation is qualitatively sub-substandard.

With a growing population and the steady shift of population from the rural to urban areas, the problem has become more difficult both in qualitative and quantitative terms.

According to the 28th round of the National Sample Survey for 1973-74, nearly two-thirds of urban house-holds live in pucca houses. In rural areas, however, kutcha and semi-pucca houses are the rule. Most of them, however, would require extensive repairs or replacement over a 20-year period. In urban areas, a very large number of house-holds have limited access to basic needs like water and sanitation and only a small minority of house-holds have modern facilities for their exclusive use. In rural areas, where the need for such modern facilities may be less urgent, practically all house-holds are dependent on communal sources for water and on nature for sanitation.

According to the draft Five Year Plan, increase in urban and rural population during 1978-83 period would be 2.11 crores and 4.19 crores respectively. On the basis of the average house-hold size reported in the 28th round of National Sample Survey, the requirement of dwelling units would come to 45 lakh units in urban areas and 81 lakh units in rural areas.

GOVERNMENT SCHEMES FOR HOUSING IN INDIA

In order to meet the requirement of additional house-holds due to population increase, replacement and repair of old units and to wipe out the existing backlog, a massive housing construction programme has to be undertaken. To achieve this goal, the investment has to be increased heavily as compared to the Fifth Five Year Plan investment.

To encourage house building activity, the government is taking measures to remove and eliminate the obstacles and disincentives which deter the growth of private building activities. Action has also been taken to preserve the existing housing stock as long as possible in a satisfactory condition.

Although it is the endeavour of the government to solve the housing problem as expeditiously as possible with the available resources, it is not possible to provide a house to every family at public cost, involving expenditure of several hundreds of crores of rupees, in view of the competing claims of other priority problems facing the country.

To prove the housing condition, specially for the lower income group, the Government of India has introduced from 1952 several social housing schemes providing subsidised housing on a limited scale for the economically weaker sections of the community like slum-dwellers and industrial and plantation workers. It provides financial assistance to state governments for undertaking composite projects of land acquisition and house construction to cater to the needs of low and middle income groups.

HOUSING SCHEME UNDER PLANS

Housing is an activity that is typically labour intensive and, therefore, fits in well with the pattern of development envisaged in the various plans in India. Housing construction also creates much needed employment for the unskilled and, therefore, income for the relatively poor.

Apart from the houses constructed for the government employees, till the Fourth Plan, the role of public sector in the provision of housing has been small. Subsidised dwellings had been provided to certain selected economically weaker sections of the community. It was only during the Fifth Plan that provision was made to provide house sites to the rural landless as well in addition to the schemes operating in urban areas.

The Sixth Plan clearly states that the provision of shelter is a basic need which must be met. The objectives in respect of housing in the plan are: (*i*) provision of house sites and assistance for the construction of dwellings for rural landless labourers, (*ii*) in view of the severe constraints of public resources, public sector social housing schemes will be designed to benefit the maximum number of people, and (*iii*) specific efforts must be made to secure reduction in cost in public housing schemes by reviewing standards and by using cheap and alternative building materials.

For the Sixth Plan period the combined public and private investment is expected to be about ₹ 13,000 crore. Additional investment by public sector enterprises, departmental undertakings and grants in-aid to institutions may be of the order of ₹ 250-300 crore.

Social Housing Schemes

Housing has long been an area of Central and State governments concern and this reflects its vital importance for both individual and social welfare. Since Independence, the Government has accepted that the State has to play an important role in housing provision; consequently State's involvement has grown and an increasing amount of public expenditure has been spent on housing.

The role of the Central Government *vis-a-vis* the social housing schemes in operation in the country is confined to laying of broad principles, providing necessary advice and rendering financial assistance in the form of loans and subsidies to the State governments, Union Territory administrations and watching the progress of the schemes. The State governments/Union Territory administrations have been vested with full powers to formulate, sanction and execute the projects under these schemes and also to release financial assistance therefore to the concerned construction agencies. Since the beginning of the Fourth Plan, all Central financial assistance is given to the states in the form of block grants and block loans for all state sector schemes, including housing schemes, without being tied to any particular head of development or scheme. Besides financing the schemes, the Ministry of Works and Housing, also monitors the progress of the same.

Till June 1982, the following social housing schemes (with year of introduction) were in operation in the country: (*i*) integrated subsidised housing scheme for industrial workers and economically weaker sections of community (1952); (*ii*) low income group housing scheme (1954); (*iii*) subsidised housing scheme for plantation workers (1956); (*iv*) middle income group housing scheme (1959); (*v*) rental housing scheme for state government employees (1959); (*vi*) slum clearance/improvement scheme (1956); (*vii*) village housing projects scheme (1957); (*viii*) land acquisition and development scheme (1959); and (*ix*) provision of house sites to landless workers in rural areas (1971).

From July 1982, the existing social housing schemes, except the subsidised housing scheme for plantation workers, which continues to be in the central sector and the scheme for provision of house sites to landless workers, have been reclassified in 4 categories on the basis of income criteria as: (*i*) housing scheme for economically weaker sections, (*ii*) low income group housing scheme, (*iii*) middle income group housing scheme, and (*iv*) rental housing scheme for state government employees.

House Sites-*cum*-Construction Assistance Scheme

The house sites-*cum*-construction assistance scheme for rural landless workers is in operation in 18 states and 6 union territories. In the Sixth Plan, provision of about ₹ 354 crore has been made for this scheme ₹ 170 crore for the provision of house sites and about ₹ 184 crore for construction assistance. The Plan provides for ₹ 250 per family for developed plots, approach roads, a masonry well for a cluster of 30-40 families and also construction assistance of ₹ 500 per family. All labour input is to be provided by the beneficiaries themselves.

It is estimated that the number of eligible families needing housing assistance would be around 145 lakh by March 1985. Of these, 77 lakh families have already been allotted house-sites before the commencement of the Sixth Plan, leaving about 68 lakh families to be covered with house sites. The Sixth Plan also proposed to provide house-sites to all the remaining landless families. Upto March 1983, 108,95 lakh families have been provided house-sites. The Sixth Plan also proposed to provide construction assistance to 25 per cent of eligible families *i.e.* 36 lakh families. The construction of houses/huts is being done by the state governments and the individuals by their own efforts. By way of these efforts upto March 1983, 23.5 lakh houses/huts had been constructed.

Housing Finance

Housing finance is the most crucial element in house construction and building activities. In the field of housing, the public sector has a marginal though promotional role to pay. The bulk of the investment in housing is, however, expected to come from the private sector.

A number of specialised agencies have come up in recent times in the country, yet the bulk of the finance for housing originates from a selected group of Central financial institutions comprising the Life Insurance Corporation of India (LIC), the General Insurance Corporation of India (GIC), Housing and Urban Development Corporation (HUDCO), the Employees Provident Fund Organisation, etc. Funds are also provided and channelised through the state apex co-operative housing societies, state housing boards and housing and urban development authorities, nationalised commercial banks, etc.

Urban Development

The Sixth Plan emphasises the development of small, medium and intermediate towns. Urban development is seen as complementary to rural development so that policies affecting the process of urbanisation would strengthen the links between the cities and their hinterland. The objective of the Sixth Plan was to strengthen the small and medium towns for increased investments in housing, water supply, communication, education, medical care, recreation, etc. It is envisaged that positive incentives would be given for setting up new industries and other activities in these towns accompanied by improvement in power and telecommunication facilities. With this objective in view, a Centrally-sponsored scheme for the development of small and medium towns with population less than one lakh has been in operation since December 1979.

The Sixth Plan has made a provision of ₹ 96 crore in the Central sector in order to support the integrated development of 231 small and medium towns during the plan period. The Central Government would finance schemes for shelter, transportation and economic activities to the extent of 50 per cent of the project cost or ₹ 40 lakh, whichever is lesser, subject to matching funds from the state agencies. The State governments would further undertake investment in water supply, sanitation, slum improvement and social facilities as a part of the integrated project. Low cost sanitation has also been introduced as an item for Central assistance under the scheme. State governments will be entitled to ₹ 15 lakh over and above ₹ 40 lakh available under the scheme for low cost sanitation, provided they propose to spend at least ₹ 12 lakh on low cost sanitation schemes out of their own funds. The projects are appraised by the Town and Country Planning Organisation. 232 towns had been approved out of 236 towns and a Central loan assistance of ₹ 47.84 crore had been released upto 31 March, 1984.

Socialisation of Urban Land

The Urban Land (Ceiling and Regulation) Act, 1976 came into force on 17 February, 1976. It provides for: (*i*) imposition of a ceiling on both ownership and possession of vacant land in urban agglomerations, the ceiling being on a graded basis according to the classification of the urban agglomeration; (*ii*) acquisition of the excess vacant land by the State governments with powers to dispose of the vacant land to subserve the common good; (*iii*) payment of an amount for the acquisition of the excess vacant land in cash and in bonds; (*iv*) granting exemptions in respect of certain specific categories of vacant lands, and (*v*) restricting the plinth area for the construction of future residential buildings. The Act provides for granting permission to hold land in excess of the ceiling limits for utilising them for the construction of dwelling units for the weaker sections of the society.

The Act applies to all the union territories and all the states except Jammu and Kashmir, Kerala, Nagaland and Sikkim, which have not adopted the Act so far; and also excludes Tamil Nadu which had enacted its own law in 1978.

Environmental Improvement of Slums

Under the programme for the environmental improvement of slums, the Sixth Plan envisages an investment of ₹ 151.45 crore in the state sector for the provision of basic amenities to about one crore living in slums in different urban areas in the country. The scheme forms part of the minimum needs programme. This is in continuation of the scheme introduced in 1972 under which amenities like water supply, sewerage, sanitation, paved pathways, community latrines and street lighting were provided to slum dwellers in selected urban areas. Out of the estimated slum population of about 3.3 crore in 1985, it is reported that about 69 lakh had been covered till the end of March 1980.

Water Supply and Sanitation

Water supply and sanitation are state subjects and the schemes relating to these are drawn up and implemented by the State governments.

Supply of drinking water to all the identified problem villages is a part of the Revised 20-Point Programme. The objective is to ensure at least one round the year source of same drinking water villages suffering from chronic scarcity or those with unsafe sources of water. Of about 2.31 lakh villages identified as problem villages at the beginning of the Sixth Plan, 1,01,659 villages are provided with protected water supply by the end of March 1983.

National Capital Region

It has been decided to revitalise the plan for the development of National Capital Region by the establishment of a statutory board at the Central level. An agreement to this effect has been reached between the Union Minister of Works and Housing and the Chief Ministers of Uttar Pradesh, Haryana, Rajasthan and Lt. Governor of Delhi. A Central legislation for this purpose is proposed to be introduced after obtaining the resolutions of the concerned State legislatures.

Jhuggi and *Jhonpri* Removal Scheme

The *jhuggi* and *jhonpri* removal scheme is designed to provide alternative accommodation to unauthorised occupants of government and public lands in Delhi and New Delhi. About two lakh tenements and plots have been constructed/developed under the scheme so far. Another scheme for developing 25,000 plots for re-settlement of squatter families left in residuary areas of Delhi has been sanctioned by the Government.

CONSTRUCTION AGENCIES

National Buildings Construction Corporation

The National Buildings Construction Corporation Ltd. (NBCC), was set up in 1960 with the specific objective of developing quality consciousness and reducing the cost of construction as well as for undertaking construction works in difficult and inaccessible areas. NBCC undertakes construction of specialised and complicated works on a turn-key basis, including planning and designing. NBCC has also undertaken considerable works in Libya and Iraq, which involve construction of airports, housing colonies, hostels, hotels, universities and sewerage works.

Housing and Urban Development Corporation

The Housing and Urban Development Corporation (HUDCO), a Government of India enterprise, under the Ministry of Works and Housing, was set up in 1970 as an apex organisation mainly to provide loan finance for housing and urban development programme in the country with a primary emphasis on the promotion of housing for the persons belonging to low income groups and economically weaker sections.

The main sources of finance for HUDCO are equity contribution by the Government, borrowing from LIC and floating of debentures. The Sixth Plan envisages an investment of ₹ 600 crore by HUDCO during the Plan.

Hindustan Prefab Ltd.

The Hindustan Prefab Ltd. (earlier known as Hindustan Housing Factory Ltd.) New Delhi, a Government of India company, apart from manufacturing pre-fabricated houses, specialises in producing several other items, such as pre-fabricated reinforced cement concrete components, pre-stressed cement concrete transmission poles, foam concrete panels and partition and insulation blocks. It undertakes wooden joinery work and has the largest seasoning kilns for timber in north India. It has standardised certain pre-cast building components for use by individual house-builders and construction agencies. The pre-fabricated components for industrial structures by the factory have not only effected saving in steel and resulted in quicker construction but also brought down the construction cost to some extent.

Research National Buildings Organisation

The National Buildings Organisation (NBO), an attached office of the Ministry of Works and Housing, was set up in 1954 as an advisory and co-ordinating body for all technical matters concerning housing and building. NBO promotes housing and building research and its application with the objective of making it readily acceptable by the construction departments and the building industry. It documents and disseminates information on the latest advances in building technology with a view to effecting reduction in cost and improvement in the quality of building and housing construction. The Organisation also tries to stimulate the production of traditional building materials and the introduction and establishment of new building material industries. It is responsible for the compilation of housing and building statistics at the national level and monitoring of the implementation of various social housing schemes. It undertakes research studies in the sociological and economic aspects of housing. Twelve rural housing wings at Vallabh Vidyanagar (Anand), Bangalore, Calcutta, Chandigarh, Srinagar, Trivandrum, Varanasi, Jodhpur, Shimla, Ranchi, Madras and Guwahati are functioning under NBO for research, training and extension work in rural housing and village planning.

NBO also functions as the United Nations Regional Housing Centre for ESCAP region.

Town and Country Planning Organisation

The Town and Country Planning Organisation (TCPO) is a technical advisory body on all matters pertaining to urban and regional development. It provides technical guidance and assistance to all state governments and union territories. TCPO also undertakes project work for development on consultancy basis from public undertakings and local bodies.

Central Public Works Department

The Central Public Works Department (CPWD) designs, constructs, maintains and repairs all works and buildings of the Central Government, except those belonging to railways, communications, atomic energy, defence services and All India Radio. It also maintains national highways in Delhi and exercises technical control over the public works departments of union territories. Public undertakings which do not have their own civil engineering organisations, have to entrust their construction works to CPWD or public sector construction and consultancy organisations. The CPWD also works on behalf of semi-government organisations on a deposit basis.

The CPWD has developed considerable expertise in the architectural landscaping, structural and horticultural fields, as well as in civil construction and the installation of services. The Department has a well developed architectural wing, a central designs organisation for complex structural design work, field units for the execution of projects and an electrical and mechanical wings to handle a variety of service installations.

QUESTION FOR EXERCISE

1. Discuss the problem of housing with particular reference to Industrial personnel in India. Suggest remedies.

22

Training and Development of Personnel

Definition of Training of Workers

1. *Dale S. Beach*: "Training is the organised procedure by which people learn knowledge and/or skill for a definite purpose."

2. *Edwin B. Flippo*: "Training is the act of increasing the knowledge and skill of an employee for doing a particular job."

3. *Michael J. Jucius*: "The term training is used here to indicate the process by which the aptitudes, skills and abilities of employees to perform specific jobs are increased."

4. *L.L. Steinmetz*: "Training is a short-term process utilising a systematic and organised procedure by which non-managerial personnel learn technical knowledge and skills for a definite purpose."

5. *J.P. Campbell*: "Training refers only to instruction in technical and mechanical operations. Specifically stated, training is the organised procedure by which people learn knowledge and skills for a definite purpose. The objective of training is to achieve a change in the behaviour of those trained. In the industrial situation, this means that the trainee shall acquire new techniques, skills, problem-solving abilities and develop work attitude. It is expected that the employees apply their newly acquired knowledge on the job in such a way as to help them in the achievement of organisational goals."

Importance of Training of Workers

A vital and necessary activity in all organisations training plays a large part in determining the effectiveness and efficiency of the establishment. Following is the need or importance of training to a business firm or industry:

1. Increase in productivity: Increase in productivity is possible only when there is an increase in quantity of output. Training programmes, by increasing skills, aptitude and abilities of workers result in increased productivity.

2. Improvement in performance: Training applies not only to new employees but to experienced people as well. It can help employees increase their level of performance on their present job assignments.

3. High morale: Possession of needed skills helps to meet such basic human needs as security and ego satisfaction. Elaborate personnel and human relations programme can make a contribution towards morale, but does not work if there is no solid core of meaningful work done with knowledge, skill and pride.

4. Reduced supervision: A trained employee is one who can supervise himself. Both the employee and the supervisor want less supervision, but greater independence is not possible unless the employee is adequately trained.

5. Reduced dissatisfactions, complaints, absenteeism and turnover: Through this the employees can experience the direct satisfactions associated with a sense of achievement and knowledge that they are developing their inherent capabilities at work.

6. Less accidents and wastage: An important advantage of training is that accidents, which spoiled work and damage machinery and equipment can be kept to minimum by well trained employees.

7. Fulfilment of manpower needs: When technical skills are required by a company it often finds it most practical to select and train from within the organisation rather then seek the skilled personnel from the outside labour market.

8. Benefits to employees: As employees acquire new knowledge and job skills they increase their market value and earning power. The possession of useful skills increases their value to their employer and thereby increase their job security. Training may also qualify them for promotion to more jobs. This, of course, increase their pay and status.

9. Increase in organizational stability and flexibility: Stability, the ability of an organization to sustain its effectiveness despite the loss of key personnel, can be developed only through creation of a reservoir of trained replacements. Flexibility, the ability to adjust to short-run variations in the volume of work, requires personnel with multiple skills to enable their transfer to jobs where the demand is highest. There is no greater organizational asset than the trained motivated personnel.

10. Prevention of obsolence: Training and development programmes foster the initiative and creativity among employees and help to prevent manpower obsolesce which may be due to age, temperament, lack of motivation or the inability of a person to adapt himself to technological changes.

11. Reduction in learning time: A well-knit training programme reduce learning time to reach the level of acceptable performance.

Thus, training is a must for all concerns. The management has no choice between 'training' or 'no training'. The only choice is to select a suitable method of training.

METHODS OR TECHNIQUES OF TRAINING

1. On-the-job methods: On-the-job means while working on a job. Numerous training methods may be used while the man is engaged in the process of productive work. These on-the-job training methods are suitable for all levels of personnel. Following are the various methods of on-the-job training:

1. On specific job: (*i*) Experience; (*ii*) Coaching; (*iii*) Understudy; 2. Position rotation; 3. Special projects; 4. Selective reading; 5. Apprenticeship; 6. Vestibule school; 7. Multiple management.

2. Off-the-job training methods: In these off-the-job training methods, the trainees have to leave their work, place and devote their entire time to the development objective. Development of trainees is primary in these methods and work of production during training is secondary. Following are off-the-job training techniques:

1. Special courses and lectures; 2. Conferences; 3. Case studies; 4. Brainstorming; 5. Laboratory method—A. Simulation (*i*) Role-playing; (*ii*) Gaming B. Sensitivity Training; On-the-job Training Methods.

On-the-job Methods

1. On specific job: Training for a specific job is the most common and formal on-the-job training programme. Current practice in job training has been strongly influenced by the war time training within industry (T.W.L.). This was first designed to improve the job performance through job instruction training. It also included training for supervisors to improve job performance. Following are the methods of training on specific job:

(*i*) *Experience*: Experience is the oldest method of on-the-job training. Learning by experience cannot and should not be eliminated as a method of development, though as a sole approach, it is wasteful, time consuming and inefficient. It has proved to be very efficient in some cases though it should be followed by other training methods to make it more meaningful.

(*ii*) *Coaching*: On-the-job coaching by the superior is an important and potentially effective approach. It is superior, properly trained and oriented. It involves direct personnel instruction and guidance, usually with extensive demonstration and continuous critical evaluation and correction. It has the advantage of increased motivation for the trainee and the minimisation of the problem of learning transfer from theory to practice. In this method the danger lies in the possible neglect to coaching by superior.

(*iii*) *Understudy*: It is considered a somewhat different approach from those described above. In it a person is specifically designated as the heir apparent. It makes the trainee an assistant to the current job holder. The trainee learns by experience, observation and imitation. If decisions are discussed with him he can become informed on the policies and theories involved. The training is conducted in practical and realistic situation. However, it tends to perpetuate mistakes and deficiencies of existing managerial practices. Moreover, the understudies are frequently neglected by those they assist.

2. Position rotation: It is the broadening of the background of trainee in the organisation. If a trainee is rotated periodically from one job to another job, he acquires a general background. The main advantages of position rotation are: providing a general background to the trainee, training in actual situation, stimulating competition among the rotating trainees and stimulating a more cooperative attitude by exposing a man to other fellow's problems and viewpoints. A disadvantage of this method is that productive work suffers because of the obvious disruption caused by such changes. As Specialisation proceeds rotation becomes less useful as few people have the breadth of technical knowledge and skills to move from one functional area to another.

3. Special projects: These assignments grow ordinarily out of an individual analysis of weakness. The trainee may be asked to perform special Assignment, in which he learns the work procedure. Sometimes a task force is created which consists of a number of trainees representing different functions in the organisation. Trainees not only acquire knowledge about the assigned activities, but also learn how to work with others.

4. Selective reading: Through this method the individual in the organisation can gather and advance their knowledge and background. Selective reading may include professional journals and books. Some business organisations maintain libraries for their executives. Some executives become members of professional associations. They exchange their ideas with others. This is a good method for assimilating knowledge. However, some executives point out that it is very difficult to find time to do reading other than that absolutely required in the performance of their jobs.

5. Apprenticeship: This method may be traced back to medieval times when those intended on learning trade skill used to bind themselves to a master craftsman to learn by doing the work under his guidance. During earlier periods, apprenticeship was not restricted to artisans. It was used in training for the professions including medicine, law and teaching etc. Today's industrial organisations require large number of skilled craftsmen who may be trained by this system. Apprenticeship training is either provided by the organisation or it is also imparted by government agencies. Most concerns have apprenticeship laws with supervised plans for such training. Such arrangements usually provide a mixed programme of class-room and job experience.

6. Vestibule schools: Large organisations frequently provide vestibule schools, a preliminary to actual shop experience. As far as possible, shop conditions are duplicated. But here major objective is instruction, not output. Vestibule schools are widely used in training for clerical and office jobs as well as for factory production jobs. Vestibule training is usually shorter and less complex than that adaptable to the apprenticeship system. It is relatively expensive, but these costs are justified if the volume of training is large, or if uniform, high standard results are important.

7. Multiple management: This method emphasises the use of committees to increase the flow of ideas from less experienced managers and to train them for positions of greater responsibility. Such a programme was developed by the McCormik & Company of Baltimore, U.S.A. This company claimed that the plan has increased employee efficiency, reduced labour turnover and absenteeism, and enabled the company to pay higher wages than those prevailing in the area and industry. A junior board was authorised to discuss any problem that the senior board may discuss, and its members were encouraged to put their mind to work on the business as a whole, rather than to concentrate to their specialized areas.

Off-the-Job Training Methods

1. Special Course and Lectures: Special courses and lectures are presented by business organisations in numerous ways as a part of their development programmes.

(*i*) *Own Regular Instructor*: There are courses which the organisations themselves establish to be taught by members of the organisations. Some organisations have regular instructors assigned to their training and development departments such as Tata and Hindustan Lever in private sector; Life Insurance Corporation, State Bank of India and other nationalised commercial banks, Reserve Bank, Hindustan Steel, Fertilizer Corporation and many others in public sector.

(*ii*) *Instructions by Instructors from Institutes*: Courses and lectures in organisations to work with university or institutes in establishing a course or series to be taught by instructors by these institutes.

(*iii*) *Sending Personnel to Programmes*: Courses for the organisations to send personnel to programmes established by the universities, institutes and other bodies. These courses are organised for a short period ranging from 2-3 days to a few weeks. The first such programme was the Slogan Fellowship Programme, established in 1931 at the Massachusetts Institute of Technology, U.S.A. In India, such courses are organised frequently by the Institutes of Management, Administrative Staff College of India, National Productivity Council, NITIE, All India Management Association and some other organisations and universities.

2. Conferences: Holding Conference is a favourite training method. Many organisations have developed guided-discussion type of conferences in their training programmes in order to escape the limitations of lectures. In Conference the participants pool their ideas and experience in attempting to arrive at improved methods of dealing with the problems which are common subject of discussion. Conference may include buzz sessions that divide the conference into small groups of four or five for intensive discussion. These small groups then report back their conclusions or questions to the whole conference. Conference method allows the trainees to look at the problem from a broader angle. However, unless the discussion is directed to the felt needs of the participants, they may feel that whole exercise is useless.

3. Case Studies: It is one of the most common form of training. A case is a written account of a trained reporter or analyst seeking to describe an actual situation. Some cases are merely illustrative, others are detailed and comprehensive demanding extensive and intensive analytical ability. Cases are widely used in a variety of programmes. This method increases the trainees power of observation. It helps him to ask better questions and to look for broader range of problems. A well chosen case may promote objective discussion. However, the lack of emotional involvement may make it difficult to effect any basic change in the behaviour and attitude of trainees.

4. Brainstorming: Brainstorming which stimulates trainees to creative thinking was developed by Alex Osborn inhibiting forces by providing for a maximum of group participation and a minimum of criticism. In Brainstorming a problem is posed and ideas are invited. Quantity rather than quality is the primary objective. Ideas are encouraged while criticism of any idea is discouraged. Often chain reactions develop from idea to idea. Later, these ideas are critically examined. There is no trainer in brainstorming. The introduction of known experts into it reduces the originality and practicability of the group contribution. Brainstorming favours divergence. This explains why Brainstorming is so little used in developing countries where no solutions carry the highest premium. Its immediate use is limited to new ideas only. It does not lead to change in behaviour.

5. Laboratory training: Adding to conventional training, laboratory training provides situations in which trainees themselves experience some of the conditions they are talking about through their own interaction. Thus, they more or less experiment on themselves. More concerned about changing individual behaviour and attitude. Laboratory training is more successful in changing job performance rather than conventional training methods. Following are two methods of laboratory training: simulation and sensitivity training.

(A) *Simulation*: Its performance is an increasingly popular technique of management development. In it, instead of taking participants into the field, the field can be simulated in the training session itself. Simulation is the presentation of real situation of organisations in the training session. It covers situations of varying complexities and roles for the participants. It creates a whole field organisation. It relates participants through key roles in it. It exposes them to simulated specific situations of a kind they encounter in real life. There are two common simulation methods of training: role-playing and business game.

(*i*) *Role-playing*: It is a laboratory method which may be used rather easily as a supplement to conventional training methods. Its purpose is to increase the trainee's methods. Its purpose is to increase the trainee's skill in dealing with other people. One of its greatest use is in connection with human relations training. It is also used in sales training as well. It is spontaneous acting of a realistic situation involving two or more persons under class-room situations. Dialogue spontaneously grows out of the situation. It is developed by the trainees assigned to it. Other trainees in the group serve as observers or critics. Since people act roles every day, they are somewhat experienced in this art. With a certain amount of imagination they project themselves into roles other than their own. As a manager is regularly acting roles in his relationship with others, it is essential for him to have role awareness and to do role thinking so that they may size up each relationship and develop the most effective interaction position. By role-playing a trainee can broaden his experiences by trying different approaches, while in actual situation, he often has only one chance.

(*ii*) *Gaming*: It simulates the problems of running a company or even a particular department. It is used for a variety of training objectives, from investment strategy, collective bargaining techniques, to the morale of clerical personnel. It is used at all the levels, from the executives to the production supervisors. It is a laboratory method in which role-playing exists. But it focuses attention on administrative problems, while role-playing tends to emphasise feeling tone between people in interaction. It involves several terms, each of which is given a firm to operate for a number of periods. Usually the period is short one, one year or so. In each period each team makes decisions on various matters such as fixation of price, level of production, inventory level, and so forth. Since each team competes with others, each firm's decisions are fed into a computer which is programmed to behave somewhat like a real market. The computer provides the results. The team which has accumulated largest profit is the winner. Strength and weakness of decisions are analysed in the light of such result.

(B) *Sensitivity Training*: It is the most controversial laboratory training method. Some of its advocates exhibit an almost religious zeal in their enhancement with the training group experience. Some of its critics match this fervour in their attacks on the technique. As a result of criticism and experience it is somewhat revised. It was first used by National Training Laboratories at Bethel, U.S.A. The training groups called themselves 'T Group'. Since then its use has been extended to other organisations, universities and institutes.

DIFFERENT TRAINING FOR DIFFERENT LEVELS

The basic objective of training programme for a particular level differs from that of other level. Rank and file employees need specific job training while management group needs broad-based training. Thus, a particular training programme would be suitable only to a particular group of people. Again, within a particular group, an individual may need a particular training while others may need some other programme. Thus, the training programme would be determined by the level of an individual in the organisation and his own personality characteristics. The level is more emphasised to assessing the suitability of training programmes.

Levels of Employees

The entire personnel of an organisation may broadly be classified into the following three levels:

1. Rank and File Level: Most extensive of all training programmes are those designed to meet the needs of rank and file employees. They require training either at the time of entry or to keep pace with the technological development at subsequent time. Such training is mostly of technological nature. Pre-employment training may involve preparation, not for a single job, but for the many types of related jobs that may be given to workers subsequently. Retraining or refresher courses may be given as a means of avoiding personnel obsolence.

2. Supervisory Level: The practice of management begins where a trainee is assigned to supervisory position. The new incumbent practises with full responsibility for results over a range of time what he has learned about supervision. He thus refines his peculiar techniques of inter-personnel relationships. His career depends upon his developed skills. Outstanding men become candidates for promotion to middle-management positions. Candidates for frontline supervisory positions and incumbent supervisors need the same kind of training opportunities. They need to know how to develop and carry out approved programmes within a budget to obtain and use service and staff help, and to meet the requirements of their superior managers.

3. Management Level: Management level differs from supervisory groups in the training need. People at this level do not have any direct contact with working force. Their outlook is broad-based. Management group may further be divided into following two levels—middle management and top management.

(*i*) *Middle Management*: The men to enter the middle management group are generally supervisors who have had several years of on-the-job practice. These are most in need of knowledge of management theory. On the practical side, they know much about management informally. Now, when they are about to manage managers and not technicians, they can no longer rely on their technical proficiency to get things done. To manage managers, they need a comprehensive understanding of the functions of managers because these are the means they must utilise to accomplish their job.

(*ii*) *Top Management*: Men to be trained at top management level are normally functional managers who are candidates for general management positions. They have stepped up the promotion ladder within their division. They require training in the management of functions which are strange to them. They are required to have a substantial grounding in the fundamentals and techniques of management. As the knowledge and technical aspects of managing are rapidly changing, it is one of the objectives of top management training to review management theory and principles and the updating of knowledge and technical development in managing.

TRAINING PROGRAMMES FOR VARIOUS LEVELS

Following specific training programmes may be recommended for people at various levels:

I. **For rank and file employees:** 1. Job training 2. Apprenticeship 3. Pre-employment training 4. Retraining.

II. **For supervisory levels:** 1. Supervisory skills training 2. Coaching 3. Special courses and classes 4. Conferences 5. Job rotation 6. Brainstorming 7. Case studies 8. Special projects and task forces 9. Simulation role-playing 10. Sensitivity training.

III. **For management level:** 1. Coaching 2. Special courses and classes 3. Conferences 4. Job rotation 5. Brainstorming 6. Committee assignments 7. Selective reading 8. Understudy 9. Case studies 10. Multiple management 11. Simulation role-playing, gaming 12. Sensitivity training.

IV. **For All Levels:** 1. Job experience 2. Induction and orientation.

STAGES OF ORGANISATION OF TRAINING PROGRAMME IN A LARGE CONCERN

1. Assessing training needs in the enterprise: This is done on the basis of identifying organisational and production problems, analysing jobs and men, anticipating future problems, using check-lists for nature and extent of training. This assessment will help in determining as to how many persons are to be trained and what kind of training is necessary for them.

2. Contents of training: This depends upon the major types of employees who are to be trained. Five distinctive groups of employees may be noted: rank and file, supervisory staff, middle management and top management. Rank and file employees have no administrative or supervisory duties. Supervisory staff is composed of specialised technical and professional persons attached to the operating line to provide counsel and aid. Various types of training should be outlined on the basis of these distinctions. Organisational analysis, operational analysis and workers analysis techniques help in determining the contents and scope of training.

3. Selection of training method: Training method should be ascertained with the advice of personnel manager and high officials about the system which will suit the training.

4. Preparation of training: This involves two stages:

(*i*) *Preparation of the trainer*: A trainer must be ready before the start of the training. He should ascertain as to what is to be taught and by which method. The success of a training programme depends to a large extent on the interest and capabilities of the instructors.

(*ii*) *Preparation of trainees*: A trainee is the person to whom training is to be imparted. Trainee must be mentally prepared to learn. Training must recognize individual difference in abilities, interest, learning speed and other significant personnel characteristics.

5. Rule for conducting the training: The following rules should be observed while imparting training:

(*i*) *Proper time-table*: The instructor must prepare time-table of the training and only one sub-job should taught in one instance.

(*ii*) *Orderly jobs*: All jobs should be orderly. This order should be made to understand and time for each sub-job should be distributed.

(*iii*) *Personal care of trainee:* Every trainee should be personally cared.

(*iv*) *Clear work*: Work should be made clearfully and legibly. Important points should be stressed. For this all orders should be clear.

(*v*) *Timing*: Work should be clearly and slowly told, *i.e.*, one action or sub -action told at a time.

(*vi*) *Employment on job*: Trainee should be employed on work. He should be asked questions while working and mistakes should be removed.

(*vii*) *Left alone for working*: After some time, when the trainee works he should be left alone for working.

6. Examination of the trainee's job: Trainee's job should be examined while working. It he makes mistakes, he should be told. After that he should be asked to repeat the whole work again. He should repeat the work till he gets competence in it.

7. Follow-up: The trainee should be allowed to work after the whole training. Later on, his work should be checked. He should be provided necessarily guidance and help in case of any difficulty. Regularity and vigilance are the key to a successful training programme.

PRINCIPLES OF TRAINING

1. Objectives and needs: Training programme should be designed so as to achieve the pre-determined objectives, goals and needs of the organisations.

2. Universal applicability: Training programme should be developed for all in the organisation and not for a particular group.

3. Well organised: Taking in view the objectives, training programme should be pre-planned and well organised. For this purpose, the whole task should be divided in various sub-activities. Such sub-activities should be arranged in a systematic order.

4. According to traits of the concern: Training programme should be designed according to the traits of the concern such as size, natural and financial position. A small-scale enterprise cannot afford a training programme.

5. Flexible: Training programme must be flexible.

6. Conducted by senior and experienced officer: Training programme must be conducted by a senior and experienced officer of the concern. In large-scale enterprises, training is conducted by the training director who is incharge of the training section under personnel department. The training director is well-trained and experienced in the art of training.

7. Consideration to both theoretical and practical: Both the theoretical and practical aspects of training must be given due consideration while preparing a training programme. Theory and practice must go hand in hand. Teaching of theory without the knowledge of its application looses the interest of trainees. Practice without theoretical knowledge may not enable the trainees to think for themselves.

8. Incorporation of recent trends: Training should be designed in such a fashion as to incorporate the recent trends developed in the industrial field. Psychological researches may guide the conducting of a programme. The main purpose of the training programme should be to enable the employee to pick up the training.

9. Catering to all Interests: Training programme should be designed after taking in view the interests of both the employer and the employees. Their group interests should not suffer.

10. More than one methods: It is not necessary to follow a single method of training for all employees. As the purpose of training is to develop the men and not the methods, therefore, more than one method may be followed side by side for different groups.

11. Motivation of workers: The main purpose of the training programme should be to motivate the worker to learn something to improve his job performance. Therefore, monetary and non-monetary reward such as promotion or a better job must be expected at the conclusion of the learning process.

12. Allowance for individual difference: This should be made because training needs differ from person to person depending upon the ability, learning capacity, interests and traditional and emotional make-up of trainees.

A sound training programme should be developed on the basis of above principles. Incidentally, these are also traits or qualities of a proper training programme.

EVALUATION OF TRAINING EFFECTIVENESS

The effectiveness of training is determined by all the three partners in it: 1. The institution imparting formal training, 2. The participants, and 3. The word organisation. All the three should be evaluated before and after the training. This may be done as follows:

1. Training programmes: The basic question for evaluation of the training programme is: to what extent did the programme achieve its objectives? A training programme is started with certain objectives. Its success can be measured in this context after the programme is over.

McMurry has suggested eight tests that must be met by any successful management training programme: (1) train candidates for specific positions, (2) define necessary qualities and skills, (3) include only trainees with adequate potential, (4) carefully determine which qualities can be developed through training, (5) use tested and proved techniques and procedure, (6) assure qualified trainers, (7) assure adequate trainee motivation, and (8) demonstrate results of the programme.

Evaluation at the end of the programme disclose the new knowledge, understanding and skill that the participants have gained during training. At various stages of the post-training phase the same kind of data show how stable these gains are and to what extent they have survived transfer to the work situation.

2. Training objectives: If the objectives were inadequately formulated even a good training programme has no chance to be effective. Sometimes this is due to faulty job analysis. Sometimes participants are shifted from one work to another so frequently that no one job analysis or training may be relevant to their future work. For example, I.A.S. personnel exposed to civil administration in their training programmes, fail miserably when they are given charge of business organisations. Thus, training failure happens whenever training objectives are not rooted in definite plan. Thus, changes on the job or when the change occurs as a whole, failures happen through inadequate organisational commitment and support.

3. Deliberate policy: A deliberate policy is required which may guide the establishment and revision of training objectives. If the policy is realistic, clear, regular and of frequent evaluation followed by marginal adjustments it can keep training objectives in tune with shifting needs. This assumes a close relationship between he training institution and the work organisation.

4. Training Institution: Evaluation of training objectives is the responsibility of the work organisation. The training institution may contribute procedural experience and consistent and sustained interest. Collaboration between the organisation and the institution ensures rapid use of evaluation results in selection and preparation of participants in programme designs and in preparing the organisation for change.

5. Participants: With the training objectives formulated clearly in terms of changes to be effected at work, the work organisation is in a position to evaluate the effect of training on individual participants. This can be done in the context of precisely defined training objective. The objective may be changed in behavioural approach. Some behavioural approach may be immediate and direct, and the other secondary, less direct, and more obviously subject to hazards of contamination. The impact of training may be to evaluate in parts by direct measurement of the time required for the trainee to reach the accepted standard of productivity. It may also be expected to influence through less direct behaviour, work attitudes, morale and turnover. All these secondary outputs are subject in the influence of many other factors. Some of these may not become evident for some time.

TRAINING PROGRAMME

Exchanges for Physically Handicapped

There are 18 special exchanges for the physically handicapped, functioning at Ahmedabad, Banglore, Bhubaneshwar, Bombay, Calcutta, Chandigarh (one for Punjab and another for Haryana), Delhi, Hyderabad, Jabalpur, Jaipur, Kanpur, Madras, Patna, Shimla, Gawahati, Trivandrum and Agartala.

Ten vocational rehabilitation centres for the physically handicapped are functioning in Ahmedabad, Bombay, Calcutta, Delhi, Hyderabad, Jabalpur, Kanpur, Ludhiana, Madras and Trivandrum.

In order to divert educated youth to channels of gainful employment, vocational guidance and career advising programme of the Directorate General of Employment and Training (DGE&T) have been expanded and streamlined.

(*i*) *CIRTES*: A career study centre at the Central Institute for Research and Training (CIRTES) provides career literature for the occupational orientation of the youth and other guidance seekers. CIRTES also imparts training in employment services, procedure, vocational guidance and seminars for the personnel of national employment service. It is also engaged in conducting research studies in several areas and fields of employment service.

(*ii*) *Training Programmes*: In an endeavour to build up the career of young persons in their adolescence, the DGE&T has evolved various training programmes. These are formulated within the national framework as far as possible and also in collaboration with foreign countries.

(*iii*) *Studies/Surveys*: During 1977-78, the DGE&T completed the survey on the employment status of apprentices trained under the Apprentices Act, 1961. Besides this, two important surveys *viz.*, (1) Study on the margin of error in the employment data collected under the EMI Programme, and (2) study on the characteristics of the hard core of job seekers on the live register of employment exchanges, are under progress.

(*iv*) *Craftsmen Vs Training*: Industrial training institutes have been set up all over the country to impart skills in 32 engineering and 21 non-engineering trades to youngmen and women in the age group 15-25. At present 466 such introduced aptitudes tests are applied for the selection of craftsmen. Training is also conducted in 274 private institutes affiliated to the National Council for Training in Vocational Trades. To promote the efficiency of craftsmen-trainees, the DGE&T has introduced aptitude tests which are applied for the selection of craftsmen-trainees in engineering trade. During 1977, aptitude tests were conducted in 19 engineering trades for the selection of trainees in industrial training institutes including model training institutes in state. The aptitude testing programme has also been extended to industries in different regions for selecting suitable candidates as apprentices under the Apprentices Act, 1961.

The duration of the courses varies from one to two years for engineering trades, but is one year for all non-engineering trades. Successful candidates are awarded National Trade Certificates.

2. Industrial Training Institutions: Besides 53 trades, the State governments and union territories have introduced training in additional trades to meet the requirements of the new industries established in their areas.

The educational qualification for admission in the industrial training institutes in most of the trades under the Craftsmen's Training Scheme is 8th standard or two classes below the matriculation or its equivalent. For some trades, such as electronics, radio and TV, electricians, Draftsmen (mechanical/civil) and surveyors, the minimum qualifications is matriculation or its equivalent with mathematics and science.

The industrial training institutes have also started a scheme to train other ranks in the Indian Army to facilitate their rehabilitation in civil life on their release and retirement from service.

3. Craft Instructors Training: Six central training institutes at Bombay, Calcutta, Hyderabad, Kanpur, Ludhiana and Madras craft instructors required by the Industrial Training Institutions and the Apprenticeship Training Establishment. The six institutes, with an admission capacity of 1,136 impart training in a number of trades. Facilities for the training of instructors have also been provided in chemical group of trades at the Bombay Institute, and in hotel-catering the Hyderabad institute. Facilities for training in printing, weaving and farm mechanics trades are also being provided at institutes in Kanpur, Bombay and Ludhiana respectively. A model training institute is attached to each of the Central Training Institute, which provides practical training for instructors.

4. Advanced Vocational Training System: A project called 'advanced vocational training system' has been launched for training of highly skilled workers and technicians in a variety of advanced and sophisticated skills not available from other vocational training programmes. The system has been introduced in vocational training Institutes for Instructors located at Bombay, Calcutta, Hyderabad, Kanpur and Ludhiana, Advanced Training Institute at Madras and 16 selected Industrial Training Institutes located at Coimbatore, Bangalore, Vadodara, Dhanbad, Durgapur, Faridabad, Guwahati, Jabalpur. Jammu, Jodhpur, Kalamessary, Meerut, Patiala, Pune, Rai-Bareily and Visakapatnam. These institutes are being modernised and developed into Model Training Institutes to enable them to conduct various advanced courses under the scheme. The Advanced Training Institute at Madras is functioning as the Apex and the five Central Training Institutes where the system has been introduced serve as Regional Institutes for the country as a whole. So far about 3,000 highly skilled workers have been trained under the scheme.

An advanced training institute for electronics and process instrumentation has been established at Hyderabad to train highly skilled technicians in field such as domestic/industrial/medical/electronics and process instrumentation.

5. Foremen's Training: An institute to train foremen was establishment in Bangalore in 1971. It trains existing and potential shop foreman and supervisors in theoretical and managerial skills and workers from industry in advanced technical skills. The facilities generated at this institute are being made available through the Central Training Institute, Bombay, also. A part time evening course has also been introduced on the modular system at the Foremen Training Institute, Bangalore.

6. Apprenticeship Training Scheme: The Apprentices Act, 1961 makes it obligatory for employers in specified industries to engage apprentices. The training consists of basic training followed by on-the-job or shop-floor training in accordance with standards prescribed by the government in consultation with the Central Apprenticeship Council. So far 217 industries and 131 trades have been brought under the Act. The Apprentices (Amendment) Act, 1973 provides for reservation of seats for scheduled caste and scheduled tribe candidates as well as for improving the employment potential of engineering graduates and diploma holders.

About 16791 establishments are implementing the Act. About 1.22 lakhs trained apprentices undergo training in various trades. Fiftyseven subject fields in engineering/technology have been designated and about 11,396 graduate and diploma holders apprentices undergo training in the various subject fields.

7. Part Time Training to Industrial Workers: Along with the expansion of facilities for the training of craftsmen in institutes and through the apprenticeship programme, even classes have been organised to improve the standards of industrial workers who may enter the industry without any systematic training.

Industrial workers, irrespective of their age, but possessing two years' workshop experience in a particular trade and sponsored by their employers are eligible for admission to this course. The period of training is two years and the fee charged is ₹ 2 per month. Courses are conducted in six Central Training Institutes and 32 Industrial Training Institutes.

8. Vocational Training Research: A Central Staff Training and Research Institute was set up at Calcutta in 1970 for developing indigenous training techniques. The Institute conducts training programmes for officers and staff of the central and state governments as well as from industry who control, regulate and direct training programmes. It also carries out research in trades and training techniques, prepares training aids, and advises industry on industrial training methods.

9. Vocational Training Programme for Women: The Central Training Institute for Women at New Delhi has been upgraded into a National Vocational Training Institute for Women. The Institute provides instructor training, basic training and advanced training in selected trades particularly suitable for women. Two Regional Vocational Training Institutes for Women have also been set up at Bombay and Bangalore.

QUESTIONS FOR EXCERCISE

1. What do you understand by training of workers? Describe the different methods of training?
2. What is the importance of training in industry? Explain the different methods of training which are generally used in industries now-a-days.
3. Explain the importance of workers' training. How will you organise a training programme in a large industry?
4. Explain the utility of training as a tool to the management control. Evaluate the various methods of training the industrial workers.
5. What is the relationship between training programmes and employee level? Discuss.
6. How will you organise a training programme in a large industry? Explain the importance of workers training.
7. What are the principles of training? How will you evaluate training effectiveness in an organisation?

23

Industrial Disputes

The industrial dispute is unrest in labour which expresses itself in many ways and forms. The most striking feature of the labour unrest expressed itself in the form of strikes or stoppage of work. As a result of strike the factories are closed down and this proves harmful both to employees and employers. In order to prevent such colossal waste the government tries to prevent or minimize the strikes. A strike by workers is followed by lock out by the industrialists. Both strike and lock out are manifestations of industrial conflict and tension between the employer and employees. Besides strikes, the unrest among labour may manifest itself in demonstrations, taking out processions, enlisting support of politicians etc. Many political parties today are vying with each other to gain domination over labour movement and capture the control of trade unions.

CONSEQUENCES OF INDUSTRIAL DISPUTES

1. Unrest: As we have already mentioned, industrial conflicts and disputes lead to widespread unrest in social life and also disruption of political harmony and peace.

2. Economic loss: The industrial disputes most obviously injure the economic interest of both the employees and employers. This effect is direct and palpable. Both indirectly and in a subtle way these also prove economically harmful to nation as a whole. Everyone is ultimately affected.

3. Economic depression: The industrial disputes are not only harmful to the industry involved but lead to all-round economic depression. A closure of one industry lead to the reduction of demand of goods of other industries or trades. For example, closure of textile industry would lead to drastic reduction in the demand of cotton.

4. Workers' hardships: The majority of workers in India do not earn enough to be able to save something for the rainy days. They are hand to mouth, if not worse. Therefore, strikes and lock outs put unbearable burden on them and they are reduced to the level of beggars.

5. Threat to social security and public peace: If industrial disputes spread in an epidemic form they pose threat to public peace.

If the tension among workers and employers mounts and takes serious form, the workers are liable to become violent or indulge in sabotage. This may compel the employer to take the help of police force and this may still further aggravate the tension which may manifest itself in the form of rioting, looting and arson. This surely disturbs the public peace. If a strike becomes a prestige issue and is long drawn, the workers may face starvation. This may compel them to beggary and other social crimes.

CAUSES OF INDUSTRIAL DISPUTES

1. Low wages: In India, the remuneration paid to workers for their work is not adequate to meet their expenses. They can neither provide for the education of their children nor can they feed them properly. Their living conditions are deplorable. Their future is uncertain and a deep sense of insecurity pervades their life. With the death of the earning member the dependents are reduced to penury and compelled to take to beggary, prostitution and other social evils. The low wages are the main reason of discontent among the workers. It is this discontent which ultimately expresses itself in the form of industrial disputes and tensions.

2. Rising prices: If we review the statics regarding the wages of workers in India we find that in most states the wages have doubled. For example, in 1954, the average annual income of workers in Andhra Pradesh was ₹ 595 which in the year 1964 rose to ₹ 1,097. However, the doubling of income has brought no relief to the workers; because whereas the wages have gone up by 200%, the prices have risen 400%. Thus, the real income of the workers has in fact dropped sharply. After the Second World War, the prices of commodities have been steadily rising, eroding the real earning of the workers. Therefore, this inflationary spiral has made the workers poorer still. This obviously produces tension and conflict among workers.

3. Absence of link with D.A, and price rise: The various trade unions in India have been clamouring for 100% neutralization of prices rise by corresponding increase in the dearness allowance. This, however, has not happened in all industries. This is a great source of conflict and tension between workers and their employers.

4. Unsatisfactory working conditions: Another cause of industrial disputes is the fact that the working conditions in most of the factories are unhygienic and poor in respect of lighting and ventilation. This tells upon the health of the workers. They are mostly suffering from some or the other chronic ailment. Being ill and unhealthy they are depressed and irritable. This makes them permanently discontented.

5. Demand for leave with pay: Like workers everywhere the industrial workers, too, need holiday from work from time to time. Therefore, Trade Unions press for a permanent provision of regular leaves with pay. This is also a source of contention among workers and employers.

6. Resistance to misconduct of officers: Today there is sufficient awakening among the workers and they are very conscious of self-respect and preserve it jealously. Therefore, any slight or insult by officers provokes them. Such incidents many at time ignite fire of conflict and tension which takes the form of gheraos etc.

7. Demand for adequate bonus: The political leaders and trade unionists have inspired the workers to think and believe that they are partners in mills and factories and that they are fully entitled to share the profits earned by the factory as a result of their labour. Though in many industries bonus is being paid now, but the amount or percentage of bonus is a source of frequent disputes among workers and employers.

8. Demand for re-instatement: At times the employers arbitrarily retrench many workers and this naturally is resisted by the affected workers. Besides, other workers are made to feel insecure. Therefore, the workers resist such moves. They stand united and agitate for the re-instatement of the retrenched colleagues.

9. Non-recognition of Trade unions: Sometimes employers refuse to recognise the trade unions in their factories. This too becomes a source of contention and conflict and may result in strikes etc.

10. Retrenchment due to sophisticated machinery: In modern industries many new and sophisticated machines are installed. These machines are labour-saving, Naturally, therefore, as a result of these there is retrenchment of workers. Recently there was great hue and cry in the Life Insurance Corporation of India due to installation of computers.

11. Political causes: A major cause of industrial disputes is political machinations. Now-a-days various political parties in India vie with each other to gain sympathy and support of workers and for this reason go out of way to support all types of agitations and even foment discontent among them.

12. Misconduct of intermediates: In many industries there is no direct contact between the employer and the workers. The workers are recruited through intermediaries or brokers. These brokers usually subject workers to various kinds of humiliation and exploitation. In resentment to these foul tactics the workers start agitations and launch other forms of protests.

The foregoing discussion of the causes of industrial disputes in India makes it clear that the problem of labour unrest is quite complex. The worker is a human being and as a human being he feels discontented and frustrated if his day-to-day needs are not met properly. If the workers are given adequate wages, there is improvement of working conditions. If brokers and political agents are eliminated the chances of conflict and tensions among workers and employers will be greatly minimized.

METHODS OF REDUCING INDUSTRIAL CONFLICT

1. Trade unionism: Usually the workers face problems of which the employers are the least aware. The brokers subject them to humiliation and emploit them in so many ways. This does not come to the notice of the employers or authorities. Unless the workers are well organized they cannot get their problems redressed. It is the task of trade unions to keep watch on the workers and help them to get redress for their grievances. In the presence of trade unions the workers feel mentally secure and this indirectly boosts production.

2. Direct contact between workers and employers: As we have had the occasion to refer to earlier, in many industries there is no direct contact between the employer and the workers and the employer is usually unaware of the problems faced by his employees. Therefore, even when the employers are considerate and sympathetic to workers they are unable to render great help because they are unaware of the real problems faced by the workers. Exploiting this lack of contact between workers and employers, the political parties and brokers exploit the workers against the employees to grind their own axe. The best means of resolving this problem is to establish direct contact between the employees and employers.

3. Conciliation Boards: A modern method of reducing industrial tension and conflicts is the establishment of Conciliation Boards. Such Boards are constituted by persons nominated by workers, employers and Government. Whenever there is some point of dispute between workers and employers the matter is referred to these Boards. They try to resolve the dispute and the finding common ground between the points of view of workers and employers. Such Boards have already been established all over India. In the Centre the Chief Labour Commissioner and in the states the Labour Commissioners head such Boards.

4. Joint Committees: Another method usually employed to resolve disputes among employers and workers is to set up Joint Committees consisting of the representatives of employers, workers and public. These committees meet from time to time and try to remove misunderstandings between the workers and employers. Such Joint Committees were established in 1957 and now their number is above 145.

5. Tripartite Committees: As the word tripartite implies, these committees are composed of labour experts besides the nominees of the employers and workers. These persons try to sort out amicably the various misunderstandings and disputes which crop up from time to time.

6. Labour Courts: Sometimes the disputes between workers and employers cannot be amicably resolved by any of the above-mentioned committees or the Conciliation Board. In order to decide such complex issues government has set up labour courts which decide the issues according to law. In India the Chief Labour Court is in Dhanbad. In Delhi, Dhanbad and Bombay there is one Industrial Tribunal each.

7. Industrial Truce: Under emergency conditions governments can declare industrial truce for a specified period. During this period there can be no strike or lock outs or any other form of agitation.

By the above-mentioned means an attempt is made to settle industrial disputes. However, the conditions are still not very satisfactory. The government of India has enacted many laws to improve the condition of workers. In 1881, 1891, 1911, 1922, 1934 and 1943 government made factory laws and in 1923 and 1952 it enacted laws regarding workers in the mining industry. In 1951, a law was passed governing the conditions of work of workers working in orchards. In 1923, Shipping law was enacted; this was modified in 1942 and 1951. In 1948, an Act was passed to improve the working conditions of P and T workers. Besides the above central legislations, the States have also passed many laws protecting the interests of workers in shop establishments etc.

In spite of the above measures the condition of workers is not satisfactory, because by money and prestige the employers are able to exploit workers in numerous ways without attracting the provisions of law. In spite of Compensation Act 1923, the workers do not receive adequate compensation. There are apparently many improvements made by employers but in fact conditions remain more or less as before.

SETTLEMENT OF INDUSTRIAL DISPUTES

Before independence Government was not concerned over the settlement of industrial disputes as conflicts were looked upon as a problem of law and order. But since independence, Government paid attention in this direction and passed the Industrial Disputes Act, 1947. It was amended several times under which was outlined machinery for the prevention and settlement of disputes. These provisions are as under:

1. Establishment of Works Committees: In every industrial establishment employing 100 or more workers, it is compulsory to establish a works committee to promote the measures for securing and preserving unity and good relations between the parties. There are equal number of representatives of workers and employer on the committee. The main function of the committee is to remove causes of friction between the two parties which concern the factory life of workers. No mention of functions of works committee have been made in the Act. However, in 1960 a tripartite committee of Indian Labour Conference prepared two lists of functions, one for works to be dealt with and the other for works not to be dealt with by the works committees. The works committee is to discuss such problems relating to grievances, complaints, matters of discipline, welfare problems such as health, safety, training, education and other personal problems which vitally affect the interests of the workers in general. The functions of these committees are purely of advisory character. No legal obligation is imposed upon employers to carry out the decisions arrived at in the meeting of the works committee.

2. Grievance Settlement Authority: The Industrial Disputes (Amendment) Act, 1982 has provided for the setting up of a Grievance Settlement Authority and for reference of certain individual disputes to such authorities. Any employer employing 50 or more workers is required to provide for a Grievance Settlement Authority for settlement of industrial dispute relating to an individual. Where such dispute arises, the concerned worker or the trade union, of which he is member, may refer the dispute to the Authority for settlement. Any such reference shall not be referred to Board or Tribunal.

3. Conciliation Officer: The appointment of conciliation officer is made by the State Government for a particular region or industries in the state. This officer is to bring the two parties together and help them resolve their differences. He can do everything to settle the dispute between the two parties amicably. He is bound to take decision within 14 days or such period as extended by the State Government from the date of registration of dispute. If the dispute is settled through his good offices and an agreement is reached, he should send a report to the Government along with a memorandum of settlement signed by the parties to the dispute. If the dispute is not settled he should inform the Government about his failure, steps taken and the reasons for not being successful.

4. Conciliation Board: In case, the conciliation officer fails to resolve the dispute, the Government appoints a board of conciliation on *ad hoc* basis for a particular dispute consisting of a chairman and two to four persons representing the employer and the employees to bring the parties to disputes to sit together and thrash out their differences as referred to by the Government. The board reports the Government about the success or failure of its efforts, steps taken and reasons for its failure to bring about a settlement within 2 months from the date of reference of the dispute.

5. Court of Inquiry: Whenever an industrial dispute remains unresolved by the conciliation officer and the board of conciliation, the matter is referred to a court of inquiry. The court may consist of one or more independent persons. It will investigate the whole dispute and submit its report to the Government on the matters referred to it ordinarily within 6 months from the date of commencement of inquiry.

If settlement is not arrived at by the efforts of the above machinery, a three-tier machinery for compulsory adjudication is provided under the Act. These are three types of semi-judicial bodies, *i.e.*, Labour Courts, Industrial Tribunals and National Tribunals.

(*i*) *Labour courts*: Labour courts have been set up by the State governments to go into the disputed orders of the employer's dismissal, discharge and suspensions of employees by the management, legality or otherwise of any order passed by an employer under the standing order, withdrawal of any concession or privilege, legality or otherwise of any strike or lock out etc. These courts will award decisions and send report to the Government.

(*ii*) *Industrial tribunals*: The State Government have been empowered to appoint as many industrial tribunals as they think proper, for the adjudication of disputes selecting to wages, hours of work and rest, intervals, leave with pay, holidays, compensatory and other allowances, bonus, profit sharing, provident fund, gratuity, discipline, retrenchment, closure of establishment etc. The tribunal will consist of a person of the rank of a high court judge. The adjudication of these tribunals is binding on both the parties.

(*iii*) *National tribunal*: National tribunal is set up by the Central Government for the adjudication of industrial disputes which involve questions of national importance or which affect industrial establishments situated in more than one state. It gives decisions on matters referred to it by the Central Government. If any matter is referred to the National Tribunal by the Central Government the labour courts and industrial courts are barred from entertaining such disputes and if any such dispute is pending before labour courts or tribunals, it shall be deemed to be quashed.

QUESTIONS FOR EXERCISE

1. Explain the nature and consequences of industrial disputes. Analyse their causes.
2. What are the methods of reducing industrial conflict? How are industrial disputes settled in India?

24

Trade Unionism in India

DEFINITION OF TRADE UNION

1. *R.A. Lester*: "Trade union is an association of employees designed primarily to maintain or improve the conditions of employment of its members."

2. *G.D.H. Cole*: "In common parlance a trade union means an association of workers in one or more occupation, carried on mainly for the purpose of protecting and advancing the member's economic interests in connection with their daily work."

3. *Webb*: "Trade Union is a "continuous association of wage earners for the purpose of maintaining and improving the conditions of their working lives."

Thus, A labour union or trade union is an organisation of workers to promote, product and improve, through collective action the social, economic and political interests of its member. The workers form an association in order to protect and safeguard their economic interests and put up a united resistance against exploitation by the industrialists. The most outstanding feature of the trade unions is their own accord. Generally, all workers in a particular occupations are the members of the trade union representing their occupation. But there is no element of compulsion in membership. If a worker so desires he can stay away from the trade union.

OBJECTIVES OF TRADE UNIONS

1. To increase the co-operative feeling: In sophisticated modern industrial complexes, thousands of workers are engaged simultaneously. However, the modern industrial system is so complex that all jobs are highly specialized. As a consequence of extreme departmentalization and division of work there is growth of individualism in modern industry. The relations between workers are ceasing to be personal and are becoming increasingly impersonal and formal. There is no common or uniting thread or unifying bond between workers. Even in one industry there is no homogeneity among workers, they hail from different regions, speak different tongues and profess different religions. Under these circumstances the first and foremost task of the trade unions is to promote friendliness among workers and bind them in the thread of fellowship and brotherhood. The Trade unions provide a forum for the workers to come together and know each other. All common problems are discussed in one form. Besides discussing problems connected with jobs, the trade unions also provide opportunity for play, relaxation and entertainment to workers. Thus, trade unions promote intimacy of relations among workers; make them sweet, personal and informal.

2. To secure facilities for workers: The majority of industrialists are indifferent to the comforts and needs of the workers. They pay no attention to making the working conditions healthy and hygienic, to mental and physical relaxation of the workers. They are interested only in getting maximum work from the workers like toilet facility, canteen etc. Under these circumstances trade unions agitate for the provision of various facilities and see to it that these are provided for.

3. To establish contact among workers and employers: The industrial complexes today have grown into giants. A single unit may employ hundreds of workers. Under these circumstances the line between employers, high managerial cadre and employees gets broken down. Many a time workers may not have seen even the face of their employer. Under these conditions the workers are not in a position to express their grievances before their employers nor do the employers have any means to know the difficulties being faced by their employees. The trade unions play the important role of bringing to the notice of employers the grievances and difficulties of the employees. The trade unions also try to arrange face to face meeting between employers and employees. Thus, better relations are established between employers and employees through the medium of trade unions.

4. To work for the progress of employees: The urban life is much different from the rural life. Most of the workers hail from villages; but after finding jobs in cities they have no residences in the cities. In cities they need a good bit of money for establishing themselves. The trade unions try to improve the economic conditions of workers and remove their hardships and handicaps. For increase in their wages, the unions represent their case before the employers and also try to get adequate bonus for the workers. The unions also try to get overtime wages to the workers.

5. To safeguard the interests of workers: Under ordinary conditions the employers tend to exploit the workers to the maximum. They care nothing for the employees; they do not give them any paid leaves and if a worker goes on leave the wages for the period of leave are deducted from the monthly wage bill of the workers. Besides, workers are denied all chances of promotion. For a very long period the workers have to work on the same post. In many industries the workers are not made permanent even after a long period of service. They are removed from services summarily. The trade unions try to protect the workers from all such eventualities. They try to secure to workers the benefits of leave, permanency and promotion. The trade unions see to it that the workers under their aegis are not shunted out summarily and that they receive all the benefits due to them.

6. To provide for labour welfare: In India the economic condition of the industrial workers are not too good. The labour class is backward in every respect. The standard of living is very low. The majority of workers are illiterate or semi-liberate. Moreover, they have large families and their condition is therefore much worse. They live in slums and eat coarse food only. It is the task of trade unions to promote the social and economic welfare of the labourers. The trade unions try to get them housing facilities and also try to arrange for the education of the children of workers. The trade unions also try to protect workers from evil habits.

FUNCTIONS OF TRADE UNIONS

Mr. Broughton has classified the functions of trade unions into three categories: (1) Inter-mural activities, (2) Extra-mural activities; and (3) Political activities.

1. Inter-mural activities: These include those activities of the trade unions which are carried on within the four walls of the organisation for the welfare of the members. These activities also include the efforts of the union which improve the employment and working conditions within the organization. Such activities are bargaining with the employer for better wages and working conditions and for workers participation in management, providing labour welfare activities, getting share in the profits of the organisation. Collective bargaining, group discussions, gherao and strikes are some of the tools which help the trade unions in getting their functions performed.

2. Extra-mural activities: Extra-mural activities are those which are performed outside the compound of the organisation for the general welfare of their members. Their main object is to seek their cooperation and help them in time of crisis. These include the provisions of sanitary houses, fair-price shops, library and reading rooms, entertainment etc. Trade unions provide facilities for the education of workers and their children and medical facilities etc. Such functions are also known as 'Fraternal activities or functions'. These activities very much depend upon the availability of funds.

3. Political activities: In today's world of democracy, trade unions play a very important role in the politics of the country. They send their representatives to the Legislative Assembly and Parliament through general elections so that they may safeguard their own interest.

CONDITIONS TO MAKE TRADE UNIONS USEFUL

1. Compulsory membership: The mainstay of a trade union is its organisational. In order to fortify and consolidate an organisation, it is essential that a trade union should have maximum membership. A trade union is an organisation of industrial workers. In order to make trade unions forceful instruments of labour welfare, it is essential that the workers should compulsorily become its members. It must be borne in mind in this connexion that a nominal membership is not enough. In order to render a trade union useful all workers should be actively associated with the work of the trade union. Every worker should consider the trade union as his or her own organisation and work relentlessly for its success.

2. Strong economic base: A trade needs not only members but money for its successful functioning. A trade union must have a strong economic base. The trade unions need large funds to support their members in emergency and during protracted strikes and lockouts. The trade unions have to support their members in the event of accident, disablement or in the event of suspension of workers by the employers. The trade unions have no special means of collecting funds. It is necessary therefore that each member must make his contribution regularly. The membership fee can be determined after taking various factors into account.

4. Freedom from external pressure: The trade unions must function as independent organizations; they should not be under any external pressure or control The various political parties try to bring trade unions under their domain by extending various baits. These political parties are not genuinely interested in workers' welfare; they have their own axes to grind. Besides, the pressure of political parties, trade unions should also safeguard themselves against any other type of pressure.

4. Spirit of unity and sacrifice: The true basis of a trade union is the spirit of unity and sacrifice in its members. It is on the strength of unity that trade unions are able to function. Besides general problems, the members of a trade union also have personal problems. For the redress of personal problems, unity among workers is most essential. Besides unity, the spirit of sacrifice is also needed. The money collected from all members may be very largely spent on few workers. Without a spirit of sacrifice such as action may not be feasible.

5. Capable leadership: Capable leadership is a *sine qua non* for the success and usefulness of the trade unions. The average worker in India is still illiterate. He is innocent of the complexities of urban life and the clever tricks of employers to exploit him. Therefore, it is very necessary that a group of such simple fellows should have capable and selfless leadership. Some trade union leaders are quite selfish and they are dangerous to the well being of workers. Instead of giving workers proper guidance these leaders use them for their narrow selfish ends. Thus, it is very necessary that the leadership of trade unions should be in the hands of selfless workers and persons genially interested in the welfare of workers. Besides that, it is also very necessary that the leadership of workers should be in the hands of workers and not professionals. Only a worker is capable of understanding fully the problems of workers; a professional has not first-hand knowledge of their difficulties. Above all, a labour leader should be fully conversant with labour laws and bye-laws.

6. Practical outlook: The main task of trade unions is to defend the interest of labour and to promote their economic and social welfare. But while trying to achieve these laudable aims it should also be borne in mind that these aims can be achieved only in the context of overall industrial prosperity. Therefore, the economic and monetary conditions prevailing in the industry have to be taken into account while trying to achieve economic propriety and the social well-being of workers. Thus, a trade union should adopt a practical and pragmatic attitude to all problems. Only if the demands are practical and relative to actual conditions can these be met; unreasonable demands will create unnecessary friction, disharmony and hardship to all concerned. The trade unions cannot afford to be wholly oblivious of the interest of the industrialists. The employers are entitled to legitimate profits and gain. Besides, it must also be borne in mind as to what sort of economic and social conditions are being faced by the society at any particular time. For example, during war the workers should not demand more wages nor should they press for reduction of workload. At times there is international economic depression. Under these conditions the demand of higher wages will be most unrealistic. In short, trade unions should relate their demands to prevalent conditions and not make extravagant and unrealistic demands.

7. Democratic outlook: The success of trade union requires democratic structure. By democratic structure what is meant is that in all crucial matters the opinion of each and every member of the trade union should be taken into account. This has another purpose. The worker in a vast industrial complex comes to look upon himself as a non-entity and feels sense of humilitation, whereas by exercising the privilege of vote in trade union affairs etc., he develops a sense of dignity and feels his importance. This feeling helps to keep up his morale. The leaders of trade unions should also be democratically chosen by workers themselves.

8. Constructive outlook: The trade union try to have the demands of workers fulfilled and this is their real aim. But it is essential that the trade unions should adopt constructive outlook for achieving this goal. Indeed the workers need not deem their industrialist bosses to be enemies but should try to settle their problems by mutual consultation in an amicable way. Some trade union leaders incite the workers, poison their minds against employers and instigate them to violence and subversion. This negative attitude is not desirable. Indeed the trade unions should adopt a policy which is mutually beneficial. As a matter of fact subversion does not pay. It is harmful for all concerned parties as well as for the whole society.

9. Freedom from policies: The utility of trade unions is greatly undermined by outside political interference. At times trade union leaders forget their true aims and indulge in politics. Such leaders deliver no benefit to workers, indeed they harm their interest. Thus, trade unions have limited resources and these should not be frittered away in politicking.

10. Aim of welfare: The welfare of workers should be the primary aim of trade unions. They should refrain from all such activities as are detrimental to the welfare of workers. The trade unions should spend their money on projects which are likely to contribute to the workers' welfare and help to raise their standard of living. Besides, they could provide for education and entertainment of workers.

HISTORY OF TRADE UNIONS IN INDIA

The history of trade union movement in India is not very long. From the industrial point of view India is very backward; and accordingly the history of trade union movement is relatively short. Indeed the trade union movement comes into being with industrial growth and development. In India the industrial development took place in the middle of the 19th century. After industrial development the first organization that came into being in industry was that of industrialists. The owners of the industries formed an organization. The industrialists organized themselves in order to protect and safeguard their interests; but there was no organization for the protection of interests of labour class. With further industrialization the exploitation of labour increased and a need for separate labour organization was felt. In organizing labour, the initiative was taken by certain social reformers. It is not very long since the labour organized itself. This history of labour movement is not more than one hundred year old. A systematic study of labour movement in India can be made by dividing it into two parts. In the first part the initial stages of labour movement would be studied and in the second the modern period.

History of Initial Stage of Labour Movement

The honour of organizing labour in India goes to M. S. S. Bengali. Mr. Bengali made first yeoman effort in 1875 to reform the deplorable conditions prevailing among the Indian labour. He also drew the attention of authorities to the pitiable situation of the labour. However, the efforts of Mr. Bengali did not bear much fruit and there was no substantial improvement in the lot of Indian labour.

In India the first Industries Act was promulgated in 1881 by Government of India. In 1881, Mr. Narayan-Meghji Lokhande made renewed efforts for reform in the conditions of Indian labour. Mr. Lokhande summoned a summit conference of workers engaged in mills in Bombay Presidency. In this conference the essential demands of labour were considered and a number of resolutions were passed. The major demand of this conference was that the workers should be granted a weekly holiday and given half an hour rest every day. Besides it was also insisted that workers suffering accidental injuries should be adequately compensated. The efforts of this conference bore some healthy fruits. Some industrialists accepted some of the above demands. As a consequence of success achieved by the conference Mr. Lokhande felt encouraged and he established a trade union in Bombay. He christened this organization "Bombay Mill Hands Association". He also helped publication of a labour magazine. This magazine was christened "Deenbandhu". Thus. Mr. Lokhande stood by the working class and did a great deal to improve their lot. But after the death of Mr. Lokhande, the momentum of the work being done by him was lost. Afterwards Railway employees organized themselves into a union.

In 1905 British Government, as a result of the diplomacy divided Bengal in two parts. The partition of Bengal was stoutly opposed by workers and social reformers. As a result of this protest a wave of awakening swept the working classes and they got organized. After the partition of Bengal and till 1909 a number or strikes on various issues were organized. In 1908 an eminent national leader Shri Lokmanya Tilak was imprisoned for six years. As a protest against this injustice a veiy big strike was organized. In this period a number of trade unions came into being. In Calcutta in 1905, the workers of printing presses organized themselves into a trade union. In Bombay in 1907, postal workers formed a trade union. A Labour Welfare Association was established in Bombay in 1910. This association did a number of good things for workers.

Modern History of Labour Movement

The modern history of labour movement in India dates from First World War. During war a wave of awakening swept the labour; they became conscious of their importance, role and worth. They also realized that they were entitled to certain rights and privileges. There were various causes of this awakening. Firstly, as a result of war there were radical changes in the industrial system and economic conditions. Secondly, many national leaders devoted particular attention to working classes. As a result of the efforts made by Lokmanya Tilak, Annie Besant and Gandhi, the working classes began to get organized. The non-co-operation movement launched by Gandhi deserves special mention in this connexion. As a result of the efforts made by Gandhiji, Ahmedabad Textile Labour Association was established. During these days a branch of International Labour Organization was established. After this, regular conferences of I. L. O. were started being held in India.

In 1920, Indian National Trade Union Congress was established. With the establishment of this trade union the labour movement in India received tremendous fillip. A special step towards progress was made in 1923. In 1923, the then Government passed Indian Trade Union Act. With the passage of this Act, the trade unions greatly benefitted. According to this Act all registered trade unions were granted constitutional recognition. The organization of trade unions underwent great change in 1926. In 1926, the leadership of trade unions went over to communists. The communists made radical changes in the policies and organization of trade unions and as a consequence of this the trade union divided itself into two. The workers owing allegiance to old leadership had peaceful and constructive outlook, whereas those owing allegiance to communists, had radical outlook. Owing to difference of outlook the two trade unions were virtually always at loggerheads. The mutual strife between unions was advantageous to the employers.

The mutual strife among trade unions went on increasing. In 1929, Indian National Trade Union Congress held its 10th session in Nagpur. This session was presided over by an eminent social reformer Pandit Jawaharlal Nehru. Subsequent to this session, some trade unions severed their connexion with the parent body. The unions which separated themselves from INTUC formed their own all India body under the name All India Trade Union Federation. The internecine struggle between trade unions did not limit itself upto here only. As a result of the mutual strife in 1931 a new all India Trade Union under the label All India Red Trade Union Congress came into being.

The mutual bickerings and strife among trade unions proved advantageous to employers and hurt the interests of workers. At Length in 1934, this mutual strife ended. In this year a grand session of Indian Trade Union Congress took place. This session was presided over by Pandit Harinath Shastri. In this session an agreement was reached between All India Red Trade Union Congress and Trade Union Congress. According to this agreement, All India Red Trade Union Congress was abolished. Subsequently in 1938 Trade Union Federation was also merged in Indian National Trade Union Congress. The credit for this agreement is due to a former President of India Shri V.V. Giri. Thus, once again in 1940 a united body of trade union was established. However, this mutual amity among unions proved to be short-lived and the Second World War brought to surface once again mutual dissensions and disagreements. Indian National Trade Union Congress opposed the war and condemned the government. However, leaders like M.N. Roy were opposed to this attitude and as a consequence, rift developed among leaders of INTUC. As a sequel to this rift 'Indian Trade Union Labour Federation' came into existence. This was headed by M.N. Roy. For a long time two parallel labour unions continued to function. The dissensions and conflicts among communists and Congressmen persisted and ultimately due to the efforts of Gulzarilal Nanda and Sardar Patel Indian National Trade Union Congress was established. An official survey in 1948 revealed that the membership of Indian National Trade Union Congress was 9,73,179 and that of All India Trade Union 8,15,011. As a result of this survey

Indian National Trade Union Congress was declared the representative union of Indian labour. Subsequently Communists also set up an all India Trade Union. This trade union was labelled Hind Mazdoor Sabha. This trade union of Communists did not also escape the scourage of rifts and dissensions and in 1949 it also split up into two groups. As a result of this split a new trade union came into being and this was named United Trade Union Congress. This trade union was headed by Professor K.T. Shah. In 1955, Jan Sangh also established a labour organization. The trade union under the aegis of Jan Sangh was known as 'Bhartiya Mazdoor Sangh'. Its headquarter was in Bhopal. Bhartiya Mazdoor Sangh was not a popular trade union. Another trade union has been established by Socialist Party and this is known as Hind Mazdoor Panchayat.

Thus, it is clear that there are four All India Trade Unions functioning in India at the moment. All India Trade Union Congress is wholly dominated by communists. According to the leaders of this union all industries must be nationalized. They support all types of freedom and facility for workers. The second Indian National Trade Union Congress is under the influence of Congress party. This trade union has conciliatory attitude and wants to settle problems peacefully and by mutual negotiations. It also believes in the government launched five year plans. It also supports the idea of partnership of workers in industry. The third important trade union is 'Hind Mazdoor Sabha' which is under the influence of Socialist Party. This trade union also favours nationalization. The fourth union is United Trade Union Congress. This union is not directly connected with any party but holds radical views. The aim of this union is to establish government of workers and peasants.

OBSTACLES IN THE PROGRESS OF TRADE UNIONISM IN INDIA

Sufficient time has elapsed since the founding of trade unions in India. But unlike Western countries, the Indian trade unions have not made the expected progress. They suffer from a number of lacunas. They have not developed on proper lines. There are various reasons for this. Certain conditions must be met if there is to be a proper growth of trade unions. In Indian industries all these conditions are not fully met. There are various types of obstacles in the development of Indian labour unions. Chiefly these fall into two categories: internal and external difficulties. The internal difficulties are related to labour and the external difficulties pertain to industrialists, intermediaries and official laws. Following discussion will make the nature of these two types of difficulties clear.

(*a*) Internal Obstacles

Indian labour has certain traits peculiar to it. Some of these traits have proved to be obstacles in the way of the growth of labour unions. Mainly, following traits of labour prove to be hindrances in the way of labour union's development and growth:

(1) Majority of Indian labour is illiterate: For any organization it is vitally important whether its members are educated or not. The educated members are an asset and the illiterate members a liability to the organization. Education broadens the outlook of individuals. An educated person understands what is beneficial and what is harmful to him. But the majority of Indian labour is illiterate. The illiteracy of labour is a hindrance in the growth of labour unions. It is difficult to keep the illiterate labour disciplined. Besides, illiterate workers are not fully conscious of their duties. They fall easy prey to the machinations of opposite groups. Without any proper reason they go on strike and indulge in subversion. They do not understand the true role and function of trade unions.

(2) Migratory habit: The majority of Indian labour hails from rural areas. The families of most of them reside in villages. Under these circumstances workers do not reside permanently in cities. As and when they get leaves or holidays they go to their wives and children. Thus, they are unable to participate regularly in the confabulations and discussions of trade unions. A number of workers do not enroll themselves as members of trade unions for this very reason. They are under the impression that if they become members of trade unions they cannot easily go to their villages. Even if they become members of unions they rush back home in the event of strikes and lock outs. On account of this habit of workers trade unionism in India does not work properly.

(3) Heterogeneous character: From the above discussion it is plain that Indian labour has a tendency to migrate from place to place. In every big industrial centre one can find workers coming from almost all regions of India. These workers are of veiy heterogeneous character. They differ *inter se* in regard to language, religion, habits of food and dress. On account of wide heterogeneity of the workers, a sense of unity cannot easily take root among them. But for the success of trade unions the trait of unity is of paramount importance. Many workers even today practise untouchability. Thus, it is plain that the heterogeneous character of Indian labour proves to be a stumbling block in the progress and development of Indian trade union movement.

(4) Low economic standards: The economic condition of Indian labour is not good. The average Indian worker's earnings are so low that he can barely meet the expenses of his family with his wages. On account of low wages he is usually under debt. On account of their poverty the workers are unable to take active part in trade union activity. Due to poor economic conditions they are unable to bear the strain of strikes and lock outs. Thus, it is clear that the poverty of workers come in the way of the growth and development of trade unions.

(5) Mutual strife: In India there are numerous trade unions functioning independently. Each of these trade unions is under the influence of one or other political party. The political parties are usually at cross purposes and pursuing contradictory policies. The political parties misuse trade unions to further their own political ends. This tendency foments dissension and strife among trade unions. The mutual strife among trade unions weakens them. If there is unity among labour all over India the labour organizations can work effectively and need not pursue contradictory and mutually harmful ends. Due to mutual dissension among trade unions each agitation is supported by some and opposed by others. This results in half-hearted action or utter failure Obviously, mutual strife is a big impediment in the way of the development of trade union activity in India.

(6) Lack of able leadership: The majority of Indian workers are illiterate and ignorant. None of these illiterate workers has the courage to take up the leadership of trade unions in his hands. Besides not possessing courage, these persons lack the ability and capacity for leadership. Under these circumstances outsiders are usually the leaders of Indian trade unions. Generally, social reformers, lawyers or politicians hold these posts. These persons are professional, well-qualified and clever people. They are well-informed about legal intricacies. However, these persons are as a rule selfish and self-seeking. They have no intimate or first-hand knowledge of labour problems. They are therefore indifferent to the true interests of labour. There are instances when these persons have been found to have worked in collusion with industrialists and to have been receiving regularly money from them. These persons do not let any real protest against industrialists build up. As and when there is agitation they cleverly sabotage it.

(7) Unemployment problem: The problem of unemployment in India is getting worse every day. The workers have to toil hard in order to find a job. Once a person finds some job he is most reluctant to leave it. This is so because finding alternative job is both uncertain and hazardous. An average Indian worker labours under the impression that by joining trade unions he is putting his job in danger. He is afraid he may be shunted out of job or his promotion stayed. Influenced by this fear psychosis the Indian worker does not participate actively in trade union activity. This indifference obviously is an obstacle in the way of the progress of trade union movement.

(*b*) External Obstacles

Besides internal impediments, there are certain external obstacles which impede and thwart the growth of trade unionism in India. The more important of these obstacles are concerned with the role of intermediaries, recruitment of workers, the industrialists management boards and labour and industrial laws. In the absence of active cooperation among various factors no trade union movement can make much progress. In the following lines these will be discussed in detail:

(1) Opposition and non-cooperation of intermediaries: Even at present the recruitment of labour in industry is not direct but is in the hands of intermediaries. These intermediaries are mostly the agents of the industrialists. They receive money from industrialists. These intermediaries are ever opposed to and unreconciled with the growth of trade unions. This is quite understandable because once trade unions become strong the role and importance of these intermediaries will be finished. That is why they are ever conspiring against workers and eager to eavesdrop on worker's conferences and pass on all information to the industrialists. Thus, it is evident that the opposition and non-cooperation of intermediaries is an obstacle to the growth of trade union activity.

(2) Opposition and non-cooperation of industrialists: The Indian industrialists deem trade unions their enemies. They are of the view that the growth of trade unions is not in consonance with their interests. Therefore, they try to undermine and sabotage all efforts designed to strengthen trade unions. They try to wean the workers from trade unions by bribing their leaders. At times the industrialists try to win over professional leaders of trade unions by giving them huge bribes.

(3) Lack of legal support: There is not enough support to workers by governmental laws and machinery. There are no adequate provisions to safeguard the interests of workers. In the event of strike there is not much protection of workers by law's. The industrialists are better placed to take advantage of law. Therefore, the growth of trade unions is impeded.

TRADE UNIONISM IN PRESENT INDIA

Labour protests on an organised scale were not unknown in India prior to the First World War (1914—18). Organised action by workers was reported in the first fourteen years of this century in many parts of the country; in some it was in response to the demand of the workers, in others the motive was political.

The establishment of the ILO in 1919, had its influence on the growth of unions in the country. While some unions chose to operate independently and confined their activities to an industrial centre/unit, others felt the need for coordination of their activities at the national level. A section of the Indian working class thought in terms of the even wider international unity of the working class through the opportunity offered by the ILO. The formation of an all-India federation in 1920, *viz.*, the All India Trade Union Congress, was the result of all these urges. The passing of the Trade Unions Act, 1926 gave a formal recognition to the workers' right to organise.

Trade Unions Act

The Trade Unions Act, 1926 provides for the registration of trade unions. Any seven or more members of a trade union may, by subscribing their names to the rules of the trade union and otherwise complying with the provisions of the Act with respect to registration, apply for registration of the trade union under the Trade Unions Act. The Act gives protection to registered trade unions in certain cases against civil or criminal action.

Membership of Trade Unions

Verification of membership of central trade union organisations for the purpose of giving representation on tripartite consultative bodies, development councils, boards, etc., at national and international levels, including International Labour Organisation, is done by the office of the Chief Labour Commissioner. The last general membership verification, as on 31 December 1968, of unions affiliated to four central trade union organisations, *viz.*, 1NTUC, AITUC, HMS and UTUC was undertaken during 1969.

With the emergence of new trade union organisations claiming all-India character and membership strength, it was decided to undertake verification of membership, as on 31 December, 1977 and 31 December, 1979, of unions affiliated to 10 central trade union organisations, *viz.*, (*i*) Indian National Trade Union Congress (INTUC), (*ii*) All India Trade Union Congress (AITUC), (*iii*) Hind Mazdoor Sabha (HMS), (*iv*) United Trade Union Congress (UTUC), (*v*) Centre of Indian Trade Unions (CITU), (*vi*) Bhartiya Mazdoor Sangh (BMS), (*vii*) United Trade Union Congress (UTUC) (LS), (*viii*) National Front of Indian Trade Unions (NFITU), (*ix*) Trade Union Coordination Centre (TUCC), and (*x*) National Labour Organisation (NLO).

However, verification could not be undertaken in the absence of consensus amongst the central organisations of workers. On account of strong differences in their views, the Government evolved a procedure. Accordingly, the 10 central organisations were addressed for submission of their claims as on 31 December, 1980 for the purpose of general verification. All the central organisations except AITUC and CITU submitted their claims. Membership figures of unions, affiliated to AITUC and CITU were collected from the records of the Registrar of Trade Unions. The general verification work initiated in November 1981 has since been completed and provisional results declared. The final results are being compiled.

ADVANTAGES OF TRADE UNIONS

1. Advantages to Workers:

(*i*) *Promotion of unity*. It promotes unity among workers members.

(*ii*) *Increase in efficiency*: Worker's efficiency is increased by improving working conditions and providing better welfare facilities.

(*iii*) *Less exploitation*: Employer's attitude of exploiting workers changes.

(*iv*) *Self-reliance*: Trade unions include self-reliance and self-respect among the workers thereby helping to build up national character. They are paid fair share of the results based on the actual work produced.

(*v*) *Better wages*: Trade unions help maintain the wages at a uniform level in terms of the actual economic value.

(*vi*) *More bargaining*: Trade unions negotiate better with the employers through collective bargaining. Being an organised body it may avoid strike and dispute honourably by putting pressure on the employers to solve the problem on the bases of self-respect.

(*vii*) *More workers' participation*: If trade union is strong, it can participate in the working of the industry.

2. Advantages to Employer Producers

(*i*) *Less disputes*: Industrial disputes can be avoided or may be solved amicably by developing mutual interests and thus employers can maintain work flow.

(*ii*) *More peace*: Trade unions may develop a sense of responsibility and loyalty among workers through counselling and collective bargaining. In this way, they help maintaining industrial peace.

(*iii*) *Promotion of democracy*: They protect the social resources and make best use of them by promoting industrial peace.

(*iv*) *Healthy policy*: Trade unions may associate the employers in framing healthy labour policies which may weaken the chances of dispute in future.

3. Advantages to Society

(*i*) *Gain in public sympathy*: In crises, they can put their viewpoint before the public to gain their sympathy. If they are fighting for a good cause, they can have sympathy of the general public.

(*ii*) *Proposals to Government*: Trade unions can purpose to the Government to enact labour policies to protect and develop labour force of the country in a better way.

(*iii*) *Better economy*: Trade unions can play a very significant role in the development of industrial economy by maintaining good industrial relations. It will result in higher and better production at lower costs.

In this way labour unions play an important role in developing labour force, promoting industrial peace, increasing production and improving working conditions.

SUGGESTIONS FOR IMPROVEMENT OF TRADE UNIONS IN INDIA

1. Education of workers: For the proper growth of Indian trade unions, a comprehensive scheme for the education of workers is necessary. The majority of Indian workers are thumb-embossers; they cannot write or read anything whatsoever. Such workers are unskilled and technically untrained. They should be given the opportunity for technical training. Besides literary and technical education, the Indian workers should also be told about labour laws relevant to his services. He should know his rights and privileges as well as his obligations. If the average worker becomes educated and knowledgeable, the progress and development of trade unions is bound to be automatic.

2. Proper election of labour leaders: The success of any organization depends upon its leadership. If the quality and calibre of leadership is available the success is most assured; but on the other hand, if the leadership is of indifferent quality, not much can be expected from it.

The workers in India blindly follow their leaders. Therefore, the interests of workers are safe only if the leader is a selfless person dedicated to the upliftment of the downtrodden. Another essential condition for the success of labour union is that the labour leader should know the problems of workers intimately and at first hand; only then can be expected to give the proper leadership. A professional who knows little about workers' problems first-hand is more often a misleader. To ensure that workers get proper leaders, they must be elected directly by them and should not be nominees of somebody.

3. Mutual co-operation: In spite of the fact that all labour unions pursue same ends, it is regrettable that there is little co-operation among them. For a comprehensive development of trade unionism in India it is imperative that there should be a broad-based mutual cooperation and give and take among the various labour unions. If all trade unions work jointly they will be such a force that the role of intermediaries will be over and the industrialists will listen to them most cautiously. Indeed unity is strength and a united organization is a formidable force.

4. Internal co-operation: Besides cooperation among various labour unions, it is equally, if not more important, that there should be internal unity and co-operation within a trade union. There is a great diversity among Indian workers. They come from different regions, speak different tongues, profess different religions. Under these circumstances a great effort is needed to weld this disparate amalgam of individuals into cohesive force. It is required that workers should develop class consciousness. They should realize that as workers their interests lie in unity among workers and that differences of religion, language etc., must be forgotten. In order to develop unity among workers labour leaders will have to strive very hard.

5. Provision of permanent residence: For the proper development of trade unions it is necessary that the majority of workers must be permanent residents of towns and cities in which they work. By staying with other workers each worker will come to know each other intimately and this will foster a sense of unity and brotherhood among them. If the workers have to stay permanently in industrial towns it is necessary that vast labour colonies should be constructed. This will put an end to the migratory habit of workers and secondly they will be able to stay with their families.

6. Economic and social upliftment of workers: It is a *conditiosine qua non* of success of labour movement that there should be improvement of the economic and social conditions of the workers. An average worker is perennially under the threat of starvation and bankruptcy and social action has no meaning for him. Even socially the workers are looked down upon. They suffer from inferiority complex. It is essential in this context that people should realize the dignity of labour and a sense of self-esteem be restored to the workers.

7. Appointment of paid officials: Generally the persons working in trade unions and welfare associations have to work gratis; they are paid nothing for their services. Under these circumstances these persons do not function efficiently and are liable to avail any opportunity of embezzlement etc. In order to eliminate such temptation and in order to give reward there should be remuneration commensurate with the nature of their work.

8. Appointment of specialists: In order to ensure the success of labour unions it is necessary that certain specialists be appointed to assist these unions in intricate matters. In modern industry very complex problems arise. There can be disputes regarding leaves, bonus, arrears and matters of recruitment, promotion and retrenchment. In these cases the services of specialists are much in need.

9. Co-operation of industrialists and government: The success of labour union is not possible without certain amount of co-operation of industrialists. The employers should consider labour unions not as adversaries but think of them to be useful instrument of individual progress. In the long-run, a satisfied labour is an asset. Besides employers, the government should also keep development of labour movement.

10. Freedom from politics: It is most important for the success of labour unions that they should be free from deleterious political influences. The political parties are more interested in promoting their own ends than those of the labour. They are not well-wishers of labour; therefore to keep them at an arm's length.

11. Confidence of public: Over and above the conditions listed above it is equally essential for the success of labour movement that it should win the public confidence. Public confidence is an almighty force. Whosoever has it is assured of success.

QUESTIONS FOR EXERCISE

1. Define Trade Union and describe its objectives and function.
2. What are the conditions necessary for making trade unions useful?
3. "The obstacles to the development of trade unions in this country

are largely internal, they come from the labour itself." Elucidate these obstacles and suggest remedies.

4. "It is said that outside leadership and political interference have been two main hurdles in the healthy development of Trade Union Movement in India." Discuss this statement in detail.
5. "Strong trade unions are a must to safeguard the interests of workers and attaining production goals." Explain this statement and discuss the weakness of Indian Trade Unions.
6. Point out the advantage of Trade Unions. Give suggestions for improvement of Trade Unions in India.

25

Labour Legislation

Labour Policy

India derives its philosophy and content from the Directive Principles of the Constitution and has been evolving in response to specific needs of the situation to suit requirements of planned economic development and social justice. It has been envisaged that growth of the economy would not only increase production but also absorb the backlog of unemployment and under-employment and a substantial proportion of additional labour force. Seventh Plan laid emphasis on harassing country's abundant human resources and improving their capabilities for development. Objectives of manpower planning are to ensure proper linkage of economic planning with manpower and educational planning so that no plan programme suffers from lack of trained manpower.

LABOUR LEGISLATION

1. Regulation of Wages Act, 1936: Payment of wages is governed by the Payment of Wages Act, 1936 and Minimum Wages Act, 1948, as amended from time to time. The Payment of Wages Act extends to whole of India. The Payment of Wages Act, 1936, applies to persons employed in any factory including establishments declared as factories under the Factory Act, 1948 and in any railway and industrial establishment such as tramway or motor transport service, air transport service, docks, inland vessels, mines, quarries or oil-fields, plantations, workshops in which articles are produced and establishments in which any work relating to construction, development or maintenance of buildings, roads, bridges or canals, etc., is being carried on. It applies only to those who are in receipt of wages, average of which falls below ₹ 1,600 per month.

Employers cannot withhold wages earned by workers nor can they make any unauthorised deduction. Payment must be made before expiry of specified day after the last day of wage period. Fines can be imposed for only those acts of omission which have been approved by appropriate authority and must not exceed an amount equal to three per cent of wages payable. If payment of wages is delayed or wrongful deductions of overtime in scheduled employment is governed by the Minimum Wages Act, 1948.

2. Minimum Wages Act, 1948: The Minimum Wages Act, 1948 empowers Government to fix minimum wages for employees working in specified employments. It provides for review and revision of minimum wages already fixed after suitable intervals not exceeding five years. However, Labour Ministers' Conference in July 1980, recommended that a revision of minimum wages should be made within two years or on a rise of 50 points in consumer price index, whichever is earlier.

The Central Government is the appropriate agency in relation to any scheduled employment carried on by or under the authority of it or in railway administration or in relation to mine, oil-field or major port or any corporation established under the Central Act. State Governments are the appropriate agencies' in relation to other scheduled employments. The Central Government is concerned to a limited extent with building and construction activities mostly carried on by Central Public Works Department, Ministry of Defence etc. and agricultural farms under the Ministries of Defence and Agriculture. Bulk of employment falls in state spheres and state governments are required to fix/revise wages and ensure their implementation in respect of scheduled employments within their spheres. Enforcement of the Minimum Wages Act in Central sphere is secured through the Central industrial relations machinery.

3. Working Journalists Act, 1955: The Working Journalists and other Newspaper Employees (Conditions of Service) and Miscellaneous Provisions Act, 1955 regulates conditions of service of working journalists and other persons employed in newspaper establishments. In 1985, the Government had set up two wage boards—one for working journalists and other for non-journalists employees under the Chairmanship of Justice Shri U.N. Bhachwat. The two wage boards submitted a final combined report on 30 May, 1989. The Government issued notification on 31 August, 1989 accepting the recommendations of the Bachawat Wage Boards regarding pay scales. An other notification regarding House Rent Allowance and Compensatory City Allowance was issued by the Government on 22 January, 1990. From time to time, the Central Government has been impressing upon the state governments/ union territory administrations for speedy implementation of the recommendations of Bhachawat Wage Boards and advising them to establish tripartite committee/special cells at state level in this regard.

4. Payment of Bonus Act, 1965: The Payment of Bonus Act, 1965 provides for a minimum bonus of 8.33 per cent and the limit of salary for eligibility is ₹ 2,500 per month. The payment is subject to stipulation that the bonus in respect of employees drawing wages or salary between ₹ 1,600 and ₹ 2,500 per mensum would be calculated as if their salary or wage is ₹ 1,600 per month. A number of representations have been received for enhancing the above ceilings. No final view has been taken so far on the issue.

5. Contract Labour Act, 1970: The Contract Labour (Regulation and Abolition) Act, 1970 which became applicable to whole of India in February 1971 provides for regulation of employment of contract labour in certain establishments and for its abolition in certain circumstances. It fixes responsibility on the principal employer for payment of wages in case of defaults. The Government has set up eight tripartite committees to advise on abolition of contract labour in certain employments.

6. Child Labour (Prohibition and Regulations) Act, 1986: Legislative provisions have been made in various laws to protect children from exploitation at work and to improve their working conditions. In addition, the Child Labour (Prohibition and Regulations) Act, 1986 prohibits employment of children in certain hazardous occupations and process and regulate their employment in some other areas.

A National Policy on Child Labour has been formulated in 1987 which apart from enforcement of legal provisions, envisages focusing on general development programmes for the benefit of child labour and project-based plan of action in areas of high concentration of child labour. National Child Labour Projects have been set up in nine such areas. Financial assistance to voluntary organisation is provided for taking up action-oriented projects. In addition, with ILO's assistance, two projects for tackling the problems of child labour within the framework of national policy, namely International Programme on the Elimination of Child Labour (IPEC) and Child Labour Action and Support Programme (CLASP) have also been taken up.

6. Equal Remuneration Act, 1976: The Equal Remuneration Act, 1976 provides for payment of equal remuneration to men and women workers for "the same work or work of similar nature" and for prevention of discrimination against women not only in matters of recruitment but also in relation to conditions of service subsequent to recruitment, such as promotions, training or transfer. Provisions of the Act have been extended to all employments. The Act provides for setting up of advisory committees by the appropriate Government on increasing employment opportunities for women. Such committees have already been set up under the Central Government as well as in most states and union territories. An enforcement machinery has been set up at Central and state level under the Act. The following four social welfare organisations have also been recognised under the Equal Remuneration Act, 1976 for the purpose of filing complaints in the court against employers for violation of the provisions of the Act: (*i*) The Centre for Women's Development Studies, New Delhi, (*ii*) The Self-Employed Women's Association, Ahmedabad, (*iii*) The Working Women's Forum (India), Madras, and (*iv*) The Institute of Social Studies Trust, New Delhi. Some state governments have also recognised certain voluntary organisations under the Act for the same purpose in the state sphere. Under the Act, any person aggrieved by the offence can also file complaint in the court.

7. The Factories Act, 1948: It is the principal legislation for regulating various aspects relating to safety, health and welfare of workers employed in factories. This Act is a Central enactment which aims at protecting workers employed in factories from industrial and occupational hazards. State governments and union territory administrations frame rules under the Act and enforce provisions of the Act and rules through their factory inspectorates. The Directorate General, Factory Advice Service and Labour Institute, Bombay which is an attached office of the Ministry of Labour renders technical advice to states/union territories in regard to administration and enforcement of the Factories Act. The Directorate General also organises annual conferences of chief inspectors of factories of states/union territories to review the position regarding implementation and enforcement of the Act.

The Act prescribes a 48 hour week for adult worker and forbids employment of children under 14 years of age in any factory. Minimum standards of lighting, ventilation, safety and welfare services which employers must provide in their factories have also been laid down. Factories employing over 30 women workers are required to provide a creche for their children. Shelters, rest rooms and lunch rooms are required to be provided by factories employing over 150 workers. Factories with more than 250 workers have to provide canteens for their workers. Factories employing 500 workers or more have to appoint welfare officers. The Factories Act was amended in the year 1987 in order to impose a general duty on occupiers to ensure health and safety of workers and on designers, manufacturers, etc., are without risk to health and safety of workers. A new chapter for regulating safety and health aspect in hazardous process industries was incorporated in the Act.

An International Labour Organisation-aided project on "Establishment and Initial Operation of a Major Accident Hazards Control System" executed by the Ministry of Labour through the DGFASLI, Bombay concluded on 31 December 1990. Under this project, a multi-disciplinary major accident hazards control advisory cells in the three regional labour institutes were established. To enable the personnel of the above division and the cells to perform their specialist roles effectively, their capabilities were developed through various means such as in-country training seminars/programmes, fellowships abroad, attachment with the experts and hands-on-experience of investigation of accidents involving hazardous chemicals and inspection of chemical plants jointly with the factory inspectorates, walk through surveys, study and review of on-site and off-site emergency plans documents prepared by the management of major accident hazards installations and district emergency authorities etc. The Division and the cells are fully operational and are functioning as the national and regional resources centres on major accident hazards control. Constant efforts are made by the personnel to keep themselves abreast of the latest information and development in the field.

A USAID project on industrial safety and health development (ISHD) is being executed with a view to strengthen communication functions of DGFASLI in occupational safety and health, data base and the capabilities for conducting safety audit.

9. Dock Workers Act, 1986: Provisions relating to safety, health and welfare of workers employed in docks are contained in the Dock Workers (Safety, Health and Welfare) Act, 1986 and rules and regulations framed thereunder. The Act came into force on 15 April, 1987. Enforcement of this Act in all the major ports is the responsibility of the Ministry of Labour and this responsibility is discharged through the Directorate General, Factories Advice Services and Labour Institutes, Bombay.

The DGFASLI being the Chief Inspector of Docks, is also entrusted with the responsibility of enforcing in major ports the Manufacture, Storage and Import of Hazardous Chemical Rules, 1989 framed under the Environment (Protection) Act, 1986.

10. Mines Act, 1952: Provisions for safety, health and welfare of workers employed in mines are contained in the Mines Act, 1952 and rules and regulations framed thereunder. These provisions are enforced by the

Ministry of Labour through the Directorate General of Mines Safety. The main functions of the Directorate General are: inspection of mines, investigation of all fatal accidents and also certain serious accidents depending upon gravity of the situations; grant of statutory permissions, exemptions and relaxations in respect of various mining operations; approval of mines safety equipment, appliances and material to conduct to examinations for grant of statutory competency certificates, safety promotional incentives including organisation of national awards and national safety conferences etc.

11. The Emigration Act, 1983: The Emigration Act, 1983, which came into force with effect from 30 December 1983, regulates emigration of citizens of India for employment in other countries on contractual basis and seeks to ensue welfare and safeguard the interest of workers. As on 30 December, 1992, number of Indian workers who had gone abroad for employment, in terms of the provisions of the Emigration Act, 1983, was about 3.80 lakh as compared to 2.00 lakh in 1991. Under the provisions of the Act, an employer can recruit any citizen of India for employment in any country or place outside India either through a recruiting agent competent under the Act to make such recruitment or directly in accordance with a valid permit issued by the Central Government under the Act. The competent authorities to grant permit for deployment of Indians abroad are Protector General of Emigrants (PGE) and Heads of Indian Missions abroad. The Act also provides that anyone intending to recruit Indians for employment abroad can do so after obtaining a Registration Certificate from the PGE under the provisions of the Act.

Certain categories of persons are not required to obtain emigration clearance for seeking employment abroad. They are entitled to get the Stamp of 'Emigration Check Not Required' (ECNR) on their passports from the passport offices by showing proof of their eligibility. Such individuals are: (*i*) persons going abroad in managerial capacity in hotels, restaurants, tea-houses or other places of public resort, etc., possessing specialised degrees in these fields; (*ii*) all gazetted government servants; (*iii*) all income-tax payers (including agricultural income-tax payers) in respect of their individual capacity. Proof of assessment to income-tax and actual payment of income-tax for last three years (net merely payment of advance tax); (*iv*) all professional degree holders, such as doctors holding MBBS degree or degrees in Ayurveda or Homoepathy, accredited journalists, engineers, chartered accountants, cost accountants, lecturers, teachers; scientists, advocates, etc. (*v*) spouses and dependent children of category of persons listed from (*ii*) to (*iv*); (*vi*) all persons who have been staying abroad for more than three years (the period of three years could be either in one stretch or broken) and spouse, and children of such persons; (*vii*) seamen in possession of CDC and sea cadets; (*viii*) all diplomatic/official passports holders; (*ix*) dependent children of parents whose passports are classified as ECNR, below 24; (*x*) persons holding permanent immigration visas such as in UK, USA and Australia; (*xi*) Persons holding graduation or higher degrees; (*xii*) Persons holding diplomas from recognised institutions like polytechnics; (*xiii*) nurse possessing qualifications recognised under the Indian Nursing Council Act, 1947; (*xiv*) all persons above the age of 60 years; (*xv*) all visitors to Pakistan and Bangladesh; (*xvi*) all persons going to any country in Europe or North; and (*xvii*) persons possessing certificates of vocational training from government recognised institutions.

The pilgrims going for Haj and Umrah in Saudi Arabia and those pilgrims travelling with the declared purpose of performing 'Ziarat' to Saudi Arabia, Syria, Iran and Jordan have been exempted from the requirements of obtaining suspension from Emigration Check Requirement' from Protectors of Emigrants/passport offices with effect from 12 May, 1992 and 8 January, 1993 respectively.

12. Industrial Disputes Act, 1947: The lay-offs, retrenchments and closures are regulated under the provisions of the Industrial Disputes Act, 1947. The Government have taken steps to further regulate lay-offs, retrenchments and closures through the Industrial Disputes (Amendment) Acts of 1982 and 1984. Accordingly, under the Act, any worker who has completed not less than one year of continuous service is entitled for a minimum amount of compensation for retrenchment/closure.

Bonded Labour System stands abolished in the country from 1975 through the Bonded Labour System (Abolition) Act, 1976. The Act envisages release of all bonded labourers, liquidation of their debts and their Rehabilitation. Incidence of bonded labour system has been reported from 12 states *viz.*, Andhra Pradesh, Bihar, Gujarat, Haryana, Karnataka, Kerala, Madhya Pradesh, Maharasthra, Orissa, Rajasthan, Tamil Nadu and Uttar Pradesh.

Under the Bonded Labour System (Abolition) Act, 1976 identification and release of bonded labourers and rehabilitation of freed bonded labourer is the direct responsibility of the state governments concerned. For the purpose of implementing the provisions of the Act, state government may confer necessary powers on the District

Magistrate. With a view to supplementing efforts of state governments a Centrally-sponsored scheme has been in existence since 1978-79 under which state governments are provided central financial assistance for rehabilitation grant upto a ceiling limit of ₹ 6,250 per bonded labourer, half of which is given as Central share. The pattern of assistance under this scheme can be either land-based, non-land-based or skill/craft-based.

QUESTION FOR EXERCISE

1. Describe the legislation made by the Government of India to promote labour welfare in the country.

26

Labour Welfare

WHAT IS LABOUR WELFARE

1. *Royal Commission on Labour*: "The term welfare, as applied to the industrial worker, is one which must necessarily be elastic; bearing a somewhat different interpretation in one country from another, according to different interpretations in the degree of industrialization and educational development of workers."

2. *Encyclopaedia of Social Sciences*: "Labour welfare implies the voluntary efforts of the employers to establish within the existing industrial system, working and sometimes living customs of the industry and the conditions of the market."

3. *International Labour Organization*: "Workers welfare should be understood as meaning such service facilities and amenities which may be established in, or in vicinity of, an undertaking to enable the persons employed there to perform their work in healthy congenial surrounding and provided with amenities conducive to good health and high morale."

4. *Labour Investigation Committee, India*: We prefer to include under welfare activities betterment of the workers, whether by employers, by Government agencies or by other agencies over and above what is laid down by law or what is normally expected as part of the contractual benefits for which the workers may have bargained. Thus, under this definition, we may include medical and educational facilities, nutrition (including provision of canteens) facilities for recreating, cooperative societies, day's nurseries and creches, provision of sanitary accommodation, holidays with pay, social insurance measures, undertaken voluntarily by employers alone or jointly with workers, sickness and maturity benefits schemes, provident funds, gratuities, bonuses and pensions etc.

All the above mentioned definitions of social welfare agree on this point: it includes all voluntary acts by employers aimed at improvement and betterment of workers' social, moral, economic and intellectual conditions. Those acts which the employer is compelled, on pain of legal actions, to undertake, however beneficial these may be for the workers are not included in the province of labour welfare. By welfare scheme the industrialists give evidence of their morale and social enlightenment and help all-round development of workers. This in turn, helps him in the long run, because, as it has been well observed, a well-paid and satisfied worker is an asset and the low-paid unsatisfied worker is a liability.

Responsibility of Labour Welfare

Having discussed the problem of Labour Welfare, the question that is likely to come up in anyone's mind is: who is responsible for Labour Welfare? Whose moral obligation is it to promote labour welfare? The most popular view in this regard is that it is the duty of the employer to look after the social welfare of the workers employed by him. This seems to be the most responsible and well considered view because though the industrialist has to make big investment in the labour welfare schemes, it is by no means a dead investment. A well-fed, well-clad and satisfied worker is an asset. He makes no loss of man-hours by absenteeism, strikes, slow tactics etc. Besides he feels a sense of allegiance to the organization in which he works. Therefore, though a costly investment, it pays very rich dividends in the long run. It is a moral duty of every mill owner or industrialist to provide fully for the good and other amenities for the families of the workers who suffer grievous injury in accidents met during working hours. He must also provide medical benefits, pensions, bonuses, incentive etc. However, the industrialist alone is not responsible for labour welfare. It is also the duty of welfare state to look after zealously the interests of the workers and initiate schemes for improvement in their working conditions, raising their morale etc. The Government should strictly enforce the benefits provided by law. It should also prevent any instance of exploitation of women workers and any abuse of children. In all progressive countries the workers have their trade unions which look after anything done for the intellectual, physical, moral and economic and safeguard and promote the interests of workers. They can compel government and employers to agree to improved benefits for the country. An example of this is the recent announcement of Government of India to allow for 8.33% bonus to all industrial workers. All three, that is, the employer, the Government and the Trade Unions are jointly responsible for labour welfare.

HISTORY OF LABOUR WELFARE IN INDIA

The following are the different stages in Labour Welfare movement in India.

1. Development Since 1870 to 1914: The first industrial undertaking in India was established in 1854. During the following fifteen years, cotton textile, jute and coal industries and railway made considerable progress and employed a sizeable workforce. The industrial progress was accompanied by usual inhuman conditions of work and exploitation of women and children. Major Moore published his report on the 'Administration of Bombay Textile Departments' in 1872. Public response to the shocking findings of Major Moore expressed itself into organised labour work on one hand and agitational activities on the other. A Brahmo Samaj preacher, Mr. P.C. Majumdar established eight night schools for industrial workers of Bombay in 1872. In Calcutta, the Brahmo Samaj established a Working Men's Mission in 1878 which preached practical religion and established nine schools for working men and depressed classes. For promoting education and social welfare activities among the jute mills workers, Mr. Sasipada Banerjee also started the Baranagar Institute during the same year.

Agitational Activities

Agitational activities to press for demands for legislative provisions regarding health and safety of mill hands were started by Mr. S.S. Bengalee and his colleagues in Bombay in 1872. In 1874, Miss Carpentar, founder of the National Independence Association of Bristol, visited India to enquire into the conditions of factory employees and published her report. This led the Government of India to set up a Factory Commission in 1875 and enact the Factories Act, 1881 on the basis of its recommendations. In 1890, the first Internal Labour Conference met at Berlin and recommended the regulation of women and child labour. The Government of India was forced to amend the legislation in 1891 and introduced protective Clauses in respect of women and children. In 1905 the Berne Conference, the forerunner of the ILO made recommendations pertaining to hours of work and working conditions. Armed by these recommendations, the British industrialists pressed the government once again and prevailed upon the latter to enact the Factory Act, 1911, introducing measures to regulate hours and conditions of work. During three decades following the first Factory Act in 1881, voluntary action in the Field of labour welfare also made considerable progress and moved from individual to organised group efforts. Formed in 1897 the Amalgamated Society of Railway Servants of India and Burma started a number of friendly benefits schemes. Organised in 1905 and 1907 respectively the Printers Union, Calcutta and Postal Union, Bombay in 1910 the Kamgar Hitawardhak Sabha (Workers Welfare Association) was established to help workers in a variety of ways such as the payment of compensation for accidents to industrial workers and improving labour housing conditions.

2. Between Two World Wars: During this period the labour welfare movement got established on a continuous and regular basis. The important factors were the formation of the ILO, All India Trade Union Congress in 1919, the emergence of the Labour Party and the British Trade Union Congress in Britain, the new orientation of the freedom movement under Mahatma Gandhi's leadership, the increase in industrial activity and the size of workforce and the militant mood of organised labour. Reforms in labour legislation were made in many directions. The Workmen's Compensation Act was passed and enforced. A significant development during the twenties was the beginning of labour welfare activities by the leading companies. The Royal Commission of Labour (1931), and the assumption of office by the Congress ministries in most of the provinces exercised great influence. The Royal Commission recommended shorter and convenient working hours for women and children, health, insurance, maternity benefits, creches, elaborate health rules, labour welfare officers, minimum wages etc. The Congress ministries, particularly of Bombay, Bengal and U.P. pursued a vigorous policy for setting labour welfare programmes in major industrial cities in their provinces in 1937,1939 and 1940 respectively. In 1936 Sir Dorab Tata School of Social Work, now known as the Tata Institute of Social Sciences, was established in Bombay.

3. After Second World War: The Second World War proved a boon to the development of Indian industry and to the labour welfare movement. In 1962, the Central Government appointed a Labour Welfare Adviser and a few labour welfare officers in the Department of Labour. Provisions were made for the establishment by amending the Factories Act, 1934. Labour welfare funds were started in establishments run by various government departments. The Mica Mines Labour Welfare Fund and the Coal Mines Labour Welfare Fund were constituted for providing housing, medical, recreational and education facilities to workers and their families employed in mica and coal mines, all over the country. In 1942, a special officer was appointed in the Department of Labour to draft a scheme of health insurance for factory workers, maternity benefits, pithead baths and creches were introduced in the mining industry.

4. Independence and After: The labour welfare movement acquired a new perspective after independence. The Indian National Congress had made many commitments to industrial workers. It naturally tried to honour them. The Labour Department of the Central Government worked out a five year programme in 1946. This was followed by Five Year Plans. Labour Welfare Advisory Boards now functioned in all States.

PATTERNS OF LABOUR WELFARE SERVICES

1. Basic standards: Activity of the State in relation to the creation of basic welfare standards for workers employed in undertakings, culminated in the passing of the Factories Act, 1948; Mines Act, 1952; Plantation Labour Act, 1951 and similar other enactments regulating working conditions in other groups of industries like railways, airways, sea-fares, CPWD, shops and commercial establishments and banks and insurance companies.

2. Activities to meet particular needs: Principal measures concerning the general welfare of particular groups with special needs include Coal Mines (Pithead Bath) Rules, Creche Rules, Coal Mines Labour Welfare, Office Establishment Rules, Tea Districts Emigrant Labour Act, 1933 and Dock Workers (Regulation of Employment) Act, 1948. Owners of all coal mines are required to construct bath rooms near the head of pits and to provide adequate quantities of water and soap for workers to bathe after they come out of the pit. Likewise, all mine owners are required to provide a creche at the premises wherein women workers can leave their children below the age of six during working hours. The rules lay down standards of services and staff as well as specifications of accommodation. The Tea Districts Emigrant Labour Act, 1933 regulates the recruitment of plantation labour, its movements to Assam and repatriation. It abolished the 'indenture' system and thereby stopped gross exploitation of his labour. The Dock Workers (Regulation of Employment) Act, 1948 is a scheme of providing guaranteed minimum employment and welfare facilities to dock workers.

3. Particular labour welfare services: Labour welfare services of a specialised nature pertain to indebtedness, housing and industrial co-operatives. Indebtedness Relief Acts of most of the States provided that the industrial workers in receipt of wages of less than ₹ 100 per month will not be subject to imprisonment under Section 51 of the Code of Civil Procedure, except where the debtor has been proved to be both able and unwilling to pay.

4. Housing: The need to improve the housing conditions of industrial workers was suggested for the first time in 1919 by the Indian Industrial

Commission. The Royal Commission on Labour laid further stress on this need in 1931. Later the Bombay Textile Labour Enquiry Committee, the U.P. Labour Enquiry Committee, the Kanpur Labour Enquiry Committee and the Bihar Labour Enquiry Committee pointed out in their reports the deplorable housing conditions in most of the industrial centres and made various recommendations for improving them. The Labour Investigation Committee suggested that the State Governments should provide necessary finance for housing while the recurring expenses should be borne by the parties concerned. The problem was discussed at the seventh meeting of the Standing Labour Committee in 1945 and an Industrial Housing Sub-committee was appointed to go in the details of the problem. The report of the Committee was discussed and approved by the Standing Labour Committee in July, 1946. Various schemes and enactments were framed both by the Central and State Governments for providing housing accommodation to industrial workers.

5. Protection of children and women: One of the major concerns of the state is to protect and safeguard children and women against exploitation and victimisation. It was in 1881 that concerted steps were first taken to regulate working hours for children. The Factories Act, 1881, defined 'child' as a person below 12 years of age and prohibited the employment of children below 7. Child workers were to work nine hours a day. Through repeated amendments, the conditions of work were made more favourable to children. The Factories Act, 1934 introduced the concept of adolescent (between the age of 15-17 years) as a 'protected' person and required that children should not work for more than 5 hours a day with a maximum spread-over of 7 hours. The position was made still better in the Factories Act, 1948. This Act defined child as a person who has not completed 12 years of age and prohibited the employment of children below the age of 14 in factories. Young persons (between the age 15-18) could be employed in factories subject to certain conditions. The occupier of a factory, before employing a young person must be in possession of a certificate of age of 14, and a certificate of medical fitness issued by the certifying surgeon, on the general physical fitness of the 'young person'. The 'young person' must be issued a token marked 'P' (protected person) which he must carry on his person during all working hours. He will work one shift only and shall not be allowed or required to work for more than 5 hours a day. He also earns leave with wages at the rate of one day for 15 days of work. Again, a young person cannot be employed in cleaning, oiling and repairing jobs as well as in hazardous occupations. He is also not allowed to work during night.

The Mines Act, 1952 makes provisions for 'young persons' which are similar to those made in the Factories Act, 1948. Further it prohibits the employment of 'young person' below ground and requires that they be given safe work under the supervision of adult workers.

In 1938, the Government of India enacted the Employment of children's Act prohibiting employment of children in certain occupations. It laid down that no child who has not completed 15th year of age shall be employed or permitted to work in any occupations concerned with the transport of passengers, goods or mail on the railway and in ports. It also prohibited the employment of children below the age of 14 in any workshop where *bidi* making, carpet weaving, cement manufacturing, printing, dyeing and weaving of cloth, cutting and smelting of mica, manufacturing of matches and fire works, shellac works, soap making, tanning and cleaning of wool are carried on.

The Act also prohibited night work for children. It does not apply to those establishments where manufacturing is carried on by the occupier with the aid of his family members.

Another Act that protects children against exploitation is the 'Pledging of Children Act, 1933'. This Act declares an agreement to pledge the labour of children whereby the parent or guardian of a child, in return for any payment or benefit to be received, undertakes to cause or allow the services of a child to be utilised in any employment, to be void. However, an agreement made without detriment to the interest of the child and not made in consideration for any benefit other than reasonable wages to be paid for child's services and terminable at a week's notice will not deemed illegal. The Tea Districts (Immigration of Labour) Act, 1933 lays down that no children shall be employed and immigrated to the districts unless accompanied by his parents and guardians. The Mines Act, 1952 holds the guardian responsible if a young person is found engaged in double employment on any one day.

Most of the Acts make special provisions for women workers. The Factories Act, 1948 provides for separate toilet, washing and resting facilities for them. It prohibits their employment during night and in hazardous occupations. It makes special safety provisions by disallowing them to clean, oil or repair moving machinery or to lift in the factory creche, she has to be given time off at stated frequencies to go and suckle her baby. The Mines Act, 1952 makes all of the above provisions besides prohibiting their employment below ground. The Indian Merchant Shipping Act prohibits women to take employment on board of sea-going ships, except as nurses.

6. Labour welfare funds: The labour welfare funds are one of two major activities of the state. In 1946, the Government of India initiated a scheme to finance welfare activities in industrial undertakings out of specially created funds. In pursuance of this scheme, a number of enactments were made. The Mica Mines Labour Welfare Fund Act was passed in 1946 followed by the Coal Mines Labour Welfare Act in 1947. The Government of India also framed rules to introduce such funds in industrial undertakings owned and controlled by them. Similar funds have also been instituted by some of the State governments. The principal amongst these are the Bombay Labour Welfare Funds and the Gorakhpur Labour Welfare Funds.

7. Labour welfare centres: The Labour welfare centres are one of the common activities of the Labour Departments of different State governments. Started in 1986 in Bombay, the idea has spread resulting in the establishment of similar centres in the principal industrial cities. Such centres are found in Bombay, Delhi, Kanpur, Calcutta and a few other places.

Welfare Activities by Employers

Welfare services provided by the employers vary from place to place depending upon the location, size and financial position of the undertaking, manufacturing process, structure of workforce, philosophy of the management, etc. Little is known of the welfare activities in small and medium size undertakings. So far as big employers are concerned, they provide a variety of services. It will not be out of place to maintain a few outstanding examples.

1. Tata Iron and Steel Company, Jamshedpur: It maintains almost the whole of the city including dwellings, a general hospital, two dozen primary schools, a training institute, parks, roads and a local broadcasting system. Social services provided by the Company are in addition to those run by the State government. The Company has special funds to give grants for tribal land, Harijan welfare and to employees for educational needs of their children. The Company has a department of Urban Community Development which runs ten urban centres in the town.

2. Delhi Cloth and General Mills Delhi: It has a department called Welfare Trust. The Trust undertakes to grant scholarships to children of employees who are in educational institutions. It also maintains a Daughter's Marriage Fund. An employee can make monthly contributions towards it. At the time of the marriage of his daughter, he gets back his own money with interest plus employer's contribution.

Many companies provide lunch and transport to their employees at subsidised rates. Nearly ten thousand industrial consumer co-operative societies function in India, where workers can buy consumer goods at prices much lower than the market prices. Associated Central Company in some of its works gives land to workers, provides technical know-how and encourages workers to supplement their wages.

LABOUR WELFARE IN INDIA

A report of International Labour Organisation defined labour welfare thus: "Workers Welfare should be understood as meaning such services, facilities and amenities which may be established in, or in vicinity of, an undertaking to enable the persons employed there to perform their work in healthy congenial surroundings and provided with amenities conducive to good health and high morale." Thus, the labour welfare schemes aim at the maintenance and betterment of workers' health and raising of their moral standards and efficiency. A report of Labour Investigation Committee set up by the Government of India have observed, "We prefer to include under Welfare activities anything done for the intellectual, physical, moral and economic betterment of the workers, whether by employees, by Government agencies or by other agencies over and above what is laid down by law or what is normally expected as part of the contractual benefits for which the workers may have bargained. Thus, under this definition we may include medical and educational facilities, nutrition (including provision of canteens) facilities for recreation, co-operative societies, day nurseries and creches, provision of sanitary accommodation, holidays with pay, social insurance measures, undertaken voluntarily by employers alone or jointly with workers, sickness and maturity benefits schemes, provident funds, gratuities, bonuses and pension etc." Thus, all above mentioned definitions of social welfare agree on this point. It includes all voluntary acts by employers aimed at improvement and betterment of workers' social, moral, economic and intellectual conditions. Those acts which the employer is compelled, on pain of legal action, to undertake, however beneficial these may be for the workers, are not included in the province of labour welfare. By welfare scheme the industrialists give evidence of their moral and social enlightenment and help all-round development of workers. This, in turn, helps him in the long run, because, as it has been well observed, a well paid and satisfied worker is an asset and the low-paid unsatisfied worker is liability.

Responsibility of Labour Welfare

Having discussed the problem of Labour Welfare, the question that is likely to come up in anyone's mind is: who is responsible for Labour Welfare? Whose moral obligation is it to promote labour welfare? The most popular view in this regard is that it is the duty of the employer to look after the social welfare of the workers employed by him. This seems to be the most responsible and well considered view because though the industrialist has to make big investment in the labour welfare schemes, it is by no means dead investment. A well-fed, well-clad and satisfied worker is an asset. He makes no loss of man hours by absenteeism, strikes, slow tactics etc. Besides, he feels a sense of allegiance to the organization in which he works. Therefore, though a costly investment, it pays very rich dividends in the long run. It is a moral duty of every mill owner or industrialist to provide fully for the food and other amenities for the families of the workers who suffer grievious injury in accidents met during working hours. He must also provide medical benefits, pensions, bonuses, incentives etc. However, the industrialist alone is not responsible for labour welfare. It is also the duty of welfare states to look after zealously the interests of the workers and initiate schemes for improvement in their working conditions, raising their morale etc. The Government should strictly enforce the benefits provided by law. It should also prevent any instance of exploitation of woman workers and an abuse of children. In all progressive countries the workers have their Trade Unions which look after and safeguard and promote the interests of the workers. They can compel government and employers to agree to improved benefits for the country. An example of this is, the recent announcement of Government of India to allow for 8.33% bonus to all industrial workers. All three, that is, the employer, the Government and the Trade Unions are jointly responsible for labour welfare.

LABOUR WELFARE IN PRIVATE SECTOR

The factory system of manufacture came to be established in India in the later half of the 19th century. When about the middle of the century, organised industries, worked by means of machinery and power, came to be established, and, in particular textile mills and other factories affording employment to thousands of persons were installed, poor people from rural parts flocked to industrial towns, lured by the money income or the ready means of livelihood available. They were illiterate and ignorant and ordinarily incapable of organisation. These poor folk from rural environment formed the bulk of the workers.

The new mechanical processes made it possible and profitable to employ large numbers of women and children at the machines and it also became evident that work under factory conditions involved special dangers to the health and safety of factory workers. Thus, during this period the efforts of philanthropists, public-spirited individuals and social workers were wholly directed in trying towards enacting provisions specifying the minimum age of employment of children and their hours of work, the regulation of hours of work for women and the basic provisions relating to safety and guarding of machinery. These were followed much later by provisions relating to health and sanitation. The safety and health provisions were elaborated in the successive Factories Acts. Though the requirements relating to health and safety cover matters such as cleanliness, ventilation, lighting, drinking water, latrines and urinals, fencing and precautions against fire, these various provisions are to be considered as measures required for the proper organisation of the work-place. It was only in the Factory Act, 1948 that specific provisions relating to welfare at the work-place were incorporated as a separate chapter. This is so far as statutory provisions go. During the intervening period, 'belated though it was, social consciousness was slowly being aroused and in many quarters there was growing appreciation of the need for the provision of welfare measures and other amenities for ameliorating the lot of the workers torn away from their rural surroundings. The first two decades of the present century saw the beginning of conscious and organised welfare work by a few progressive industrial units. Some social service agencies were also active in the field. It could be said that many of these welfare schemes were models of their kind, established as they were voluntarily out of certain convictions or particular interest or social attitudes coupled with knowledge of the immediate benefit that would accrue to the enterprise itself.

Concept and Scope

The Encyclopaedia of Social Sciences states that industrial welfare work is a term "used to describe the voluntary efforts of an employer to establish within the existing industrial system, working and sometimes living and cultural conditions of his employees beyond what is required by law, the customs of industry and the conditions of the market."

The Labour Investigation Committee in its Report published in 1946, defines welfare activities as "anything done for the intellectual, physical, moral and economic betterment of the workers whether by employers, by government, by other agencies, over and above what is laid down by law or what is normally expected as part of contractual benefits for which the workers may have bargained."

These are broad definitions which emphasise the scope and extent of welfare work as including all types of activities which go to help the worker in leading a fuller life. Even in a given situation, it would be difficult to define the term 'welfare' as applied to industrial workers. As pointed out by the Royal Commission on Labour in India in its Report published in 1931, the concept of welfare work must necessarily be elastic, bearing a somewhat different interpretation in one country from another, according to the different social customs, the degree of industrialisation and the educational development of the workers. For the purpose of this article we may look to the I.L.O. documents for a more workable definition of welfare since these are the results of tripartite discussions and are based on the practices in vogue and the felt needs of the workers.

The Resolution concerning Welfare Facilities for Workers adopted at the International Labour Conference in 1947, refers to the amenities which the employers are urged to provide in undertakings, whenever appropriate, in co-operation with the representatives of workers. These are "such services, facilities and amenities as adequate canteen, rest and recreation facilities, sanitary and medical facilities, arrangements for travel to and from work and for the accommodation of workers employed at a distance from their homes, and such other services, amenities and facilities as contribute to improve the conditions under which workers are employed."

The Asian Regional Conference of the International Labour Organisation held in Ceylon in 1950, devoted considerable attention to the provision of facilities for the promotion of workers' welfare. It considered the Resolution concerning Welfare Facilities for Workers adopted in 1947, but felt that special conditions in Asian countries must be taken into account. Taking into consideration that in the Asian countries public welfare services are not yet developed and that there was a wide diversity in the amplitude and quality of the welfare services and amenities provided in the individual undertakings, the Resolution adopted at this Conference recommended that the basic requirements in respect of workers' welfare facilities, such as occupational health and reasonable medical and maternity facilities, canteens and other feeding arrangements and child care services should be prescribed by legislation thus subjecting them to adequate control and careful and regular supervision to ensure that the minimum standards prescribed were observed. Resolution recognised that this was dealing with only a part of the problem and urged that public policy should ensure that "adequate medical care and educational and recreational facilities, housing and other accommodation are progressively made available for all workers". It also recommended the provision of welfare facilities administered by public authorities financed by welfare funds, and the establishment of various types of co-operatives catering to the needs of the workers.

These two Resolutions sum up the basic requirements in respect of workers' welfare both inside and outside the undertakings. Based as they are on the felt needs of the workers, they seem to point to the very direction in which welfare activities in this country have developed and reinforce our own concepts in the matter. As early as in 1918, the Indian Industrial Commission in its Report stated that "measures for the welfare of operatives in India fall under the heads of co-operation, the provision of open spaces and other facilities for recreation, medical attendance and instruction by various methods and in various subjects. Steps in these directions are being taken by Government departments, by the more enlightened mill-owners, and by private associations like the Servants of India Society and the Social Service League. The necessity of providing open spaces for recreation is generally recognised; medical facilities, when on the right lines, are freely resorted to by the labouring classes, and we would emphasise the urgency for a further extension of these. Co-operative work among labourers and especially among mill hands presents serious difficulties, owing to the fluctuating nature of the population and to the lack of a common interest. But their indebtedness and the extent to which they are exploited by the shop-keepers from whom they buy their daily supplies furnish a very strong case for a special effort. Employers may give most valuable aid in all these directions, and, in particular, by starting benefit and provident funds and by the provision of compensation for injuries etc., received by their employees, a measure, which though already taken by a few public-spirited industrialists, should be much more generally followed." The welfare measures mentioned in the I.L.O. documents were among the subjects discussed in the Report of the Royal Commission on Labour in India and incorporated in its recommendations. It would, therefore, be adequate for the purpose of this chapter if the discussions are confined broadly to these specific measures.

Welfare Programmes

Industrial welfare work has taken numerous forms and so have the agencies responsible for giving effect to them. The welfare facilities now available to industrial workers may be classified into two categories: (A) welfare facilities provided at the work-place, and (B) welfare facilities provided outside the work-place; and these may be discussed under the following heads:

1. Statutory;
2. Voluntary;
3. Mutual; and
4. Other (by Government Agencies, Statutory Welfare Boards and Social Welfare Agencies).

Statutory

Welfares facilities at the work-place: Before we discuss the statutory provisions relating to welfare as such, a review of the provisions of the Factories Act, 1948, relating to health and safety might be attempted to serve as a background. In fact, it is difficult to draw a line where the provisions relating to these might be considered as basic requirements for organising the setting up at the work-place and where they might be deemed to be measures for the welfare and general well-being of the workers. This would very much depend on the standard of the amenities provided.

The basic provisions relating to health and safety cover cleanliness of the work-place, proper ventilation and lighting, removal of dust and fumes, supply of cool drinking water and provision of adequate sanitary facilities, separate for men and women. The provisions in the Act relating to safety are up to the accepted standards of the more industrially advanced countries not only in the safeguarding of dangerous machinery but also in securing safe methods of working in the case of hoists and lifts, lifting gear, safe means of access to work, precaution against dangerous fumes and dust and explosion of gases and vapours.

The standard of compliance with these requirements varies considerably. There are factories in which conditions can be said to compare favourably with the best factories elsewhere in the world and there are also factories, particularly small ones where standards are barely sufficient even to maintain production at a reasonable level. These are indeed "slum factories" in which no regulations, however well conceived, can be of avail in improving working conditions. Such factories do exist elsewhere in the world also.

Sanitary regulations have not eradicated slums so far as housing is concerned and it is accepted that there moval of slums needs recourse to special measures requiring State assistance, the measures generally adopted being demolition of condemned building and rehabilitation of the slum dwellers. The problem of slum industry would have to be dealt with on similar lines. This is today in fact being attempted in a small way with the setting up of industrial estates making it possible for the industries located in congested areas to move to more congenial surroundings. But, in practice, this has had very little effect.

It is, however, a matter of satisfaction that the newer industries that are coming up are much better designed and cater more fully to the basic needs of the workers and provide an environment conducive to the general efficiency and the well-being of the workers. This development has to a great extent been influenced by the new industries set up with foreign collaboration. The high standing and industrial traditions of the collaborators have had their influence on the layout and design of factory building and the standards of amenities provided. A number of foreign firms of high standing have also set up their own manufacturing units in this country bringing with them their own industrial experience. The standards of welfare in most of these new large industrial undertakings are far above the basic requirements laid down under the statute.

These have had necessarily to be in keeping with the general layout and design of building.

The chapter on welfare in the Factories Act covers provision of washing facilities, for storing and drying clothes, facilities for sitting, first-aid appliances, canteens, shelters and rest rooms and creches. It is accepted that the carrying out of these provisions will depend mainly on effective supervision provided within the factory. Government supervisor can never provide the detailed maintenance and day-to-day inspection that is required for the proper maintenance and proper use of safeguards and amenities. In small factories this supervision will have to be the personal duty of the manager and he has to learn that it is not beneath his dignity to give real attention to these matters which are an essential part of good management. In the larger factories such work must of necessity be delegated to a personnel manager or labour welfare officer and provision has been made in the Act that the larger factories must have on their staff a duly qualified officer for this purpose. Many of these facilities are required to be provided only in the larger establishments. A canteen is required to be provided only where 250 or more workers are employed. A creche is required to be provided only where 250 or more workers are employed. These welfare facilities were not new to industry. Such amenities could be found in many progressive undertakings long before the provisions were incorporated in the Factories Act. A few were praiseworthy examples of their own kind. However, even among these few establishments only a small number of the welfare provisions listed characterised the welfare work of a particular undertaking and this was the main reason for incorporating these provisions in the modern Factories Act.

Many of the modern factories have well planned and designed sanitary blocks with toilet facilities, wash-basins and lockers. Canteens, however, have taken the pride of place. These are generally well constructed and well equipped with modern cooking facilities and there seems to be a growing realisation that the time spent in a canteen should serve as a period of relaxation from the working atmosphere of the rest of the building. The creche seems to be the one item which many of the modern factories would prefer to avoid setting up, regulating the employment of women or by employing unmarried women or widows.

In discussing these statutory requirements relating to safety, health and welfare, reference has been made only to the Factories Act. These provisions first appeared in the Factories Act and have since been incorporated with very minor modifications in the Mines Act and Plantations Labour Act.

Welfare facilities outside the work-place: The Plantations Labours Act also provides for certain welfare facilities and amenities outside the work-place such as recreational facilities, educational facilities. But in other industries there are no statutory requirements about the provision of welfare facilities outside the work-place.

Voluntary

Many employers have introduced programmes supplementing the welfare activities under the statutory obligations or by way of extention of these amenities. They include facilities, such as medical care, reading rooms, indoor games, educational film shows, dramas, grain shops, retail shops of their own products, and in a few cases, co-operative banks and provision stores. This is an enumeration of various types of welfare amenities seen in operation in many industries, but all these facilities are not necessarily provided at all undertakings.

Medical care is one important amenity which was being provided by employers on a fairly wide scale covering many sectors of industry and which is now gradually disappearing with the extension of the Employees' State Insurance Act and Scheme. The standards of medical care differed widely but the basic services were provided by many. In some undertakings the standards of the amenities available to the workers were far above those which they could hope to get elsewhere.

The pressing need of workers for adequate medical facilities had been stressed by the Indian Industrial Commission and the Royal Commission on Labour in India. The industry had responded well. The medical departments which were set up, however, confined themselves to treatment of ordinary ailments, paying hardly any attention to the preventive aspects of their work, safeguarding the health of the worker in his working environment. When the Employees' State Insurance Scheme took over the responsibility for medical care, it was hoped that the existing medical departments in industry would take over the functions of an occupational health service for promoting the general health of the workers and protecting them from ailments that may be due to abnormal environmental conditions and the hazards of the occupation. It is only in a few industrial undertakings that this development has taken place.

In the forties of this century, welfare schemes in larger industrial centres received attention from a number of employers. Some schemes were in elementary stage, many were advanced, and a few were a model of their kind. There were schools, meal-sheds, co-operatives, workmen's stores, workers institutes and clubs, societies for cultural activities, etc. In some places playgrounds, dispensaries, maternity and child welfare centres, segregation hospitals, community halls, were provided. These schemes were, however, better operated in conjuction with housing schemes. This was possible in industrial towns in early stages of development where civic amenities were lacking and land was available in plenty.

In older congested rapidly growing industrial towns and cities it was impossible for individual employer to provide these facilities to his own workers. Rapid urbanisation had widened labour market and there was no obvious advantage that the employer saw in providing welfare facilities. Because of this and other difficulties, increasingly, government agencies, statutory boards and welfare funds came to be entrusted with the organisation and administration of welfare activities. But welfare centres continued on the factory premises, wherever possible. These were extensions of welfare facilities statutorily provided.

A new trend was noticed in relation to the provision of welfare facilities to workers with emphasis on the development of basic industries in the national policy. These basic industries were located close to the sources of raw material, power, water, coal, ores, etc. They brought up new towns with new housing, schools, hospitals, recreation facilities, etc. The management discharged in such settings the responsibilities of progressive civic authorities.

Mutual

Workers organised themselves for mutual help. Activities that workers organisation took up so far are of co-operative type like savings banks, credit societies, provision stores, canteens, etc. In some places trade unions undertook in addition to these, literacy work, running libraries, and reading rooms and organisation of religio-cultural programmes, etc.

Though a few workers organisations have made a work in this direction, the range of their activities has been confined to a very limited field, particularly co-operatives. Viewing the problem as a whole, it can be said that there has been no significant or marked increase in these activities during the course of these many years.

WORK OF ORGANISATIONS

However, the conditions brought about by the rapid development of industries and the high degree of urbanisation, not only made development in this direction impossible but made existing amenities in the industrial towns less easily available to the workers because of pressure of population and overcrowding. In the circumstances, obviously, the possibility of improvement could be through the efforts of the State or public authorities. In this connection a suggestion made by the All-India Trade Union Congress in their memorandum to the Investigation Committee is pertinent. It stated: Some of the essential items of welfare should be provided in the Act itself and further regulations regarding details may be kept to be made by rules. As there will be difficulties in enforcing some of the welfare activities such as canteen, creches, washing and bathing facilities in the case of small factories, we suggest that some of these welfare activities should be made available in industrial areas for the general body of workers for whom no separate provision could be made by the employers, and these facilities should be under municipal or governmental control, but may be financed by employers. It was, however, during the war years that the government concerned itself directly with the welfare measure. The Bombay and the U.P. governments were the first to embark on a policy of providing welfare measures for industrial labour. Their welfare activities were organised through welfare centres located in the various industrial centres in the State. The example of these two States has since been followed by almost all the other States and the Union Territories.

The welfare centres are graded according to the importance of the industrial centres in which they are located and cover a wide range of activities such as recreational, educational and cultural and other specific amenities such as creches and shower baths. In some of the States the centres also provide medical care. Formerly the centres were run by Government as a departmental activity, but recently in a number of States Statutory Boards have been constituted for the purpose. The activities of the Maharashtra Labour Welfare Board and the Labour Welfare Schemes run by the Department of Labour, Uttar Pradesh, may be considered as illustrative of the welfare activities carried out through these agencies. The Maharashtra Labour Welfare Board maintains 72 welfare centres—4 *Mahakendras* and 69 *Kendras.* The centres are kept open from 8.00 a.m. to 11.00 a.m. and 4.00 p.m. to 8.30 p.m. for men and boys and from 11.00 a.m. to 4.00 p.m. for women and girls. The *Kendras* are divided into two groups each under the administrative and supervisory control of an Assistant Welfare Commissioner assisted by six Workers' Welfare Officers, each in charge of 5 to 8 *Kendras.* The total staff—executive, supervisory, field level, clinical and other—numbers 412. The *Mahakendras* are located in spacious and well planned buildings with gymnasium, wrestling pits, shower baths and open spaces for games and sports. The *Kendras* are housed in hired buildings with provisions for indoor games and limited facilities for outdoor recreational activities.

Games and sports feature as an important activity of the centres. All centres are provided with facilities for indoor games and outdoor games. Inter-centre competitions are periodically organised. Besides, cultural activities are organised. Music programmes by top-class artists, who offer their services at a nominal charge, are arranged at the welfare centres. Occasionally such programmes are also staged by workers, and this activity has received an added impetus being linked up with Kamgar Sabha Programmes of the All India Radio. Talented men and women artists are picked up from these programmes for further opportunities on the Radio. Educational film shows are held at regular intervals.

Educational activities include nursery schools in some centres (on grant-in-aid basis) for children between the age of three and six and in some centres creches are provided. Scholarships are awarded to deserving and needy students from working class families. The scholars are paid at ₹ 10 per month for 10 months and are required to put in at least one hour's work at a centre for group activities. Workers are encouraged to participate in the Workers' Education Programme. Selected workers are also deputed to a similar programme of the Bombay Labour Institute.

In Bombay, groups of women members are deputed to a *Samsar Shastra Course.*

There is another scheme intended to provide supplementary incomes to working class families living around the centres. The scheme seeks to obtain part-time work of different types essentially unskilled or semi-skilled nature to unemployed workers.

A Library-*cum*-Information Centre is maintained at each *Kendra.* Voluntary groups from industrial areas are encouraged to become its members.

The total membership at the Centres under Maharashtra Labour Welfare Board is over 1,13,000, out of which 20,000 are non-industrial workers and their dependents.

The Labour Welfare Scheme of the Uttar Pradesh Government covers almost the same range of activities as are being provided by the Maharashtra Labour Welfare Board. However, the scheme also provides for medical care—Allopathic, Ayurvedic, Unani and Homoeopathic. The Labour Welfare Centres are classified into three categories, *viz.* Class A, Class B and Class C on the basis of the activities provided in them. There are at present 65 Centres—26 of Class A, 33 of Class B and 6 of Class C. There are two seasonal centres. The Government incurs an annual expenditure of 24 lakh rupees on these.

In Plantations in Assam, considerable headway has been made in the provision of welfare amenities. The Assam Plantation Employees' Welfare Fund Act provides for the constitution of a Fund for financing the activities to promote measures for the welfare of plantation workers in the State. The welfare activities include recreational centres, creches, canteens, hospitals and dispensaries.

Among welfare work carried out by Statutory Welfare Funds the activities of the Coal Mines Welfare Fund stand out very prominently. The principal activities financed by the Fund may be broadly divided into two categories, *viz.*, General Welfare and Housing. A substantial portion of the expenditure under 'General Welfare' account is spent on the provision of medical facilities including specialised treatment in cases of eye, ear, nose, throat and dental diseases and venereal diseases. Surgical facilities are also available. For the treatment of simpler cases a number of regional hospitals with attached maternity and child welfare centres are run by the Fund. Special facilities are provided for T.B. patients and for the treatment of leprosy patients and patients suffering from mental diseases. Grants are made to the colliery owners for the maintenance of dispensary services. Antimaterial operations in the mining areas was one of the major projects undertaken by the Fund. The recreational and educational activities include Miners' Institutes which are the nucleus of the general welfare activities of the Fund and 56 such Institutes have been set up. In addition, 61 Adult Education Centres are functioning in the various coal-fields. The other important welfare activities include pithead baths and creches, grants to collieries for water supply schemes and promotion of co-operative movement in the coal-fields.

The Mica Mines Welfare Fund is responsible for welfare in the Mica Mines, and the agency set up under the recent Iron Ore Mines Labour Welfare Cess Act will assume responsibility for the promotion of welfare in the iron ore mines.

The Company townships do not present a serious problem as the enterprise itself assumes responsibility for providing the civic amenities. They are newly built. These townships are not confronted with the insurmountable difficulties which civic authorities in the industrial towns have to face because of the rapid haphazard growth.

In other industrial towns and cities further development in the field of labour welfare lies in the promotion of activities through Labour Welfare Funds.

It is being increasingly realised by the newer industries today that painting of the factory supplemented by properly designed lighting system is not merely providing a protective coat against weather for the building and the machinery but a means to make the surroundings more pleasant. Many amenities are introduced to make work less irksome and motivate the worker to greater effort. But all these provisions are available to workers in the larger enterprises. Under the Factories Act, only factories employing 10 or more workers with power and 20 or more without power, are covered. Thus, the workers employed in a considerably large number of smaller factories are not in receipt of any benefits emanating from the legislative provisions.

The welfare amenities provided through the Government agencies of Welfare Funds could be availed of by workers irrespective of their employment in a factory covered by the Factories Act or in an unregulated factory. It is, therefore, a welcome feature of the activities of the Maharashtra Labour Welfare Board that the facilities provided can be availed of by non-industrial workers as well.

For the development of small-scale industries a number of Industrial Estates are being set up. The factory buildings are much better constructed and well laid out here than would be the case if they were put up by the entrepreneurs themselves. But so far little thought has been given to the welfare of workers in the Industrial Estates.

WELFARE PROGRAMMES IN INDUSTRY—PUBLIC SECTOR

The Public Sector is a comparatively new arrival on the Indian industrial scene. Not that it was ever absent, wholly. Apart from the employees in their civil and defence departments, Governments employ a large number of workers in many undertakings which are industrial in character. This is also the case with other public authorities. But by and large, these undertakings are either in the nature of public utilities or related to defence. In recent years, however, Governmental industrial venture in India has entered fields of production many of which used to be the traditional preserve of private industry. This development has followed the declaration of Government's Industrial Policy, enunciated in its Resolution on the subject in April, 1948, and later restated in April, 1956. As a result, a growing number of industrial workers are finding employment in Government and other public undertakings. Between 1960 and 1962 alone employment in different branches of the public sector went up from 69 lakh to about 77 lakh. This figure includes administrative, medical, educational and other services; the number of persons employed in this group during 1962 was about 40 lakhs. The welfare of this large number of workers has become the direct concern of the public authorities.

Government's Industrial Policy has been designed to give content to the concept of the 'welfare state' envisaged in the Preamble to the Indian Constitution and its Directive Principles: Thus, the public sector has come to be an instrument of policy for realising the new social order.

It is, therefore, not surprising that the performance of enterprises in the public sector is watched with interest and expectation. One important aspect of their performance relates to the maintenance of high standards of labour welfare. The Industrial Policy Resolution itself lays down that proper amenities should be provided for all those engaged in industry and that their living and working conditions should be improved. The Five Year Plans also emphasise that conditions of work in public undertaking should set the pace for the private sector. These are the basic considerations that guide the public sector undertakings in their efforts to promote welfare of their workers.

Concept and Scope

Labour welfare is an imprecise concept. Taken comprehensively, factors that affect the worker like life in the factory or outside, his earnings, conditions of work, his relations with the management or the trade union, social security, housing and community life have impact on his well-being and, therefore, come within its purview. In fact, the Labour Investigation Committee in its Report published in 1946 defined labour welfare as "anything done for the intellectual, physical, moral and economic betterment of workers". But to deal with the subject in such a comprehensive manner would be going too far afield for the purpose of this article. In a restricted but more commonly understood sense, however, labour welfare relates to the provision of specific amenities at the work-place and outside, through legislative action or otherwise.

According to the resolution concerning welfare facilities for workers, adopted at the International Labour Conference in 1947, welfare amenities were "such services, facilities and amenities as adequate canteens, rest and recreation facilities, sanitary and medical facilities, arrangements for travel to and from work and for the accommodation of workers employed at a distance from their homes, and such other services, amenities and facilities as contribute to improve the conditions under which workers are employed". Again, the resolution on the promotion of facilities for workers' welfare in Asian countries adopted at the ILO Asian Regional Conference in 1950 covered the following specific amenities: (*i*) occupational health facilities; (*ii*) maternity and child care facilities; (*iii*) canteens and other feeding arrangements; (*iv*) medical care; (*v*) educational and recreational facilities; and (*vi*) housing and other accommodation. The ILO recommendation (No. 102) concerning welfare facilities for workers, adopted at the International Labour Conference in 1956, also restricts itself to feeding, rest, recreational and transport facilities.

For the purpose of this chapter, therefore, the term 'Labour Welfare' has been taken in this restricted sense, *i.e,* in the sense of amenities provided within the precincts of the work-place or outside to ensure a better working and living environment to the industrial workers.

The public sector comprises a vast and varied field of activities. Apart from the undertakings run departmentally by the Central and State Governments and other public authorities like the port trusts, local bodies, etc., there is a growing number of public enterprises functioning in different branches of industry. These are run mostly as companies and corporations. Complete data on labour welfare in these numerous undertakings are not readily available. This chapter is, therefore, confined, in the main, to an account of the welfare facilities provided in undertakings run by or under the control of the Central Government.

At the Work-place

Welfare facilities at the work-place, provision of which has been made a statutory obligation of the employers in the Factories Act, 1948, the Mines Act, 1952 and the Plantations Labour Act, 1951, all Central Acts, include facilities such as first-aid appliances, canteens, creches, rest shelters, supply of wholesome drinking water and washing facilities. These enactments do not make any distinction between the public and private sector undertakings in the matter of application of their various provisions; their requirements in regard to the provisions of such facilities apply equally to the public sector undertakings.

Under the Factories Act and the Rules framed thereunder, managements have to ensure general cleanliness of the work-place, proper lighting and ventilation and provide facilities such as: (*i*) first-aid appliances, (*ii*) canteens in factories employing 50 or more workers, (*iii*) creches, if employing more than 50 women, (*iv*) rest shelters, (*v*) seats for occasional rest for workers obliged to work standing, (*vi*) supply of wholesome drinking water, (*vii*) washing facilities, and (*viii*) suitable arrangements for keeping workers' clothing. The statutory requirements in the Act are enforced by the factory inspectorates set up in the State for the purpose.

The Mines Act and the Rules framed thereunder provide for the supply of cool and wholesome drinking water, maintenance of first-aid rooms of the prescribed standard and of first-aid boxes kept in the charge of qualified personnel and located at conveniently accessible places and provision of latrines and urinals separately for men and women workers. The other amenities to be provided by the mine managements are maintenance of creches, provision of canteens in mines employing 250 or more persons, rest shelters and pithead baths equipped with showers. The responsibility to enforce the welfare provisions in the Mines Act and the Rules framed thereunder is that of the Chief Inspector of Mines, Dhanbad. The requirements in regard to the provision of creches and pithead baths in coal mines are, however, enforced by the Coal Mines Welfare Commissioner, Dhanbad.

Plantations Labour Act, 1951 and the Rules framed thereunder also provide for the supply of wholesome drinking water, canteens, creches, medical facilities and suitable housing accommodation for workers as prescribed by the State Governments, The statutory requirements of the Act are enforced by the State Governments through their Chief Inspector of Plantations appointed by them for the purpose.

In the Case of transport undertakings and docks too the provision of welfare facilities such as maintenance of general cleanliness of the work-place, proper lighting and ventilation, facilities for drinking water, provision of canteens and rest shelters, etc. has not been left for voluntary action but is regulated by the relevant enactments. Under the Motor Transport Workers Act, 1961, which is a Central Act, undertakings are required to provide canteens of the prescribed standard and to provide clean, comfortable, well lighted and ventilated rest rooms at places where workers are required to halt at night. The facilities to be provided by the Dock Labour Boards under the Dock Workers (Regulation of Employment) Schemes framed under the Dock Workers (Regulation of Employment) Act 1948, include canteens, supply of drinking water, washing, bathing and toilet facilities and rest shelters.

Reports on welfare activities during 1962-63 received from the Central Government undertakings show that statutory welfare amenities such as the provision of canteens, rest rooms, latrines, washing facilities, first-aid appliances, etc., are being provided in almost all of them. The standards in respect of certain amenities being provided by some of the public sector undertakings are better than the prescribed minimum. For instance, the Sindri unit of the Fertilizer Corporation of India has provided an air-conditioned canteen for the benefit of its workers; it has a seating capacity for about 500 persons. In the National Instruments Ltd., the canteens provided by the management are subsidised by the company towards the cost of fuel and a part of the cost of food stuffs, up to ₹ 7,500 per annum; this is in addition to the establishment charges. While all the undertakings ensure the supply of wholesome and cool drinking water, some of them have recently installed water coolers.

Outside the Work-place

Provision of welfare facilities outside the work-place is not regulated by law. Increasing attention, is, however, being paid by the managements of public sector undertakings to the provision of welfare amenities and programmes in the community, aimed at the promotion of their workers well-being. The welfare facilities provided by them outside the work-place generally include provision of housing, medical, educational and recreational facilities, and transportation to and from the work places. Medical facilities are in addition to those available under the Employees' State Insurance Scheme wherever it applies. Promotion of co-operatives is another measure which generally forms an essential part of the labour welfare programmes and has been receiving increasing attention in recent years. Mention may also be made of the Labour Welfare Funds constituted in 1946 in Central industrial undertakings (excluding Railways and Dock Yards) for financing welfare measures in these undertakings. Besides the provisions made by managements and the activities of these Funds, there are a number of schemes sponsored by other agencies whose welfare activities cover, though not specifically workers in the public sector undertakings. These are the Coal Mines Labour Welfare Fund, the State Governments and the Standardised Industrial Housing Scheme Administrations.

Welfare Amenities in the Railways

The activities of the Welfare Organisation of the Railways cover a wide range of welfare, educational and recreational programmes for the benefit of railway employees. The sources of finance for meeting the expenditure on staff welfare are: (*a*) the Railway revenues, and (*b*) the Staff Benefit Fund which also is financed from these revenues. The activities of the Staff Benefit Fund include: (*i*) relief distress among staff and their children, (*ii*) schemes for sickness and maternity benefits and child welfare, and (*iii*) provision of educational and recreational facilities. The per capita annual contribution from the railway revenues to the Staff Benefit Fund of the Zonal Railways was increased from ₹ 2 to ₹ 4 from April 1, 1958, to provide for an expansion in the welfare activities of the Fund. The rate was enhanced further to ₹ 4.50 from April 1, 1960. The Fund is managed by the Staff Benefit Fund Committees set up at the headquarters and the divisional levels. These committees comprise the representatives of recognised unions, staff and administration.

'Education' is one of the important activities carried out by the Railways for the benefit of their staff. The railways maintain a network of schools located in different parts of the country. The total number of such schools during 1961-62 was 701 of which 641 were primary, 24 middle, 34 higher secondary/high schools and 2 of the intermediate standard. The number of pupils on the rolls in these schools was over 90,000. The railways, during 1961-62, also maintained 12 subsidised hostels for the benefit of railway employees' children.

Some other welfare amenities being provided by the Railways include: (*i*) provision of canteens, (*ii*) vocational training centres to provide technical training facilities for non-skilled and semi-skilled workers during their off-duty hours, (*iii*) handicraft centres for the benefit of Railway men's families, (*iv*) recreational and medical facilities, (*v*) holiday homes, (*vi*) housing, and (*vii*) co-operatives. The recreational activities of the Railways include: (*i*) organisation of tournaments and sport meets, (*ii*) maintenance of recreation clubs and railway institutes set up for the benefit of Railway employees posted at wayside stations, and (*iii*) holiday homes. The 16 holiday homes maintained by the Railways during 1961-62 were quite popular among the employees; over 3,000 employees made use of these homes during 1961-62. This gives an idea of the medical and health facilities being provided by the Railways for the benefit of their staff.

The amount spent by the Railways on the provision of medical and health services during 1961-62 was ₹ 7.51 crore.

Posts and Telegraphs

The Posts and Telegraphs Department have set up a welfare organisation which has been functioning since 1948 and deals with matters relating to the welfare of its employees. The Department also set up in 1960-61 a Welfare Fund for the benefit of its employees, with a Government contribution of ₹ 7 lakh per year for the first three years. The Fund is administered by a central committee and 25 circle committees set up for the purpose. The welfare facilities provided by the Fund include: (*i*) financial and medical assistance in cases of proved hardship resulting from serious illness or major surgical operation, (*ii*) holiday homes, (*iii*) community centres, and (*iv*) sports and recreation clubs.

Apart from the amenities under the Fund, the welfare organisation of the Department also provides a wide range of other welfare and recreational facilities. Important among these are: (*i*) medical facilities, (*ii*) provision of canteens, (*iii*) rest rooms, (*iv*) organisation of sports and cultural meets, (*v*) financial assistance to staff for house building through the staff co-operative housing societies, and (*vi*) organisation of consumer and credit co-operative societies.

Docks and Ports

The agencies for the provision of welfare amenities for dock workers and port employees are: (*i*) the Dock Labour Boards constituted under the Dock Workers (Regulation of Employment) Act, 1948 to administer the schemes framed thereunder for dock workers, and (*ii*) the Port Trusts. Such Boards are at present functioning in Bombay, Calcutta, Madras, Visakhapatnam and Cochin The welfare amenities provided by these agencies include: canteens, rest shelters, dispensaries, hospitalisation and first-aid, drinking water, washing and toilet arrangements, educational and recreational facilities and housing.

The expenditure on welfare amenities, health measures and recreational facilities provided by the Dock Labour Boards is met from a separate fund called the Dock Workers Welfare Fund maintained by the Boards. The Fund is financed from the contributions made by the registered employees at rates determined by the Boards from time to time.

Labour Welfare Funds in Central Government Undertakings

These Funds were created in 1946 for financing welfare measures in Central industrial undertakings excluding the railways and dockyards. The Funds are contributory in nature and are mainly financed from voluntary contributions of the workers and contributions from Government. Its other sources of income include: (*i*) receipts from fines, (*ii*) profits from canteens, and (*iii*) proceeds from cinema shows and dramatic performances organised from time to time. The rate of Government contribution in recent years has been rupees two per worker or an amount equal to the worker's contribution whichever is less. The Funds are administered by bipartite committees comprising representatives of managements and employees of the undertakings.

These Funds organise a wide range of welfare and recreational activities which include: (*i*) medical aid, (*ii*) relief in cases of distress on occasions like death, sickness, accidents and other natural calamities, (*iii*) grant of scholarships to workers' children, and (*iv*) recreational facilities such as sports, maintenance of recreation clubs, reading rooms and screening of films. Besides these amenities, the Funds also grant interest-free loans to needy workers on occasions—like marriage, sickness and funerals.

Apart from the above amenities provided under the Welfare Funds, some of the Government undertakings have also drawn up schemes for providing facilities not covered by these Funds. For instance, about 30 undertakings have set up Death Benefit Schemes on voluntary basis. The purpose of the scheme is to provide financial help to the dependents of deceased workers. Other such amenities provided by some of the undertakings are transport facilities and help in promoting cooperative societies.

Welfare Programmes in the Steel Plants

Apart from compliance with the statutory provisions concerning welfare, the three steel plants in the public sector have paid a good deal of attention to the formulation and implementation of other welfare programmes. Important among these are programmes concerning the provision of housing. To enable the workers to live in a healthy and clean environment, the Steel Projects at Durgapur, Bhilai and Rourkela had drawn up from the outset plans for the construction of townships, with all the essential amenities, near the main steel works. This indicates the progress in regard to the construction of houses in the three Steel Projects (including expansions).

Provision of medical facilities forms another essential part of the welfare programmes of the steel plants. For instance, the Rourkela Steel Project has built up a 250 bed hospital for the benefit of its workers. In addition to this, there are one general hospital and four health centres. Free medical facilities are provided to the workers in these hospitals. Similar medical facilities are available to the employees at the medical units functioning in the Durgapur and Bhilai Townships.

Other amenities provided by the Steel Projects include: (*i*) educational facilities, (*ii*) shopping centres, (*iii*) libraries, (*iv*) children's parks, (*v*) recreational facilities such as cinema shows, open air theatres and recreation clubs, (*vi*) transport facilities to workers—travel at concessional rates for their journey to and from their work-place, and (*vii*) promotion of co-operative societies.

Other Public Sector Undertakings

Apart from the Railways, Posts and Telegraphs, Docks and Ports, Steel Projects, etc., which have been covered earlier; there are a number of other undertakings functioning in different branches of industry as mentioned earlier. These undertakings also have welfare programmes similar to those described earlier. Some of the special features of these programmes, however, may be mentioned here. The National Coal Development Corporation has 23 hospitals and 17 sectional dispensaries. It provides free electricity to workers drawing salaries upto ₹ 400 P.M. Assistance is also given to the dependants of the deceased workers on compassionate grounds. Advances for purchasing bicycles are given by the Hindustan Aircraft Ltd., Bangalore. Heavy Electricals (India) Ltd., Bhopal, pay special attention to the contract labour. Relief is given to the dependants of deceased workers by the Indian Telephone Industries Ltd., Bangalore, under its Death Relief Fund. Hindustan Machine Tools Ltd., Bangalore, has a Fine Arts Society, a stadium and a swimming pool for its workers.

Housing facilities are being provided by almost all the undertakings though the proportion of workers housed varies. In the Sindri Unit of the Fertilizer Corporation of India, for instance, housing accommodation has been given to nearly all workers; the percentage of workers covered during 1962 in the National Coal Development Corporation was about 30.

Contribution of Other Agencies

In the foregoing paragraphs an attempt has been made to give an idea of the welfare amenities provided outside the work-place by (*i*) the managements, and (*ii*) under the Labour Welfare Funds constituted in the Central Government's industrial undertakings. Apart from these, there are a few other agencies *viz.*, (*a*) Coal Mines Labour Welfare Fund, and (*b*) State Governments whose welfare activities cover workers in the public sector undertakings, though not specially. The welfare facilities provided by the Coal Mines Labour Welfare Organisation set up to administer the above Fund and the welfare centres run by the State Governments are available equally to the workers in the public sector undertakings located in areas covered by the programmes of these agencies.

Welfare Personnel

While the responsibility to secure the implementation of the various statutory provisions concerning welfare is that of the Inspectorates set up for the purpose, these enactments also contain provisions concerning the appointment of Welfare Officers in undertakings. The employment limit as prescribed in the Factories Act and the Mines Act is: 00 or more persons in the case of factories and mines, and 300 or more workers in the case of plantations covered by the Plantation Labour Act. The qualifications laid down for such Officers generally are: (*i*) a university degree, (*ii*) degree or diploma in social work, and (*iii*) adequate knowledge of the language spoken by the majority of workers in the undertaking where they are to be appointed. The Union Ministry of Labour has a list of labour officers who are available for posting in Central Government undertakings. The Labour Officers (Central Pool) Recruitment and Conditions of Service Rules, 1951, prescribe the duties, qualifications, etc., of such officers. Their duties include securing provision of amenities such as canteens, creches, drinking water, housing, educational and recreational facilities, etc., for the workers. The qualifications prescribed for them are the same as stated above. Similar qualifications have been prescribed for the welfare personnel appointed by the Coal Mines Welfare Organisation.

There seemed to be a shortage of trained and experienced personnel for labour welfare work. In recent years, however, the facilities for the training of such personnel have increased substantially. Some of the universities and independent institutions offer courses in social work. Generally, these courses are open to university graduates and their duration is two years. The trainees are awarded a degree or diploma after completing the prescribed period of training. With the professionally trained personnel manning all the services, it is hoped, that the quality of service rendered to work would be better.

While the survey attempted here is not exhaustive it can at least be said to be illustrative.

WELFARE PROGRAMMES OF TRADE UNIONS

In the Indian trade union movement there are more schools of thought than one, The trade union organisations which are run by the communists or which work according to communist line do not appear to believe very much in the efficacy of social welfare programmes. Their whole approach to the question is different. The second group of trade unions and the organisations to which they are affiliated are essentially financially weak and do not appear to have been able to undertake social welfare programmes on a sizeable scale. Indian National Trade Union Congress has affiliated unions in Ahmedabad, Bombay, Indore, Jamshedpur, Madras, etc. These unions do undertake social welfare programmes. It may, however, be said that it is only at Ahmedabad that social welfare activities have found a permanent and extensive place in the work programmes of the trade unions. The Textile Labour Association of Ahmedabad has been conducting social welfare activities for the last 45 years or so and now spends annually as much as four to five lakh rupees on social welfare programmes. There must be other unions of workers in private and public sectors, in other parts of the country who might have been doing similar work. The total assessment of this work is, however, not available. In the absence of such a comprehensive assessment this chapter might enable the readers to have a glimpse into what the trade unions might have been doing in the field of social welfare programmes, by and large, throughout India.

The Trade Union Movement has its origin in Western countries. As a result of industrial revolution in the West, large scale industries came into existence and the workers all of a sudden realised that they had ceased to be the owners of the tools belonged to the employers. The employees had to work with those tools in return of wages paid to them. The worker was reduced to a mere wage slave. Thus, started the capitalist system of exploitation of man by man. In course of time, however, the workers realised that if they had to combat this exploitation, they should form associations of the working classes. These associations soon began to be known as "trade unions".

Trade union movement was primarily organised to relieve the workers from their chains of exploitation. The trade unions, therefore, made demands on behalf of workers, entered into collective bargaining, settled disputes, called out and conducted strikes to secure redressal of their various grievances.

Marx and Trade Union Movement

When large-scale industries began to be established in the early years of the 20th century in our countiy, trade union movement was born as a necessary corollary. Methods employed in the Western countries were more or less copied in our country. But at the end of the First World War a novel idea which was put into practice in Russia caught the imagination of the world. Karl Marx was the Father of this idea. He pointed out that in a capitalist society, exploitation of workers was bound to take place. As a result of exploitation, class war is bound to follow. In order to win this war, the workers should unite, and the trade unions should form the vanguard of this movement which would bring about revolution in the society and ultimately destroy the exploitation of this class. This theory of Karl Marx was put into practice by Lenin in Russia where under his leadership, Russian working class brought about a revolution and the dictatorship of the proletariat was established. This experiment gave entirely a new colour to the trade union movement. People began to think that as was done in Russia, workers can bring about a revolution and destroy the capitalist society through their trade unions.

Gandhiji's Concept of a Trade Union

When Mahatma Gandhi returned to India, after his stay and successful experiments in the practice of 'Truth' and 'Non-violence' in South Africa, he was probably conscious of both these concepts of the trade union movement; but he did not approve of either of them. He felt that the methods employed by the Western trade unions while taking care of workers' wages, their conditions of work and other material things, basically ignored the building up of their character. He also felt that the trade union movement in Western countries was not conducted for securing justice to the workers but for obtaining largest number of benefit for them by resorting to any means. As for the Russian experiment, he fell that the whole experiment was divorced from 'Truth' and 'Non-violence' and the workers were exploited by the trade unionists for achieving their political ends. He, therefore, did not desire that the trade union movement in our country should be organised either on the Western or on the Russian pattern.

When Smt. Anasuyaben Sarabhai asked Mahatma Gandhi in 1917, whether he could help her in forming a trade union of textile workers of Ahmedabad, he very candidly asked her as to why she wanted to form a union? He further asked whether she wanted a union of thieves or of robbers, or a union of men? According to Mahatma Gandhi, if workers were united, and as a result of their union they became strong, and their strength was used to deprive the employers or the society of their legitimate rights it was a union of thieves or robbers. But if the workers were united and were taught to become men—that is, responsible citizens of the country—and if their unions were to insist on securing justice and nothing but justice, and further more, if the unions were to advise the workers even to make sacrifices for the larger interests of the society as a whole, then it was a real union of men and if Smt. Anasuyaben would undertake to form such a union, he would gladly guide and help her.

Experiment in Ahmedabad

Smt. Anasuyaben agreed to accept Mahatma Gandhi's advice and thus commenced a novel experiment of 'Truth' and 'Non-violence' in the field of trade union movement. A union of textile workers was formed in Ahmedabad. Its constitution was drafted by Mahatma Gandhi himself. The workers had to pay regular subscription to maintain their office-bearers and to conduct union's various activities. Office bearers were not to act as lawyers who would take up any case for a fee, but would espouse the cause of the workers only if they made a just and reasonable demand. All false demands had to be rejected. For settlement of a demand, firstly, negotiations had to be undertaken. If negotiations failed the matter had to be referred to the arbitration whose decision would be binding to both the parties, and only when arbitration was not available, workers were to be advised to go on strike. But strike had to be completely peaceful. There should be no violence or coercion. The trade union had to bridge the gulf between the employers and employees. Their hearts had to be changed. Means to be employed were 'Truth' and-Non-violence'. Method to be used was that of arbitration. The battle was to be won with the help of public opinion. Mahatma Gandhi took active interest in the working of the Textile Labour Association, Ahmedabad. He himself used to say that he was making experiment in Ahmedabad, and if the experiment succeeded, he would allow the movement to be spread all over the country, In 1948, nearly three decades after the experiment started in Ahmedabad, Gandhiji felt that it had more or less succeeded and then he allowed the Ahmedabad workers to expand their activities in various other industries throughout the country. Thus, was born the Indian National Trade Union

Congress which today happens to be a big representative organisation of the workers in the country.

Plight of Workers

One of the clauses in the constitution of the Textile Labour Association, Ahmedabad, as drafted by Mahatma Gandhi reads as follows:

"(4) To raise the status and improve the conditions of life through internal efforts."

Smt. Anasuyaben Sarabhai had to implement this clause of the constitution and to carry out the promise made to Mahatma Gandhi according to which she had pledged herself to build up the character of workers. What was the condition of Ahmedabad workers and that of the workers in the country in those days, that is, before 1920? Workers were illiterate, their children were not sent to school, wages were so low that the whole family, husband, wife and children, had to work for the maintenance of the family. Workers were addicted to drinking. Child marriage, bigamy and polygamy were prevalent amongst the working class and customs resulting out of their backwardness were rampant. The society was plagued with untouchability. Women-folk were illiterate. Birth-rate and infant mortality rate were very high. Workers were living in slums and they had little knowledge of hygienic habits needed for a city dweller. They were ignorant about rules of health. They were victims of superstition. They were suffering from inferiority complex and they believed that they were born to be slaves of the rich. This was the plight of workers more or less in our country when the new experiment was commenced.

Literacy Drive

There were no primary schools in the working class localities, Even if schools were opened workers' children would not attend the schools as they were required to help their parents by working on some odd jobs to augment the meagre family income. Smt. Anasuyaben Sarabhai, therefore, first of all, directed her energies to tackle this problem. Adult education classes were opened. In the light of a kerosene lamp on the verandah of a sympathetic worker or in an open space under the sky, she would collect the workers and teach them how to read and write. Soon the movement gathered momentum and adult education classes became the main activity of the Textile Labour Association, Ahmedabad, in the initial stage of its organisation. After 25 years or so, that is, in 1942, the Textile Labour Association conducted an inquiry about the literacy among the workers, and it was found that as many as 85 per cent of the textile workers, as a result of the efforts of the Textile Labour Association, had learnt to read and write.

Opening of the Closed Doors

The Textile Labour Association's concept of adult education was not only to impart knowledge of letters but to ensure all-round education. The closed doors of their minds had to be opened. They had to be equipped with knowledge which would enable them to think for themselves and to distinguish right from wrong. And whatever was learnt in the adult education classes had to be absorbed and expanded also. In order to achieve this objective, the Textile Labour Association began to open libraries and reading rooms in various working class localities. Adult education classes are no longer necessary now but the libraries and reading rooms are in great demand. At present as many as ninety libraries and reading rooms are maintained by the Textile Labour Association in various working class localities of Ahmedabad.

Primary Schools

Should adult education classes form a permanent activity of the Textile Labour Association programme? A question was asked: If the parents could not be persuaded to send their children to schools, it would become necessary to have adult education classes for all time to come. This was not only a social problem, but it was a ticklish economic question also. In those days parents to earn from ₹ 20 to ₹ 25 per month between themselves and the children were also earning from about ₹ 7 to ₹ 10 per month. The family was maintained with the help of the children's earnings. And if the children were sent to the schools, how could the family be maintained? The union had first to tackle this economic question. A demand for wage increase was made and the wages were increased. Then started a whirlwind campaign amongst the workers to send their children to schools, but there were not adequate number of schools. The Association decided to open its own primary schools. School after school was opened. At one time, out of an annual subscription of nearly ₹ 2,50,000 as many as ₹ 50,000 were spent on primary education by the Association. Demands for opening fresh schools were every day increasing. How can a trade union afford to open as many primary schools as would fulfil the needs of all the children of the workers? The union, therefore, started persuading the local Municipality to open primary schools wherever they did not exist. But this was also of no avail, for children would not go to schools merely because a school was opened in their locality. The school-going habit had to be inculcated in them. The union, therefore, devised a new plan. A school was opened by the union. The union staff used to visit the working class localities to bring the children to the school, and when the parents got accustomed to sending their children to schools and the children were habituated to attending the school, the school was handed over to the Municipality. This process went on for years and all the schools started by the union were handed over to the Municipality in course of time. Even before compulsory primary education was introduced in Ahmedabad, the children of working classes had accustomed themselves to going to schools and it was considered a matter of shame for the parents if their children were not going to school.

Prohibition

The British Government did not believe in the policy of Prohibition. Excise duty was levied on all intoxicants and a large revenue was collected from that source. The Government was not interested in reducing or abolishing the consumption of liquor. Liquor was freely available everywhere in the country. A large number of liquor shops were also opened in the working class localities. Hours of work in factories were long, working conditions were miserable, living conditions in worker's house were also pitiable. When they left the factories in the evening the workers were completely exhausted and since the atmosphere at home was unattractive, they would go to the liquor shops, indulge in drinks and thus try to forget their miseries. Major part of the earning of the workers was thus spent away on drinks on pay-day and there was hardly anything left to feed the members of the family till the next payment. Hence, debts had to be incurred. The workers addicted to drinking were suffering in health and their efficiency in the factories was also affected. The drinking habit made the workers not only inefficient but also unsocial. They were becoming irresponsible to their family, to the industry and to the society. The Textile Labour Association, therefore, decided that workers must be freed from the habit of drink. The Association started prohibition propaganda among the workers, house-to-house visits were undertaken, and pledges not to drink were given by the workers. *Mohalla* organisations were formed to introduce prohibitions were also utilised for the purpose. The union passed a resolution asking workers to give up their drinking habit, and it was further decided that if a member was found drunk he would be expelled from the union. The prohibition movement gathered great impetus when Mahatma Gandhi started his march to Dandi from Sabarmati Ashram to commence the *Salt Satyagraha*. Thousands of workers to whom Mahatma Gandhi was a friend, philosopher and guide, followed him in this historic march and they would not turn back. About four miles away from Sabarmati Ashram, near Chandola Lake, Mahatma Gandhi halted for a while and addressed the textile workers. He asked them to go back to Ahmedabad, and advised them to completely stop drinking, remove untouchability and wear Khadi. As advised by Mahatma Gandhi, the workers returned to Ahmedabad and the union vigorously started the three activities named by Mahatmaji. In a year's time, Ahmedabad was completely free from the habit of liquor drinking. When Government auctioned licences, nobody came forward to make a bid. The Government then arranged to hawk liquor from tenement to tenement in working-class localities. However, nobody would buy it. Prohibition had come to stay in Ahmedabad. Workers were free from the vice, and later on when the Government of Bombay decided to introduce partial prohibition in the province, Ahmedabad was selected as the first 'Dry Area' in Gujarat Region. Besides making prohibition propaganda, alternative recreation programme had to be evolved to lead the workers away from liquor-shops. Physical culture centres, libraries and reading rooms, recreation clubs were started; musical and dramatic societies were also promoted. A volunteer corps was formed.

Khadi

The Textile Labour Association felt that khadi was the link between industrial workers living in urban areas and the unemployed or underemployed population living in rural areas. Even though the textile workers were producing cloth in the mills, they were advised by the union to use as much khadi as they can, and thereby help their brethren in rural areas. The union started a *Khadi Hat* (khadi-shop) to enable the workers to buy khadi conveniently. A large number of textile workers are today habitual wearers of khadi and the shop which was started in 1930 has since flourished having an annual sale of khadi to the extent of ₹ 10 lakh.

Untouchability

A section of workers in the textile mills came from the so-called class of untouchables. In the interest of solidarity of workers and to secure social justice for them, it became the duty of the trade union to see that untouchability among the workers was eradicated. A two-fold programme was undertaken. The union started propaganda among the Harijans for their uplift. They were taught the value of cleanliness and hygienic habits. They were taught how to cook nutritious and tasteful food. They were also advised to give up undesirable social practices; For all these purposes, the assistance of caste organisations was secured. Child marriage and bigamy were condemned. On the other side, among the so-called *Savarna* people, that is the rest of the working classes, a vigorous propaganda was undertaken to remove untouchability. Canteens and dining sheds in the factories were opened to Harijans. Harijans were also taken to temples by the *Savarnas.* As a result of this propaganda undertaken by the union, it may be stated without any exaggeration that untouchability has more or less disappeared from the textile workers of Ahmedabad.

Social Reforms

Mention was made in the preceding paragraph about use of caste organisations to remove untouchability. The Textile Labour Association felt that if uplift work had to be done among the backward communities, their caste organisations could not be ignored. The caste organisations had their own constitutions and rules which were respected by the people. It was felt that if the constitutions of these caste organisations could be modified and rules changed, the organisations could become effective vehicles for introducing social reforms on a large scale. Among the textile workers, there were three or four castes which were depressed and backward. Besides, the Harijans who suffered from untouchability, there were *Vagharies* and *Thakardas* who, though they were not considered untouchable, were, however, as backward as Harijans. The union, therefore, decided to utilise the organisations of these castes. Thus, 'Sudharak Mandate' of these castes came to be established. Through the agencies of these bodies, the leaders of castes were persuaded to introduce reforms in their own communities. Resolutions were adopted by these Mandate regarding sending their children to schools. It was, however, with great difficulty that the leaders of these castes were persuaded to send their girls to schools. Parents even used to give differential treatment to boys and girls. A girl was supposed to marry and go to somebody else's house. She was, on this account, not properly fed or clad and was also not sent to school. With special efforts in this direction, the mental approach of parents towards their children was suitably modified. Marriage customs made marriages very costly. Resolutions were adopted to reduce the cost and strict watch was kept by the organisations to see that these resolutions were acted upon. Women were very rarely sent to the maternity homes for deliveries. In single ill-ventilated dark rooms, deliveries took place. Birth-rate was high and death-rate of children was also very high. Large number of women were becoming victims of diseases and were losing their lives immediately after deliveries. To begin with, one, and later on, several maternity homes were opened in the city through the efforts of the union, and active propaganda was undertaken with the help of these caste organisations to send women to the various maternity homes. It is gratifying to note that at present not a single bed remains vacant in the numerous maternity homes, in Ahmedabad. Women rarely succumb to death on account of maternity, and death-rate among children has also been considerably reduced.

Worker's Wife

The problem of emancipation of women was very complex. As a daughter in the parent's house, she was neglected; as a wife in her husband's house, she was more or less treated as a slave. Being a member of the weaker sex, she was always exploited, ill-treated and very frequently beaten by her husband. In a number of cases husbands used to punish their wives by marrying second time.

The Textile Labour Association felt that unless the status cf woman in the house was raised, there would be no happy domestic life in the working class family. The easy way was to help women form their association and advise them on their problem. However, it was felt that this might destroy the family life of thousands of workers. The union, therefore, chose to take to a difficult path which was likely to take some time to achieve results but once the results were achieved, the domestic life of the workers would indeed be a happy one. The Association started propaganda among men and women simultaneously. Men were told to respect womenfolk, to abstain from beating their wives and to treat mother of their children as their equals. Women were advised on how to keep their houses clean, how to spend their time usefully, how to cook tasty food, how to rear up their children well and how to create conditions where their husbands might never think of disrespecting them. This method worked well and brought forth good results. It may not be correct o draw a conclusion from the above episode that the textile workers have totally stopped beating their wives, but it can safely be stated that the practice is fast disappearing and the workers have realised that it is improper to beat their wives, and they feel ashamed now to admit that they are beating their wives.

Co-operative Housing

Trade unions in Western countries generally concentrate their energies on the improvement of working conditions in factories. If a worker has to be a responsible citizen of the State, the trade union as conceived by Mahatma Gandhi cannot ignore the living conditions of workers. As early as 1929, the attention of the Textile Labour Association was drawn to the slums which were unfit for human habitation, and in which the textile workers were then living. The union felt that unless clean, well ventilated and sufficiently spacious houses were provided to the workers their health could hardly be maintained. Women who had to live in such houses could not feel happy, and the menfolk would hardly have any attraction for their homes. The union drew out a ambitious programme. A survey was made. It was found that 60,000 houses were required to be built. The employers were persuaded to build some houses. They could build hardly 2,000 tenements. The Municipality was then requested to build some houses. Hardly a thousand houses could be built by the Municipality. The gap was too large. What was to be done? The union felt that a way had to be shown to the working class. The union, therefore, formed the first Co-operative Housing Society in the year 1931. Workers immediately understood the significance and implications of co-operative effort. They began to save and more and more co-operative housing societies began to be formed. Later on after achieving independence, the Government introduced the subsidised Industrial Housing Schemes and today in Ahmedabad, the workers have formed over 200 co-operative housing societies, probably the largest number of co-operative housing societies in any industrial city in India. The union's activity on this score is, no doubt, satisfactory; yet slums do exist today and, therefore, this becomes even today one of the important activities of the trade union.

Textile Labour Association

The Textile Labour Association, Ahmedabad, is now 46 years old. The problems and difficulties which confronted social workers 30 years back no longer exist today. The workers are well-organised, their wages have increased, their working conditions have improved, their social customs have changed, they are educated and their children also receive education. They have become politically conscious, their representatives are elected to the Municipal Board, Legislative Assembly and to the Parliament, and they manage their union too. But a trade union cannot afford to be contented with the progress achieved. The process of reformation in the social field has to be continuous. The work among men, women and children and youth as also health activities are to be carried on for all time to come. The five main activities mentioned above are carried on by the Textile Labour Association. Keeping these activities in the centre, physical culture centres, libraries and reading rooms, dispensaries and maternity homes, boarding houses, a co-operative bank, co-operative society and co-operative housing societies are organised.

Workers' Duty Towards Society

All these activities surely build up the character of the worker, but it was felt that something vital was lacking. Man must realise that his ultimate duty in life is to help other human beings. Instead of hatred, we must have love for our fellow-beings. Love must be translated into help, and help should come out of sacrifice. A worker earning a living wage, having a decent house, and enjoying political freedom may be a good worker, but he cannot be considered as a good man unless he realises that there are human beings in this country who are not as well placed as himself and deserve some help from him. To inculcate this idea among the workers, the Textile Labour Association has the *Seva Patras* and *Seva Mandals* (Societies of Service) Committees in working class localities. Workers spare a coin, or handful of grain everyday and periodically such accumulated savings are handed over to these *Seva Mandals* who help those who are needy by way of giving food, books and fees to the needy and medicine to the sick. The Chawls or Bastis where *Seva Mandals* are formed present a picture, to the visitor, of a society where everybody feels like a member of a large family.

The afore-mentioned activities are being carried on by the Textile Labour Association for the last 46 years. It is rather difficult to assess the exact results of all these activities. But if one were to compare the textile worker of Ahmedabad of 1917 with the worker of today, he will obviously observe a vast difference between the two. To what extent the experiment made by Mahatmaji in Ahmedabad has influenced the Indian Labour Movement? As mentioned above, the Indian National Trade Union Congress (INTUC) was started in 1947. About 1,600 Unions with a membership of eighteen lakh workers from all over the country in various industries are affiliated to this national organisation. Have all these workers imbibed the spirit of Mahatma Gandhi? One cannot give a definite reply, but one may safely say that continuous propaganda is made by the INTUC to lead the workers in this direction. All the sixteen hundred Unions affiliated to the INTUC may not, however, be able to achieve what the Ahmedabad Textile Labour Association has been able to achieve.

QUESTIONS FOR EXERCISE

1. What is Labour Welfare? Who is responsible for Labour Welfare?
2. Trace the history of Labour Welfare in India.
3. Explain the pattern of Labour Welfare Services in India.

27

Workers' Participation in Management and Profit Sharing

MEANING OF WORKERS' PARTICIPATION

Workers' participation in management has been interpreted as the joint consultation prior to decision-making by the management. Workers take it as equivalent to co-decisions. Expert regard it as association of labour without the final authority or responsibility in decision-making. However, it is a process of delegating authority or responsibility in the general area of managerial functions. It is a forum for the formal and informal communication and consultation by which the employees are kept informed about the affairs of the concern and through which the workers present their opinions, suggestions etc. to contribute to management decisions.

It has been laid down in India's Third Five Year Plan that "The success or failure of an undertaking is not the concern of management alone. For the peaceful evolution of the economic system on a democratic basis, it is essential that workers' participation in management should be accepted as a fundamental principle and on urgent need."

As a human being every worker wants that his opinion and voice should carry some weight in the working and management of the enterprise in which he is working. In the words of Prof. F.S. Walpole, "It is not a matter of man being accorded the privileges to an employee, of stating a complaint or offering a suggestion, but of being bestowed with a responsibility to do so, because he is investing not money but life.

The scheme of workers' participation in management has been devised to ensure effective consultation with workers on points of their concern. It makes the workers feel that they have better understanding of the industrial process in which they take part. It gives them a sense of direct participation in industrial decisions. Increasingly associated with the management of industrial undertaking the workers develop an awareness of the problems of industry. They feel that they have to make a positive contribution towards the goals of business organisation. Workers participation meets the psychological needs of the workers, brings them closer to the management, promotes their interest in self-education, gives them an insight into the economic and technical conditions and the purpose of the undertaking where they work and serves to bridge the gulf between the perceptions management and the workers.

OBJECTIVES OF WORKERS' PARTICIPATION

1. To increase production and welfare: The primary objective of workers participation is to increase the production and the productivity of the workers by improving the industrial and human relations industry. It takes the minimum economic welfare instead of 'maximum profit' as the object of industrial production. Job satisfaction brings about increased production and leads to higher profits to the industry.

2. To achieve better social status: This system gets the workers a respectable status in the society. It assures the human dignity because workers become a partner in the gains of productivity. It reflects in terms of maintaining healthy industrial relations by reducing industrial strifes and creating positive conditions in which industrial harmony and peace can grow.

3. To achieve change in attitude: Workers' participation seeks to bring about a change in their attitude, they think themselves part and parcel of the unit. This system is promoted through the changing attitude of employers towards labour. It brings a basic change in the thinking of the workers. Psychologically, workers accept their responsibility as they feel themselves the partners in taking the decision on the matters concerning them. Participation makes them a responsible employee.

FORMS OF WORKERS' PARTICIPATION

1. Co-partnership: Under co-partnership workers are involved in the shareholding of the company for which they are working. They become a part owner of the company. They take part in the internal matters of company as a shareholder. They may elect their representatives to the board of directors in the management of the concern. They share the profits of the company in the form of dividend.

2. Suggestion scheme: 'Suggestion scheme' is one of the ways of encouraging workers interest in a concern. Under this scheme, suggestions are invited from the workers to improve the methods of working in the concern and to pay suitable reward to the worker whose suggestion proves useful. The management gets new ideas and workers feel important. In India, Dalmia and D.C.M. have introduced such schemes successfully.

3. Employees' representation on the board of directors: This ensures a full-fledged participation of workers in management, one or two workers' representatives are nominated or elected on the Board of Directors, the apex body in decision-making. As directors they have the same authority. This scheme has been successfully implemented in several countries of the world. In India, it was introduced by the election of two directors from among the employers on the Board of Directors of the nationalised banks under 'Nationalised Banks Management and Miscellaneous Provisions Scheme' in 1970. One such director was from the clerical and non-supervisory cadre and another from the supervisory cadre.

4. Joint management councils: Joint consultative committees are set up comprising the representatives of the workers and the employers to discuss various matters concerning the working conditions of workers in industry. The decisions of such committees are purely of advisory character though the management generally implements the decision because it is the outcome of the deliberations between the representatives of the management and the employees. The matters which are generally taken up by these committees are prevention of accidents, management of canteens, water, meals, safety etc., issue and revision of work rules, avoidance of waste of time and materials, absenteeism, indiscipline, training etc. Such committees may be formed on plant or shop level. The matters which are to be settled through collective bargaining such as wages, bonus, etc. are excluded from the scope of the committees.

5. Works committees: In establishment employing 100 or more workers, establishment of works committees were made compulsory by Industrial Disputes Act, 1947. This introduced the system of labour management participation through legislation. Such committees consist of equal number of representatives of workers and employer. Its main purposes are to provide measures for securing and preserving amity and good relations between the employer and employees. However, these committees have failed in the attainment of their avowed objectives due to unchanged outlook.

MERITS OF WORKERS' PARTICIPATION

1. Mutual understanding: In a capitalistic economy, workers and capitalists have different interests. Both doubt the integrity of each other. Both are ignorant of each other's problems and never try to know them. The workers' participation in management extends mutual understanding between the workers and employers who come nearer to each other and understand each other's viewpoint. To employees it gives a better understanding of their role in the working of the industry and of the processes of production.

2. Increase in production: Better understanding and good relations are the pre-requisites of higher and better production. Production and productivity increase by effective co-operation of the workers. Increased production benefits both the employers and the workers.

3. Solution of industrial disputes: As the workers become partners of the industry and take part in the decision-making they extend full co-operation to the management in carrying out the decision. They have a sense of loyalty and better understanding. This reduces to the minimum the possibility of dispute based on irrational grounds.

4. Increased efficiency of workers: Under the scheme workers abide their own decisions and work with their full zeal to carry out the decision. Their efficiency and productivity are increased. This benefits both the parties in shape of increased wages to labour and in the form of increased and better production to the management.

5. No outside intervention: As employees become responsible for carrying out the decision industrial relations are improved and industrial disputes become negligible. In the absence of any dispute there is no question of outside intervention.

6. Industrial democracy: Industrial democracy means participation of all parties in the management of industries. True industrial democracy is established when workers participate in the management. Their ego is satisfied and they contribute something positive in the interest of the industry and of the country as they can express themselves better.

7. No resistance to change: Change is generally resisted by the workers because every change is regarded by them as a threat to stability. But, if workers are given a right to participate in the decision-making bodies, they adjust themselves to the changed environment. Once the workers are taken into confidence introduction of change is very smooth.

8. Spotting out creativity of employees: Participation offers an opportunity to intelligent employees to demonstrate their knowledge, skill, initiative as well as creativity. It enables the management to capitalise the talent and ability of employees. It offers an opportunity for the advancement of employees and of management executives.

OBSTACLES IN WORKERS' PARTICIPATION

1. Inefficiency: As Indian workers are inefficient, uneducated and not competent in taking the decision, their participation will only delay the implementation of the decision. A good decision cannot be carried out unless it is supported by the workers.

2. No participation in complicated problems: Participation cannot be extended to complicated problems such as financing, marketing, production and managerial functions, such as planning, directing, coordinating, controlling etc., as these functions require specialised knowledge. Management today requires services of experts such as financiers, engineers, managers, accountants, chemists, statisticians etc., who are fully equipped and use the modern methods and techniques to the job they are assigned. This specialised knowledge is not an elective function. Therefore, it cannot be shared with workers.

3. Weak trade unions: In India trade union movement is not strong. There are multiple trade unions. They are dominated by political leaders and with political ideologies. Workers' participation can succeed only when labour is duly organised so that they can work on equal footings. It is very necessary to have one representative trade union in one unit.

WORKERS' PARTICIPATION IN INDIA

1. Pre-independence period: Before independence in India nothing sincere was done in this direction by the Government or by the private employers. For the first time the management of the Delhi Cloth and General Mills Ltd. introduced the workers representation in mills.

2. After independence period: (*i*) *Workers committees.* The Government of India passed the Industrial Disputes Act, 1947 under which workers committees were established with a view "to promote measures for securing and preserving unity and good relations between the employer and workmen." But these committees failed in the attainment of their avowed objectives.

(*ii*) *The industrial policy resolution of 1956*: It emphasised the need of associating workers with management in the following words: "In a socialist democracy labour is a partner in it with enthusiasm. There should be joint consultation and workers and technicians etc. be associated progressively in management whenever possible. Enterprises in public sector have to set up an example in this respect."

(*iii*) *The Second Five Year Plan*: It gave concrete shape to the concept of labour participation in management in India. The Government of India announced its policy as follows: "It is necessary in this context that the worker should be made to feel that in his own way he is helping to build a progressive state. The creation of industrial democracy, therefore, is a prerequisite for the establishment of a socialist society." The approach of the Planning Commission was accepted by the Government and Parliament.

(*iv*) *Study group 1956*: A First hand of workers participation was considered necessary. In 1956, the Government of India decided to send abroad a study group under the chairmanship of Mr. Vishnu Sahai, the then Secretary, Ministry of Labour. The Study Group carried out on the spot study in U.K., Belgium, France, Sweden, Germany and Yugoslavia. The group submitted its report in 1957, incorporating concrete suggestions for the implementation of the workers participation including the establishment of joint councils in Indian industries.

(*v*) *Labour conferences 1957*: The matter was placed in the agenda of the Indian Labour Conference in 1957. It was considered in detail. The conference decided that the workers participation for the present should be left to the volition of the employers. It was also recommended that the scheme should be initially tried out in 50 undertakings in both the public and private sectors. A sub-committee of the four persons was set up to consider details regarding the scheme of workers participation.

(*vi*) *Tripartite Seminar 1958*: In February 1958, a tripartite seminar on labour management cooperation was held in which participated employees and employers from undertakings chosen for setting up joint management councils, representatives from the central organisation of employers and employees and of Central/State Governments. The seminar arrived at certain conclusions regarding the constitution and functions of joint management councils and administrative problems connected therewith.

(*vii*) *A second tripartite seminar 1960*: It was held in March 1960 under the auspices of Union Ministry of Labour to exchange views on labour participation. Against a modest target of fixed in 1957 the joint management councils were set up only in 24 units, 17 in private sector and 7 in public sector.

It was agreed that a tripartite committee on labour management co-operation should be set up at the centre to review the progress of the scheme from time to time and to sort out difficulties in the functioning of joint management councils. The Government of India set up a special unit in the Ministry of Labour and Employment to deal with all matters connected with the scheme.

(*viii*) *Nationalised Banks' Scheme 1970*: In 1970 the Government of India placed before Parliament a scheme known as "Nationalised Banks' (Management and Miscellaneous Provision) Scheme." In pursuance of its terms two directors were elected on the Board of Directors of each Nationalised commercial bank, representing the employees of bank—one from amongst the clerical and non-supervisory cadre and another from supervisory cadre officers.

(*ix*) *Scheme of workers' participation in industry 1975*: On 30th October, 1975, Government of India announced a scheme of workers' participation in industry at shop and floor levels as a part of 20 point programme. The scheme was introduced in mining and industrial undertakings employing 500 workers or more. A National Apex Body was set up at national level. States also constituted Apex bodies to review the industrial relations. Bipartite National Committees were established in key industries. On 5th January, 1976 the Government extended this scheme to Government sector units employing 100 or more workers.

WORKERS PARTICIPATION IN MANAGEMENT

The Government reviewed the working of earlier schemes on workers' participation which were introduced in October 1975 and January 1977 respectively. In the light of the review and experience gained in the implementation of the scheme, the Government introduced a new and comprehensive scheme of workers participation *vide* Resolution dated 30 December, 1983 in Central public sector undertakings.

A Tripartite Committee constituted under the scheme and comprising representatives of some Central ministries/State governments, major public sector undertakings and central trade union organisations, reviews progress of the scheme from time to time and suggests remedial measures. A monitoring cell had also been created in the Ministry of Labour to assist the Committee.

The schemes relating to participation of workers in management have in the past been non-statutory and not been able to provide an effective framework for a meaningful participation of workers in management. A national seminar was, therefore, organised in New Delhi on 8-9 January, 1990 to hold a wide debate on the subject. Subsequently, regional seminars were also held in Kanpur, Thiruvananthapuram, Madras, Indore and Bombay. The subject was also discussed in the conference of the state labour ministers held on 20 April, 1990 and the Indian Labour Conference, 21-22 April, 1990. On the basis of the consensus of opinion expressed in these fora, the participation of workers in Management Bill,

1990 was formulated and introduced in Rajya Sabha on 30 May, 1990. The bill *inter alia,* provide for participation of workers in management at the levels of the shop floor, the establishment and the board of management level in industrial establishments covered under the Industrial Disputes Act, 1947.

SUGGESTIONS TO MAKE PARTICIPATION SUCCESSFUL

1. Free atmosphere: An atmosphere completely free from psychological inhibitions on the side of both the parties should be created.

2. Facilities: The management should ensure maximum security of service, maximum possible facilities, reasonable structure of wages, salaries and allowances to the workers.

3. Education of representatives: Workers and managements representatives should be educated in the mechanics of participation schemes.

4. Strengthening of unions: Workers unions should be strengthened. Free from any political pressures workers representation should be made at shop and floor levels.

5. Elimination of communication gap: Communication gap should be eliminated. Suggestion system, consultation, etc. should be introduced in the industry.

6. Collective bargaining: Collective bargaining should be introduced in industries for settling labour disputes amicably. Direct labour tactics such as strikes, gherao, etc. should be avoided as far as possible.

PROFIT SHARING

What is Profit Sharing?

1. *International Labour Organisation*: "Profit sharing is a method of industrial remuneration under which an employer undertakes to pay his employees as share in the profit of the enterprise, in addition to their regular wages."

2. *Henry R. Seager*: "Profit sharing is an agreement freely entered into, by which the employee receives a share, fixed in advance, of the profits."

3. *U.K. Profit Sharing Co-partnership Report*, *1920*: "Profit sharing" is used "as applying to those cases which an employer agrees with his employees that they shall receive in partial remuneration of their labour and in addition to their wages a share fixed beforehand in the profits realised by the undertaking to which the profit sharing scheme relates."

Characteristics of Profit Sharing

1. Added remuneration: Profit sharing scheme is not a method of wage payment because it is based neither on time nor on output. It may be described as a form of an added remuneration.

2. Share in profits not losses: Only profits are shared and not the losses. The amount to be distributed among workers depends primarily on the profits.

3. Advance agreement: The proportion of profits to be distributed is determined in advance under an agreement and the management can make no change in it later on.

4. Extended to all workers: The scheme is extended to all the workers in the industry, irrespective of their nature of job.

Bases of Profit Sharing

1. Individual basis: Each worker must be paid that share of the profit which the concern has earned due to his efforts. This is established a direct relationship between effort and reward. But it is very difficult to find out individual's contribution to the profit.

2. Departmental basis: The profits earned by a particular department are shared by its employees. Thus, each department may have its own arrangement.

3. Unit basis: The profits earned by the unit are distributed among the employees and the employer of the unit. Thus, efforts of the workers are duly rewarded.

4. Locality basis: The profits of all the industrial units in a particular locality are pooled and divided among the workers and employers of the locality in a pre-determined ratio.

5. Industry basis: The profits of all units belonging to a particular industry are added together and divided in the given ratio between the employers and the employee. Thus, the workers of the unit having losses may also get the share in the profits of the industry.

Advantages of the Profit Sharing Scheme

1. Increased productivity: Profit sharing scheme creates an interest and a desire among the workers to work whole-heartedly for the concern. They realise that increase in output or reduction in cost will benefit not only the employer but also the workers. Thus, the scheme induces the workers to produce more at lower cost of production.

2. Improved industrial relations: Replaced by the community of interests industrial unrest and strife come to an end. The management and workers cooperate to maximise the profits of the concern. Thus, are ensured industrial peace and better industrial relations.

3. Workers welfare: Increased earning for workers as an additional earning contributes materially to the welfare of the workers. The lumpsum paid to them can be used for some constructive purposes. It ensures greater economic security.

4. Stabilisation of labour force: As the workers who leave the concern during the course of year, lose their share profit, hence, the scheme is a positive incentive to the workers to stick to their jobs. Thus, it ensures Stabilisation of labour and reduces labour turnover.

5. Improvement in supervision and administration: As the workers are directly linked with the share of profit and their morale is kept high they do not need strict supervision. Disciplined workers alone keep the standard of administration high.

6. Realisation of social justice: Profit sharing scheme achieves social justice by relating earning of the workers to the company's financial position and by affording them the place of equal partners in an industrial enterprise.

7. Sense of responsibility: Due to profit sharing scheme the worker is self-motivated. He feels a sense of responsibility as he is interested in the prosperity of the concern.

8. Advantages to the society: Society is benefited by the reduction in industrial disputes, reduction in the cost of production, improvement in the quality of the goods, low price of the commodity and minimisation of the wastage of men, material and machines.

9. Increased national income: Lesser industrial disputes, more production, better quality, increased income of workers and employers due to profit sharing scheme lead to the increased national production and national income.

Limitations of Profits Sharing

1. Not well founded: The profits do not result merely from the availability of capital or efforts of labour. It depends on several other factors such as efficiency of management, market conditions, economies of size and location and other factors beyond the control of the workers. Thus, profit sharing does not maintain any healthy relationship between effort and reward.

2. Lack of distinction: Profit sharing does not distinguish between efficient and inefficient workers. Irrespective of individual's efficiency all workers share equally. This lowers the morale of efficient workers and their productivity comes down.

3. Delay in reward: A share of profit is paid to the worker only at the end of a specified period. Thus reward comes long after the exertion has been made. This reduces the eagerness to get something for the efforts.

4. Industrial unrest: The profits of the concern are either very low or are turned into losses during the lean years of depression. Instead of eliminating industrial disputes, profit sharing scheme may well be a cause of industrial unrest.

5. No proper determination of profit: The determination of exact amount of profit and the workers share therefore may pose a number of complex problems, because the management tempers the account. Trade unions may have their own doubt about the correctness of accounts even if the management is honest.

6. Opposition by trade unions: Trade unions generally put up stiff opposition to the scheme on the plea that it is a mischievous move on the part of the management to create disunity among the workers. The workers of the concern making good profits lose their interest in trade union movement.

7. Opposition by employers: Employers object to the profit sharing scheme, arguing that profit is partly the reward of the risk which the employer runs. Further, why should the workers not bear the share in loss as well?

8. Reduced labour mobility: Profit sharing ensures the stability of workers. It reduces the mobility of workers which is always not in the interest of the workers and the organisation.

9. Negligible motivation: If the total profits amount to a small sum the share of each worker would be negligible to induce him to greater efforts.

10. Unscientific base: The scheme has no scientific base or formula to allocate the profits. The workers share of profit have been allocated on an arbitrary basis usually a percentage of pay.

11. Low wages: It is generally found that where the scheme is in operation, the wages are paid low.

To conclude, profit sharing schemes are not good in themselves nor do they create good industrial relations between workers and management. The relations depend upon the basic attitude of both the parties.

QUESTIONS FOR EXERCISE

1. What is the meaning of workers' participation in management? What are its objectives and forms?
2. Explain objectives of workers participation in management.
3. What are the merits of workers' participation in management? How far has this been successful in India?
4. State the case for and against the participation of workers in the management of industry.
5. Would you recommend labour participation in management? If so, at what level and to what extent?
6. What is the meaning of profit sharing? Discuss its advantages and limitations.
7. Assess the importance of profit sharing scheme in improving the industrial relations.

28

Collective Bargaining

DEFINITION OF COLLECTIVE BARGAINING

1. *Michael J. Jucious*: "Collective bargaining refers to a process by which employers on the one hand and representatives of employees on the other, attempt to arrive at agreements covering the conductions under which employees will contribute and be compensated for their services."

2. *Encyclopaedia of Social Services*: "A process of discussion and negotiation between two parties one or both of whom is a group of persons acting in concert. The resulting bargain is an undertaking as to terms and conditions under a continuing service is to be performed."

3. *Edwin B. Flippo*: "Collective bargaining is a process in which the representatives of labour organisation and the representatives of business organisation meet and attempt to negotiate a contract or agreement which specifies the nature of the employee-employer union relationship."

ROLE OF COLLECTIVE BARGAINING

1. Management point of view: From the management viewpoint the main object of an organisation is to get the work done by the employees at minimum, cost and thus earn a high rate of profits. Maximum utilization of workers is the objective of effective management. This co-operation from the side of the employees required collective bargaining as a device to get and promote co-operation. The labour disputes are mostly due to certain direct or indirect causes based on rumours and misconceptions. Collective bargaining is the best remedial measure for maintaining cordial relations between the employer and employees. Strikes and go-slow tactics are avoided resulting in increase of production. It promotes industrial democracy.

2. Labour point of view: Labour has poor bargaining power. Individually a worker has no existence. As labour is perishable, the employers succeed in exploiting the labourers. In united form the working class becomes a power to protect its interests against the exploitation of the employers through the process of collective bargaining. The collective bargaining imposes certain restrictions upon the employer. It prevents unilateral action. All employees are treated on equal footings. The conditions of employment and rates of wages are changed only after negotiations with labour. Employer is not free to make and enforce decisions arbitrarily.

3. Trade union point of view: Collective bargaining can be made only through the trade unions, who are the bargaining agents for the workers. Trade unions protect the interests of workers through constructive programmes. Collective bargaining is one of the devices to attain this objective through negotiations with the employers. Trade unions negotiate with employer for better employment opportunities and job security through collective bargaining.

4. Government point of view: Government is also concerned with the process of collective bargaining. It passes and implements labour legislation to be implemented in its true sense. It enforces the rules and laws, by force. Collective bargaining deters the Government from using the force because an amicable agreement can be reached between employer and employees for implementing the legislative provision. Labour problems are minimised through collective bargaining and industrial peace is promoted without any use of force.

Essential Pre-requisites for Collective Bargaining

1. Strong trade union: Existence of a strong representative trade union in the industry that believes in constitutional means for settling the disputes.

2. Enlightened management: Existence of a strong and enlightened management which may integrate the different parties, *i.e.*, employees, owners consumers and society or Government.

3. Agreement on objectives: Agreement on basic objectives of the organisation between the employer and the employees and on mutual rights and liabilities.

4. Constructive method of negotiation: Existence of a fact-finding approach and willingness to use new methods and roles for the solution of industrial problems. The negotiation should be based on facts and figures and both the parties should adopt constructive approach.

5. Proper records: Proper records for the problem should be maintained.

6. Starting at plant level: Collective bargaining should be best at plant level. If there are more than one plant of the firm, the local management should be delegated proper authority to negotiate with the local trade union.

7. Avoiding unfair practices: In order that collective bargaining functions properly, unfair labour practices must be avoided by both the parties.

8. Arbitration clause: The contract must include arbitration clause in case there is a dispute. The institution of collective bargaining represents a fair and democratic attempt at resolving mutual disputes. Wherever it becomes the normal mode of settling outstanding issues, industrial unrest with all its unpleasant consequences is minimised.

PROVISIONS OF COLLECTIVE BARGAINING CONTRACT

Collective bargaining is a form of collective agreement. It should include every matter defining the relationship between the management and the workers. Usually two types of provisions are included in a collective bargaining agreement.

(*i*) *Economic provisions*: Economic provisions involve provisions which affect the economic and working conditions of the workers.

(*ii*) *Political provisions*: The political provisions include the provisions relating to the general administration such as divisions of authority and responsibility between the management and the employees or workers' participation in decision-making bodies or powers to challenge the decisions taken by management etc.

Terms in Contract

1. Wage rates, including shift and overtime wage rates, the method and the period of payment of wages and incentive wages.
2. Allowance, holiday pay, leave with pay etc.
3. Hours of work, holidays, vacations, leave rules etc.
4. Lay-off of workers, rationalisation, demotion, discharge, promotion or transfers, covering particularly the nature and effect of security.
5. Grievance-procedures including steps, time limitations and provisions for arbitrations.
6. Safety and health facilities.
7. Setting up of standards for production, methods and procedures.
8. Workers' representation in management, profit sharing and co-partnership.
9. Recognition of trade union and its authority.

10. Maintaining discipline, penal provisions for indiscipline.
11. Provision for retirement benefits such as pension, gratuity provident fund etc.
12. Performance appraisal, job analysis and job evaluation.
13. Bonus.
14. Labour welfare and social security measures etc.
15. Arbitration clause.

In India collective bargaining got impetus from statutory provisions which laid down general principles of negotiation, procedures for collective agreements and the character of representation of the parties negotiating disputes. Among the voluntary measures, tripartite conferences, joint consultative boards, industrial committees and working parties at the industrial level played a vital role in the development of collective bargaining in India. The Code of Discipline enforced in 1958 by voluntary agreement between workers and employers aimed at avoiding work stoppages as well as litigation, securing settlement of disputes and grievances by negotiation, conciliation and arbitration facilitation, free growth of trade unions. It attempted to establish faith of the parties in the voluntary approach. It provided a suitable climate for the growth of the collective bargaining in India.

Types of Collective Agreements

Collective agreements concluded in India may broadly be placed under three types:

(*i*) Voluntary Agreement which have been drawn up after direct negotiation between the parties and are purely for purpose of their implementation. From the industrial point of view, cotton textile industry, plantation industry, coal industry, chemicals, petroleum, oil refining and distribution, automobiles and electric equipment manufacturing industry are the examples where voluntary agreements have been common.

(*ii*) Agreements which combine the elements of voluntaries and compulsion both; and

(*iii*) Agreements which acquire legal status because of successful discussion between the parties and under legal reference to industrial tribunals or courts. In port industry, port-level agreements have been concluded while in banking and insurance industry, industry level agreements have been more common. Collective bargaining has made recently its headway and post and telegraphs too.

Assessment of Collective Bargaining in India

1. Pre-Independence: (*i*) *Lack of unions recognition*: Except for the industrial relations legislation in some States where arrangements for recognition of unions exist, there has been lack of statutory recognition of unions for the country as a whole.

(*ii*) *Lack of good faith*: There is also the lack of provisions requiring employers and workers to bargain in "good faith".

(*iii*) *Historical factors*: Some historical factors have also stood in the way of collective agreements having a greater share in maintaining industrial harmony. The Whitley Commission found that the only attempt made to set up machinery for regulating the relations between a group of employers and their work-people was at Ahmedabad. Although the assessment of the Whitley Commission was made soon after the Trade Unions Act, 1926 was enforced, the situation did not change significantly in the period 1931 to 1947.

2. Since Independence: Since independence trade unions have been growing and agreements with employers have become more common. The changing attitude of employers and the emergence of a new generation of employers and workers have also been helpful in this direction. Despite their limitations legal measures have lent as much support to collective agreements as joint consultations in bipartite and industry levels. As laid down in the First Plan, the concept of collective bargaining could derive its reality only from the organized strength of the workers and genuine desire on the part of the employers to co-operate with the workers. Recently the Government of India have given encouragement to collective bargaining in this country by providing a scheme of workers' education, participation of labour in management, evolving Code of Discipline, framing works committees, joint councils and grievances procedure at the plant level. Besides, tripartite conferences and committees have also provided an ingenious mechanism for promoting collective bargaining practices.

QUESTIONS FOR EXERCISE

1. What is Collective Bargaining? What is its role in industry? Describe its pre-requisites and provisions.
2. Discuss the role of collective bargaining in personnel management. What are the essential conditions for successful collective bargaining?
3. How can you make collective bargaining effective at Plant level? Write short note on 'collective bargaining'.

29

Grievance Procedure and Discipline

Definition of Grievances

1. *R.P. Calhoon*: "A grievance is defined as anything that an employee thinks or feels is wrong generally accompanied by an actively disturbing feeling. It does not have to be justified."

2. *M.J. Jucious*: "A grievance can be any discontent or dissatisfaction, whether expressed or not whether valid or not and arising out of anything connected with the company that an employee thinks, believes or even feels as unfair, unjust or inequitable."

3. *Dale Beach*: "Grievance is any dissatisfaction or feeling or injustice in connection with one's employment situation that is brought to the attention of management."

CAUSES OF GRIEVANCES

1. Difference of opinion: An important reason of grievance is the difference of opinion on any particular point between the workers and the management. Different interpretation of legal provisions lead to such difference of opinion.

2. Status of trade union: The determining age, strength and status of trade union is also a leading factor in grievance. If a trade union is comparatively young and it has substantial strength, it is more militant and it gives air to the grievances of the workers in a big way.

3. Working conditions: A large number of workers grievances are about the bad and unhealthy working conditions in the organisation such as frequent break-up of machines, disruption in the supply of material, continuous and unjustified cut in wages, more rejection of goods, etc.

4. Doubts and fears: Many grievances arise due to conservative attitude of the managers and supervisors. For example the partial attitude of the manager to the workers may create fear and dissatisfaction in the minds of workers.

NEED FOR A GRIEVANCE PROCEDURE

What is grievance procedure?

Grievance procedure is a problem-solving, dispute setting machinery which has been set up following an agreement between labour and management. It is the means by which a trade union or an employee makes the claim that there has been a violation of the labour agreement by the company.

According to Mangurlkar "a grievance procedure is essential because it brings uniformity in handling the grievances," It is a device by which grievances are settled generally to the satisfaction of the trade union or employees and the management. It is an important part of labour relations. It is essential, even if the plant is not organised. It enables a management to detect defects or flaws in the working conditions or in labour relations, to detect defects or flaws in the working conditions or in labour relations, and undertake suitable corrective measures. In order to create a good morale and a code of discipline, it is essential that the grievance procedure is applied honestly and without prejudice, failing which there is likely to be an explosion, and employees would be irretrievably impaired. It gives confidence to the workers. If he does not get a fair deal, he knows what to do and whom to approach to ensure that he does get justice. It gives him confidence that "his complaint will be investigated and a decision given in a reasonable period of time."

Objectives of Grievance

1. To attend to grievance: Most grievances seriously disturb the employees and affect their morale, productivity and willingness to cooperate with the organisation. If an explosive situation develops, it may be promptly attended by the grievance handling procedure already in existence.

2. Limitations of supervisors: It is not possible that all the complaints of the emplyees would be settled by first-line supervisors. These supervisors may not have a proper training for the purpose, or they may lack authority. Moreover, there may be personality conflicts and other causes as well.

3. To check on arbitrariness: It serves as a check on the arbitrary action of the management since the supervisors know that employees are likely to see to it that their protest does not reach the higher management.

4. To serve a pressure valve: It acts like a pressure valve on a steam boiler. It serves as an outlet for employee gripes, discontent and frustrations. It makes employees entitled to legislative, executive and judicial protection. Grievance redressal procedure, which also act as a means of upward communication gives this protection.

5. To create awareness of top management: Due to Grievance Procedure the top management becomes increasingly aware of employees problems, expectations and frustrations. It becomes sensitive to their needs and cares for their well-being. While formulating plan that might affect the employees for example, plant expansion or modification, the installation of labour saving devices, etc., the management should take into consideration the impact of such plans on the employees.

6. To give way to protest: The management has complete authority to operate the business as it sees fit-subject to its legal and moral obligations and the contracts it has entered into with its workers or their representative trade union. But if the trade union or the employees do not like the way the management functions, they may submit their grievances in accordance with the procedure laid down for that purpose.

Advantages of Grievance Procedure

1. It is a channel or avenue by which any aggrieved employee may present his grievance.
2. It is a procedure to handle every grievance systematically.
3. It is a way to relieve the worker from his dissatisfaction with his job and working conditions.

TYPES OF GRIEVANCE PROCEDURE

The grievance procedure may be of an open door type or of a step-ladder type.

1. Open-door type: In an open-door policy the management asserts that no employee is prevented from going to it directly with his grievance, and even meet the head of the concern in an effort to have his grievance properly attended. Open-door policy may be useful in the casê of small units.

2. Step-ladder type: In a large organisation, however, it is not possible for the top man to attend to each grievance at a personal level. Therefore, most companies prefer the step-ladder type of procedure for an expeditious processing of the grievances of their employees.

GRIEVANCE PROCEDURE STEPS

1. Grievance procedure steps in unionised organisations

(*i*) *To the supervisor*: The aggrieved employee verbally communicates his grievance to his immediate supervisor or in a conference or a discussion specifically arranged for the purpose and seeks satisfactory solution. The grievance may be settled if the supervisor has been properly trained for the purpose, and if he adheres to a basic problem-solving method.

(*ii*) *To the manager*: If the grievance is not settled by the supervisor it is sent to a higher level manager with a note in which are mentioned the time, place and nature of the action to which the employee objects. The higher level manager may be the chief business manager, a superintendent or an industrial relations officer who goes into the grievance and gives his decision on the issue.

(*iii*) *To the committee*: If the decisions of the supervisors and of the higher level manager have not solved the problem, the grievance is to be submitted to the Grievance Committee, The committee is composed of some fellow employees, the shop steward or a combination of union and management representatives. It considers the record and suggests a possible solution. It may ask the aggrieved to accept the employer's proposed settlement. It may advise that the trade union will not press for procuring anything more than has already been suggested. It may recommend that the issue be submitted for arbitration.

(*iv*) *To the corporation executive*: If the decision or suggestion of the Grievance Committee is not accepted by the aggrieved, he may approach the corporate executive.

(*v*) *To the arbitrator*: The last step is, grievance is taken when the grievance is referred to an arbitrator who is acceptable to the employee as well as the management. They may agree that the arbitrator's award will be final and binding on both the parties.

2. View of the Indian Institute of Personnel Management, Calcutta

(*i*) *To immediate supervisor*: In the first instance, the grievance should be settled at the lowest level; that is, the employee should raise his grievance with his immediate superior.

(*ii*) *To next to immediate superior*: It should be made clear to the employee that he may appeal if he does not get satisfaction from his immediate superior. He should know who the next person in the echelon of management is to whom he should refer his grievance.

(*iii*) *Speedy solution*: The grievance should be speedily dealt with.

(*iv*) *According to instruction*: If the grievance is against any instructions issued by the supervisor, the employee should clearly understand that, in the interest of discipline, the instructions must first be carried out before the grievance can be considered and decided upon. It is only when this has been done that the employer will register his protest and set the grievance handling procedure in motion.

(*v*) *Terms of settlement*: It should be clearly understood by the employee that there will be no recourse to any official machinery till the grievance redressal procedure has been set in motion and that, in the event the employee is still dissatisfied, there will be no direct action by either party which might prejudice the case or raise doubts while it being investigated.

ELEMENTS OF A GOOD GRIEVANCE PROCEDURE

1. Sound Channel: If the previous stage or channel has been found to be inadequate, unsatisfactory or unacceptable the existence of a sound channel through which a grievance may pass for redressal. This stage may comprise three, four or five sub-stages.

2. Simple, definite and prompt procedure: The procedure should be simple, definite and prompt, for any complexity or vagueness or delay may lead to an aggravation of the dissatisfaction of the aggrieved employee.

3. Clearly defined steps in handling grievance: The steps in handling a grievance should be clearly defined comprising the following:

(*i*) *Definition*: Receiving and defining the nature of the grievance;

(*ii*) *Data*: Getting at the relevant facts about the grievance;

(*iii*) *Analysis*: Analysing the facts, after taking into consideration the economic, social, psychological and legal issues involved in them;

(*iv*) *Decision*: Taking an appropriate decision after a careful consideration of all the facts; and

(*v*) *Communication*: Communicating the decision to the aggrieved employee.

4. Following the decision: Whatever the decision, it should be followed up in order that the reaction to the decision may be known and in order to determine whether the issue has been closed or not.

5. Proper search and records: There must be a full search of facts and a proper maintenance of records.

INDUSTRIAL DISCIPLINE

Meaning of Industrial Discipline

1. *W.R. Spriegel and Edward Sohelge*: "Discipline is the force that prompts an individual or groups to observe rules, regulations and procedures that are deemed necessary to the attainment of an objective."

2. *Richard P. Calhoon*: "Discipline may be considered the force that prompts individual or groups to observe rules, standards and procedures deemed necessary for an organisation."

3. *Michael J. Jucious*: "Discipline used as a noun and preceded by the objective 'good' means that the workers winningly abide by company rules and executive order. To set right the indiscipline or improve its causes provided punishment provisions are known as discipline."

Objectives of Discipline

1. To get voluntary acceptance: To get voluntary acceptance to rules, regulations and policies of the organisation in members so that the objectives of the organisation are achieved surely, certainly and economically.

2. To develop adjustment: To develop the feeling of adjustment so that they work according to situations.

3. To provide direction: To provide direction, right of leadership and getting co-operation.

4. To arouse endurance and co-operation: To arouse the feeling of endurance and mutual co-operation among the workers and management.

5. To instigate respect for humanity: To instigate the feeling of respect of human being and human relations and create the atmosphere favourable to that.

6. To increase morale, efficiency and production: To increase the morale and efficiency of the organization so that it can give maximum production on minimum cost.

Principles of Discipline

1. Code of conduct: With the consent of both parties for the establishment of discipline a code of rules and regulations should be made. It should be such that every one may understand and follow it easily. It should be properly communicated.

2. Equal treatment: On the basis of this code all workers should be equally treated. Disobedience to the provisions of the code should be punished without any partiality.

3. Responsible person: On the basis of the code, responsibility of disciplinary action should be in the hands of a responsible person who may give orders to the subordinates.

4. Full knowledge of rules: Workers should have full knowledge of the rules and administration. It should be clear as to which punishment is applicable on the violation of a rule.

5. Preventive measures: Stressing the positive discipline, the management exercises preventive measures for maintaining discipline.

6. Appeal: The supervisor or foreman should be responsible for discipline. It is his duty to punish the indiscipline. However, the person accused should have a right to appeal to the high officials.

7. Natural justice: The causes of indiscipline should be examined impartially. Discipline should be based on natural justice. The accused person should be given a chance to hearing and then only any decision is to be taken.

8. Prompt action: Disciplinary action should be taken promptly. There is no effective control on accusation punishment if decisions are delayed.

9. Instrument of progress: Official disciplinary action is to be calculated as an interment of progress of the organization.

10. Confidential proceedings: Disciplinary proceedings should be confidential and not in the presence of other persons. Otherwise he loses faith in organization and respect for high officials.

Kinds of Discipline

According to Dale Yoder, 'Discipline is to regulate the human behaviour through reward or punishment'. This definition stresses upon two types of discipline—positive and negative.

1. Positive Discipline: It is an arrangement where a worker is motivated to work himself and he is eager to obey and abide by the rules. It is a mental action to influence the mind of the worker in such a way that he grows faith and esteem for the organization. Positive discipline has a deep connection with the human relations aiming reaction.

According to Spriegel, "Positive discipline does not re-establish the comprehension but brings it to use for the completion of a general of objective. Positive discipline does not obstruct a person but makes him suitable to get more freedom without any extra formality. Positive discipline instigates effective co-operation. It depends on the proper acceptance by workers an efficient management of the organization and supervisor's efficiency. It is a voluntary effort by workers and the management.

2. Negative Discipline: Negative approach to discipline is the opposite of positive discipline. It stresses more on punishment rather than co-operation. The accused worker is given warning. Its objective is to establish discipline through fear and punishment. The worker is not instigated to work, but deterred from doing or wrongly doing or doing against instructions. He is told the nature and quantity of punishment well in advance before actual punishment is given to him.

Which type is better?

As a policy matter the management should follow the policy of positive discipline, because it is not restrictive in nature. It prompts individuals or groups to observe rules, standards and procedures deemed necessary for an organisation. But negative approach is also necessary to maintain discipline in the industry.

Causes of Indiscipline in Industry

(A) Internal Causes

1. Lack of effective leadership: Discipline needs effective leadership. Effective leadership keeps a balanced influence over all classes of management, labour union, workers, government and consumers.

2. Lack of personnel development opportunities: Workers are disappointed if an industry has no chances of development or chances are not equally available due to partiality in appointments and promotions.

3. Defective supervision: Supervisor is the nearest managerial authority over workers whose human and sympathetic behaviour keeps discipline. If he lacks these traits the worker will not be disciplined.

4. Biased attitude: While giving facilities or taking disciplinary actions if the management does not treat all workers alike, it breeds dissatisfaction and non-cooperation among the workers leading to indiscipline.

5. Lack of code of conduct: Non-existence of a code of conduct or lack of its knowledge to workers, leads to indiscipline.

6. Avoidance of grievances: If officers do not care for the complaints made for the bad working conditions, ill-behaviours of supervisors and other conditions, it leads to indiscipline and dissatisfaction.

7. Divide and rule policy: Management also sometimes grows dissensions among the workers so that they are engaged in mutual complaints and conflicts. This is the policy of divide and rule. Condemning this policy Fayol says, "To weaken the enemy, it is intelligent to divide the army but to divide in one's own group is a crime to the business."

8. Personal factors: Indiscipline may also be due to personal factors such as selection of wrong persons, lack of capability control and co-operation. This creates disinterest in work and spoils the discipline.

9. Victimization and excessive pressure: Management grows prejudices about some persons. It tries to perplex and crush them and in retaliation this increases indiscipline.

Thus, the causes of indiscipline among the employees are discriminating behaviour by management, non-compliance and complaints, wrong decision regarding selection and promotions, etc., lack of effective communication, wrong type of leadership and supervision. Sometimes, management is itself responsible for creating indiscipline among the employees. Hence, H. Fayol has very aptly said that, "Discipline is that what leaders make it." To keep the workers in discipline the management should itself exhibit disciplined behaviour.

(B) External Causes

These relate to the factors outside the concern itself. Various non-economic, social and political factors influence the discipline in industries as a whole. If the whole country is passing through violence and disturbance, the industry's discipline will also be affected.

CODE OF DISCIPLINE IN INDIA

In India code of discipline was evolved in broad outline at the 15th Indian Labour Conference held in 1957. It was scrutinised later on by a Sub-Committee on Workers Participation in Management and Discipline in Industry. It was ratified at a meeting of the sub-committee held on 14 and 15 March 1958. It was finally adopted at the 16th session of the Indian Labour Conference held in 1958. It came into operation with effect from June 1, 1958. It is applicable to both public and private sectors.

1. Objectives: The code aims at bringing about greater industrial harmony and as such expects "a just recognition by employers and workers of the right and responsibilities of either party as defined by law and agreements (including bipartite, tripartite agreements arrived at all levels from time to time) and a proper and willing discharge by either party of its obligation consequent on such recognition. The Central and State Governments on their part, will arrange to examine and set right any shortcoming in the machinery they constitute for the administration of the labour laws."

2. Provisions: The provisions of the code of discipline may be divided into two broad categories. The first category consists of positive obligations placed on the employers and unions. The other category includes provisions in the nature of dont's which can be regarded as negative obligations of both unions and management in general.

3. Essential elements: The striking feature of the code is that emphasis has been put on mutual agreement rather than on compulsory arbitration on adjudication. There is no legal sanction behind the code. The code is not supperimposed. Nor has it a statutory basis. However, the code has a value for it is essential for industrial democracy in India. According to the code, representatives of management and unions should agree to encourage constructive co-operation between their representatives at all levels and as between workers themselves. Code of discipline must be observed because its non-observance would cause harm to the individual worker as well as the whole nation. Indian code of discipline provides that there should be no strikes and lock outs without notice and neither the employers nor the employees or labour union should have recourse to coercion, intimidation, victimisation or go-slow as also litigation and stay-in strikes.

Suggestions to Check Indiscipline

1. Condonation of past offences: As the real purpose of disciplinary action is to prevent the recurrence of future offences of similar nature, they should be allowed to be condoned after a prescribed time limit. As far as the past offences are concerned, an opportunity should be given to employees to rectify their faults. The employer should try to seek co-operation from the employees.

2. Agreement about disciplinary rules: The code of discipline should be prepared and adopted with the approval of employees. In framing the rules and regulations for maintaining discipline, unilateral action should not be taken by the management. A code of discipline duly approved by the representatives of the trade unions and by the management avoids certain unhappy consequences and imposes self-discipline.

3. The discipline committee: While the minor cases in which reprimand, rebuke or warning is required may be settled by the supervisor or the manager, a discipline committee should adjudge the case to ensure the unbiased justice to the employees and the employer where the offence requires a greater punishment.

4. Investigations by personnel department: The Discipline Committee cannot successfully work unless it gets the full facts of the case. These facts should be collected and supplied by the personnel department, as it has the specialised staff for rendering expert service and advice on personnel matters in the organisation. The personnel department acts as a safety valve for the smooth operation of the Discipline Committee.

QUESTIONS FOR EXERCISE

1. Define Grievance and describe its causes. What is the need of a Grievances Procedure.

2. What do you understand by Grievances? Discuss their various causes.
3. Explain the types and steps of Grievance Procedure.
4. What is the meaning of discipline in industries? Define its objectives and principles.
5. "Too often discipline is thought of only in the negative sense, in reality, positive discipline is immeasurably more effective and plays a larger role in business management." Discuss the statement and indicate the principles to be borne in mind while taking disciplinary action.
6. Explain the causes of Indiscipline in Industry. What is the Code of Discipline in India? Suggest improvements in it.
7. "Discipline is what leaders make." Comment.

30

Social Welfare in India

Development of India's vast human potential is essential for achieving the basic objectives of economic growth, equity and self-reliance. Much has been accomplished in the decades since independence. But much still remains to be done. As the economy emerges from a major economic crisis and transits to a path of strong, broad-based growth, it is vital to reinforce the process of social sector development and take special care to protect the weakest and poorest segments of society from the rigours of structural adjustment and stabilisation policies during the transition.

Central Plan Allocations

Recognizing these imperatives, Government has substantially increased the Central Plan allocations for social sectors and poverty alleviation programmes in the last two budgets. As Table 30.1 shows, the budgetary allocation for Education has been increased by 62 per cent over the past two years, with the outlay for Elementary Education going up by 84 per cent and that for Adult Education increasing by 78 per cent. The allocation for health was hiked by 91 per cent. The Central Plan outlay for Rural Development, which encompasses the major programmes for poverty alleviation and employment generation, was raised by 126 per cent over the past two years to a level exceeding ₹ 7000 crore in 1994-95 (BE). Two new schemes, the Employment Assurance Scheme (EAS) and the Prime Minister's Rozgar Yojana (PMRY), were launched in 1993-94 and are being strengthened and expanded.

Employment Growth

In addition to these major increases in Central Plan allocations for social sectors and poverty alleviation programmes, the Government has accorded the highest priority to promoting sustainable employment intensive growth in its economic reform policies. As a result, total

TABLE 30.1

Central Plan Outlay for Social Sectors

(₹ crore)

Ministry/Department/Scheme	1992-93		1993-94		1994-95	Per cent 1994-95 (BE) / 1993-94 (BE)	change 1994-95 (BE) / 1992-93 (BE)
	(BE)	(Actual)	(BE)	(RE)	(BE)		
1	2	3	4	5	6	7	8
1. **Education**	952	964	1310	1314	1541	17.6	61.9
of which							
(*a*) Elementary Education	284	307	442	389	523	18.3	84.2
(*b*) Adult Education	120	98	178	178	214	20.2	78.3
2. **Health**	302	383	483	402	578	19.7	91.4
3. **Family Welfare**	1000	1190	1270	1523	1430	12.6	43.0
4. **Women and Child Development**	452	481	569	573	662	16.3	46.5
of which							
Integrated Child Development Services	360	372	474	474	537	13.3	49.2
5. **Welfare**	530	532	630	747	705	11.9	33.0
6. **Rural Development**	3100	3596	5010	5438	7010	39.9	126.1
of which							
(*a*) Jawahar Rozgar Yojana (JRY)	2046	2545	3306	3306	3855	16.6	88.4
(*b*) Employment Assurance Scheme (EAS)	–	–	1	438	1200	–	–

Contd...

1	2	3	4	5	6	7	8
(*c*) Integrated Rural Development Programme[2]	390	394	654	657	675	3.2	73.1
(*d*) Rural Water Supply and Sanitation	480	481	770	770	950	23.4	97.9
7. **Other Programmes**							
(*a*) Nehru Rozgar Yojana (NRY)	71	71	75	75	70	–6.7	–1.4
(*b*) Scheme for Self-employment for Educated Unemployed Youth (SEEUY)	45	40	40	38	[3]	–	–
(*c*) Prime Minister's Rozgar Yojana (PMRY)	–	–	[1]	35	145	–	–
Total (including others)	**48407**		**63936**		**70141**	**9.7**	**44.9**

1. Provision made at RE stage, as the schemes were launched on Oct. 2, 1993. RE for EAS was ₹ 600 crore and ₹ 35 crore for PMRY.
2. BE as per the Department of Rural Development and Planning Commission. It was revised upward within total BE for the Deptt. of Rural Development. In the Budget Papers BE were ₹ 375 crore, ₹ 630 crore and ₹ 624 crore for the years 1992-93, 1993-94 and 1994-95 respectively.
3. Integrated with PMRY.

Source: Budget Papers and concerned Departments.

employment growth in the economy is estimated by the Planning Commission, to have virtually doubled to about 6 million in each of the years 1992-93 and 1993-94, as compared to only 3 million in the crisis year of 1991-92. In 1994-95, with overall economic growth having accelerated significantly, the increase in aggregate employment can be expected to be commensurately greater.

Human Development

Table 30.2 presents trends in basic indicators of human development. While too much should not be read into year to year changes in the annual data of the Sample Registration System (SRS), it is interesting to note that the all-India infant mortality rate was virtually stable in the crisis-affected years of 1991 and 1992, before resuming its pattern of decline in 1993. Similarly, the death rate rose slightly in 1991 and 1992, before reverting to a declining trend in 1993. These tentative trends are consistent with the view that while general living standards were adversely affected by the economic crisis of 1991-92, the subsequent recovery was beginning to show beneficial effects.

TABLE 30.2

Basic Indicators of Human Development

Year	Life Expectancy at birth[1] (Years)	Literacy rate[2] 1991 (Per cent)	Birth rate[3] (Per thousand)	Death rate[3] (Per thousand)	Infant mortality rate[3] (Per thousand)	Per capita NNP at 1980-81 prices[4] (₹)
1	2	3	4	5	6	7
1951	32.1	18.3	39.9	27.4	146	1127
1961	41.3	28.3	41.7	22.8	146	1350
1971	45.6	34.5	41.2	19.0	129	1520
1981	50.4	43.6	37.2	15.0	110	1630
1982	NA	NA	33.8	11.9	105	1693
1983	55.4	NA	33.7	11.9	105	1691
1984	NA	NA	33.9	12.6	105	1790
1985	NA	NA	32.9	11.8	97	1811
1986	NA	NA	32.6	11.1	96	1841
1987	NA	NA	32.2	10.9	95	1870
1988	57.7	NA	31.5	11.0	94	1901
1989	NA	NA	30.6	10.3	91	2059

Contd...

1	2	3	4	5	6	7
1990	NA	NA	30.2	9.7	80	2157
1991	NA	52.2	29.5	9.8	80	2223
1992	60.8	NA	29.2	10.1	79	2178
1993P	NA	NA	28.5	9.2	74	2226

NA = Not Available. P = Provisional.

1. Data for 1951, 1961, 1971 and 1981 relate to the decades 1941-1950, 1951-1960, 1961-1970 and 1971-1980 respectively, centred at mid-point of the decade *i.e.* 1946, 1956, 1966 and 1976. For 1983, data relate to 1981-85, centred at 1983. The estimate centred at 1988 refers to the period 1986-90. For 1992, it is based on the extrapolated values of the Standing Committee of Experts on Population Projection, centred at June 1992.
2. Data for 1951, 1961 and 1971 relate to population aged 5 years and above and those for 1981 and 1991 relate to population aged 7 years and above. Data exclude Assam for 1981 and Jammu and Kashmir for 1991.
3. Data for 1951, 1961, 1971 and 1981 relate to the decades 1941-1950, 1951-1960, 1961-1970 and 1971-1980 respectively. The estimates for 1981 onwards are based on the Sample Registration System (SRS).
4. Relate to financial years 1950-51, 1960-61 and so on.

Source: (*i*) Registrar General & Census Commissioner of India, (*ii*) Central Statistical Organisation.

5. There are wide inter-State variations in indicators of human development (Table 30.3). For instance, in Kerala the life expectancy at birth at 69.5 years and male literacy rate at 93.6 per cent have reached high levels as compared to States like Bihar, Madhya Pradesh, Orissa, Rajasthan and Uttar Pradesh, where concerted efforts are required for improving the quality of life. Similarly, Kerala's infant mortality rate of 13 per thousand is less than a fifth of the all-India estimate of 74 and less than one-eighth of rates prevailing in Madhya Pradesh and Orissa. Indeed, the indicators of human development in Kerala are comparable with several Asian developing countries like China, Malaysia, Indonesia, Thailand and Sri Lanka which have done well in human development. (Table 30.4).

Decline of Poverty

The incidence of poverty declined from 37.4 per cent in 1983-84 to 29.9 per cent in 1987-88 (Official Planning Commission estimates based on the recently released 48th Round of the National Sample Survey have not yet been finalised). These are the averages for the country as a whole and tend to hide disparities among States. States like Punjab and Haryana had the lowest incidence of poverty of about 7.12 per cent in 1987-88, as against Bihar and Orissa, where more than 40 per cent live in poverty (Table 30.5). This indicates that sustained efforts have to be made to reduce poverty in more populous States with higher proportions

TABLE 30.3

Selected Indicators of Human Development for Major States[1]

State	Life expectancy at birth (years)[2] (1986-90)	Literacy rate[3] 1991 Total	Male	Female	I.M.R.[4]	Death rate	Birth rate
		(Per cent)			(prov. esti. of the SRS-1993) (Per thousand)		
1	2	3	4	5	6	7	8
1. Andhra Pradesh	59.1	44.09	55.13	32.72	64	8.4	24.1
2. Assam	53.6	52.89	61.87	43.03	81	10.2	29.5
3. Bihar	54.9	38.48	52.49	22.89	70	10.6	32.1
4. Gujarat	57.7	61.29	73.13	48.64	58	8.1	28.0
5. Haryana	62.2	55.85	69.10	40.47	65	7.8	30.6
6. Karnataka	61.1	56.04	67.26	44.34	67	8.0	25.5
7. Kerala	69.5	89.81	93.62	86.17	13	6.0	17.3
8. Madhya Pradesh	53.0	44.20	58.42	28.85	106	12.6	33.4
9. Maharashtra	62.6	64.87	76.56	52.32	50	7.2	25.0
10. Orissa	54.4	49.09	63.09	34.68	110	12.2	27.2
11. Punjab	65.2	58.51	65.66	50.41	55	7.9	26.3
12. Rajasthan	55.2	38.55	54.99	20.44	82	9.0	33.6
13. Tamil Nadu	60.5	62.66	73.75	51.33	56	8.0	19.2
14. Uttar Pradesh	53.4	41.60	55.73	25.31	93	11.4	36.0
15. West Bengal	60.8	57.70	67.81	56.56	58	7,3	25.6
All India	**57.7**	**52.21**	**64.13**	**39.29**	**74**	**9.2**	**28.5**

1. Major States include States with population of 10 million and above as per 1991 Census.
2. Data relate to average over 1986-90 as estimated by the SRS and centred at 1988.
3. Relate to population aged 7 years and above and excludes Jammu & Kashmir for All India.
4. Infant Mortality Rate.

Source: (1) Cols. 2, 6, 7 and 8—Occasional Paper No. 1 of 1994, Sample Registration System (SRS), the Registrar General of India.

(2) Cols. 3, 4 and 5 are based on Final lPopulation Total of 1991 Census, Series-1, Paper No. 2 of 1992, the Registrar General of India.

of people below the poverty line, in order to bring about a significant reduction in the poverty ratio for the countiy as a whole.

Welfare of Weaker Sections

Some social sector programmes have been strengthened and reoriented in favour of weaker sections. Specific minimum weightage is being given to Scheduled Castes/Scheduled Tribes and women in special programmes of poverty alleviation and employment as well as in several other programmes.

TABLE 30.4

Indicators of Human Development for Some Asian Countries—1992

Country	Life Expectancy at birth (Years)	Infant Mortality rate (Per thousand births)	Adult Literacy (Per cent)
1	2	3	4
China	70.5	27	80.0
Indonesia	62.0	66	84.4
India	60.8	74	52.2
Kerala State (India)	69.5	13	89.8
Malaysia	70.4	14	80.0
Philipinnes	64.6	40	90.4
Pakistan	58.3	99	36.4
Republic of Korea	70.4	21	96.8
Singapore	74.2	8	92.0
Sri Lanka	71.2	24	89.1
Thailand	68.7	26	93.8

Note: For India and Kerala State the estimates are from Tables 30.2 and 30.3 respectively.

Source: UNDP-Human Development Report, 1994

Women Welfare

1. PDS: The Public Distribution System (PDS) has been revamped in 1775 blocks to augment the supply of essential (STEP), about 1.37 lakh women have benefited up to December 1994. Rashtriya Mahila Kosh (RMK) was set up in 1992-93 for meeting the credit needs of poor women. The Kosh was set up with a corpus of ₹ 31 crore. Over a year, the Kosh assisted 39 voluntary organizations and extended credit to 44186 women with the financial assistance of ₹ 7.05 crore. The Mahila Samriddhi Yojana (MSY), launched on October 2, 1993, aims at promoting saving habits amongst rural women. Under the scheme, for saving up to ₹ 300 with a one year lock-in-period, a rural adult woman will get a Government incentive of ₹ 75. The scheme has received an overwhelming response from all over the country. Since its inception up to December, 1994 about 72 lakh MSY Accounts have been opened with a total deposit of ₹ 65.90 crore.

2. DWCRA: The Programme for Development of Women and Children in Rural Areas (DWCRA) is now in operation in 450 districts of the country with UNICEF assistance. During 1993-94, 15483 groups with a membership of 2.69 lakh women, were formed to take up economic

TABLE 30.5

Number and Percentage of Population below the Poverty line by States

State	1983-84 Population		1987-88 Population	
	(Lakh)	Per Cent	(Lakh)	Per Cent
1	2	3	4	5
1. Andhra Pradesh	205.1	36.4	195.7	31.7
2. Assam	49.8	23.5	52.9	22.8
3. Bihar	365.5	49.5	336.4	40.8
4. Gujarat	87.6	24.3	73.3	18.4
5. Haryana	27.7	15.6	18.2	11.6
6. Himachal Pradesh	6.1	13.5	4.5	9.2
7. Jammu & Kashmir	10.3	16.3	9.8	13.9
8. Karnataka	137.6	35.0	136.5	32.1
9. Kerala	71.5	26.8	49.0	17.0
10. Madhya Pradesh	254.9	46.2	224.9	36.7
11. Maharashtra	232.0	34.9	214.1	29.2
12. Manipur	1.9	12.3	1	1
13. Meghalaya	4.0	28.0	1	1
14. Orissa	118.1	42.8	135.1	44.7
15. Punjab	24.4	13.8	13.9	7.2
16. Rajasthan	126.2	34.3	99.5	24.4
17. Tamil Nadu	200.2	39.6	176.9	32.8
18. Tripura	5.1	23.0	1	1
19. Uttar Pradesh	530.6	45.3	448.3	35.1
20. West Bengal	255.1	39.2	173.5	27.6
21. Small States & UTs	32.3	27.1	14.2	7.7
All India	**2710.0**	**37.4**	**2376.7**	**29.9**

1. Included in small States/UTs.

Notes:

(*i*) The estimates for 1983-84 are derived by using the poverty line of ₹ 101.8 per capita per month for rural areas and ₹ 117.5 per capita per month for urban areas at 1983-84 prices, corresponding to the poverty lines of ₹ 49.1 and ₹ 56.6, respectively, for 1973-74.

(*ii*) The estimates for 1987-88 are derived by using the poverty line of ₹ 331.8 per capita per month for rural areas and 150.1 per capita per month for urban areas at 1987-88 prices, corresponding to the poverty lines of ₹ 49.1 and ₹ 56.6, respectively, for 1973-74.

(*iii*) The number of persons below the poverty line relate to the population as on March 1, 1984 and 1988, respectively.

Source: Planning Commission.

activities. During 1994-95 (up to November, 1994), over 19000 groups with a membership of 3.19 lakh were formed.

3. Reservation and Priority: There is reservation and priority for women in special employment and poverty alleviation programmes as well. Under the Integrated Rural Development Programme (IRDP), 40 per cent of beneficiaries have to be women. The achievement during 1993-94 was 33.6 per cent. Similarly, under the Jawahar Rozgar Yojana (JRY), 30 per cent of employment generation is meant for women. As against this, the share of women in employment was about 25 per cent in 1993-94. Other schemes to support and improve working conditions for women are: Hostels for Working Women, Day Care Centres/Creches, Employment-*cum*-Training-*cum*-Production Centres, etc.

Child Development

1. Integrated Child Development Services (ICDS) is a comprehensive scheme for the development of children and expectant/nursing mothers. The scheme has gradually been extended to 3381 projects covering 3657 blocks and 240 urban slums. There are 3.4 lakh Anganwadis under ICDS. The beneficiary coverage of ICDS is as high as 1.75 crore children and 0.36 crore mothers, as on September 30,1994. Out of 3381 ICDS projects, 755 projects are being implemented with the World Bank assistance in predominantly tribal and backward areas of Andra Pradesh, Bihar and Madhya Pradesh. The ICDS has made a perceptible improvement in the nutrition and health status of children. In 507 ICDS blocks, services have been extended to cover adolescent girls in the age group of 11-18 years, particularly school dropouts. Other main programmes for the development of children include Early Childhood Education, Balwadi Nutrition Programme, Special Nutrition Programme, etc.

2. Another significant step has been the adoption of a National Nutrition Policy in April 1993 to eliminate/reduce widespread malnutrition. For this, Special Action Plans are being drawn up. A National Nutrition Council under the chairmanship of the Prime Minister, has been constituted to oversee the implementation of the policy.

Welfare of Weaker Sections

The strategy followed for the development and welfare of weaker and vulnerable sections of the society has been to initiate special target-group oriented programmes by earmarking funds, providing subsidies, and reservations in service and educational institutions, etc. Other benefits envisaged for the Scheduled Castes/Scheduled Tribes population include scholarships for studies, free coaching for competitive examinations and training, etc.

1. SCP: The Special Component Plan (SCP) strategy has been followed to channelise the flow of funds from Central and State Plans for the development of Scheduled Castes (SCs), at least in proportion to their population to total population. The SCPs of States are supplemented with Special Central Assistance to fill the gap between requirement and normal flow from Central/State Plans. During 1994-95, of the total State Plan Outlay of ₹ 39194 crore, a sum of ₹ 4312 crore (*i.e.*, about 11 per cent) was earmarked for the Special Component Plan. Special Central Assistance of ₹ 274 crore has been provided for this purpose. The Central Ministries also earmark funds for the development of Scheduled Castes under different programmes. Under the IRDP, 50 per cent of families assisted/funds utilised should be SC/ST families. Similarly, under Jawahar Rozgar Yojana (JRY), priority in employment is given to SC/ST families and about 50 per cent of employment generation goes to them. There is also reservation of 22.5 per cent for SC/STs in the Prime Minister's Rozgar Yojana.

2. TSP: An area based approach of 'Tribal Sub-Plans' (TSP) is being implemented for the development of Scheduled Tribes (STs). The TSPs are implemented through 194 Integrated Tribal Development Projects (ITDP) and 250 Modified Area Development Projects (MADP). Funds for TSP are pooled from State Plans, Special Central Assistance and allocation for various programmes made by Central Ministries. During 1994-95, out of total State Plan, a sum of ₹ 3061 crore was earmarked for TSP and ₹ 275 crore as Special Central Assistance.

3. Incentives: Various incentives like scholarships, hostels, free coaching, etc. are given for the educational development of SC/ST children. Under the Post-Matric Scholarship Scheme, during 1993-94 about 13.38 lakh Scheduled Castes and 3.37 lakh Scheduled Tribes children got financial benefits.

NSFDC: The National Scheduled Castes and Scheduled Tribes Finance and Development Corporation (NSFDC), which was set up in 1989, supplements the efforts of the Government for improving the economic status and quality of life of SC/STs. The Corporation channelises funds through State/UTs level SC/ST Development Corporations and other agencies to assist SC/STs for procuring loans at reasonable rates of interest for income generating and self-employment projects. Up to September 1994, the NSFDC had sanctioned 609 projects costing ₹ 491 crore for assisting 1.79 lakh SC/ST beneficiaries. Out of the NSFDCs share in sanctioned loans of ₹ 243 crore, an amount of ₹ 137 crore was disbursed. The Tribal Cooperative Marketing Development Federation of India (TRIFED) was set up in August 1987, primarily to provide facilities for the marketing of produce, especially minor forest produce from tribal areas. The total turnover of sales and Procurement of TRIFED increased from ₹ 22 crore in 1988-89 to ₹ 86 crore in 1992-93 and to ₹ 106 crore in 1993-94.

5. Reservation: The Government has implemented reservation of 27 per cent of vacancies in civil services and jobs under the Government of India for Other Backward Classes (OBCs), subject to the exclusion of the 'creamy layer'. A National Backward Classes Finance and Development Corporation, with an authorised share capital of ₹ 200 crore, was set up in 1992-93 for promoting economic development of OBCs. During 1993-94, a sum of ₹ 106 crore was sanctioned for assisting 76289 beneficiaries.

6. Other initiatives: Other important initiatives taken recently to improve the well-being of Other Backward Classes and Minorities, include: (*i*) setting up of a National Commission for Backward Classes for examining the requests for inclusion of certain castes in the Central list of OBCs; (*ii*) setting up of a National Commission for Safai Karamacharis to look into specific problems of scavengers, flayers, tanners, etc.; (*iii*) setting up of a National Minorities Development Corporation with a share capital of ₹ 500 crore to promote economic and developmental activities for the backward sections amongst the minorities; and (*iv*) setting up of a Maulana Azad Education Foundation to promote education amongst educationally backward sections of society, minorities and backward classes in particular, and others in general.

HOUSING

The Policy

The National Housing Policy was adopted by the Parliament in August, 1994. The long-term goal of the policy is to reduce houselessness and to provide minimum level of basic services and amenities to all. It is recognised that the magnitude of the problem calls for the involvement of various agencies including the Government, cooperatives, communities and private sector. The policy envisages a major shift in the Government's role towards being a facilitator rather than a provider. The needs of vulnerable sections will continue to be taken care of by the Government. The housing development strategy, covering technological, financial and

TABLE 30.6

Performance of Rural Housing for Weaker Sections and Lower Income Groups

(In lakh)

Scheme	1992-93	1993-94		1994-95	
	Achievement	Target	Achievement	Target	Achievement (Up to Aug. 1994)
1	2	3	4	5	6
1. Rural House-sites-*cum*-House Construction:					
(*a*) House-sites (Families)	8.88	5.53	9.21	4.98	3.26
(*b*) Construction Assistance (Families)	5.31	2.95	4.66	2.97	1.26
2. Economically Weaker Sections (Dwelling Units)	1.14	0.96	1.22	0.92	0.23
3. Low Income Group Housing (Dwelling Units)	0.54	0.48	0.60	0.40	0.09

Source: Ministry of Programme Implementation.

institutional aspects has been included in the policy framework. The thrust has however shifted from a project-based approach to a sectoral one, by treating it as an integral part of economic development.

The Central and State Governments have been operating various schemes for providing institutional and research support for the housing sector. The scheme for allotment of house-sites-*cum*-construction assistance as part of the Minimum Needs Programme in rural areas is under the purview of the State Sector. Indira A was Yojana (IAY) was introduced in 1985-86 in the Central Sector for the poorest of the poor belonging to Scheduled Castes and Scheduled Tribes and freed bonded labourers in rural areas. Non-SC/ST poor families are also eligible now under the scheme subject to certain conditions. Houses under the Indira Awas Yojana, as far as possible, are built in clusters along a microhabitat approach, so that common facilities can be provided for the clusters. Under IAY, 3.06 lakh houses were built during 1993-94, as against the target of 2.51 lakh.

Rural Housing

The physical performance under the scheme of rural house sites-*cum*-construction assistance indicates that the weaker sections have been given due priority (Table 30.6). The achievement of 1.22 lakh dwelling units for economically weaker sections well exceeded the target of 0.96 lakh units in 1993-94.

Loans for Housing

In order to encourage housing activity, the Reserve Bank of India has announced that bank lending to the housing sector (up to ₹ 2 lakh in case of new house and ₹ 25000 for repairs) would be treated as priority sector lending. The ceiling for housing loans is fixed at ₹ 10 lakh.

NHB

To augment the flow of institutional credit for the housing sector and to promote and regulate housing finance institutions, the National Housing Bank (NHB) was established in July 1988 as a subsidiary to the Reserve Bank of India. It mobilises resources and channelises them to various schemes of housing and infrastructure, and provides refinance for direct housing loans given by commercial banks and non-banking institutions. The NHB also finances housing finance institutions for direct lending for construction/purchase of new housing/dwelling units, public agencies for land development and shelter projects, primary co-operatives, housing societies, professional developers and also allottees of plots/dwelling units under Land Development and Shelter Projects. Since its inception and up to March 1994, the NHB had provided refinance assistance of the order of ₹ 1929 crore apart from ₹ 196 crore advanced for various land development and shelter projects.

HUDCO

The Housing and Urban Development Corporation (HUDCO) also provides loans and technical support to State and local agencies for housing and infrastructure development. Since its inception in 1970 and up to October 1994, total loans amounting to ₹ 9476 crore were sanctioned, and ₹ 6522 crore actually disbursed for the construction of over 5.66 million residential units. The HUDCO also provides concessional finance for housing projects for the benefit of Economically Weaker Sections (EWS) and Low Income Groups (LIG). During 1994-95 (up to October 1994), ₹ 85 crore and ₹ 64 crore were sanctioned for EWS and LIG, respectively.

WATER SUPPLY AND SANITATION

Considerable progress has been made in providing safe drinking water facilities, particularly in under-served villages, yet the magnitude of the problem is such that large areas are still to be covered. A backlog of

8365 'hard-core' and 'no-source' problem villages was left uncovered at the end of the Seventh Five Year Plan. Out of this backlog villages were covered during 1990-94. Against the current year's target of 278 villages, 59 villages were covered by November 1994.

TABLE 30.7

Population Covered with Drinking Water and Sanitation Facilities (Percentage coverage as on March 31)

Item/Area	1985	1990	1993[1]
Drinking Water Supply			
Rural	56.3	73.9	79.2
Urban	72.9	83.8	84.9
Sanitation Facilities			
Rural	0.7	2.4	3.26
Urban	28.4	45.9	47.9

1. *Provisional.*

Source: Planning Commission.

Since 1985, the coverage of population for drinking water supply and sanitation facilities in rural and urban areas has increased rapidly (Table 30.7). The budgetary allocation for the Central sector plan for rural water supply was increased from ₹ 770 crore in 1993-94 to ₹ 950 crore in 1994-95, an increase of 23 per cent.

LABOUR AND EMPLOYMENT

Trends

By stressing the growth of employment intensive sectors, the employment strategy envisaged in the Eighth Plan is expected to bring about a rate of growth of employment of the order of 2.6 per cent to 2.8 per cent per annum corresponding to expected average annual rate of overall economic growth of 5.6 per cent. On an average, 8.5 million additional employment opportunities per year are expected to be generated during the Eighth Five Year Plan. It is now estimated that additional employment opportunities of the order of 6.4 million and 5.6 million were created in 1992-93 and 1993-94 respectively. This lower than target average annual increase in additional employment is mainly because of lower GDP growth than targeted. On the other hand, the average increase of 6.0 million in the first two years of the Plan is significantly higher than the average of 5 million additional employment opportunities generated per year during the period 1985-86 to 1991-92. These trends indicate that the employment content of growth has increased during the first two years of the Eighth Five Year Plan.

Advisory Committee

A Standing Advisory Committee on Labour has been constituted by the Planning Commission to facilitate consultation with trade unions and experts in labour matters in formulating plans and policies concerning labour and employment.

Child Labour

Despite constitutional requirements and legal deterrents, child labour continues to be a serious problem. Current efforts to progressively reduce and eventually eliminate the use of child labour comprise mainly National Child Labour Projects initiated in several areas of concentration of child labour for rehabilitation of children withdrawn from work. Following the announcement made by the Prime Minister on August 15, 1994, a new scheme for eliminating child labour in hazardous employment by the year 2000 is being prepared. A National Authority for Elimination of Child Labour has been established in October, 1994 under the chairmanship of the Minister of State for Labour with the following functions:

(*i*) To lay down policies and programmes for elimination of child labour, particularly in hazardous employment.

(*ii*) To monitor the progress of implementation of programmes, projects and schemes for elimination of child labour.

(*iii*) To co-ordinate implementation of child labour elimination-related projects of various Ministries of the Government of India.

It has also been decided that steps should be taken to institute State Level Child Labour Advisory Boards, State Authorities for Elimination of Child Labour and District Level Child Welfare Committees. Each State will draw up a master plan of action for elimination of child labour within a specified time frame. For this purpose, areas and industries with child labour concentration will be identified. Non-Government Organisations (NGOs) will also be actively involved in these programmes.

SPECIAL EMPLOYMENT AND POVERTY ALLEVIATION PROGRAMMES

Special employment and anti-poverty programmes like Integrated Rural Development Programmes Training of Rural Youth for Self-Employment (TRYSEM), Jawahar Rozgar Yojana (JRY) and Nehru Rozgar Yojana (NRY) have been a central feature of India's development strategy. In 1993-94, two new programmes namely the Employment Assurance Schemes and the Prime Minister's Rozgar Yojana were introduced. In addition, some State Governments have special employment programmes of their own, such as the Employment Guarantee Scheme (EGS) in Maharashtra and the Self-Employment Scheme for Registered Unemployed (SESRU) in West Bengal.

The EAS

The EAS is implemented in 1778 backward blocks in the country. It aims at providing 100 days of unskilled manual work up to two members of a family in the age group of 18 to 60 years normally residing in villages within the blocks covered under EAS. It is a need-based programme; hence no target of employment generation has been fixed. Since 1993-94, the JRY has been made more target-oriented and expanded substantially through increased budgetary allocations. It has been divided into three streams *viz.* (*i*) JRY-Ist stream with 75 per cent of total allocation; (*ii*) JRY-2nd stream with 20 per cent of total allocation for 120 selected backward districts, and (*iii*) JRY-3rd stream for innovative projects, aimed at prevention of migration of labourers, enhancing women's employment, special programmes through voluntary organisations and those aimed at drought proofing and watershed development.

JRY

For better targeting, cost effectiveness and judicious selection of assets under JRY, the allocations for two sub-schemes of 1st stream of JRY, have been increased for the Indira Awas Yojana (IAY) from 6 per cent in 1992-93 to 10 per cent in 1993-94 and for the Million Wells Scheme (MWS) from 20 per cent to 30 per cent during the same period. Along with SC/ST and freed bonded labourers, poor non-SC/ST families have also been included for assistance under IAY and MWS subject to the condition that their share not exceeding 4 and 10 per cent of allocation respectively.

IRDP

Under IRDP, all families in rural areas below the poverty line are eligible for assistance. There is reservation for SC/ST up to 50 per cent of total families assisted. 40 per cent is reserved for women and 3 per cent for those who are physically handicapped.

SEEUY

The Scheme for Self-Employment for Educated Unemployed Youth (SEEUY) has been integrated with the PMRY from 1994-95. The target under PMRY for 1994-95 is fixed at 2.2 lakh micro-enterprises to generate about 4.4 lakh employment opportunities.

Suggestions

Wide prevalence of open unemployment and the large proportion of population below the poverty line, warrants strengthening of these programmes. However, there is urgent need for qualitative improvement in the programmes through better targeting, flexible allocation of funds in favour of more deserving States and dovetailing of these programmes with sectoral and area development programmes. Proper planning, identification of thrust areas at grassroot level, viable projects within the management capacities of poor families, and effective tying up of forward and backward linkages, credit and marketing, are also essential for bringing about qualitative improvements.

Outlook

Various policies and programmes adopted for development in social sectors have started showing results in positive direction. The quality of life has improved. The employment content of growth has increased.

The higher budgetary allocations for social sectors in recent years have helped to minimise the short-term social costs of structural adjustment. To ensure sustainability of higher budgetary allocations to social sectors, adequate resources will have to be mobilised by both the Centre and the States. Furthermore, available limited resources have to be better targeted. As a corollary to this, those who can afford to pay, must be charged for the services rendered. To augment resources, more innovative options, including private sector participation and greater support from NGOs have to be explored.

The process of decentralization in the implementation of various social sector programmes has been facilitated by the 72nd and 73rd Constitutional Amendments. What is now required is involvement of Panchayati Raj institutions and NGOs with the overall coordinating responsibility of the Government for coast effective implementation of various programmes.

QUESTIONS FOR EXERCISE

1. Write an essay on Social Welfare in India.
2. Discuss the problems of Housing in India.

31

Social Security in Other Countries

SOCIAL SECURITY IN GREAT BRITAIN

Poor relief in England started in the middle ages. It was recognised during the reign of Queen Elizabeth that it is a part of the State's duty to provide the citizen against the wants. The Christian monastries used to dispense relief to the destitute. With their abolition it became necessary for the State to arrange for poor relief. This resulted in the enactment of Poor Law. It was renamed Public Assistance, in which form it survives even today. Thus, the present social security measures in England are a modified form of Poor Law. The basis of the two, however, are different. The social services in modern times are less deterrent, differently financed and without the stigma attaching to poor relief.

Social Services in 20th Century

Social services are an important feature of the British social life. They have exercised immense influence upon the industries. In 1890 the total expenditure for social services including the cost of administration, in Great Britain was to the tune of 23 million pounds. In 1900 it increased to 26 millions pounds. In 1920 it was over 8 million. In 1935 it was estimated at 463 million. In 1938-39 expenditure on social security amounted to 342 million. In 1955-56 this amount raised to 1795 million pounds. At the same time public authorities were spending 2000 million pounds a year on social services. The expenditure on social services in 1935 was 53% of the total expenditure granted by the Parliament. Thus, it is clear that in 20th century expenditure on social services considerably increased in England. This was an example for other countries, particularly for India which has been always veiy much influenced by life in Britain.

Pre-Beveridge Poor Relief

As has been already pointed out, Poor Relief existed in England for a long time. Before 1601 it was generally believed that poverty is a proof of laziness since the able-bodied persons could find work if they wish. Therefore, those able-bodied persons who did not work were used to be punished. For example, in 1530 it was a custom that able-bodied men and women found begging were tied with the end of a cart, naked and beaten with whips till their bodies used to bleed. An Act was passed in 1547 which provided that the able-bodied vagabonds should be branded with the letter 'V' and were to be attached as property of any master who could give them food and clothes in return for their services. If they attempted to escape before two years, they were branded with the letter 'S' and condemned for a life of slavery. If they again attempted to run away they were given death sentence.

As has been already pointed out, progress in Poor Relief was made during the reign of Queen Elizabeth. Justices of the Peace were given power to assess the wages of the workers and decide their rates. Several Acts were passed for the purpose. An Act was passed in 1601 which provided for compulsory assessment for the relief of the poor. In every town of the poor overseers were appointed who used to raise taxation for poor relief and provide relief to those who could not find employment due to old age or infirmity. Those who were able-bodied and yet did not work, were punished. With certain modifications, this Act governed poor relief till 1834. In 1834 an Act was passed under which the administration of the Poor Law was placed under the direction of a Central Board of Poor Law Commissioners. This Act provided for work house tests for the able-bodied persons, grouping of Parishes in Unions, election of a Board of Guardians in every Parish, Relief to all able-bodied paupers by admission to the work houses and outdoor relief to the persons above 60 years of age and deceased. A Poor Law Board was constituted in 1847. It supervised the administration of Public Relief upto 1871. Afterwards, it was substituted by Local Government Board. In 1919 the Ministry of Health was created. It undertook the administration of Public Relief. An Act was passed in 1834 which provided that a man must earn livelihood by his labour. In 1895 Friendly Societies used to provide help to unemployed workers. A Royal Commission on Poor Law was appointed in 1905, In its report in 1909 the Commission stated that pauperism was prevalent in the country. It condemned the retention of children in work houses. It pointed out that the administration of outdoor relief was not properly supervised. A Local Government Act was passed in 1929 which inaugurated a new system of Poor Law. Now, the work of Poor Law Administration was transferred to Country Councils and Country Borough Councils which were to act through Public Assistance Committees. The administration of Poor Law was now the responsibility of the Local districts. It was hoped that this measure would result in economy and efficiency in social services.

Unemployment Insurances

In 20th century again, public attention was diverted towards Unemployment Insurance. In the past unemployment was not recognised and the able-bodied idlers were punished. Now, it was realised that it is the prime duty of the State to provide work to every citizen. If some persons were unemployed they must be helped by the government. In 1919 a scheme based on contributory principle entitled Compulsory State Insurance was introduced. It was utilised in industries employing about 2.25 million workers. The contribution in this scheme were 2½ from the employer, 2½ from the worker and $1^2/_3$ by the state in the total of $6^2/_3$. This benefit was to be 7 shillings for adult for a maximum of 15 weeks in 12 months. Workers under 18 years of age were to receive half benefit. In 1916 this scheme was extended to several other rates. Another scheme known as "out of work donations" was launched to cover ex-servicemen, unable to find jobs, together with all other unemployed workers.

Compulsory State Insurance

In 1920 the Compulsory State Insurance was extended to all manual workers and non-manual workers earning not more than 250 pounds annually. This, however, did not cover agricultural and domestic workers. A fund was created by the contributions of the employers, the workers and the State. The unemployed workers were helped out of this fund. The rates of contributions and benefits were raised from time to time. The main condition for the payment of the benefit was that the workman should have made at least 30 contributions in the last two years. If 8 or more contributions were paid during the last 2 years or 30 contributions at any time, transitional benefits were provided. Depending upon the income and the means of household, public assistance was provided. In 1931 National Economy Act was passed which increased unemployment insurance contributions and reduced the benefits. The benefits of workers below 21 years and benefits for dependents were reduced. A new system of transitional benefit was introduced. This system was abolished in 1934. The rate of benefits was restored upto pre-1931 level. In 1936 a scheme of unemployment insurance for agricultural workers was introduced. It was, however, criticised as very expansive and was replaced by social security scheme after the war.

Compulsory Health Insurance

The British Government introduced Compulsory Health Insurance system in 1911. This system was contributory in principle and covered earning members between 16 and 65 years of age, whose income did not exceed 250 pounds a year. Benefits were in the form of cash and medical treatment.

Provision for Pensions

In 1908 Britain introduced the scheme of old age pensions. This was provided from funds raised by general taxation without any contributions from employers and workers. In 1914 every British subject, over 70 years of age, who has been a British resident for 12 years and a British subject for 20 years was entitled for pension provided he did not receive poor relief and his income did not exceed 31 pounds and 10 shilling. Under the Act passed in 1925 and 1929 the Health Insurance System covered all the persons who were included in old age contributory pension scheme. Pensions for widowed mothers and for orphans on a contributory basis was introduced in 1925. Under this scheme the pension to a widow is payable until she attains the age of 70 or remarries. But remarriage did not affect the allowances for children.

Workmen's Compensation Act

In 1906 was passed the first Workmen's Compensation Act in England. This Act provided that the employers should pay compensation to the workers without distinction of age or sex, who became unemployed due to some accident or industrial disease. The payments were to be made weekly in the case of temporary and permanent disablement and lumpsum to dependents in the case of death. This Act was amended in 1923. Now, the amount of compensation was raised and the scope of the Act was extended. This had no provision for introducing compulsory insurance in case of compensation. However, many employers used to protect themselves by insuring with companies for the purpose.

Benefit Schemes of Employers

Besides the Acts passed by the States the British employers started several benefit schemes such as pension schemes, saving schemes and unemployment benefit schemes. The payment under these schemes was different in different companies. Most of these schemes were covered by industrial welfare schemes, which were later on determined by such Acts as Public Health Act, Shop Act, Factories Act etc. The schemes were concluded between employers and trade unions by agreements about health, welfare and hours of work etc.

The above mentioned system of social insurance in Great Britain suffered from several defects, of which the more important are as follows:

(1) A large number of needy workers were left outside the scope of these social insurance schemes.

(2) There was no uniformity regarding means test to determine the eligibility for achieving social insurance benefits.

(3) The benefit rates used to vary without sufficient justification. All these defects were removed by Beveridge Plan.

In June 1941 the British Government appointed Sir Wm. Beveridge to make a survey of the National schemes of social insurance and allied services and make recommendations. His report was known as Beveridge Plan. It was presented to the Parliament in December 1942. Since then it was put into practice by various Acts of the Parliament.

General Characteristics of the Plan

The Beveridge Plan aimed for the provision of a unified system of income maintenance to cover needs arising from a variety of causes. It was based on a uniform rate of provision which could be varied to meet special cases. The questions of children and adult dependents were treated separately. The man and wife however, were treated together while making special provision for divorce, separation and widowhood. The variation in contributions and benefits with the variations of wages was abolished. The Plan started from the idea of a National Minimum, which was to be ensured by the State as far as possible to everyone in all the contingencies of life.

Three Assumptions

The Beveridge Plan was based upon three assumptions considered as pre-requisites for its success. These were as follows:

(1) Children Allowances: There was no relation between the size of the workers family and his wages under the existing industrial system. According to Beveridge Plan children's allowances were to be graded with age. These allowances were to be received by the children due to their age. They were not subject to any conditions for their use by the children or the parents. They were also not subject to any means test.

Their cost was to be borne by the State out of tax revenue. They were, therefore, non-contributory.

(2) Comprehensive Health Service: In England Health Service was provided by the government, the medical practitioners and the private bodies. The National Health Insurance Scheme started in 1919. It covered about half the British population in 1941. Again, different authorities administered maternity and child welfare scheme. Further, there were the Poor Law School Medical Service etc. However, there was no co-ordination in these schemes before Beveridge Plan. Beveridge Plan assumes a comprehensive health service for disease and disability for every citizen irrespective of the ability to pay. The Plan emphasizes that the state ought to pay high benefits in disease and disability. The State should try to remove conditions which bring about disease and disabilities. Medical treatment should not depend on a person's ability to pay. It should be paid for by the community. It is so since in its actions productive power is reduced and idleness is increased. According to Beveridge Plan in the contributions forming part of the social security plan a compulsory payment should be included to cover those services for every citizen without any further charge. The assumption was accepted by the Government.

(3) Full Employment: The Beveridge Plan assumes the full employment as a necessary prerequisite for its success. It, however, points out that 8.5% of the British population or 15,00,000 of persons would normally remain unemployed. Therefore, it suggested that unconditional unemployment benefit should be given for short period only, because unless full employment is guaranteed the plan of social securities would break down.

Coverage of the Plan

Beveridge Plan covers everybody. It takes into consideration all the primary causes of needs. It does not leave out any risk. It divides the entire population into 6 classes based on the means of livelihood of the people. These 6 classes cover the entire population. Every citizen is covered by one or the other class. Thus, every one receives benefits. The employers and rich people must play their contributions even though they do not get any benefit. No contributions were to be paid by the children, the retired persons and the housewives. The six classes mentioned above are: (*i*) employees, whatever their income: (*ii*) employers and other persons, working for gain: (*iii*) housewives of working age, *i.e.* not gainfully employed and below pensionable age; (*iv*) other persons of working age but are not gainfully employed; (*v*) persons below working age, *i.e.*, children below 16 years; (*vi*) retired persons above working age.

Rates of Contribution

All insured persons, whatever their means, are to pay a flat rate of contribution. The standard rates proposed in the Plan are 4s 3d male and 3s 6d female. The employer's contribution is 3s 3d for a man and 2s 6d for a woman. Contributions vary according to age groups.

Benefits under the Plan

As has been already pointed out, the benefits under the plan were available for housewives, children, unemployed and sick persons, disabled workers and old persons unable to work. These benefits are not dependent on contributions. The housewives, the children, the unemployed and the sick, the disabled and the old reap the benefits without paying any contributions. These benefits are as follows:

(1) Benefits for housewives: (*i*) A marriage grant upto £ 10. (*ii*) A maternity grant of £ 4, when children are born. If she is gainfully occupied, she will further get an additional maternity benefit of 36s a week for 13 weeks without paying contribution, (*iii*) A widowhood benefit of 36s a week for 13 weeks, (*iv*) After 13 weeks and as long as she has dependent children, she will get guardian's benefit of 24s a week, and, in addition, children's allowances. If she has no dependent children, she will have to qualify herself for work under the training scheme when she will get training benefits, (*v*) If she is divorced through no fault of her own, she will get benefit as a widow gets, (*vi*) When she is ill, help will be given to her in the form of sickness benefit.

(2) Children's allowances: The Plan provides an allowance of 8s for all children except the first dependent child in any family, irrespective of the parents' status of income. Allowance for the first child is also provided, if the parents are unable to earn.

(3) Unemployment and sickness benefits: In this case, a payment of 24s a week is to be given for a single person, and 20s for a married couple. An unemployed man with wife and two children will receive 50s a week. The qualifications for these benefits is the training scheme for those who remain unemployed for 6 months. They have to join a training centre where work would be taught to them for a certain period, during which they will receive training benefit which will be the same as unemployment benefit.

(4) Workmen's compensation: Under the Beveridge Plan, for 13 weeks of incapacity, the worker will be treated as a sick person and will get a sickness benefit. Thereafter, the weekly payments will be increased to two thirds of the former earnings but will not be less than the standard rate. The Plan proposes a special machinery to deal with compensation cases instead of by ordinary law courts. If the accident is fatal, a lumpsum grant of £ 300 w ill be given to the dependents.

The Plan also provides a funeral grant of £20 to be paid when the adult dies, £15 between £10 and 21, £10 between 3 and 10, and £6 under three years.

(5) Old age pensions: Men will get old age pension at 65, and women at 60. The rates are 24s for a single person and 40s for married couple, irrespective of the age of the other partner.

Cost of the Plan

In 1945 the cost of the Plan was estimated at 697 million pounds. In 1965 it was estimated at 858 million pounds (₹ 1100 crores). This estimate is based upon a price level of 25% higher than that of 1938.

Administration and Implementation

Sir William Beveridge proposed for a unification of the administrative responsibility and the establishment of a single Ministry of Social Security with a single Social Insurance Fund. This suggestion was not initially accepted by the British Government. However, now a separate Ministry of National Insurance has been created. The plan aroused wide interest. The government accepted it as the basis for building up the social security structure in the country. In post-war years a series of Acts introduced a comprehensive system of social security. This system became operative on 5th July, 1948. In subsequent Acts further adjustments have been made. At present the social security system of U.K. includes Family Allowances, National Insurance, Industrial Injuries Insurance, National Assistance and the National Health Service. This system ensures that no one may fall below a minimum standard of life at any time in the country. The payment of family allowances was made from the Exchequer. This allowance was at the rate of 8 shillings per week for each child after the first under the age limit which was normally 15 and later on extended to 31 July after the 16th birthday. The scheme was first started on 6th August 1946. In 1952 the allowance was raised by almost 50% under the Family Allowances and National Insurance Act, 1952.

National Insurance

The National Insurance Act, 1946, came into full operation on the 5th July, 1948. It has been amended six times since then, in 1949, 1951, 1952, 1953, 1954, and 1955. The Act applies to everyone over school-leaving age living in Great Britain. Everyone is required to pay contribution at fixed weekly rates, except old people, children, married women and persons with very small incomes. Contributors are divided into three classes: (*i*) Employed persons; (*ii*) Self-employed persons; and (*iii*) Non-employed persons. The scheme provides sickness, unemployment, maternity and widow's benefit, guardian's allowance, retirement pension and death grant. Persons in Class 1 are covered for all benefits; those in class 2 for benefits other than unemployment and industrial injuries benefits; and those in Class 3 for benefits other than sickness, unemployment, industrial injuries and maternity benefits. The qualifying condition is a minimum number of contributions over a specified period except for guardian's allowances and industrial injuries for which there are no contribution conditions.

Industrial Injuries Insurance Scheme

It replaced the Workmen's Compensation Scheme in July 1948. The relevant Acts are the National Insurance (Industrial) Acts, 1946 to 1954. Benefits are provided for personal injuries caused by accidents, arising out of, and in the course of, employment, and for prescribed diseases.

National Assistance

According to the National Assistance Act of 1948, Financial Assistance is being given to those who are in need of it, from the State Exchequer. Welfare services for the aged, the infirm, the homeless and the handicapped have been provided. Grants or Allowances have been advanced to those who are unable to maintain themselves and who are not covered by other social security services. The National Health Service provides for full medical care for all residents in Britain generally at the cost of the Exchequer. This is according to the National Health Service Acts of 1946, 1949, 1951 and 1952. For the administration of the national plan, a Ministry of National Insurance has been created with headquarters in London with a staff of 500. Its Central Record Office at Newcastle includes 7000 persons. Regional Offices and Local Offices have also been created. The total staff employed to administer the National Insurance Schemes is between 35,000 an 43,000 and is highly efficient.

Thus, there is a comprehensive social security system in Great Britain. Besides the above-mentioned governmental measure, several voluntary charitable societies and institutions are furthering the cause of social security in the country. These include National Council of Social Service, the Family Welfare Association, The National Old People's Welfare Committee, The Standing Conference of National Voluntary Youth Organisation, The National Council of Associated Children's Home, The Nation Council of Maternity and Child Welfare and many other associations for maternity and child welfare and benefits for disable people. Other important societies doing valuable work include British Red Cross Society, Marriage Guidance Council and British Federation of Social Workers. Thus, in U.K. the State has recognised full obligation towards providing social security to the greatest possible extent for all the people. The high standard laid down by the Beveridge Plan however, could not be achieved. In fact the practical form of Beveridge Plan amounts to almost communist society. It lays down full employment ideal which is difficult to achieve in any country other than communist. Some thinkers have even disputed the plan's claim of improving efficiency and checking a tendency to curtailment of population. Recently, a new phenomena has been noted. Some young men and women do not work at all and make unemployment allowances their sole means of livelihood. Thus, the problem of social security is not easy as the planners assume. However, U.K. presents an example to the non-communist world.

SOCIAL SECURITY IN U.S.S.R.

On 14th November, 1917 the Soviet Government issued the first decree on social insurance in the country. This was a few days after the Communist government assumed office. This decree intended to improve the inadequate social insurance system under the preceding government. The new scheme provided for (1) an extension of insurance to all workers and employees in town and countries; (2) the covering of all loss of earning power from any cause whatever, including unemployment; (3) the payment of insurance contribution by the employing enterprise; (4) the payment of full wages in cases of disablement; and (5) complete self-administration of all insurance organisations by the insured.

Due to certain difficulties, the basic principles of social insurance scheme were actually enforced in 1922 under the New Economic Policy. For this purpose, the government announced a Labour Court which provided medical help, benefits to disabled, feeding of children, help to destitutes, funeral allowances, old age pensions and family pensions in case of death of the wage earner. In USSR insurance premiums are paid by the employers in the form of deductions of sums equal to a percentage of the wage bills of the enterprises and paid into the insurance funds of the trade unions. Medical help does not belong to social insurance but to social services. The social insurance system applies to industrial workers only. Agricultural workers are protected by the peasant's collective organisations.

The main principles of social insurance in USSR are as follows:

(1) Since 1933 it is administered by the trade unions alone.

(2) It insures only employed persons.

(3) It is insurance with premiums paid by the employers.

(4) Trade union membership is a condition for the enjoyment of full insurance benefits. However, non-members receive half of the benefit of insurance scheme.

(5) Social insurance is connected with the government's drive for viability of labour and increased production. Those who have worked in the same enterprise for the longest period of time receive maximum benefits. On the other hand, persons terminated from the job receive less benefits.

(6) Insurance against unemployment was abolished in 1930 when almost full employment was ensured by First Five Year Plan.

Thus, the social insurance scheme of USSR provides relief to temporarily disabled workers and pensions to disabled and old workers. The former category of workers receive upto 100% of the average earnings if disablement is due to employment. In other cases relief is provided on the basis of period of service. For example, it is 100% for 6 years or more, 80% from 3 to 6 years, 60% between 2 and 3 years and 50% under two years of service. The amounts are 50% for those who are not members of any trade union. Those terminated from the jobs or leaving them on their own are entitled to benefits only after working in a new place for at least 6 months. Pensions are granted only in the case of permanent disablement and old age. This disablement should be connected with the employment. In other cases it varies according to the age and period of employment. The amount of pension depends upon the last wage or salary earned by the worker. The highest pension amounts to 66% of the last wage.

Other Social Security Schemes

Besides the above mentioned social insurance system, the social security system in USSR includes the following: (1) Medical treatment for everybody free of charge in hospitals working under the People's Commissariat of Health, (2) The right of two weeks paid leave per year after having worked at least 11 months continuously in the same enterprise, (3) The use of rest homes and sanatoria run partly by the trade unions and partly by the industrial enterprises themselves for the workers employed by them. The use of these rest homes and sanatoria is restricted according to the length of service, and a charge is made according to the wages. (4) The use of parks of rest and culture in the towns and in the suburbs, which are frequented on Sundays and other public holidays, (5) Educational services provided for all and free of charge in primary stages, (6) Maternity benefits are provided to the expectant mother or to the mother immediately after confinement by the employer as a legal obligation.

Social Security of Women and Children

In USSR the social security of the women and children is one of the primary functions of the state. Labour laws guarantee right to work to every woman. Refusal to employ a woman on the basis of pregnancy is punishable by imprisonment upto 6 months or a fine upto 1000 Roubles. A repetition of the offence is punishable by 2 years imprisonment. Thus, every woman, pregnant or otherwise gets work and wages. During the period of pregnancy she is given lighter work without any reduction in her wages. Overtime for the expectant mothers is forbidden after the fourth month of pregnancy The woman has a right to leave her work for 35 days before confinement. She has a right to receive money grants from the state. In July 1944 this period of absence was extended to 42 days with leave on full pay which may be extended upto 91 days. During the war the expectant mothers were assured of supply of rations. They are allotted special seats in trams, buses and railways. They can enter without waiting in a queue. There are thousands of welfare centres for women and children. There are separate rooms particularly 'women's hygiene rooms' in every factory. Women are provided special working conditions on joining work after child birth. They are allowed additional time during working hours to feed their children. If a child, under the age of two years, falls ill, the mother is granted special leave of absence. She is also given money-allowance for buying the first outfit for the child.

The state also protects unmarried mothers and their children. All the measures described above also apply to them. They are citizens of the country with full rights. The state provides the punishment for anyone causing any insult to them. Special allowances are given to mothers bearing a large number of children.

The above brief outline of the social security system in USSR shows that it is the leader and the most forward country in the world in this respect.

SOCIAL SECURITY IN AUSTRALIA

The social security measures beginning in Australia at the start of the present century earned her a reputation of being, "The Social Laboratory of the world". Even before the Federal Constitution of 1901 the social security measures were the responsibilities of the states. But since the establishment of Federation, the Commonwealth Government is taking more and more interest in social security measures. The first Federal Social Service was the old age pension which began in 1909. In 1910 it was followed by the introduction of pensions for the invalid. In 1912 maternity benefits were provided. From 1939 there has been a great extension of social services. In 1941 child endowment was introduced. In 1942 followed widow's pension scheme. In 1943 started maternity allowance and funeral benefits. In 1944 an Employment and Sickness Benefit Act was passed. In 1946 by a referendum, the responsibility of social services were shared both by the Federal Parliament and the various states and the right of the Federal Parliament to legislate on social service scheme has been established.

Maternity Allowances

According to the legal provisions in Australia, maternity allownces mean the payments made by the Government to Mothers to provide financial assistance towards expenses associated with the birth of children. This payment is in addition to the free care, treatment and accommodation which a mother receives in a public ward of a public hospital. If she is confined in a non-public ward, allowance of 8s a day is paid towards the cost. These maternity allowances are not subject to any means test. Where there are no other children the payment is £15. It is increased with the number of children. In the case of the birth of twins or more children, an additional amount of £5 is paid in respect of each child in access of one born at a birth. On application, 4 weeks before the expected birth an advance payment of £5 is made as maternity allowance.

Child Endowment

In Australia, any person who has under his care more than one child under the age of 16 years, may claim a child endowment. Child endowment is 10s a week for each child and payments are made at the interval of 4 weeks. There is no means test. The payment is made to all the qualified claimants irrespective of their financial position.

Widow's Pensions

Widow's pensions are paid at different rates. The term widow includes not only a woman whose husband is dead but also a deserted wife, a divorced woman or a woman whose husband is in jail or in hospital as well as certain other dependent females. A widow, who has the custody of one or more children under the age of 16 years, is given a pension of £2, 7s 7d a week. A widow not less than 50 years, having no children under sixteen, gets £ 4, 17s, a week. A widow under 50 years of age, who has no children under 16 years but who is in necessitous circumstances, within 26 weeks after the death of her husband, is paid £2, 2s. 6d, a week. A woman whose husband has been serving a term of imprisonment for at least 6 months and she has one or more children under 16 or if she is not less than 50 years, is entitled to a pension of £1,17s a week.

Benefits against Unemployment, Sickness and Accident

These benefits are available to every Australian citizen between the ages of 16 and 65 in case of men and between 16 and 60 in case of women. There is a means test about income but not about property. The maximum payment to a married claimant is 25s a week with an allowance of 20s a week for a dependant spouse and 5s a week for one child making a total payment of 50s a week. The maximum payment to an unmarried claimant is 25s a week, and he can have other income of 20s a week. Any qualified claimant with a child of 16 years of age in his custody is entitled to an additional benefit of 5s a week in respect of the child. Sickness benefit is payable from the seventh day after the day on which the claimant becomes incapacitated, provided a claim is lodged within six weeks after that day. Unemployment benefit is payable from the seventh day after the day on which the claimant becomes unemployed or lodged his claims whichever is the later, and continues so long as he is able and willing to undertake suitable work and is otherwise qualified.

Old Age Pensions and Other Benefits

Old age pensions are given to men at 65 years of age and to women at 60 years of age under certain means tests as to both income and property. The maximum rate of old age pension is £110, 10s a year or £2, 2s 6d a week.

QUESTIONS FOR EXERCISE

1. Describe the growth of Social Security in U.K.
2. Evaluate Social Security measures in U.S.S.R.
3. Discuss Social Security measures in Australia.

32

Social Security in India

The Meaning of Social Security

No man in any society is so capable and versatile as to be able to satisfy all his needs. Everyone is dependent on others for the fulfilment of some or other needs. In particular, the aged, the helpless, the unemployed and the ones suffering from difficult chronic diseases are badly in need of help from others. The pregnant women need assistance during last period of pregnancy and for the delivery of the child. If the above mentioned persons are not given adequate help and assistance, chaotic conditions will result in the society and the social order will be upset. Moreover when the aged, the sick, the pregnant and other helpless persons have rendered help to others when they were able-bodied, young, healthy and strong, the society owes them a debt for their earlier services and they must receive social assistance in the hour of their need. It is for this reason that all progressive civilized people provide for social security for all those who are helpless. The various legal, official and non-official sanctions which ensure help to the desolate and forlorn persons, make up the concept of Social Security. Accordingly the meaning of Social Security is that a society guarantees help and assistance to sick, disabled, destitute, aged and those who are temporarily incapacitated and need other's help.

The Definition of Social Security

In order to appreciate fully the meaning of social security, one needs to examine some eminent definitions of the concept of social security.

1. *Sir William Beveridge*: "Social security is an attack on five giants, namely, Want, Disease, Ignorance, Squalor and Idleness". As is evident from this definition that social security implies protection from want and hunger, ignorance and idleness and removal of dirt, filth and disease from society. Thus, social security helps to maintain high standards of

health and immunity, cleanliness and purity of food-stuffs. In 1942 Sir Beveridge prosecuted a detailed plan on social security which came to be known as *Beveridge Plan 1942*. In this he suggested measures directed to attack on five above mentioned giants which spread a sense of insecurity.

2. *The International Labour Organization*: Social Security is "the security that society furnishes through appropriate organization against certain risks to which its members are exposed. A man is utterly dependent upon others twice in his life time, one when he is a child and for the second time during his old age. Besides these periods, there are certain times during intervening period when he becomes helpless and has to rely on others. This is when for some unforeseen causes he meets an accident or is wounded in war or has fallen prey to some epidemic etc. The children are lovable creatures and many people feel instinctively moved to nurture them and provide them assistance. But nature has not endowed man with an instinct to help others during their emergency. Man does show sympathy but more often than not the sympathy is lip-confined and does not translate itself into actual action. The social security is a collective name for those measures which a society has provided to meet such contingencies."

3. *The First International Seminar on Social Security*: "Each country must create, conserve and build up the intellectual; moral and physical vigour of its active generation, prepare the way for its future generations and support the generation which has been discharged from productive life. The Social Security is a genuine and rational economy of human resources and values."

Thus, Social Security is a planned commitment of a society to ensure bright future for the new born generation, active development of the present generation and lastly, but no less importantly, to relieve the discomforts of the retired generation and help them live in peace and harmony.

SOCIAL SECURITY AND SOCIAL INSURANCE

Social Security protects a man from hunger and want, squalor, disease, unemployment and ignorance. Social Insurance makes the Social Security possible, that is, it creates and initiates a mechanism which is *sine qua non* of the realization of Social Security. Thus, social insurance is an important feature of social security; as a matter of fact social security includes in it social insurance, the concept of social security is wider than that of social insurance. It includes in it, besides social insurance, social assistance programmes. Sir William Beveridge has defined social insurance thus: "Social insurance is the giving, in return for contributions, benefits upto subsistence level, as of right and without means test, so that the individual may freely build upon it." By the virtue of social insurance the persons are insured and their dependents are given financial grants and other benefits like free medical aid and children education so that their standard of living is not allowed to fall beyond a minimum level. The situations or contingencies in which such aid and benefits are allowed are: (1) unemployment; (2) protracted illness; (3) pregnancy and child birth, accidents and incapacitation due to disease, shock or accident; and (4) death. In the 4th alternative, dependents of the deceased are provided sufficient money to maintain subsistence level and receive medical aid and educational facilities for children. Thus, social insurance is primarily aimed at protection from want and hunger, whereas social security, besides want and hunger, also help removal of squalor, disease, ignorance and exploitation. The benefits of social insurance are admissible only to those who are so insured and make their regular contributions towards it. On the contrary, the benefits of social security are admissible to everyone irrespective of contributions towards it. Social insurance is an institution jointly operated by industrialists, workers and government. Social security is exclusively operated by the government. In social insurance the benefits are allowed to the insured persons irrespective of their status and economic need, whereas the benefits of social security are allowed strictly on the basis of needs and requirements. A comparison between social insurance and social security is made below:

Social Security	*Social Insurance*
1. Protects against want, squalor, disease, ignorance and unemployment.	1. Protects against want only.
2. Its benefits are admissible to all.	2. Its benefits are admissible only to contributors.
3. Benefits according to economic needs of the person.	3. Benefits without reference to economic need.
4. Social assistance a part of social security—completely government operated.	4. It is operated jointly by the workers, industrialists and government.
5. It is a complete institution.	5. It is partial and is included in social security.

SOCIAL SECURITY IN INDIA

There are several schemes providing social security to the workers against such contingencies as ill-health, industrial accidents, maternity etc.

(1) Employees' State Provident Scheme: The passing of the Employees State Insurance Act, 1948 marks the most important step in the provision of social security benefits. Till recently it covered non-seasonal factories using power and employing 20 or more persons but now it is being gradually extended by the state governments to smaller factories, hotels, restaurants, shops, cinemas, etc., employing 20 or more persons. It covers employees drawing wages not exceeding ₹ 1,000 per month.

The Act provides for medical care in kind and cash, benefits of maternity, employment injury and pension for dependents on the death of a worker because of employment injury. Full medical care including hospitalisation is also being progressively made available to the members of the family of the insured persons.

As on 31 December, 1983 there were 84 ESI hospitals and 42 annexes with 22,552 beds and 1,167 dispensaries under the scheme. The number of employees covered was about 63.02 lakh.

(2) Employees' Provident Funds: Retirement benefits are available to the employees under the Employees' Provident Funds and Miscellaneous Provisions Act, 1952. As on 30 September, 1983 it covered 173 industries/ classes of establishments, employing 20 or more persons all over India, except Jammu and Kashmir. The Act does not apply to establishments registered under the Co-operative Societies Act, 1912 or under any other law relating to co-operative societies employing less than 50 persons and working without the aid of power. The scheme is at present applicable to those drawing wages up to ₹ 1,600 per month.

The employees contribute 6.25 per cent of the basic wages and dearness allowances including cash value of food concessions and retaining allowance payable to the employees. The employers make a matching contribution. The Government has enhanced the rate of contribution to 8 per cent in respect of 108 industries employing 50 or more persons.

As at the end of 30 September, 1983 the number of subscribers under the scheme was 125.74 lakhs. The total amount of provident fund contributions received was ₹ 9,572.60 crore while the total amount refunded was ₹ 4,932.28 crore.

(3) Death Relief: A Death Relief Fund was set up under the Employees' Provident Fund Scheme in January 1964, with a view to affording financial assistance to the nominees or heirs of deceased members of unexempted establishments whose pay (including basic pay, DA, etc.,) does not exceed ₹ 1,000 per month at the time of death. The quantum of benefit is restricted to the amount by which amount payable on account of provident fund falls short of ₹ 1,250.

(4) Employees' Deposit Linked Insurance Scheme: Another important social security measure, the Employees' Deposit Linked Insurance Scheme, 1976 was introduced for the members of the Employees' Provident Fund and the exempted Provident Funds with effect from 1 August, 1976. On the death of a member, the person entitled to receive the provident fund accumulations would be paid an additional amount equal to the average balance in the provident fund account of the deceased during the preceding three years, if such average balance was not below ₹ 1,000 during the said period. The maximum amount of benefit payable, under the scheme, is ₹ 10,000 and the employees do not have to make any contribution for it.

(5) Family Pension: To provide long-term financial security to the families of industrial employees in the event of their premature death, the employees' Family Pension Scheme was introduced from 1 March, 1971 by diverting a portion of the employees' contribution to the Employees' Provident Funds with an additional contribution by the Central Government. The amount of family pension payable ranges from a minimum of ₹ 60 to maximum of ₹ 320 per month depending on the period of membership of the fund.

(6) Gratuity Scheme: The Payment of Gratuity Act, 1972 is applicable to employees in factories, mines, oil-fields, plantations, ports, railways, motor transport undertakings, companies, shops and other establishments under the Act. The employees drawing wages not exceeding ₹ 1,000 per month are entitled to payment of gratuity at the rate of 15 days wages for each completed year of service, subject to a maximum of 20 months' wages. However, in the case of seasonal establishments, the gratuity is payable at the rate of 7 days' wages for each season. The Act does not affect the right of an employee to receive better terms of gratuity any award or agreement or contract with the employer.

WORKING CONDITIONS AND WELFARE

Working conditions in factories are regulated by the Factories Act, 1948, which prescribes a 48-hour week for adult workers and forbids the employment of children under 14 in any factory. Minimum standards of lighting, ventilation, safety, health and welfare services which the employers must provide in their factories have also been laid down. Factories employing over 30 women workers are required to provide a creche for their children. Shelters, rest rooms and lunch rooms are to be provided by factories employing over 150 workers. Factories with more than 250 employees have to provide canteens for their workers. Factories employing 500 employees or more workers have to appoint welfare officers. Amenities have also been provided in mines and plantations covered by the Mines Act, 1952, and the Plantations Labour Act, 1951, and the Bidi and Cigar Workers (Conditions of Employment) Act, 1966, Contact Labour (Regulation and Abolition) Act, 1970, Motor Transport Workers' Act, 1961, etc.

To provide housing, medical, recreational and other welfare facilities on a planned basis, statutory welfare funds have been created for the benefit of workers in coal, mica, iron ore, manganese ore, limestone and dolomite mines and in the *beedi* industry. The welfare facilities provided under these funds include provision of housing, hospitals, medical, educational and recreational facilities.

The finances for the funds are raised through the levy of a cess, an *ad valorem* cess as customs duty on mica exports, a cess as a duty on mica exports of iron ore and manages ore and duty of excise on internal consumption and a cess on the limestone and dolomite consumed by the iron ore and steel plants and cement and other factories. The welfare fund for *beedi* workers is being financed by levy of cess on manufactured *beedis.*

Acts under which' funds have been established are: The Iron Ore Mines and Manganese Ore Mines Labour Welfare Cess Act, 976; Iron Ore Mines and Manganese Ore Mines Labour Welfare Fund Act, 1976; the Limestone and Dolomite Mines Labour Welfare Fund Act, 1972; Coal Mines Labour Welfare Funds; the Mica Mines Labour Welfare Fund Act, 1946; and the Beedi Workers Welfare Cess (Amendment) Act, 1981.

Plantation Labour

The Plantation Labour Act, 1951 provides for the welfare of plantation labour and regulates the conditions of work in plantations. The Act is administered by the state governments. The Act was passed in 1951 but was brought into force from 1 April, 1954. Even from this date only such sections of the Act were given effect to which could be enforced without framing of rules. The concerned state governments published their rules under the Act from September 1955 to April 1959, on the lines of model rules recommended by the Ministry of Labour.

With a view to removing some difficulties that have been experienced in the working of the Plantations Labour Act, 1951 and for enlarging the scope of the Act, the Plantations Labour (Amendment) Act, 1951 was passed by Parliament and has been brought into force with effect from the 26 January, 1982.

The Act applies to whole of India except Jammu and Kashmir and covers all tea, coffee, rubber, cinchona and cardamom plantations measuring 5 hectares or more and employing 15 or more workers. Workers drawing wages upto ₹ 750 per month are now covered under the Act. The Act now provides for compulsory registration of plantations.

Under the Amendment Act, all plantations have to provide housing accommodation to their resident workers and their families and also to those residing outside who have put in six months of continuous service and who express a desire in writing to reside in the plantations. The plantations also maintain hospitals and dispensaries for workers. Some of the plantations also run elementary schools for the education of the workers' children. Training in useful handicrafts, such as tailoring, knitting, weaving and basket-making and recreational facilities are provided in some of the tea estate centres with the help of the Tea Board.

Training

Since the Factories Act, 1948 is the main labour legislation concerning conditions of work and since the conditions of work in factories are constantly changing due to rapid advances in the manufacturing technology, there is a dire need to train the enforcing authorities at the field level so that the enforcement of the provisions under the Factories Act is done with due consideration for such changes. With this in view, the Directorate General, Factory Advice Service and Labour Institute, conducts training programmes for factory inspectors, medical inspectors and other specialist inspectors. Courses for new inspectors as well as senior inspectors and specialist inspectors are conducted on a regular basis. The inspectors are also deputed by their respective Inspectorates to attend certain specialised courses offered by various industries.

WORKERS' SAFETY

The Factories Act, 1948 contains provisions to ensure safety measures and to promote the health and welfare in factories. It also provides for the appointment of safety officers in notified factories and in factories engaged in operation involving risk of bodily injury, poisoning or disease. The Act and the rules framed thereunder are administered by the state governments through their factory inspectorates.

Under the Constitution, safety, health and welfare of workers employed in mines are the concern of the Central Government. The matter is regulated by the Mines Act, 1952, which applies to all types of mines including those of atomic minerals and oil-fields.

The Directorate General of Mines Safely has been entrusted with the function of enforcing the provisions of the Mines Act. 1952, and the rules and regulations framed thereunder. The National Council for Safety in Mines is a registered society engaged in safety activities.

The Dock Workers (Safety, Health and Welfare) Scheme, 1961 framed under the Dock Workers (Regulation of Employment) Act, 1948 provides for measures for ensuring the health and welfare of dock workers and safety measures for those workers who are not covered under the Indian Dock Labourers Regulations 1948.

The Directorate General, Factory Advice Service and Labour Institute, Bombay function as an integral body to advise Government, industry and other interests concerned with matters relating to safety, health and welfare of industrial workers.

(1) National Safety Council: The National Safety Council was set up in 1966 to promote safety measures to prevent accidents, minimise dangers and mitigate human sufferings, to conduct programmes and lectures and conferences on safety, to conduct educational campaigns, to arouse consciousness amongst employers and workers to collect educational and information data, etc. As on 31 December, 1983, the Council's membership was 1,606 corporate members, 131 individual members, 31 trade union members and 78 life members.

The National Safety Day is celebrated every year throughout the country to mark the foundation day of the National Safety Council.

(2) National Safety Awards: To give recognition to good safety performance on the part of industrial undertakings and to stimulate and maintain the interest of both the managements and the workers in accident prevention programmes, the Government instituted in 1965 the National Safety awards. The award schemes were instituted for factories registered under the Factories Act, 1971, separate schemes for factories not covered under the Act and for ports have also been introduced. At present ten schemes are in operation.

Shram Vir Awards

Shram Vir awards were instituted in 1965 for workers of factories mines, plantations and docks. They are given in recognition of meritorious performance which leads to higher productivity or economy or efficiency.

QUESTION FOR EXERCISE

1. Write an Essay on Social Security in India.

33

Employees' State Insurance

In a Welfare State striving constantly for "the greatest happiness of the greatest number" the problem of social security is of vital importance. The term 'social security' may broadly be defined as the endeavour of the community as a whole to afford relief to the utmost extent possible to any individual during periods of physical distress inevitable on illness or injury and from the economic distress consequent on reduction or loss of earnings due to illness, disablement, maternity, unemployment, old age or death of the working member. The concept of social security has been highlighted in Article 41 of the Constitution of India which envisages that "the State shall, within the limits of its economic capacity and development, make effective provision for securing the right to work, to education and to public assistance in cases of unemployment, old age, sickness and disablement and in other cases of undeserved want". The objective of social security can be achieved either by a self-balancing scheme of social insurance or by assistance from public funds or an appropriate combination of the two methods.

Historical Background

The enactment in 1923 of the Workmen's Compensation Act prescribing payment of compensation for employment injuries may be regarded as the first step towards a scheme of social security in India. Thereafter, the Maternity Benefit Acts of various States (the lead was taken by Bombay in 1929) gave some benefits to women workers during temporary incapacitation due to maternity. All these Acts were, however, based on the principle that the employer should be solely responsible for making payments of the amounts involved. Besides, the Acts did not envisage provision of medical care.

Following the conventions adopted in 1927 by the International Labour Office (ILO) in regard to health insurance for workers in industry, commerce and agriculture, the Government of India examined the question of providing for such benefits in India. In view of the financial implications involved, Provincial Governments were somewhat reluctant to assume responsibility for assistance to any scheme of insurance. The problem was further considered by the Royal Commission on Labour in 1931. Though the Commission recommended the need for benefits during sickness, several difficulties (including inadequacy of morbidity statistics) hindered further progress. The Kanpur Labour Enquiry Committee set up in 1937 and later the Bihar Labour Enquiry Committee in 1940, supported the formulation of a sickness insurance scheme on a contributory basis. The proposal received further support from the Conference of Labour Ministers held in 1940, 1941 and 1942. Meanwhile, employers and workers both expressed willingness to contribute. It was finally decided that the scheme should not throw any financial burden on Government. In March, 1943 the Government of India appointed Professor B.P. Adarkar as Special Officer to prepare a health insurance scheme for industrial workers. The Report, examined in consultation with the two experts of the ILO (Mr. Stack and Mr. Rao), formed the basis of the Employees' State Insurance Act, ESI Act of 1948.

Initial Difficulties

In view of the size of the country, the disposition of workers, the shortage of administrative and medical personnel, the inadequacy of dispensaries and indoor space in hospitals and the newness of the Scheme, it was felt that the ESI Act should be implemented only in suitable stages, the space of extension being dependent on results achieved and the experience gained. It was accordingly decided to implement the Scheme in the first instance in Kanpur and Delhi. On representations from employers in Delhi and Kanpur that their contributions would handicap them competitively against employers in non-implemented areas, who were exempt, the ESI Act was amended in 1951 to provide for payment of contributions by employers in implemented and non-implemented areas at differential rates keeping in abeyance the original schedule stipulated in the Act.

The 24th of February, 1952 is undoubtedly a Red Letter Day in the history of social security in India. The ESI Scheme was introduced on that date in Kanpur and in Delhi covering 1,20,000 workers.

Jurisdiction

The Scheme currently covers all employees working in "power" using non-seasonal factories (excluding mines, railway running sheds and defence installations) in which 20 or more persons are working on a monthly remuneration of ₹ 400 or less. The term 'employee' includes clerical and supervisory staff and casual employees engaged by or through contractors.

The Act has a built-in provision for extending its scope to "any other establishment or class of establishments, industrial, commercial, agricultural or otherwise". The very elasticity of the provision is a clear pointer to the wide prospects of further extension.

Benefits

Benefits are provided in five well recognised contingencies—benefits in cash during sickness, maternity, disablement and death and benefits in kind through medical care to insured persons (IPs) and their families. The Scheme visualises a series of contribution and benefit periods of 25-26 weeks winch go in pairs, each contribution period being followed, after an interval of 13 weeks, by a corresponding benefit period. Title to sickness and maternity benefits is determined with reference to the contributions paid in the corresponding contribution period.

(1) Sickness Benefit (SB): Sickness benefit represents the periodical payments made to an IP during a period of sickness certified by a duly appointed medical practitioner. The qualifying condition for payment of benefit in a benefit period is that in the corresponding contribution period contributions were paid or were payable for at least two-thirds of the number of weeks for which the IP was deemed to be available for employment, subject to a minimum of 12 contributions.

Sickness benefit is payable for a maximum duration of 56 days in a continuous spell of 365 days. The rate at which sickness benefit is payable is roughly half of the average daily wage of the IP during the relevant contribution period. The prescribed waiting period of 2 days is waived if the IP is certified sick within 15 days of the last spell of sickness. Details regarding extended sickness benefit are given later in this article.

(2) Maternity Benefit: Maternity benefit implies periodical payments to an insured woman in case of confinement, certified by a duly appointed doctor or midwife. The term 'confinement' means "labour resulting in the issue of a living child, or labour after 26 weeks of pregnancy resulting in the issue of a child whether alive or dead".

The qualifying conditions are similar to those for SB with the additional requirement that at least one contribution should have been paid between 35 to 40 weeks preceding the date of confinement or the date of expected confinement whichever is more advantageous to the insured woman. Maternity benefit is payable for a period of 12 weeks of which not more than 6 weeks should recede the expected date of confinement. The daily rate of benefits is double the sickness benefit rate and is therefore roughly equivalent to average daily wage of the insured woman. This is further subject to a minimum of 75 paise per day. There is no waiting period in the case of maternity benefit.

(3) Disablement Benefit: Disablement benefit comprises periodical payments to an IP suffering from disablement as a result of an employment injury sustained, as an 'employee' under he Act. For the purpose of deciding whether an accident or an occupational disease amounts to an employment injury, the principles of the Workmen's Compensation Act have been translated in the ESI Act.

Unlike sickness and maternity benefits, there are no contributory conditions and there is no limit of duration of benefit.

Disablement benefit is of two types—temporary disablement benefit (TDB) and permanent disablement benefit (PDB). Temporary disablement connotes a condition involving temporary capacity to work and requiring medical treatment and attendance. DB is paid as long as the temporary disability lasts. The daily rate of TDB is roughly one-half of the average daily wage of the IP. There is a waiting period of three days *i.e.* TDB is not paid if the incapacity does not exceed three days; where it does, however, benefit is paid from the very first day of incapacity provided this is accompained by loss of wages.

Permanent disablement implies permanent loss of earning capacity which may be either partial or total. Total disablement is said to result when the loss of earning capacity from an injury is 100 per cent, where loss of earning capacity is less than 100 per cent the disablement is described as partial. In the event of total disability, full benefit is payable to the IP for life at the TDB rate applicable to him. For permanent disablement, the beneficiary gets a pension for life proportionate to the loss of earning capacity.

The Regulations give the beneficiary, whose degree of permanent disablement has been assessed as "final" by the Medical Board, a right to opt for communication of periodical payments of PDB into a lumpsum provided that the daily rate of PDB does not exceed 50 paise. This is with a view to avoiding inconvenience to recipients of benefits of small amounts.

(4) Dependants' Benefit (DB): Dependants' benefit is in the nature of periodical payments to dependants of an IP who dies as a result of an employment injury. The dependants recognised under the Scheme are the widow or widows, legitimate or adopted son, and legitimate unmarried daughter. The widow is entitled to a benefit until she remarries, the son till he is 15 years of age, and the daughter till she is 15 years of age unless she marries earlier. Benefit to the son and to the unmarried daughter can be paid beyond the age of 15 years and upto the age of 18 years where they are receiving education.

The widow is entitled to benefit at three-fifths of the full rate (TDB) to which the IP would have been entitled during life time while the son and the daughter are each entitled to two-fifths of this rate. If the total of dependants' benefit so distributed amongst the widow/widows and entitled children exceeds at any time the full rate, the share of each dependant is proportionately reduced. In the absence of a widow and children, the benefit can be paid to other eligible dependants.

5. Medical Benefit: An insured person is entitled to medical benefit while continuing in insurable employment and for 13 weeks thereafter. Persons in regular insurable employment, *i.e.* those who have paid at least 12 weekly contributions in any contributory period, are entitled for a further period of about 9 months from the date they cease to make contributions to the Scheme. In addition, insured persons suffering from T.B., leprosy, mental and malignant diseases, fracture of lower extremity (non-employment injury cases and from rare and peculiar reaction to certain modern drugs) are entitled to extend medical care for one year over the above their normal period of entitlement. The Employees' State Insurance Corporation (ESIC) provides at its own cost artificial limbs to amputees and artificial dentures due to loss of teeth consequent on employment injury. Under the Scheme spectacles are provided free for impaired vision due to employment injury and at no-profit no-loss basis for non-employment injury cases.

Medical care is afforded through the provision of outdoor treatment, jequisite drugs, pathological and X-ray investigations, domiciliary visits, indoor treatment, ambulance services, specialists' services, ante-natal and post-natal care, emergency treatment and the like. Outdoor medical care is provided either through the 'service' system or the 'panel' system. Under the 'service' system State Insurance Dispensaries with full-time salaried doctors are set up in convenient places, mobile dispensaries are also available. Under the 'panel' system, private medical practitioners are appointed from the medical profession as Insurance Medical Practitioners at those private clinics where treatment is available. Indoor treatment is provided either in hospitals constructed exclusively for the use of insured persons or by reservation of beds in other hospitals.

The Corporation has agreed in principle to afford to families of insured persons full medical care (including hospitalisation) on the same scale as for insured persons. In view of the shortage of medical personnel and the inadequacy of hospital beds all over the country, it has not been possible to implement this objective. In all the States except Delhi, the administration of medical care is the statutory responsibility of State Governments who make the requisite arrangements for outdoor and indoor treatment. In most of the States, families of insured persons have been given outdoor medical care of the restricted type in ESI dispensaries in 'service' areas or at clinics of Insurance Medical Practitioners in 'panel' areas. Some of the States have found it possible to provide families with expanded medical care which includes all facilities (*e.g.* pathological investigations, radiological examinations, specialist consultations, ambulance service) short of hospitalisation. No State has yet been in a position to provide full medical care to families. It is expected, however, that two or more States may be able to provide such amenities before the end of the Third Five Year Plan period.

Except in Delhi (where ESIC directly runs medical care) medical care is provided by State governments who initially advance funds required for the purpose. Thereafter, the Corporation reimburses the State governments with seven-eighth of the cost where families of insured persons get medical care and three-fourth where medical care is provided only to insured persons.

The Corporation has also taken steps for the promotion of health education to industrial workers through *Yogasana*. A pilot Scheme is in operation in Delhi—it is proposed to have similar schemes in some other areas shortly.

One of the advantages of the Scheme is the availability of morbidity data (amongst industrial workers and their families) which can be utilised for future planning, action and research. Such a data would be of valuable assistance in the control of preventable diseases among insured persons and for planning future social welfare measures under the Scheme.

Additional Benefits

The Employees' State Insurance Act empowers the Corporation to enhance, from time to time, the scale of any benefit admissible thereunder. During the past few years, the Corporation has provided the following additional benefits.

(1) Extended Sickness Benefit: Insured persons suffering from tuberculosis, leprosy, mental and malignant diseases, fracture of lower extremity (non-employment injury cases), who have been in continuous employment for two years are paid extended sickness benefit for a further period of 309 days at half the ordinary rate of sickness benefit. In other words, this will enable such IPs to get benefit for a total period of 365 days (56 at full sickness benefit and 309 at half thereof). Extended sickness benefit as above is also paid to IPs who suffer disabilities as a result of rare and peculiar reaction to certain modern drugs and injections. Medical care in all such cases is provided for a total period of one year over and above what they are normally entitled to.

(2) Artificial Limbs: A set of artificial limbs consisting of a dress limb and a working limb with all accessories is provided free of cost to IPs losing a limb as a result of employment injury or otherwise. Incidental expenditure on the journey to and from the Army Artificial Limb Centre, Poona where the limbs are fitted, stoppage charges, travelling expenses for an attendant on the insured person, compensation for the loss of wages and the like are also borne by the Corporation. Repair and renewal of all such prosthesis are also provided for by the Corporation.

(3) Artificial Dentures: Artificial dentures are provided free of cost to the IPs who suffer loss of teeth due to employment injury.

(4) Free Spectacles: Spectacles are provided free of cost to IPs who sustain impairment of eye sight due to an employment injury or an occupational disease.

(5) Free Remittances: Cash benefits are, at the request of the IPs, remitted by money order at the cost of the Corporation.

(6) Family Medical Care: Medical care has been extended to members of families as stated earlier in this article.

Contribution

The Corporation administers a self-balancing scheme of social security; during the first five years, however, the Government of India met two-third of the administrative expenditure. The income of the Corporation is derived from the contribution made by employers and the employees. Under Chapter V-A (Transitory Provisions), the rate of Employers' Special Contribution consists of such percentage not exceeding five per cent of the total wage bill of the employers as may be specified by the Central Government from time to time. As stated earlier in this article, even employers in non-implemented areas have to pay a contribution. Till 31st March. 1962, the employers were paying ¾ per cent of the wage roll in non-implemented areas and 1¼ per cent of the wage roll in implemented areas. With effect from 1.4.62, however, the rate of employers' special contribution in implemented areas was raised to 2½ per cent of the wage roll; the position in non-implemented areas remains unchanged.

The responsibility for payment of employees' contribution rests, in the first instance, on the principal employer who is entitled, however, to recover the employees' share by deduction from wages. The employees' contribution is payable in unit of weeks. The usual mode of payment of employees' contribution is the affixation of ESIC contribution stamps (obtainable on payment from any branch of the State Bank of India) on the contribution cards; employers employing 250 or more workers are, however, permitted to use franking machines for the purpose. For the purpose of determining of amount of weekly contribution payable, Schedule-I of the ESI Act divides employees into 8 wage groups, each having a corresponding rate of employees' contribution. Employees drawing a wage below ₹ 1 per day are exempted from payment. In the highest wage group, the rate of employees' contribution is ₹ 1.25 per week. The average incidence of employees' contribution works out to about 2.31 per cent of the wages.

Significant Principle

The contributory principle in the ESI Scheme is significant as it stimulates a sense of self-respect among the IPs, encourages thrift, confers a basis for claiming benefit as a matter of right and provides for participation of the IPs, through their representatives in the administration of the Scheme.

The ESI Act provides for a budgetary or an assessment system of finance as opposed to the capitalisation or accumulation system prevailing in some other countries. The budgetary system is conducive to maintaining an equilibrium between contributions and benefits by a process of adjustments between the expenditure. The Corporation prepares a budget each year indicating the estimated income and the expenditure anticipated. The budget estimates have to obtain the approval of the Central Government. The accounts of the Corporation are maintained in the form prescribed by the Central Government and are audited by the auditors appointed by the Central Government. Under the Act the annual report, the audit report and the budget as finally adopted have to be placed before Parliament.

The ESI Act also stipulates evaluation of the assets and liabilities of the Corporation quinquennially by a valuer approved by the Central Government.

Adjudication Machinery

All questions relating to the insurability of an employee, rate of contribution, duration and right of any person to any benefit and other claims, any dispute between a principal employer and an employee, and allied matters are decided by an Employees' Insurance Court (EI Court) specifically set up for the purpose in various places in the States. An appeal to the High Court against the decision of an EI Court can be made only where a substantial question of law is involved.

For the purpose of deciding whether an employment injury sustained by an employee has turned into permanent disablement and for assessing the extent of diminution in the earning capacity as a result thereof, Medical Boards have been set up by the State governments in various industrial centres. There is provision for an appeal against the recommendations of the Medical Board. The forum for such an appeal is the Appeal Tribunal which consists of a judicial officer of the State government (other than the judge of the EI Court) assisted by one or more medical experts and one or more officials or members of trade unions, as assessors.

Administrative Set-up

The Administration of the Scheme vests in the Employees' State Insurance Corporation which is a body corporate having perpetual succession and a common seal. The Corporation consists of 36 members including 5 members each representing employers and employees, two representing the medical profession and two elected by Parliament. The other members represent the Central and State governments. The Union Minister for Labour and Employment is the Chairman of the Corporation while the Union Minister for Health is the Vice-Chairman.

Under the general superintendence and control of the Corporation, a representative Standing Committee consisting of 13 members has been constituted to act as an executive body. A Medical Benefit Council consisting of 26 members has also been set up to advise the Corporation on the administration of medical benefits. The Council has representatives from the Medical Services of State governments besides members representing employers, employees and medical profession; the Medical Commissioner of ESIC is also a member of the Council.

It will be evident that the ESI Corporation is basically a tripartite organisation depending for its efficiency altogether on the common endeavour of employers, employees and the Central and State governments with the assistance of the medical profession.

The Director General is the Chief Executive Officer of ESIC. The Director-General and four more Principal Officers assisting him (the Insurance Commissioner, the Medical Commissioner, the Actuary) are all appointed by the Central Government in consultation with the Corporation.

ESIC has a regional office in every State (under a Regional Director) to maintain close and constant contacts with the State governments, employers and employees. At the regional level, Regional Boards under the chairmanship of the State Labour Minister and Vice-Chairmanship of the State Health Minister have been established; the Board also has representatives of employers, employees, the medical profession and the State government concerned. Similarly, local committees have also been set up on a tripartite basis in all important implemented areas.

The basic unit for cash benefits is the local office which is responsible for disbursement of claims. Inspectors have been appointed by the Corporation to visit factories, to offer assistance to employers, to ensure executive coverage and check prompt payment of contributions. The basic unit for giving medical benefit in kind is the State Insurance Dispensary or the Clinic of the Insurance Medical Practitioner, depending on whether the industrial centre is covered by the 'service' or 'panel' system respectively. Local and inspection offices are under the control of Regional Office while State Insurance Dispensaries and Insurance Medical Practitioners are under the administrative control of the Director of Health Services of the State Governments, except in Delhi where the medical benefits are directly provided by the Corporation.

During the earlier years, the income derived by the Corporation was substantially in excess of its expenditure. This enabled the Corporation to build up a substantial reserve which is, however, expected to be expended in the near future on capital construction of hospitals and dispensaries throughout the country. There can be no better investment of funds of ESIC than in hospitals and dispensaries rendering medical service to IPs and their families. The investment will be 'gilt-edged' with the return in the form of goodwill and relief of human suffering even though such institutions will obviously cost a great deal because of individual and thorough attention to every patient.

Study Group

One of the most important developments, indicative of the future trends and developments of the Scheme, was the appointment of a Study Group by the Government of India in 1957 to report on the possibilities of having an integrated Social Security Scheme. The Study Group recommended that the ESI Scheme, the Employees' Provident Fund Scheme, the Coal Mines Provident Fund Scheme and the Assam Tea Plantations Provident Fund Scheme Act should all be unified into one and that a single agency should assume the responsibility of administering the different benefits under these schemes. The Study Group also recommended the raising of the rate of provident fund contributions from the present 6 per cent to $8\frac{1}{3}$ per cent of the wages and conversion of the Provident Fund Scheme into a pension-*cum*-gratuity scheme. The Study Group further recommended that the employers' contribution under the ESI Act should be raised to the full statutory level. The Study Group's report is under consideration of the Government of India in consultation with the various interests concerned.

The working of ESIC in its many-sided activities is under constant review. Obviously several delicate and difficult human problems arise from day-to-day as serve interests are involved—the Central and the State governments, employers, employees and the medical profession. ESIC maintains at all levels close and constant contacts with all the parties concerned. It derives advantage from its own experience even as it gains by the valuable advice tendered by those affected. Measures designed to rationalise procedures, reduce formalities and improve benefits (both medical and cash) are constantly examined. As a member of the International Social Security Association, ESIC profits by the experience of other countries in the working of social security schemes.

It cannot be gainsaid that the scope of the ETI Scheme at present is extremely limited when viewed against the general objectives of social security. To begin with, the Scheme now covers only industrial workers in perennial "power" using factories having 20 or more workers and drawing ₹ 400 or less a month; they form only a fraction of the total population. It cannot be pretended that the benefits given substantially alleviate the distress suffered. But Section 1(5) of the ESI Act is sufficiently elastic to afford wide prospects of extension to "any other established or class of establishments, industrial, commercial, agricultural or otherwise". The ESIC can, therefore claim to be a "symbol of security". Indeed, despite its limited current scope, ESIC may well be the foundation of social security over which edifices, which will progressively benefit an increasing number of citizens (men, women and children) of all classes, can safely be built in the years to come.

QUESTION FOR EXERCISE

1. Describe and discuss Employers State Insurance Scheme in India.

34

India and I.L.O

International Labour Organization (ILO) is one of the biggest International Organization today. It has been established for realising social, economic and political justice, particularly among labourers of the world. It was established as a result of the Treaty of Versailles, after the First World War. This treaty was signed by thirtytwo nations. The convention deliberated over causes of labour unrest, the problems of labourers and their remedies. On 31 January, 1919, an International Labour Enactment Commission was established in Britain, U.S.A., France, Italy, Japan as its members. This commission was entrusted the task of establishing an organisation to solve the problems of labour welfare. This Commission received co-operation from Commonwealth. During 1 Feb., 1919 and 23rd March, 1919, 35 meetings of this Commission were held. In the 35th meeting on 23rd March, 1919 it was resolved that a broad outline of International Labour Organisation may be formed. The follow up activities continued at Washington upto 29th October. Thus, in the International Labour Convention at Washington was born International Labour Organisation.

FUNDAMENTAL PRINCIPLES

The fundamental principles of International Labour Organization have been mentioned in Labour Charter or the Charter of the freedom of labourers. All the members of U.N.O. have accepted this charter. The fundamental principles in this charter are: "The regulation of the hours of work, including the establishment of a maximum working day and week, the regulation of labour policy, the prevention of unemployment, the provision of an adequate living wage, the protection of workers against sickness, disease and injury arising out of his employment, the protection of children, youth persons and women, provision for old age and injury, protection of the interest of workers when employed in countries other than their own, recognition of the principles of association, the organization of vocational and technical education and other measures."

Alongwith it some fundamental principles based upon the labour problems and their remedies have been accepted in the charter. These are as follows: (*i*) The guiding principle shall be that labour should not be regarded merely as commodity or an article of commerces, (*ii*) the rights of association for all lawful purposes by the employers as well as employed is recognised, (*iii*) the payment to the employees should be a wage adequate to maintain a reasonable standard of life, as understood in their times and countries, (*iv*) an adoption of an eight hours' day or 48 hours' week as the standard to be aimed at where it has not already been attained, (*v*) the adoption of a weekly rest of at least 24 hours which should include Sunday, whenever practicable, (*vi*) the abolition of child labour of young persons as shall permit the continuation of their education and assure their proper physical development, (*vii*) the principle that men and women should receive equal value, (*viii*) the standard set by law in each country, with respect to the conditions of labour, should have due regard to the equitable economic treatment of all workers both national and foreigners, (*ix*) each state should make provision for a system of inspection in which women should also take part in order to ensure enforcement of laws and regulations for the protection of employed.

FUNCTIONS OF INTERNATIONAL LABOUR ORGANIZATION

The important functions performed by International Labour Organisation are as follows:

1. Intensive study of international labour problems and economic system and research concerning these problems together with provision of incentives to the nations prepared to remedy them.

2. Efforts to eradicate the problems on the basis of intensive study of research.

3. Some nations are anxious to provide legislation concerning labour problems and want to encourage such organisations. The International Labour Organisation provides them expert advice.

4. Publication on dilferent subject and the accumulation on data concerning labour problems together with encouragement to labour power are some of the functions of ILO. The subjects of publications

and accumulation of data include: unemployment, social security, social welfare and labour organisation.

5. Providing suggestions from time to time to the member nations about labour welfare and industrial development.

6. Information can be secured about the problems of various countries with the help of ILO. It also provides information about remedies to these problems. It also gives information about the causes of failures and success in this direction.

7. The countries which require help apply to ILO, which sends delegations for the study of these problems and suitable advice.

OBJECTIVES OF INTERNATIONAL LABOUR ORGANIZATION

The labour charter of ILO provides an insight into objectives. The main objectives of ILO are as follows:

1. Provision of employment for each labourer who is physically and mentally qualified and who has a desire for employment and makes effort for it.
2. While providing employment two considerations are emphasised: providing job according to qualification and the work should be according to desire and interest.
3. Increase in the income of the labourer.
4. Raising the standard of living of the labourers.
5. Proving the incentive for mobility to the labourers and suitable guidance about facilities for this mobility.
6. Provision of sufficient social security to labourers.
7. Provision of life insurance for the labourers.
8. Arranging collective bargaining for labour welfare and providing security and respect to labourers right in this connection.
9. Providing educational facilities to the labourers a dependence.
10. Providing sufficient facilities for training in order to increase the efficiency of the labourers.
11. Increasing the co-operation between labourers and employers.
12. Increasing the capacity of production of the industry.
13. Provision of suitable policies in order to prescribe sufficient share to labourers in economic development.
14. Elimination of slums and provision of proper houses for the industrial labourers.

15. Provision of healthy recreation to the labourers to increase their working capacity.
16. Arrangement to provide equal wages for equal work.
17. Provision of necessary reforms in the working condition of labourers.
18. Provisions by which the employment of child labour may be restricted.
19. Protection of the health of the young labourers and provision of facilities of education of them.
20. Adequate arrangement for child welfare.
21. Proper arrangement for maternity security and benefits.

CONSTITUTION OF INTERNATIONAL LABOUR ORGANIZATION

In 1967, the membership of ILO included 118 nations. Since the number has considerably increased and today only exceptional nations are out of it. The activities of ILO are carried on primarily on the basis of the following constituents of its organization:

(1) International Labour Office: This is situated in Geneva. It is the secretariat of ILO. Its main divisions are: The Secretariat, the World Information Service and Publications. Its most important function is the study and research about labour problems. Experts from various countries contribute in this function on the basis of their knowledge and experience. It has branches in so many countries of the world. In India its branch was established in New Delhi in 1928. This branch establishes intimate relationships between ILO, Indian Government Employers and Labourers. This office has a Director General as the Chief Officer. Under him, in the International Labour Office, are workers from different countries. In 1966 there were sixteen Indians in the 1145 workers in this office. Besides these, several Indians were connected as specialists in different fields. International Labour Office publishes two magazines, *International Labour Review*, a monthly magazine and *Industry and Labour*, a fortnightly magazine.

(2) Governing Body of ILO: As is clear by the title, this body governs ILO. The most important functions performed by it include: General Survey of the office of ILO, making of budget, prescribing policy for the activities of the organisation, establishment of industrial expert committee, election for the post of Director General and other important decisions in normal times. The governing body has three sessions in a year. The election of the Chairman and Deputy Chairman is held every year. In the beginning the governing body had 32 members. In 1963 its number was 48 of which 24 were representatives of the government, 12 representatives of the employers and 12 representatives of the labourers. The governing body has ten important nations as its permanent numbers. These are: Canada, China, France, India, Italy, Japan, USSR, England, USA, and West Germany. Including these ten members the internal body has 24 representatives of which 14 are elected after every 3 years. The first session of this body was held at Mysore in 1950. During 1961-62 the Indian representative Dr. S.T. Mairany was its chairman.

(3) International Labour Conference: International Labour Conference is held almost every year. It aims at deliberation upon the problems of the labourers. It includes 4 representatives from each member nation. Of these 4 representatives, 2 are nominees of the government, one of the employers and 1 of the labourers. Besides, several experts and advisers also participate in the deliberations of International Labour Conference. It performs 2 important functions—Preparation of the agenda for the conventions and presenting recommendations. These conventions and recommendations are known by the name of International Labour Code. Upto 1966, 50 conventions were held and 127 recommendations were accepted. These recommendations are mainly concerned with: hours of work, leave with pay, jobs for the women, security of the children, prevention of industrial accidents, and their compensation, life insurance for unemployment, old age and disease, fixation of minimum wages, labour problems of colonies and problems concerning sea workers and fishermen.

Besides the above three constituent parts of the constitution of ILO, it also includes different committees by means of which its various important functions are performed. Some of more important committees are: Industrial Committee, Expert Committee, Correspondent Committee, Regional and Conventional and Advice Penal Committee and regional committees.

INTERNATIONAL LABOUR ORGANISATION AND INDIA

As one of the most populated nation in the world India has made significant contributions to the development of ILO. The most important points in this connection are as follows:

1. India has been the member of ILO since its beginning.
2. India is one of the ten permanent members of the governing

body of ILO. Therefore, it has played an important role in the determination of the policies of ILO.

3. As a member of different committees of ILO, India has taken important part in its functioning.
4. By regular financial contribution India helped meeting the financial requirements of ILO.
5. The Indian Government has taken steps to implement recommendations of ILO for the uplift and welfare of labour in India.
6. Indian Government has shown interest in the social progress of ILO.
7. Mention has been made to India in most of the annual publications of the progress of social security, in the world by ILO.
8. On the recommendations of ILO the Indian Government has taken action concerning employment bureaus, employment policy, industrial training, social security legislation, fixation of working hours, leave with pay, security of women and child labour, minimum wages, industrial security, welfare and co-operation etc.

QUESTIONS FOR EXERCISE

1. Describe the principles and functions of I.L.O.
2. Explain the objectives and Constitution of I.L.O.
3. Write short note on I.L.O. and India.

Selected Bibliography

SOCIAL CONTEXT OF INDUSTRIALISM IN INDIA

Berna, J.J., *Industrial Entrepreneurship in Madras State,* Asia Publishing House, 1960.

Buchanan, D.H., *The Development of Capitalist Enterprise in India,* MacMillan & Co., New York, 1935.

Chattopadhyay, Gauranga and Sen Gupta, Anil K., "Growth of Disciplined Labour Force: A Case Study of Social Impediments", *Economic and Political Weekly,* 4 : 28, 29, 30, 1969, pp. 1209-16.

Erdman, Howard L., "Political Attitudes of Baroda Industrialists", *Economic and Political Weekly,* 29 November 1969.

—, *Political Attitudes of Indian Industry: A Case Study of the Baroda Business Elite,* The Athlone Press, University of London, for the Institute of Commonwealth Studies, London, 1971.

Gadgil, D.R., *Origins of the Modern Indian Business Class: An Interim Report,* International Secretariat Institute of Pacific Relations, 1959.

Holmström, Mark, *South Indian Factory Workers,* Cambridge, Cambridge University Press, 1976.

Joshi, P.C., "The Decline of Indigenous Handicrafts in Uttar Pradesh", *Indian Economic and Social History Review,* 1963, 1(1), 24-35.

Kannappan, Subbiah, "Labour Force Commitment in Early Stages of Industrialization", *Indian Journal of Industrial Relations,* 1970, 5(3), 290-350.

Kester, Gerad, *Industrial Clerks: A Changing Type* (Unpublished Research Report, Shri Ram Centre, New Delhi), 1968.

Lamb, Helen B., "The Indian Business Communities and the Evolution of an Industrialist Class", *Pacific Affairs,* 1955, 28(2).

Lambert, Richard D., "Workers, Factories and Social Change in India", *Economic Weekly,* 1964, 16(32-33), 1335.

Mehta, A.B., *Domestic Service Class,* Popular Book Depot, Bombay, 1960.

Morris, Morris D., "Caste and the Evolution of the Industrial Workforce in India", *American Philosophical Society, Proceedings,* 1960, 104, 124-133.

—, *The Emergence of an Industrial Labour Force : A Study of Bombay Cotton Mills 1854-1947,* Berkeley, California, *1963.*

—, "The Recruitment of an Industrial Labour Force in India with British and American Comparisons", *Comparative Studies in Society and History,* April 1960, 305-328.

Ramanathan, G., *Indian Babu,* Sudha Publications, Delhi, 1967.

Sengupta, A.K., *Labour Commitment and Social Changes: A Micro-Study in West Bengal* (Unpublished, Indian Institute of Management, Calcutta).

Sharma, Baldev R., "The Indian Industrial Worker", *Indian Journal of Comparative Sociology,* 1969, 10(1-2).

—, *The Indian Industrial Worker,* Delhi, Vikas Publishing House, 1974.

Sheth, N.R., "The Problem of Labour Commitment", *Economic and Political Weekly,* 27 February 1971, 35-37.

Thorner, D., "Casual Employment of a Factory Labour Force: The Case of India 1850-1939", *Economic Weekly,* 1957, Annual Number.

UNESCO Research Centre, *Social Research on Small Industries in India,* Delhi, 1965.

Vaid, K.N., *The New Worker,* Asia Publishing House, Bombay, 1967.

—, *Contract Labour in Manufacturing Industries,* SRC Press, New Delhi, 1966.

—, and Singh G., *Contract Labour in Construction Industry—A Study in Rajasthan,* SRC Press, New Delhi, 1966.

Vatsal, A.B., "Managerial Ideology in India", *Economic and Political Weekly,* 22 February 1970.

INDUSTRIAL ORGANIZATION IN INDIA

Chandra, Sushil, *Sociology of Work Plant* (Aspects of Social Organization and Structure), Institute of Social Sciences, Agra University, Agra, 1963.

Rice, A.K., *Productivity and Social Organization: The Ahmedabad Experiment: Technical Innovation, Work Organization and Management,* Tavistock, London, 1959.

Sengupta, Anil K., "Some Features of Malfunctioning of an Industrial Organization", *Sociological Bulletin,* 1969, 17(2), 122-138.

Sethi, Narendra K., "Organization Efficiency Through Human Relations: Conceptual Framework for Indian Industry", *Public Administration,* 1966, 4(5), 17-18.

Sharma, Baldev R., "Absenteeism: A Search for Correlates", *Indian Journal of Industrial Relations,* 1970, 5(3), 267-290.

Sheth, N.R., "Social Implications of Wage Incentive Schemes", *Indian Journal of Industrial Relations,* 1967, 2(4), 460-475.

Shri Ram Centre for Industrial Relations, *Human Problems of Shift Work: A' Study of the Socio-psychological Processes in Worker Adjustment to Shift-Work in Industry,* Shri Ram Centre for Industrial Relations, New Delhi, 1970.

Sreenivasan, K., *Productivity and Social Environment,* Asia Publishing House, Bombay, 1964.

Thakur, C.P. and Aurora, G.S., *Technological Change and Industry,* Shri Ram Centre for Industrial Relations, New Delhi, 1971.

UNESCO Research Centre, *Social and Cultural Factors Affecting Productivity of Industrial Workers in India,* UNESCO, 1961.

Vaid, K.N., *Papers on Absenteeism,* Asia Publishing House, Bombay, 1967.

TRADE UNIONS IN INDIAN SOCIETY

Bogaert, Michael V.D., *Trade Unionism in Indian Ports: A Case Study at Calcutta and Bombay,* Shri Ram Centre for Industrial Relations, New Delhi, 1970.

Crouch, H., *Trade Unions and Politics in India,* Manaktalas, Bombay, 1966.

Johri, C.K., *Unionism in a Developing Economy,* Asia Publishing House, Bombay, 1967.

Kannappan, S., "Gandhian Model of Unionism in a Developing Economy: The TLA in India", *Industrial and Labour Relations Review,* 1962, 16(1), 86-110.

Morris, M.D., "Labour Discipline, Trade Union, and the State in India", *Journal of Political Economy,* 1955, 63(4), 293-308.

Mukherjee, Radhakamal, *The Indian Working Class,* Hind Kitab Ltd., Bombay, 1951.

Munson, Fred C., *Indian Trade Unions: Structure and Functions,* Institute of International Commerce and Bureau of Industrial Relations, Graduate School of Business Administration, University of Michigan, Ann Arbor, 1970.

Oranti, Oscar A., 'Problems of Indian Trade Unionism', *Annals of the American Academy of Political and Social Science,* 1957, 310, 151-161.

Punekar, S.D., *Trade Unionism in India,* New Book Co. Ltd., Bombay, 1948.

—, and Madhuri, S., *Trade Union Leadership in India,* Bombay, 1967.

—, and Savur, Manorama G., *Management White-Collar Relations,* Popular Prakashan, Bombay, 1969.

Raman, N., *Political Involvement of India's Trade Unions,* Asia Publishing House, 1967.

Ramanujam, G., *Under the Babul Tree: Story of Indian Labour,* INTUC, 1967.

Ramaswamy, E.A., 'Trade Unions and Politics', *Sociological Bulletin,* 1969, 18(2), 138-148.

Reindrop, Julian, *Leaders and Leadership in the Trade Unions in Bangalore,* The Christian Literature Society, Madras, 1971.

Sharma, G.K., *Labour Movement in India: Its Past and Present* (1885-1960), Department of Economics, University of Rajasthan, Jaipur, 1962.

Singh, Jaspal, "Social Background of Trade Union Leaders", *Economic and Political Weekly,* 5:34, 1970, pp. 1421-24.

Vaid, K.N., *Growth and Practice of Trade Unionism-An Area Study,* University of Delhi, Delhi, 1962.

—, *State and Labour in India,* Asia Publishing House, Bombay, 1965.

—, "Why Workers Join Unions?", *Indian Journal of Industrial Relations, 1965,* 1(2), 208-230.

INDUSTRIAL RELATIONS IN INDIA

Alexander, K.C., *Participative Management-The Indian Experience,* Shri Ram Centre for Industrial Relations and Human Resources, New Delhi, 1972.

Das, Nabagopal, *Experiment in Industrial Democracy,* Asia Publishing House, Bombay, 1964.

Dastur, Zarin and Mankidy, Jacob, *Organization in Conflict: The Strike in Andhra Bank,* National Institute of Bank Management, Bombay, 1975.

Dayal, Ishwar and Sharma, B.R., *Strike of Supervisory Staff,* Progressive Bombay, 1970.

Johri, C.K. (ed.), *Issues in Indian Labour Policy* (National Seminar on Industrial Relations in a Developing Economy), Shri Ram Centre for Industrial Relations, New Delhi, 1969.

Karnik, V.B., *Strikes in India,* Manaktalas, Bombay, 1961.

Kennedy, Van D., *Unions, Employers and Government,* Manaktala and Sons, Bombay, 1967.

Mathur, K. and Sheth, N.R., *Tripartitism in Labour Policy,* Shri Ram Centre for Industrial Relations, Delhi, 1969.

Mhetras, V.G., *Labour Participation in Management,* Manaktalas, Bombay, 1966.

Mohan Das, S.R., *The Indian Labour Scene,* S.R. Mohan Das, Bombay, 1970.

Morris, Morris David, "Order and Disorder in the Labour Force : The Jamshedpur Crisis of 1958", *Economic Weekly,* 1958, 10(44), 1387.

National Commission on Labour, *Report of the Study Group on Sociological Aspects of Labour-Management Relations,* New Delhi, 1968.

Ramaswamy, E.A., *The Worker and His Union: A Study in South India,* Allied Publishers, New Delhi, 1977.

Sheth, N.R., *The Joint Management Council: Problems and Prospects,* Shri Ram Centre for Industrial Relations and Human Resources, New Delhi, 1972.

Sur, Mary, *Collective Bargaining,* Asia Publishing House, Bombay, 1965.

Tanic, Zivan, *Workers' Participation in Management—Ideal and Reality in India,* Shri Ram Centre for Industrial Relations, New Delhi, 1969.